'Filling a gap in the social science literature, Rob Watts engages in a powerful defence of the right to dissent, which is defined as fundamental given the irreducible pluralism of ideas in every society. Bridging social theory with empirical analysis of recent forms of criminalization of acts of resistance, he convincingly challenges the myth of liberal democracy as tolerant of disagreement and points at the complex – and not always rational – relations between fear, security and liberalism'.

Donatella della Porta, Professor of Political Science and Political Sociology, European University Institute, Italy

'Rob Watts' *Criminalizing Dissent* could not appear at a more important moment. In a careful, deliberate manner, he undertakes to explain not just what dissent is and the many forms it can take in liberal democracies, but also why it is so important that we protect it. This is a timeless lesson that seems especially relevant now'.

Sophia Rosenfeld, Walter H. Annenberg Professor of History, University of Pennsylvania, USA

T0298546

Criminalizing Dissent

While liberal-democratic states like America, Britain and Australia claim to value freedom of expression and the right to dissent, they have always actually criminalized dissent. This disposition has worsened since 9/11 and the 2008 Great Recession. This ground-breaking study shows that just as dissent involves far more than protest marches, so too liberal-democratic states have expanded the criminalization of dissent.

Drawing on political and social theorists like Arendt, Bourdieu and Isin, the book offers a new way of thinking about politics, dissent and its criminalization relationally. Using case studies like the Occupy movement, selective refusal by Israeli soldiers, urban squatters, democratic education and violence by anti-Apartheid activists, this book highlights the many forms that dissent takes along with the many ways in which liberal-democratic states criminalize it. The book also highlights the mix of fear and delusion in play when states privilege security to protect an imagined 'political order' from difference and disagreement.

The book makes a major contribution to political theory, legal studies and sociology. Linking legal, political and normative studies in new ways, Watts shows that ultimately liberal-democracies rely more on sovereignty and the capacity for coercion and declarations of legal 'states of exception' than on liberal-democratic principles. In a time marked by a deepening crisis of democracy, the book argues dissent is increasingly valuable.

Rob Watts is currently a professor of Social Policy at RMIT University where he teaches politics, criminology, policy studies and applied human rights. He was a founding member of the Greens Party in Victoria, and established the Australian Center for Human Rights Education at RMIT in 2008. His recent books include *States of Violence and the Civilising Process* (2016), *Public Universities, Managerialism and the Value of the University* (2017) and *The Precarious Generation: A Political Economy of Young People* (2018, co-authored).

The Criminalization of Political Dissent
Series editor: Professor Judith Bessant, RMIT University, Melbourne, Australia

This challenging new book series explores the way governments since 9/11 from across the political spectrum intensified their efforts to criminalize both traditional and new forms of digital political dissent. The series will feature major contributions from the social sciences, law and legal studies, media studies and philosophy to document what happens when governments choose to regard activists campaigning for increased government transparency and accountability, environmental sustainability, social justice, human rights and pro-democracy as engaging in illegal activities.

The book series explores the legal, political and ethical implications when governments engage habitually in mass electronic and digital surveillance, outlaw freedom of movement real and virtual public assembly and prosecute digital activists. The books in this series are a 'must read' for anyone interested in the future of democracy.

Governing Youth Politics in the Age of Surveillance
Edited by Maria Grasso and Judith Bessant

Shooting the Messenger
Criminalising Journalism
Andrew Fowler

Criminalizing Dissent
The Liberal State and the Problem of Legitimacy
Rob Watts

For more information about this series, please visit: https://www.routledge.com/ The-Criminalization-of-Political-Dissent/book-series/CRIMPD

Criminalizing Dissent

The Liberal State and the Problem of Legitimacy

Rob Watts

Routledge
Taylor & Francis Group

LONDON AND NEW YORK

First published 2020
by Routledge
2 Park Square, Milton Park, Abingdon, Oxon OX14 4RN

and by Routledge
52 Vanderbilt Avenue, New York, NY 10017

First issued in paperback 2020

Routledge is an imprint of the Taylor & Francis Group, an informa business

British Library Cataloguing-in-Publication Data
A catalogue record for this book is available from the British Library

Library of Congress Cataloging-in-Publication Data
A catalog record has been requested for this book

ISBN 13: 978-0-367-67061-0 (pbk)
ISBN 13: 978-1-138-48871-7 (hbk)

Typeset in Goudy
by codeMantra

Dedicated to Marion Harper and Peter Abrehart of the Unitarian Peace Memorial Church of East Melbourne and to Ambrose and Sebastian.

Contents

Figures and tables

Figures

Tables

Acknowledgements

This book has taken a long time to write, partly because there were some fundamental and difficult problems involved in understanding dissent as political to say nothing of the effort involved in making sense of the attempts by liberal-democratic states to suppress those activities.

I would like to acknowledge first the intellectual assistance rendered by a former student of mine, Bao Huynh, who did some fundamental research and who helped me with some thinking as well, at a time when I needed an extra brain and an extra pair of eyes. I should also acknowledge the fact that my current academic boss Dr Michele Ruyters helped out at the right time with financial support that enabled me to pay Bao for his work.

That I continue to enjoy teaching, and the practices of enquiry and writing that nourish my teaching, has a lot to do with working with younger colleagues like James Rowe and Kara Sandri. Like other 'canny outlaws' in the new dark ages into which many universities have plunged themselves into, we work together to refuse the bizarre and chilling effects produced by the inane, crass, corporate gibberish now imposed by the 'leaders' of our universities who strive to inhibit the capacity of good teachers to inspire and promote the loving practices of critical thinking, creative enquiry and the courage to engage in good judgement, which is what universities exist to do.

More than one student of mine has remarked on the sermon-like intensity of my lecturing style. It may come as unsurprising to know that I am regularly invited to give an occasional address at the Unitarian Peace Memorial Church in East Melbourne, an activity that has become an easy, almost guilty pleasure. I love the Unitarians for their courageous and persistent commitment to the great tradition of dissent. Like the Baptists, the Unitarians belong to the great Anglo-American tradition of Dissenters. Unlike the Baptists who saw fit to trim their sails to social conformity in the pursuit of upward social mobility, the Unitarians continue to be persistently disagreeable. The value of this as a disposition is suggested by looking at their roll-call of notable Unitarians who include Isaac Newton, Ralph Waldo Emerson, S.T. Coleridge, Charles Dickens, Florence Nightingale, John Dewey, Catherine Helen Spence, Frank Lloyd Wright, Linus Pauling and Tim Berners-Lee. This is I why I have dedicated this book to Marion Harper and

Peter Abrehart, two outstanding activists and members of the Unitarian Peace Memorial Church in East Melbourne.

I have also dedicated this book to Ambrose and Sebastian – two younger Australians – and they know why.

Much of this book was composed in a study looking out across the tree-tops in the four-storey 'tree-house' I share with my life partner, Professor Judith Bessant, AM. Like the Unitarians, Judith epitomizes the value of discovering and calling out bullshit, which she did repeatedly as she read drafts of this in her capacity as the editor of the book series in which this book appears.

I would like to thank Karthikeyan Subramaniam for managing the production process and the editor Hannah Lamarre for a skilled and professional job.

Introduction

Significant and sustained political protest has become a recurrent feature of our time. In America in January 2017, the inauguration of Donald Trump as the forty-fifth President of the US triggered a series of roiling protests in Washington and across America. On Inauguration Day itself, significant numbers of people took to the streets of Washington, DC. The following day, it is estimated that over four million Americans participated in the Women's March, part of a global event involving seven million people, many expressing their view of the new President's well-publicized views about the role and status of women to say nothing of his dealings with women. By the end of 2017, the Crowd Counting Consortium, using a webcrawler that surveyed events reported on local newspaper and television sites, claimed that since the Women's March on Washington on 21 January 2017 between 5.9 million and nine million people had engaged in 8,700 protests in the US (Chenoweth and Pressman 2018).

At the same time since Trump's inauguration, the American state has instigated significant and sustained criminalization of dissent. Assuming with writers like King and Waddington (2004), Earl (2006) and MacKinnon (2014) that the criminalization of dissent refers to the policing of protest, we see repeated exercises of this kind. On the morning of the inauguration itself, Washington police surrounded or 'kettled' groups of marchers at 12th and L Streets detaining some 230 people for up to eleven hours without food, water or access to toilets or medical care. While some of those arrested were protestors, others were journalists or simply by-standers. Federal prosecutors subsequently charged them all with 'felony rioting', (a non-existent crime in Washington, DC) as well as charges like 'felony incitement to riot', 'conspiracy to riot' and property-damage crimes – mostly involving broken windows (Bromberg and Chevraud 2017). In November 2017, each defendant was facing over sixty years in prison: most of these charges were subsequently dropped.

While the American government eventually moved to dismiss all charges in July 2018, the Trump Administration's antagonism to dissent persisted. During his electoral campaign, Trump had frequently signalled his support for taking 'forceful action' against those who vocally opposed him at campaign rallies. Since the inauguration of President Trump, his administration backed by wealthy conservatives has encouraged a significant nationwide legislative exercise designed to criminalize dissent (The Real News 2018).

The anti-Trump protests remind us that the first two decades of the twenty-first century have been marked by near-global expressions of protest with significant political effects. There have been significant 'colour' revolutions beginning with the 'Orange revolution' in the Ukraine in late 2004. Even more striking was the upsurge in political protest erupting in more than seventy countries after the Great Recession of 2008: this included the so-called 'Arab Spring' in North Africa, anti-Austerity campaigns like the Occupy Wall Street movement in the US, campaigns by Podemos in Spain, the 'Umbrella movement' in Hong Kong, the 'Five Star' movement in Greece, the 'Maple Spring' movement led by students in Canada and the Chilean students who sparked the 'Chilean Spring' (The Economist Intelligence Unit 2013).

While many of these protest movements expressed a range of progressive or 'left-wing' commitments to greater equality, peace, environmental sustainability and the protection of human rights, e.g. of asylum seekers, we also saw examples of what we can call right-wing or populist protest (Mueller 2016). Some of these movements like Britain's UK Independence Party, Hungary's Civic Alliance (Fidesz), Poland's Law and Justice, and France's National Rally have redefined the liberal-democratic political cultures of these nation-states. Outside the electoral systems, a plethora of far-right and ultranationalist movements challenge the erstwhile commitment of liberal democracy to pluralism by crafting imaginaries centred on the idea of a single People or a unitary national community purged of elites and foreigners. The resurgence of populism has been driven by anger about what some people see as the 'unfair' treatment of minorities like indigenous people, gays and lesbians, or refugees and asylum seekers or as the toxic effects of economic globalization (Gerbaudo 2016, 2017). In late 2018, protestors in France wearing the 'gilet jaune', a fluorescent yellow hazard vest, began protesting ostensibly against rising fuel costs, but angered by a globalist President Emmanuel Macron promoting a Green agenda at their expense.

In most cases, much of the anger and discontent coming from both the 'left' and populist movements have been expressed in both time-honoured ways like street marches, blockades, anti-eviction actions, establishing camps in city squares 'squats' and resistance to police interventions. It has also increasingly involved the use of new technologies like mobile phones, and websites as well as social media to inform, mobilize and organize political activity. This includes new kinds of digital petitions or staging Distributed Denial of Service attacks on government and corporate websites.

Whatever the implications of this current wave of protest for the state of liberal democracy (Anastasakis 2009: 6 cf.; Mueller 2016: 68), there can be little doubt that liberal-democratic states everywhere have been quick to suppress and to criminalize protest. All too often this includes using existing legislation or passing new legislation to 'outlaw' it – or to punish it – and then using police and security agencies to regulate and suppress protest. This can involve everything from mass arrests, and varying degrees of violence including water-cannon, tear gas, dogs, massed police baton charges, percussion grenades and mounted police to tactics like 'kettling' as we saw in Washington, DC, in January 2017. We have also seen states conflating protest with terrorism, treating protest as a security problem and rolling out digital mass-surveillance systems. As Deidre Mackinnon (2014: 1–2) makes clear, moves in America in 2017–18 to criminalize the wearing of masks during protest marches or to treat environmentalists as terrorists is far from unique to America: other liberal democracies like Canada, Australia and the UK are using these and other tactics assimilated under the rubric of being 'tough on crime' (Parks and Daniel 2010).

Let me start out by saying why I have written this book. I want to emphasize the deeply political character of dissent and its criminalization. This will involve thinking about how other writers especially those working in social sciences like sociology, criminology and political science have thought about politics, dissent and criminalization. If we think about dissent as I do here, we will need to describe, understand and evaluate what happens when politics is criminalized.

I do not want to assume that protest is the only kind of dissent worth paying attention to. It is entirely characteristic, however, that a major study of the law of dissent and written at the end of one of the most tumultuous decades in twentieth-century American history should focus on civil disobedience, protest marches and riots (Bassiouni 1971). Likewise, Deidre MacKinnon's (2014) impressive work of scholarship essentially conflates dissent with political protest. When Jeff Shantz points out that the criminalization of dissent 'in an era of neoliberal governance … has been 'understudied and undertheorized' … in recent works of social science, politics and legal studies' the force of this observation is reduced when he and his collaborators weaken conflate 'protest' with 'dissent'. I will suggest that while there is a tendency to treat protest as if it is identical with dissent, this is far from being the whole story.

There are many other kinds of dissent than protests of various kinds. Though Gene Sharp preferred to talk about 'non-violent struggle', he pointed, e.g. to some 'two hundred identified methods of symbolic protest, social non-co-operation, economic boycotts, labor strikes, political noncooperation, and nonviolent intervention (ranging from sit-ins to parallel government)' (Sharp 1990: 2–3). Yet even that approach ignores the possibility that dissent may be far more diverse and may, e.g. involve both far smaller scale, often lonely kinds of dissent than the mass anti-Austerity demonstrations that erupted in southern Europe after 2008, or the millions of 'Anonymous' pro-democracy hacktivists flooding government websites after 2010.

I think, e.g. of the solitary decision taken by a man called Robert Walsh who displayed prodigious resilience and personal courage in his act of dissent. Walsh was in his thirties when he decided to report to police the fact that as a young child and a pupil at St Alipius Christian Brothers School in Ballarat, a regional city of 100,000 people in Australia, he had been repeatedly raped by a Christian Brother called Robert Best. Later another priest called Gerald Risdale repeated the abuse. Like so many other victims of priestly sexual abuse, Robert Walsh felt unable to disclose his abuse or confront his abusers until decades later, partly because he felt he was somehow to blame for the abuse he suffered. Nonetheless,

Robert Walsh finally overcame all of the reasons he had for saying or doing nothing and went to the police to allege that a Christian Brother and a Catholic priest had raped him. Robert Walsh bears eloquent witness to the purpose and value of a quite lonely and personal kind of dissent especially when it involves speaking truth to power in the name of justice.

Or there is the case of Ian Hislop, the redoubtable editor of Britain's *Private Eye* since 1986, who has made satire into an art form. Hislop rightly treats dissent as far more than protest. The magazine itself has tirelessly ridiculed the vice, folly and humbug of political, business and social elites, while the 'Street of Shame' column that appears in Private Eye is devoted to critical evaluations of British journalists, editors and publications. He has been responsible for memorable front pages in the magazine like one featuring an image of a little girl in hospital being visited by Prime Minister Thatcher who asks, 'What will you do if you grow up'? As Hislop said later, you can either write a 2,000 word piece in the Guardian about the failure of National Health or you can make a joke about it (Wroe 1995).

Hislop's larger point about dissent is made in a remarkable exhibition he curated at the British Museum in 2018 entitled 'I Object' bringing together dissenting objects from across many centuries. The images and objects include the yellow umbrellas carried by pro-democracy protestors in Hong Kong in 2014, a 1904 British penny stamped by women suffragettes with their slogan 'Votes for Women', a 1794 cartoon by Richard Newton showing John Bull farting towards the image of King George III with the one word punchline 'Treason!' to a 'Dump Trump' badge from 2017 (Hislop and Hockenhull 2018). Jonathan Jones' critical review of Hislop's 2018 exhibition is worth quoting at length:

> What is dissent? In Britain, this word started out as a term for radical religious minorities and became a political word partly because they were associated with political protest. That's one example of the infinite local contexts and nuances this show ignores. How can you speak of dissent in the abstract? People protest against, mock or subvert authority not just in very different ways but for different reasons. Authority itself takes different forms. [The Hislop] show insists that somehow it's all the same impulse. That flattens history.
> (Jones 2018)

Like Jones, I do not want to flatten history. We need a richer more inclusive idea of dissent.

Secondly dissent understood in this more general way does not always get the acknowledgement or careful thought that is warranted. The tendency to overlook dissent as an important aspect of social and political life reflects some of the 'odd' even puzzling aspects of dissent. I at least was puzzled to discover the extent to which academic research, especially on the part of those working in the mainstream of social sciences like political science, legal studies and criminology, disciplines, I assume, exist to make sense of political and legal matters, being inclined to overlook both dissent and the disposition of liberal-democratic states to repress or criminalize it. One bizarre expression of this oddness is found in a recent text with the attention-grabbing, even bold title *The Right to Dissent* (Larsen 2009). What is odd is that the book does not actually discuss dissent in any way, shape or form. Indeed, it only identifies 'disagreement' as a synonym for dissent and deals with this thought in *just one footnote* and then does this in fleeting fashion (Larsen 2009: 313). Granting the difficulty of documenting an absence, this is suggestive of the way dissent *per se* as distinct from protest or social movements leads something of a fugitive existence in the mainstream of contemporary social sciences.

Of course, this is not to deny the significant interest on the part of some scholars, e.g. in specific aspects of forms of dissent or its criminalization. There is a body of scholarship addressing free speech and/or its repression (e.g. Greenwalt 1989; Gelber 2002) or civil disobedience (Brownlee 2012). Nor is this to ignore a very substantial level of interest by political scientists, sociologists and criminologists in social movements and public disorder (e.g. Shantz 2011; Sylvestre 2014; Dafnos 2014; Della Porta 2009, 2013, 2015). In particular, political scientists like Donatella della Porta have generated an impressive body of research work both documenting and theorizing the nature of protest activity and social movements along with the reactions of states to protest (Della Porta et al., 2006; Della Porta 2009, 2013, 2015). Equally other social sciences like sociology, media studies, cultural studies and anthropology have also paid a lot of attention to social movements and protest. As Biggs (2015: 1–33) argues, an interest in what sociologists like to call 'contentious collective action' manifest in social movements, protests, rebellions, riots, strikes, and revolutions has proved to be a persistent preoccupation among sociologists (also Tarrow 2011: 7: Tilly 1995a, 1995b; Coleman 2011; Fuchs 2013). Equally, there is also a small but growing body of work exploring the criminalization of dissent (Lapham 2004; Lyon 2007; Boykoff 2007; Fernandez, 2008; Shantz 2011; Greenberg 2012). But again we come back to my starting point: when the social science does pay attention, they are preoccupied with protest.

Let me start by outlining the key questions I will address before I say something about some of the problems which have led me to write this book.

Key questions

In this book, I want to address a number of closely connected questions. To begin with, there are basic questions like: what is dissent and how should we think about it? Is dissent being criminalized and, if so, to what extent are liberal-democratic states criminalizing it? Why do liberal-democratic states criminalize dissent? How should we make sense of this exercise in criminalization?

These questions open up fundamental political and ethical issues centring on the relations between sovereignty and the idea of legitimacy. Sovereignty refers to the power and authority of the state. Joseph Strayer says 'Sovereignty requires independence from any outside power and final authority over men who live within certain boundaries' (Strayer 1970: 58).[1] Legitimacy asks the questions: why should I obey that state? Is it because the state has sovereign power? Or is it for some other reason like the goods that compliance with the law brings? Given that liberal-democratic states invariantly claim that their criminalization of dissent is legitimate, how should we think about legitimacy and its relationship to the sovereignty of the modern liberal-democratic state? Is the repression or criminalization of dissent legitimate? Why might dissent be both valuable and legitimate?

To address these questions, I will be drawing on a range of cases, evidence and theoretical perspectives with the intention to be modestly innovative in a number of ways. I do this because there are some problems with the way in which conventional social sciences deal with dissent and its criminalization.

The social sciences on dissent and its criminalization

For one thing when those sociologists, legal scholars or political scientists do acknowledge dissent, they tend to rely on some odd interpretative or explanatory theoretical perspectives and miss out on some of the truly puzzling aspects of dissent.

Consider the vast literature on social movements. As Della Porta and Daniani (2006: 1) noted more than a decade back, the study of social movements even then had become a major area of research 'with specialized journals, book series, and professional associations'. While much of this literature offers all sorts of important insights, it also suffers from some important defects which constrain how we might think about social movements *as well as all the other forms of dissent that the social movement literature overlooks*.

One key problem, e.g. begins with the premise that it is possible to both explain and to predict important aspects of social movements, a premise that points to the lingering effects of the positivist origins of the social sciences, especially to the underpinnings supplied by a tradition of 'substantialism', which treats the world as a 'world of things'. I have a lot to say about this in the following chapters.

A second but somewhat different problem has to do with how the many forms that dissent takes all seem to provoke states, including the most liberal-democratic ones, into criminalizing that dissent. Many ordinary people including the readers of this book will likely be surprised to discover the extent to which liberal-democratic states have been prepared to repress dissent by criminalizing its many forms, both old and new.

This practice has a long history. It is surely noteworthy, e.g. that barely a decade after the Americans won their War of Independence (1775–83) conventionally understood as the first instalment in the Age of the Democratic Revolution (Palmer 1959/1964), that a Federalist-dominated Congress passed the Sedition Act of 1798, making it an offence *to even criticize the American government*, an action taken in the name of national security. In our time, we now have abundant evidence that the American state has repeatedly carried out extensive and illegal surveillance of large numbers of its own citizens (Greenwald 2014; Owen 2017).

It also seems that some states will do almost anything to stamp out dissent. We have seen, e.g. quite bizarre cases of liberal-democratic states deciding that political satire is a criminal matter. On 31 March 2016, Jan Böhmermann, a German TV satirist read a poem about Recip Erdoğan, the then President of Turkey (2014–) on his show. The poem claimed that Erdoğan engaged in 'intimate relations with goats and sheep' and watched child-pornography while repressing the Kurdish people. A furious Erdoğan insisted that Böhmermann be prosecuted under Germany's penal code. Paragraph 103 of Germany's penal code prohibits German citizens from 'insulting foreign heads of state'. The same penal code also required that the German government give consent to the prosecution of such cases and the Turkish president subsequently received Chancellor Angela Merkel's permission for proceedings to go ahead (Global Freedom of Expression 2016). In October 2016, German prosecutors sensibly enough dropped the case against Bohmermann (Sauerbray 2016).

In Britain too, governments have long used a variety of laws and policing techniques to regulate, and in some cases to suppress dissent by criminalizing it. British governments have used Section 44 of the *Terrorism Act 2000* to *police non-terrorist activities*. In 2003, police used the *Terrorism Act 2000* to stop and search the belongings of a student protestor and a journalist attending a protest against an arms trading fair in London (International Network of Civil Liberties Organizations 2013: 50).

Then there are the curious ways the social sciences have addressed the practice of criminalization in general and the criminalization of dissent in particular. We might, e.g. have expected that when states rely on legal – and even more significantly illegal – practices to stamp out dissent, small but vigorous criminology of state crime would have engaged this issue. There certainly have been attempts especially coming from sociology and criminology to understand that when states suppress various kinds of dissent and harm people in the course of doing this by abolishing their human rights or even killing or wounding them, this should be understood either as 'state crime' or as 'political crime' (Green and Ward 2004; Ross 2012). However, this approach involves dropping a narrative frame based on the originary sociological idea that any social order is also a moral order and that crime *of any kind* is a form of deviance. Hence, Penny Green and Tony Ward claim that state crime is 'organisational deviance involving the violation of human rights' (Green and Ward 2004: 2), which they enlarge on to suggest that 'state crime is one category of organisational deviance, along with corporate crime, organised crime and the neglected area of crime by charities churches and other non-profit bodies' (Green and Ward 2004: 5). This somewhat odd premise then produces either what some might call a 'classic sociological account' – or what I have called a 'farrago of muddled thinking' (Watts 2016: 50). Consider, e.g. David Kauzlarich and Ronald Kramer's claim that state crime at an organizational level:

> ...[r]esults when there is a coincidence of pressure for goal attainment, availability and perceived attractiveness of illegitimate means, and an absence of or weakness of social control mechanisms.
> (Kauzlarich and Kramer 1998: 148; Ross 2012)

Jeffrey Ross (2012: 25–7) likewise offers a resolutely sociological account of 'political crime' that becomes seriously weird. This begins with the idea that some people are 'nonconformists or malcontents' who take advantage of situations inside organizations that facilitate illegal and deviant behaviour. The really unfortunate effect this has is to conflate, even render identical the actions of a state when it decides to brutally suppress some form of political dissent with the various forms of that dissent, because both involve some kind of 'deviance'. As Ross says, e.g. his theory applies 'whether we are talking about terrorist groups or national security groups' (Ross 2012: 25). The oddity of this is epitomized by Ross (2012) when a sequence of chapters surveys 'nonviolent oppositional political crimes' (i.e. protest marches by citizens) and 'illegal domestic surveillance' by the state! All of this ignores the basic problem that states routinely get to decide what is illegal (which includes the various forms of dissent they don't like) as well as what is legal like their decision to harass or suppress that dissent.

A different problem characterizes the field of criminalization studies. Broadly speaking, this field has not paid much attention to the criminalization of dissent. In spite of a burgeoning interest in criminalization (Lacey 2009, 2013; Brown 2013), we have yet to see any substantial interest in the criminalization of dissent.

A few writers have touched on aspects of what is involved when states engage in 'preventive justice' (Zedner 2007, 2009). Some scholars of constitutional law have noted how even liberal-democratic states are easily moved to declare 'states of exception' and use various 'grey' and 'black' legal holes legalizing the use of 'force' against dissent or perceived threats to 'national security' (Dyzenhaus 1997, 2006; Loughlin 2015). This can lead to the reinvention of coercive preventive justice measures and the suspension of long-cherished rights like *habeas corpus* justified by claims that the state in question is now engaged in a 'war on terror'. This last body of work begins to highlight one of the key puzzles addressed in this book.

The idea that liberal-democracies value toleration, freedom of speech and difference has long been a commonplace of political theory. The liberal philosophical narrative says that starting with the Reformation and in terms subsequently elaborated on initially by John Locke, Western states came increasingly to accept the proposition that citizens had a right to have and to express diverse religious and other opinions. At the hands of later liberal philosophers from von Humboldt, Constant and J.S Mill in the nineteenth century to modern liberals like Isaiah Berlin, John Rawls and John Gray, this evolved into the proposition that the project of human progress was best served by protecting and encouraging a plurality of attitudes and ways of living (Nederman and Laursen 1990: 2–3).

However, as some critics like Robert Woolf, Barrington Moore and Herbert Marcuse (1968) noted, there has to be more than a suspicion that the ethic of toleration that liberal-democracies are supposed to foster is at odds with the actual political conduct of these states that are intolerant of, even hostile to difference, diversity and dissent. Harbouring that suspicion is why Harriet Brabazon asks one pointed question: if liberal-democracies around the world pride themselves on principles like freedom of association and democratic rights such as the right to political expression, or freedom of movement, 'Why would these states and their decision-makers not welcome social movements and dissent of all kinds as a natural part of the rich fabric of citizen participation in decision-making?' (Brabazon 2006: 3). Brabazon's question is fundamentally pertinent to this book – and helps to explain the focus on liberal-democratic states. The fact that liberal-democratic states not only seem to disapprove of dissent but also regularly and routinely criminalize it points to a basic puzzle about the legitimacy of dissent in liberal-democratic states.

To summarize then: dissent has many more faces than is typically acknowledged, and certainly goes well beyond protest activity. Yet dissent is also an odd activity or practice and the social sciences have not handled the many faces of dissent as well as they might, or the persistent attempts by liberal-democratic states to criminalize it. As I will argue here, we need to take the idea that suppressing dissent by means that are both legal and extra-legal amounts to a practice of *criminalizing the political*. This implies that we need to think about dissent, politics and the political and to do this in terms of the relations between the state, the law, sovereignty and legitimacy.

To start with, there are puzzles about the status of dissent itself.

The problem of dissent

For one thing, governments, elite groups and even lots of ordinary citizens tend on the whole to not like dissent in any of its forms. Some research evidence suggests that many of us think that governments are indeed right to 'crack down' on protest marches because this is just plain old 'common-sense': flag waving and protest marches, especially, when they involve, violence rarely seem like a 'normal' or 'good thing' to be doing (O'Keefe and Schumaker 1983: 375–94). As Peterson and Wahlstrom (2015) point out, cases of dissent like social movement protest seem almost to provoke states to use a wide range of techniques to repress dissent.

In places like Britain or Australia, this looks a lot like a 'fear of politics'. Citizens in these countries have a long-standing experience of quintessentially democratic institutions and practices like a multi-party parliamentary system, free elections, the rule of law, free unions, a free press and so on. However, one of the problems it seems now is that many citizens don't like the adversarial style of politics involving hyper-aggression, personal hostilities and rudeness between politicians or the fact that politicians seem unable or unwilling to agree on very much. In Australia, e.g. commentators have decried the level of negativity and hostility characterizing Parliamentary debate while public opinion polls recorded a 33 per cent decline in satisfaction with the Parliament in the last year (Bull and Wells 2012). Yet this kind of criticism seems to forget that disagreement and opposition has been designed into the very institution of parliament itself, symbolized by the way Parliamentary buildings require as a fundamental that the deliberative spaces provide a place to be occupied on one side by the government and the other by an Opposition. The very idea of politics as a contest of ideas, or for votes seems by some strange alchemy, to have become a reason why many do not now like all the 'conflict' and 'disagreement' and absence of consensus said to characterize what some call a 'crisis of democracy'.

Though this defence will be considered in more detail later, we may also see in state suppression of dissent, evidence of what some call the 'pluralist prejudice'. This is the axiomatic assumption that because Western liberal-democratic political systems already provide more than enough politically expressive channels like open media, freedom of expression, or free and open elections, there is really no need for dissent or protest. This assumption is central to what can be called the 'liberal imaginary', namely the idea that politics properly understood is all about individuals engaging in rational, self-interested action oriented to consensus.

Law against liberty: the problem of dissent and its criminalization

Mindful of Helena Rosenblatt's (2018) warning about how we use categories like 'liberalism', Koshka Duff brilliantly summarizes conventional liberal political theory's animus against dissent, noting how it starts from the premise that 'history shows there is no desirable alternative to liberalism' and that dissenters therefore need to be both constructive and 'realistic', i.e. they need to specify what they would put in place of existing social arrangements' (Duff 2015: 50).[2]

Further the strong preference for consensus rather than dissensus is another important clue. As Perry Anderson noted, important liberal theorists like John Rawls and Jurgen Habermas share a common political ideal: consensus (Anderson 2006: xv). This may be why so many think that dissent is really neither necessary nor valuable. Liberal institutions are legitimate because they do not impose any particular vision of 'the good life' on individuals (unlike totalitarian or communist states), while liberal states afford a framework within which free and equal citizens can disagree – 'so long as they are reasonable about it'. Citizens can elect their representatives in free, open elections, which leads to the formation of governments bound to obey the popular will and to uphold the rule of law – which says, e.g. all must be treated as equals before the law. In liberal societies, governments are obliged to uphold the rule of law, and protect everyone's rights to free speech and other relevant civic or human rights. So anyone who steps outside these rules of the game is clearly up to no good. People who ignore or bypass the available channels must be doing so because they are 'irrational', 'deviant' or worse criminally inclined or even treasonous. Given this background of persistent official animus against protest and other forms of dissent, it is not surprising that popular anxiety, suspicion or fear swirls around protest and other kinds of dissent are based on the intuition that these kinds of activities are somehow not quite the right thing to do.

However, this puzzle about the odd status of dissent only deepens when we consider the evidence that some of this popular negativity about dissent implicates the media which has played a major role in giving protest in particular, and dissent more generally, a bad rap. The popular media in most liberal democracies tends, e.g. to report protests in terms generally unfavourable to those doing the protesting and in ways generally supportive of police responses. Much of this reportage relies on the idea, e.g. that protest is disruptive, disorderly and potentially or actually violent. BBC reporting on action by groups like AntiFacist Action (Antifa), e.g. typically stressed their violent dispositions:

> Antifa is anti-government and anti-capitalist … Unlike the mainstream left, they do not seek to gain power through traditional channels – winning elections and passing bills into law. Antifa does not shy away from militant protest methods, including the destruction of property and sometimes physical violence.
>
> (Cameron 2017)

Yet this negative representation of dissent by the media sits oddly with the long-standing self-portrait produced by the media itself. Framed as the 'Fourth Estate', the media represent themselves as the guardians of democracy and defenders of the public interest. On this account, the 'Fourth Estate' understands the mass media as a powerful watchdog in liberal democracy, revealing abuses of state authority and defending the democratic rights of citizens. At the least, it might have been expected that those working in the media would feel or express some affinity with those who dissent. However, Habermas' (1989) account of the public sphere testifies to the way that, while this idea might have been true in the eighteenth century, the modern media have morphed into industries, wholly oriented to the profit motive, and become just another corporate business.

Then there is the deep puzzle about dissent that originates within the tradition of liberalism itself, or at least that important strand of modern liberalism that links, e.g. John Stuart Mill (1859/1998) and Isaiah Berlin (1991, 2002).

Semantically we can say that 'dissent' signifies disagreement and is the opposite of 'consent'. Understood as disagreement, dissent is as normal as it is ubiquitous. This is how Berlin, one of the greatest of modern liberal theorists, understood the ubiquity and normality of disagreement. Berlin (1991, 2002) insisted that we take seriously the idea that, in any human community, there is simply an irreducible plurality of 'values' or ethical ideas. Berlin says we confront a world in which there is simply a multiplicity of values, and no rational or 'objective' way of saying that one is better or more true than another. Berlin insisted that the plurality of conflicts between our ethical ideas is 'an intrinsic, irremovable element in human life': 'the idea of total human fulfilment is a […] chimera' (Berlin 2002: 213). 'These collisions of values are of the essence of what they are and what we are'. Berlin insist that a world in which such conflicts are ever resolved or made to go away is *not* the world we live in, know or understand (Berlin 1991: 13).

In short, pluralism acknowledges that there are just different beliefs, truth claims, conflicts, and thus choices, not only between particular values or truth claims in individual cases, but even between different ways of life. For example, the beliefs and conduct of a Catholic doctor who emphasizes the 'sacred' grounds of all life are incompatible with those of a feminist woman who wants the freedom to decide what she does with her own body. The related idea is that while each of these ideas is worthwhile and valuable, there is no rational or 'objective' way of saying which is true or which is preferable, which doesn't rely on or insert into the criteria used to ascertain the criteria of rationality or objectivity assumptions that are themselves neither rational or objective, but which are used to bolster the case being made.

Berlin has not been the only major thinker in our time to point to the problem that there are many competing ethical ideas and principles and some have gone on to rethink what this implies for our conception of 'the political' and/or democracy.

Politics as conflict (*agon*)

This discussion has centred on the idea that *agon* is somehow a desirable feature of democracy and a defining feature of the political more generally. *Agon* is the Greek word for 'struggle', 'conflict', 'contest' or 'competition'. As Kalyvas (2016: 18) reminds us, the Greek *polis* hosted athletic games (*agones*) from the ninth century BCE on. In these *agones*, contestants strove to excel, to distinguish themselves to be the best and to win in a fair and open contest and in front of a public gathering of spectators (Kalyvas, 2016: 18). As Schaap (2016: 1) notes, modern theorists of the political including Hannah Arendt, Michel Foucault, Chantal Mouffe, William Connolly and Jacques Ranciere have all developed a distinctive if not always entirely consensual account of the political and/or of democracy as *agon*. Bonnie Honig (1993, 2008), along with these important theorists of the political, is inclined to treat the political as synonymous with disagreement and conflict (*agon*).

However, are we entitled to conflate Berlin's conception of the pluralism with the idea that politics or democracy is inherently and desirably agonist? What does the idea of *agon* imply for understanding the political, democracy and the practice of dissent? And what happens when *agon* becomes antagonism, even violent confrontation? This was a possibility Michel Foucault half-recognized when he suggested that rather than fussing about freedom 'it would be better to speak of an "agonism" – of a relationship which is at the same time reciprocal incitation and struggle; less face-to-face confrontation which paralyzes both sides than a permanent provocation' (Foucault 1983: 222).

The discussion about *agonism* as I suggest later in this book opens up complex questions about the extent to which *agon*, dissent and antagonism can be deemed both a legitimate and a desirable political activity in any community.

While writers like Honig, Mouffe and Ranciere are unfazed by evidence of disagreement (as was the case for Berlin), for others disagreement is a problem, possibly even a scandal. Other major liberals like John Rawls (1971), Jurgen Habermas (1996), and Amy Gutmann and Deniss Thompson (2002), while accepting pluralism as an initial position, also seem annoyed, as Bonnie Honig (1993) points out, when faced with evidence of disagreement. Honig notes, e.g. that 'most [liberal] political theorists are hostile to the disruptions of politics' and 'assume that the task of political theory is … to get politics … over and done with' (Honig 1993: 2). In consequence, they have done their level best to go beyond dissent to arrive at a place of consensus and achieve a workable political order by installing various deliberative procedures into our public life – but arguably at some cost to the robustness of our democratic culture. Here too we see something of the oddity that the preoccupation with order and consensus gives rise to.

Politics as human action

At stake here is not only the relation of *agon* to consensus but the puzzling nature of human being itself understood as 'human action' and the ways we orient to or value the relation between order/continuity and difference/change. As will become clear whatever else it is to be human, human being involves a ceaseless process of change where nothing is ever the same today as it was yesterday. Biologically our embodied-self grows, develops and then decays. Our body/mind is constantly plunging forwards from the moment of our conception, then birth and onto our decline and death. Pascal's (1670) famous evocation of the human condition may not play well in an age preoccupied with happiness, but who can gainsay the truth of it:

> Let us imagine a number of men in chains, and all condemned to death, where some are killed each day in the sight of the others, and those who remain see their own fate in that of their fellows, and wait their turn, looking at each other sorrowfully and without hope.
>
> (Pascal 1670/1995: 199)

Our communities and civic spaces are spaces likewise of restless change, difference, innovation and movement, generated in part by those biological life processes like the co-presence of many generations which shape and impel changing needs across what we call the 'life-cycle'. This is to say nothing, as Hannah Arendt (1958) reminded us of the momentum provided by the birth of new citizens as much as by the ceaseless loss to death or the admixture of strangers, peoples from other places as migrants or tourists. Our cultural processes, enabled and embedded in what we call 'consciousness', i.e. the various ways we represent the world to ourselves are communicated, exchanged and elaborated both in our embodied mind and in and across many symbolic and cultural fields of action. As Merlin Donald (1991, 2001) has shown, the evolution or unfolding of human consciousness involves the generation of new ideas, inside expressive forms like song, image and story, as well as in scientific and interpretative knowledge forms reproduced, preserved and embedded in symbolic mnemonic technologies including languages, writing books, libraries, smart phones and iPads.

This runs up against the way we conventionally understand politics and the political as processes committed to ordering, regulating and governing human communities understood often in Hobbesian terms as the requirement that we need states to regulate otherwise unruly, evil and disobedient tendencies 'hardwired' into human nature. We will have occasion soon to turn to the radical critique of 'the political' in the work of Carl Schmitt (1985; 2003) and Carlo

Galli (2015). This work poses important questions: how should we understand the obsession with order when this is set against the ontological disposition to change and impermanence that actually characterizes both the natural and human worlds? Might it not imply that order and permanence is an imaginary, a defence, or a wall constructed to defend us against what we find too terrifying to acknowledge or deal with and might this not have implications for what and how and we think about how dissent relates to the political?

If there is a good case for treating disagreement as a normal part of our life in common and of our kind of liberal-democratic communities, this is plainly not a view that appears to be widely shared by most liberals, the media, liberal-democratic states or the mass of citizens. Yet this seems to run contrary to much of that the real character of the human condition and the actual history of liberal democracies tells us about the role played by political disagreement, dissent and conflict. This suggests we need to think again about the problem of how to acknowledge and/or value the role of disagreement, conflict and dissent. If this is the case, it requires us to address one large question: if disagreement and dissent are as common as I think they are, how and why does dissent become such a problem? This is why this book is about dissent *and* its criminalization.

Overview

In what follows, I start by thinking about the ubiquity of disagreement and the bad rep dissent enjoys (Chapter 1). This is also an opportunity to think about the many problems which the conventional social science preoccupation with definitions points to. This is an opportunity to outline the problems with the doctrine of substance and why taking the 'relational turn' is a good move. As will become clear this involves treating dissent as a political practice-cum-relationship.

In Chapter 2, I begin the process of elaborating a relational account of politics, the political and dissent as a kind of free-floating energy that undermines the very institutions and practices it also constitutes (Sitze 2015: xxiii). I draw on writers like Arendt and Bourdieu to catch the peculiar relational quality of the political by twining the categories of *praxis*/practice. Arendt shows how being political entails the capacity to act (Arendt 1968: 179). Arendt relies on the classical Greek conception of act as *arche*, which means both beginnings *and* the order produced by governing/directing (Arendt 1958: 177). Bourdieu's focus on the conflict immanent to any field of action is a reminder that even the *habitus* that practice sustains is both orderly and agonistic. This opens the way to treating dissent and its criminalization as an example of the immanent polarities of order-and-disorder given the central role played by the state in criminalizing certain forms of conduct.

I return then (in Chapter 3) to outlining the many faces of dissent as political praxis. I use Engin Isin's (2005) relational account of the political in a world exhibiting a complex mix of enduring institutions, habitual conduct, and hierarchies of authority *and* an irreducible pluralism of difference and disagreement. I use one case study of Israeli selective refusers to highlight some of the ways in which dissent works inside a hierarchical and authoritarian space like a military unit. I use another case of urban squatters in various cities, to foreground other ways dissent works highlighting the possibility that different kinds of relations like solidarity *and* antagonism are at work.

In Chapter 4, I highlight the fundamental contradiction at work in liberal democracies between apparent support for freedom of speech and dissent and the ruthless suppression of dissent initially by using the Occupy Wall Street movement to highlight this tension. I then overview some of the legislative and policing techniques that the British American and Australian state has used to criminalize dissent using 'crimes' like sedition, anti-terrorism and public disorder.

In Chapter 5, I ask how has the criminalization been explained and understood so far especially by those working in the field of criminalization studies? As I will show, there has been a disposition to explain what has been called the 'punitive turn' or 'over criminalization' as a 'rational' response to a 'real' problem, i.e. increasing crime rates. Others have explained the punitive turn by treating it as a natural consequence of a particular form of liberalism called 'neoliberalism'. How well do these explanations work in relation to both 'normal' crime let alone political crime? As I suggest here, these kinds of explanations do not work all that well.

Granted that criminalization studies have been unwilling to pay much attention to the criminalization of political dissent, we need to understand how it happens. In Chapter 6, I use the British state's prosecution of the publishers of *The Little Red School Book* (1971) as a classic case of criminalizing freedom of speech. I argue that both cases illuminate the incoherence and irrationality at work in the complex and not necessarily rational relationship between liberalism, fear and security. I draw on Ian Hacking's (1998, 2001) 'historical ontological' framework to show the relational dynamics are at work in what Hacking calls ecological niches. This highlights the need to treat the modern liberal-democratic state as 'the unity of difference between consent and dissent, and fear and security'.

In Chapter 7, I begin to think about the relations between legal systems and the deep questions raised about the legitimacy of the criminalization process in general and the criminalization of dissent in particular. The chapter addresses two questions: first, what makes law 'lawful' or 'legitimate'? Second, why ought I, or we, obey a state – and its laws and policies? To answer these questions, I survey the Anglo-American legal tradition, which has tried to locate the legitimacy of the law in everything but the sovereign power (i.e. violence) of the state. As I show no-one has done better than John Austin when he argued drawing on Hobbes imperative theory of the law that say when the state orders you to do something you should do so because if you don't you will be punished. The threat of evil being done to you says Austin is the only obligation to obey that matters: sovereignty trumps legitimacy.

A parallel effort by political theorists to ground legitimacy in the democratic consent of 'The People' is explored in Chapter 8: are there political grounds for securing the legitimacy of liberal-democratic states? Because liberal democracy claims its political legitimacy rests on the consent of 'The People', dissent is always a problem because it subverts any simple idea about the point and value of popular consent. Worse as I show any defence of legitimacy of liberal-democratic states understood as the search for the implied ethical or normative basis of liberal democracy, does not stand too much close scrutiny. This may well be the point those who use Schmitt's critique of liberal democracy think they are making. However, even Schmitt missed something important. Even if Schmitt wants to use his decisionistic account of the political to deny any normative basis for the political, he has failed to do so. Human goods are always at stake in the political.

That point is made in Chapter 9, which uses Nelson Mandela's advocacy for political violence against the South African apartheid state ca. 1962–91 to address a series of questions. When, if ever is political violence justified? What does justifiable political violence look like? What particular forms or uses of violence may be just, or justifiable in political contexts or to political purposes? What distinguishes just political violence from unjust [political] violence? Writers like Uwe Steinhoff (2007) and Jason Brennan (2016, 2019) argue that we need to resist the temptation to assume that in liberal-democracies, only non-violent resistance to state injustice is permissible, and that 'we must defer to democratic government agents, even when these agents act in deeply unjust, harmful, and destructive ways' (Brennan 2016: 40).

The need to make the case for armed resistance let alone engage in it may at this time be beyond the pale in most existing liberal-democratic states. In the Conclusion I argue the more limited case that dissent is a valuable activity when dissent is part of a practice of discerning and living out the goods that make our lives good and fulfilling and worth living. It is especially valuable when it pursues the good conceived of as knowledge of truth. As such, dissent stands opposed to those many kinds of ignorance that tend to be promoted by institutions like states, or by particular regressive imaginaries promoted by people on the right and the left who want to abolish diversity and plurality. We need to remember and emulate the strong case made since Socrates through Kant, and J.S. Mill to John Finnis and Martha Nussbaum, that we need to be free to think and engage critically in public ways: this kind of practice is always going to end up in dissent especially when those with interests to protect see criticism as dangerous or a threat to those interests.

Notes

1 This approach signifies the conventional idea that state sovereignty had something to do with the Treaties of Westphalia (1648) a view contested heavily by John Ruggie (1993), Benno Teschke (2003) and Saskia Sassen (2006). As will be clear for my general thinking about sovereignty, I have drawn heavily on Jens Bartelson (1993, 2014), Steven Krasner (1999) and Jean Bethke Elshtain (2008).

2 Helena Rosenblatt (2018) reminds us in a watered-down version of Reinhart Kosselleck's (2002) 'conceptual history', that 'liberalism' is both a hotly contested category and one with a history that is frequently ignored or forgotten. She offers to fix this with 'a story that has never been told' using what is effectively a 'word history' that actually works by excising liberal discourse from political practice (Rosenblatt 2018: 2).

Chapter 1

Thinking about dissent

If there is one image from the twentieth century that seems to capture the essence of dissent, and so works as a kind of cult image, it must surely be the 1989 image of the lone Chinese protestor, often referred to as 'Tank Man'. This nameless man was photographed on 5 June 1989, by Associated Press photographer Jeff Widener from a hotel some 800 m away and just one day after the China's Red Army had literally crushed the pro-democracy movement in Tiananmen Square in Beijing underneath the steel treads of its tanks. The man was photographed standing alone just some meters in front of a menacingly large military tank at the head of a line of similarly menacing tanks. He is wearing a white shirt and black trousers and appears to be carrying what looks to be one or more shopping bags. Witnesses saw the man repeatedly block the passage of a line of very large tanks bearing down on him before he was scooped up by security forces. Like his name, his fate remains unknown.

As with other images, from the countless depictions of Christ's crucifixion, through the American sailor kissing a girl in Times Square in 1945, to Marilyn Monroe holding down her billowing white dress, any sense or meaning these 'iconic' images have, all depend on a range of prior beliefs and conceptual schemes. We need to already know what the image means, before we can 'see' it. In effect, while it is often said that 'a picture is worth a thousand words', this cliché is demonstrably untrue. You can check this by turning off the soundtrack of a TV newscast or a feature film and try to work out what is going on. As John Berger (1972) and Pierre Bourdieu (2017) remind us, a picture typically needs a thousand words – or more – to disclose its meaning. But how do words work and how do they make sense of reality?

I want to do a few things in this book. I want to make sense of dissent, and establish why and how it is often criminalized by states and whether this raises some problems about the legitimacy of doing this. So to make sense of 'dissent' or 'criminalization', I could begin by asking a simple question like, what is dissent? and then offering some sort of definition. This is a fairly standard, almost common sense approach. There is an expectation in books like this that the author will offer a formal definition of the thing s/he is interested in. However, I will have to disappoint.

There are some basic problems with this common sense approach. The problems have to do first, with how we think about using words to make sense of the world we live in. This is because we tend to assume that words name things. This points to another bigger more important assumption namely that many of us think that the world we live in is made of stuff called things.

On the face of it, this looks right. As I look around the room where I am writing this chapter, e.g. it is full of things including chairs, books, bookshelves, benches, two computers, a rug and so on. Even the room is a thing: it has walls, windows, a ceiling and a door. Then there's me. In an important way, I am also a thing: I have length, mass (too much), wear certain kinds of clothes and there are bits of me that are also things like my eyes, the feet I stand on as I work upright, or the hands with fingers which I use to type with and so on. Given that each of these things can be named, as I have just demonstrated what then could possibly be the problem?

As it turns out there are many problems: for one thing, neither dissent nor its criminalization are things. Rather they are actions or 'practices' and they need to be thought about in quite different way to the way we (and especially social scientists) normally think about things. This also has implications for the words we use. All of this matters because if we are to work out what is actually happening, we need to pay closer attention to what we are trying to describe and understand.

Let me start by saying why I have problems with definitions. This takes us to the common sense way we think about words and language which has been called the 'classical theory of language'. I then consider how the idea that the world is made of things has shaped the ways conventional social scientists in sociology, criminology or political science make sense of what is actually happening. Treating people as things, e.g. has encouraged a futile exercise in trying to measure/explain/predict what humans do. I then outline briefly an alternative perspective I am proposing for thinking about dissent (and its criminalization, that involves taking what's been called the 'relational turn'. Finally I unpack the first of several basic puzzles about the practice of dissent namely how the ubiquity of disagreement in ordinary life somehow becomes a 'problem' called 'dissent'. Let me start with definitions.

The problem with definitions?

It is a truth generally acknowledged by many social scientists that we cannot do any research till we have a clear definition. That said it seems that there are also problems when trying to define something like 'dissent'. Historian Robert Martin (2013: 3) acknowledges, e.g. that dissent is 'a very broad complicated category' and one that is also deeply 'contextual' before he plunges into the task of defining dissent declaring that:

> Dissent is any practice – often verbal, but sometimes performative – that challenges the *status quo* (the existing structure of norms, values, customs, traditions and especially authorities that underwrite the present ways of doing things.
>
> (Martin 2013: 3)

Donna Riley (2008: 20) likewise argues that dissent embodies a 'fundamental logic of social justice' and therefore 'defines itself against the *status quo*'. Riley draws on Brownlee's (2007/2013) account of civil disobedience, to highlight some of the key forms of activist dissent including civil disobedience (or non-violent direct action), legal protest, rule-breaking, conscientious objection, radical protest, revolutionary activism and then almost as an afterthought adding in industrial strikes and whistleblowing. Both Martin and Riley depends on Brownlee's assumption, made in a conventional and philosophically sanctioned way, that we can identify some *essential* features like 'a conscientious or principled outlook and the communication of both condemnation and a desire for change in law or policy' before adding other features like 'publicity, non-violence, fidelity to law'.

Roland Bleiker argues that producing an ideal-typical or abstracted definition let alone a formal, well-bounded 'model', or 'taxonomy' of 'dissent' (and I would add of categories like 'criminalization' or 'the state') is neither possible, let alone desirable. Bleiker says that the highly contingent nature of dissent means that 'grand theories of dissent run the risk of objectifying and entrenching forms of domination' (Bleiker 2000: 140). Bleiker (2000) suggests paying a lot of attention to each case of dissent rather than pursuing some 'grand theory of dissent'. Of course some will still insist that we cannot do this till we know what kinds of things count as a case or instance of dissent and that we need to enumerate or identify the core features of dissent.

Though this is not at all immediately obvious, this discussion highlights two really significant questions. The first of these is this: how do we use words to name the stuff of the world? The second of these is equally difficult: what is the 'stuff' of the world we are trying to make sense of?

It is fair to say that most conventional social scientists avoid engaging explicitly with both problems. When we look at the practices of conventional sociology and political science, we will see they think about and use language in ways that writers like Eleanor Rosch and George Lakoff say depend upon the 'classical theory of language'.[1] Equally most social scientists assume that the stuff they do their research on are things and assume that the social (or political) order is an 'order of things'. There is a significant reciprocal affinity operating between both assumptions. Both the 'classical theory of language' and the idea that our world is simply made up of things are unhelpful because untrue. Dissent is not a thing but an activity involving relations. Let me start with the 'classical theory of language' and spell out what this means and why it matters before I turn to the idea that social scientists need to stop thinking about things and to start thinking about relations and actions.

The classical theory of language

Expecting or demanding a definition depends on an old tradition of using words to define a name/thing in terms of its essential qualities or characteristics. For example, we might say that the name 'cat' is defined in terms of certain properties like being a small, typically furry, mostly domesticated, carnivorous mammal, with parts that include four legs, whiskers and a long tail. Elliot Sober points out that the search for essential defining features assumes that the world is made up of things characterized as:

> ... natural kinds. It holds that each natural kind can be defied in terms of properties that are possessed by all and only members of that kind. All gold has atomic number 79 and only gold has that atomic number ... a natural kind is to be characterized by a property that is both necessary and sufficient for membership.
>
> (Sober 1980: 148)

The expectation that we can or should define our categories entails that we can and should define the essential characteristics of the thing we are interested in as a prelude to some kind of enquiry, so that we can establish a true relationship between our truth claims and the world. In the natural sciences, this has informed the way natural scientists produce descriptions of rocks, flowers, chemicals or natural events. People working in the social sciences continue to heed Max Weber's advocacy for 'ideal types' by trying to define social and political phenomena like 'crime', 'the family', 'justice' or 'representative democracy' in ways that capture their defining properties (Derman 2012). This also informs the practice of operationalization in quantitative social science research which is based on the premise that we do not know the 'meaning of a concept unless we have a method of measuring it' (Bridgeman 1927: 5).

As Jerrold Katz says, what Lakoff calls the 'classical theory of language' has been spelled out in the twentieth century by philosophers like Frege (1952), Church (1956) and Searle (1958). This approach assumes that the practice of naming, and the idea of reference in general, relies on 'our mentally connecting a set of properties with a name, our identifying something as having each of these properties, and our applying the name to the object by virtue of this identification' (Katz 1977: 1). This 'classical theory of language' has come under deadly fire since the 1950s when Ludwig Wittgenstein (1958) laid out the problems with it.

Wittgenstein argued that traditional theories of meaning in Western philosophy had wrongly asserted that the meaning of a sentence was to be found outside the proposition and this is what gave a sentence its sense. This 'something' was located either in the world (or 'reality') or it was to be found in the mind as some kind of mental representation or 'idea'. Hence the meaning of sentence like 'The cat sat on the mat' makes sense and/or is true because there is a cat sitting on the mat. Or a sentence like 'Two plus two equals four' makes sense because we have agreed on the rule that 'Two plus two equals four'. As he argued the idea that 'the essence of human language' rested on the premise that 'the words in language name objects', and that 'sentences are combinations of such names' was nonsense because the reduction of language to representation failed to catch the complexity of what was going on. Wittgenstein argued that the meaning of the word is revealed in its actual use: in effect Wittgenstein became an anthropologist of language itself as a form of life is a practice that is part of a way of life found in all communities. If we look at the actual use of words, they reflect a rich array of language-games and practices relying loosely on rules that we use, e.g. when reporting an event, speculating about an event, forming and testing a hypothesis, making up a story, reading it, play-acting, singing catches, guessing riddles, making a joke, translating, asking and thanking (Wittgenstein 1958: 11–12). In effect, Wittgenstein was arguing against the time-honoured idea that we can produce definitions, a point he made delightfully by showing that we cannot even provide a definition of the concept of a 'language-game' because there is always something fuzzy and contingent about the way we use the idea of 'game'.

That idea, in turn, inspired scholars like Eleanor Rosch and George Lakoff, who grasped the implications of Wittgenstein's attack on the idea that language was a literal representation of reality. Lakoff argued that the 'classical theory of language' relies on many problematic assumptions including claims that:

- words only have one meaning and can be defined or be comprehended literally;
- only literal language can be – contingently – true or false;
- all definitions given in the lexicon of a language as represented, e.g. by a dictionary are literal, the concepts used in the grammar of a language.

(Lakoff 1993: 205)

As Lakoff has demonstrated none of these claims are true. Research by Rosch (1975) shows that concepts like 'fruit' or 'animal' encoded by natural languages have vague boundaries implying that propositions will most often be neither absolutely true, nor absolutely false, but rather true/false to a certain extent, or true in certain respects and false in other respects (Lakoff 1972: 183). Worse these claims ignore the central role played by metaphor (to 'see' why this is so, you might reflect on the use I have made of words like 'ignore', 'demonstrated', 'played', 'central' or 'role' in the prior sentence). Lakoff has gone on to argue for understanding the way human thought and language actually rely on metaphor and underneath that linguistic technique on a process he calls 'ontological mapping across conceptual domains'. His example is the way in which we might speak of a love relationship: *Our relationship has hit a dead-end*. Here 'love' is understood as a 'journey', which in this case implies that the relationship has 'stalled', that the lovers 'cannot keep going the way they've been going', that they must 'turn back', or must 'abandon the journey' as relationship altogether. The conceptual system used for understanding the domain of love draws on the domain of journeys. The metaphor is not just a matter of language, but of thinking. The conceptual mapping is primary, and the language is secondary. In this case, we make a mental map that translates from the 'source domain' (i.e. 'life – or love – is a journey') to the 'target domain', i.e. 'our relationship' (Lakoff 1993: 2010).[2]

This new account of language and meaning and the fundamental role played by metaphor in human thought has implications for any traditional approach in the social sciences, which says defining our terms or concepts so as to arrive at a literal or close match between concept and reality is both a good idea and possible.

If there are issues with the way we rely on dodgy assumptions about words and concepts, this is even more true when we think about what reality is made of.

How do sociologists think about 'the social'?

Let me start with an indispensable question: what is the 'stuff' that sociologists are interested in? Or to put this formally, *how* do sociologists think about 'the social'? (We could ask the same question of political scientists, criminologists, economists or psychologists and their 'objects' of study like 'the political', 'crime', 'economics' or 'the mind': I am simply using sociology as an example to highlight a more general disposition).

As will become clear, there are any number of *apparently* different answers to this question. The differences have something to do with how different sociologists identify, e.g. as 'quantitative' or 'qualitative' sociologists. 'Quantitative' sociologists do a lot of data collection about 'social facts' like rates of employment, crime or protest and then do statistical analysis of 'variables' as they strive to generate explanations that can also serve as predictions. 'Qualitative' sociologists, on the other hand, do 'ethnographies' or 'participant observation' and talk a lot about the meaning of gestures or 'the social construction of reality' and the 'rules of the game' involved in 'symbolic interaction'.

Why then do I say that the most sociologists think about 'the social' in ways that assume that different kinds of substance are constitutive of 'the social'? One immediate objection is that surely this is not possible given the distinction between 'quantitative' and 'qualitative' sociologists. Surely the fact that there are long-standing methodological disputes between 'quantitative' and 'qualitative' sociologists (or political scientists, criminologists etc.) suggests that I am making some kind of 'category mistake' by talking about 'sociology' as having a symbolic order based on an idea about substance. To put it simply, the fact that there are a number of competing narratives about what sociology is must surely mean first that we cannot talk about any symbolic order called 'sociology' (or 'political science', 'criminology' or whatever). Isn't this precisely what Hans Joas and Wolfgang Knobl (2009: 371) were getting at when they highlighted sociological research revolves around the 'structure' versus 'agency' binary that underpins the various 'structuralist' and 'phenomenological' traditions in sociology while constituting a basic point of contention (Joas and Knobl 2009: 371).

While these debates are real enough, and certainly have seen a lot of energy spent on technical methodological controversy, these debates have had the effect of diverting attention away from thinking about the 'what it is we are trying to know' – or what I am calling the question of the 'stuff' we are trying to find out about.

In sociology, the distinction made between 'objective'/quantitative and 'subjective'/qualitative sociology supports binaries like 'society vs individual' or 'structure vs agency'. While these are ostensibly binaries, each of the parts of the pairs looks for a causal connection and relies on a reduction of 'the social' to their preferred binary, i.e. either to 'society' or 'the individual or to other binaries like 'structure' or 'agency'. This is the clue that each is relying on an idea about substance. While it is easy enough to say that when philosophers refer to 'substance', this is a fancy way of talking about the 'stuff' that makes up reality, what this means may not be immediately clear or simple.

The idea of substance

This idea of 'substance' itself has a long and authoritative back-story that starts with the origins of Western philosophy (Hoffman and Rosenkrantz 1997). The idea of 'substance' originates with a curiosity about the nature of being (*ousia* Greek) giving rise to questions like 'why is there anything rather than nothing'? The Greek interest in *ousia* was translated into two Latin words *substantia* giving us the English word 'substance'. Substance means roughly 'something that stands under or grounds things' and this is the idea Western philosophers have talked about ever since. (Marc Cohen highlights the dangers in translation noting that 'substance', the conventional English rendering of Aristotle's word *ousia*, is misleading, suggesting as it does a kind of *stuff*.) As Cohen says what 'substance' and *substantia* both miss is the connection of the word *ousia* to the verb 'to be' (*einai*) from the present infinitive ('I am') (Cohen 2009: 197).

As Howard Robinson suggests, the 'substances' in a given philosophical system (or a discipline like sociology) are those 'things' which, according to that system, are the foundational or fundamental entities of reality. The history of Western metaphysics points to a disposition for some people to claim there is only one substance, while others insist there are two or more substances. Thales, e.g. thought there was only one substance – water. Spinoza thought that there was just one substance (God) which is what he thought filled up the universe. Plato set loose a story about two substances including the stuff we can see and touch that are *phenomena* which change all the time in contrast with the enduring timeless stuff that Plato represented as ideal forms found in the noumenal realm (like the idea of triangle or circle) that belong to the (noumenal) realm and be hidden from plain sight. Descartes was also a substance dualist because he thought that there were two substances: 'matter' and 'mind' and that we humans had a dual nature because we had a material body and a mental mind. Scientific naturalists like Carl Hempel imagine that there are only physical things and forces 'out there' (Botha 2001: 26–48).[3] And so the debate goes on.

Let me quickly point to the way in which this tradition of substance-talk has played out in sociology.

Substance in sociology

Andrew Abbott has highlighted the way in which sociology is a discipline preoccupied with 'units', 'attributes' and 'causes', when he says conventional sociologists assume that the world is made up of 'substances' and 'essences' (Abbott 1995: 93). When sociologists worry about the criteria for working out who is 'working-class' or who is 'adolescent' or 'elderly', or how many Americans are in a 'family', or how being 'working-class' determines the educational prospects of 'the young' we are seeing the preoccupation with substance. This is what Pierpaulo Donati calls 'entitative thought' which conceptualizes and reasons 'by entity', i.e. by things (Donati 2011: 68). As Mustafa Emirbayer notes 'large segments of the sociological community continue implicitly or explicitly to prefer to conceive of the social world as consisting primarily' in substances and static 'things' (Emirbayer 1997: 281) Emirbayer makes the point, albeit tacitly, that the signs of 'substantialism' are found at work in all sorts of seemingly different kinds of sociology from 'rational-actor and norm-based models, diverse structuralisms, and statistical 'variable' analyses – all of them beholden to the idea that it is entities that come first and relations among them only subsequently' (Emirbayer 1997: 281).

One way of seeing how the difference between 'qualitative' and 'quantitative' sociology helps to cover up the reliance on substance-talk is to use Dewey and Bentley's discussion of 'self-acting' substances and 'inter-acting' substances.

Those who think of things operating through 'self-action' conceive of 'things … as acting under their own powers' (Dewey and Bentley 1949: 108), and doing so independently of all other substances. Christian thought has long talked about an entity like the 'soul' culminating in Thomas Aquinas theology. As Emirbayer argues, many sociologists have been fascinated by socialization theory and the idea of 'norm-following individuals', as a basic unit of analysis. This depicts individuals as 'self-propelling, self-subsistent entities that pursue internalized norms' imparted by socialization (Emirbayer 1997: 284). In other kinds of sociology, we see this idea in the interest in 'agency' found in sub-genres like rational-choice theory which has had a major impact on the sociology of social movements. Rational actor theorists like Jon Elster argue that 'the elementary unit of social life is the individual human action. To explain social institutions and social change is to show how they arise as the result of the action and interaction of individuals' (Elster 1989: 13).

Equally in quite different kinds of sociology interested in holistic theories and 'structuralisms' that focus less on individuals and more on self-subsistent 'societies', 'structures' or 'social systems', the core entities like 'structures', 'class', 'nation' or 'patriarchy' are also treated as self-acting entities. As Emirbayer notes, this kind of sociology is not interested in 'individual persons, but groups, nations, cultures, and other reified substances' that do 'all of the acting in social life'. The reliance on a conception of self-acting substance is suggested when Charles Tilly, e.g. claims that social movements or nationalist struggles are best understood as driving themselves along trajectories 'that repeat … time after time in essentially the same form' (Tilly 1995a: 1596).

A different kind of sociology assumes that the social is made up of 'inter-acting' substances. This is mostly found in the domain of quantitative sociologists who are preoccupied with identifying and measuring the inter-action between variables. In models based on 'inter-acting' substances, the entities remain fixed and unchanging throughout such inter-action, each independent of the other, much like billiard balls or the particles in Newtonian mechanics. As Abbott notes, sociologists who rely on survey research practice a sociology of 'variables' which features, as he points out, a 'compelling imagery of fixed entities with variable attributes' that 'interact, in causal or actual time, to create outcomes, themselves measurable as attributes of the fixed entities' (Abbott 1988: 170; also Emirbayer 1997: 286). It also relies heavily on a variety of 'quantitative methods to test their causal hypotheses, including multiple regression, factor analysis' (Emirbayer 1997: 286).

This is neither the time nor place to say why this preoccupation with 'thing-like entities' is mistaken. As Pierre Bourdieu and Loic Wacquant say, this is part of the 'commonsensical perception of social reality of which sociology must rid itself' (Bourdieu and Wacquant 1992: 15). I assume that this critique has been developed adequately by many writers from Elias (1978), Abbott (1995), Emirbayer (1997), Donati (2011), and Dépelteau (2018).[4] More to the point the value of taking the 'relational turn' will need to be demonstrated by the case made here for treating dissent and its criminalization relationally. However, since this may seem like a story 'told by an idiot full of sound and fury signifying nothing', let me quickly spell out some of the key features involved in taking the relational turn which I then illustrate by thinking about the puzzling aspect of disagreement in modern societies.

Taking the 'relational turn'

As Seth Asch (2004: 28) notes, the relational perspective has not been well canvassed in the Western philosophical tradition. That said, Asch (2004), e.g. makes a good case that philosophers like Hegel and social theorists like Simmel, Mauss and Foucault have done a lot of the ground work.[5] This work has certainly assisted what we can call the modern 'relational' turn (Donati 2011; Dépelteau and Powell 2013; Donati and Archer 2015). Talking about the relational turn is one way of saying that we have not yet worked out all of the elements of what a relational perspective might look like. Prandini says we need to be cautious about whether a fully-fledged relational sociology is now available, suggesting that there is less a paradigm and more a 'relational turn' underway. Prandini says we will know that we have a relational paradigm when social scientists are able to specify 'accurately the ontology of society and social relation and to discover new methods and research techniques well suited to study it' (Prandini 2015: 13). That seems about right. Let me outline quickly what this seems to involve by pointing to several key aspects of the work of Norbert Elias and Pierre Bourdieu.[6]

Elias' critique of conventional sociology highlights the pervasive tendency to reduce or convert what are processes into 'things'. This disposition is seen as much in everyday language as in the specialized discourses of the sciences. Elias makes his point poetically when he says, 'We say, "The wind is blowing", as if the wind were separate from its blowing, as if a wind could exist which did not blow' (Elias 1978: 112). Elias was rightly concerned about the way this disposition when applied to social processes separates the actor from their activity, producing well-known binaries like 'structure'/'agency' to say nothing of opening up a gulf between people-objects relationships or people-people relationships.

Elias proposed that we begin our social investigations by dealing neither with the aggregate actions of isolated 'individuals', or with 'societies' as if these are external structures (or things) imposed on 'individuals', but rather focus on the processes and the connections in which we live out our lives (Elias 1978: 63). Glossing Elias, Donati says that all of us live in 'an invisible world' that we make 'but do not see or come to see very rarely. This is the world of social relations' (Donati 2011: xv). Elias says the challenge faced by the social sciences is to construct richly descriptive 'figurational models', which overcome the 'imaginary gap between the individual and society' and allow us to understand the relations between them as realities that constitute them as such. The idea of a 'figuration' is the idea of a 'network' of practices and relations which we make and remake: Elias' use of the idea of adance like the waltz catches the way in which the activity, if dancing together, creates the network or figuration for as long as those in it dance together.

This idea is analogous to Bourdieu's account of 'fields' and 'practice'. Bourdieu, e.g. defined a field 'as a network, or a configuration, of objective relations between positions' (Bourdieu and Wacquant, 1992: 97). (Note: the translation from the French 'champs' to the English 'field' misses out the resonances of 'battle' and 'conflict' signified in the translation of the Latin 'Campus' into 'champs'.) Fields are as much the product of a 'system of dispositions' that Bourdieu refers to as the 'habitus' each of us has, as a way of thinking, feeling, believing, judging and even walking or throwing a balls, just as fields constitute that habitus. Bourdieu's relational perspective means that no one 'entity'/'thing' is granted causal privilege over others, without recognizing its location within a system of relations and its consequent susceptibility to change (Emirbayer 1997).[7]

Bourdieu once said that 'the real is relational' (Bourdieu 2000). Relationality as a concept is deeply embedded Bourdieu's sociology. According to Schinkel, 'the notion of the relational' was so central to Bourdieu that he preferred to speak not of his 'theory' but rather of a 'system of relational concepts'. This relational turn, however, has a particular meaning that takes it away from the intersubjective. Bourdieu was very clear about what this focus on relations implied: 'what exist in the social world are relations – not interactions between agents or intersubjective ties between individuals, but objective relations…' (Bourdieu and Wacquant, 1992: 97).The relational perspective developed by Elias and Bourdieu underscores the point that practices constitute individuals as much as individuals engage in practices: this is simply to say that all actions are always transactional and relational (Powell and Dépelteau, 2013; Dépelteau 2018).

Let me now return to the problem of dissent and begin to tease out the point of taking a relational turn. If we ask what dissent is, we can start with the language of dissent. The point of taking a relational turn is indicated when we start to reflect on the language of dissent, and how it is relationally tied to what it is not.

The language of dissent

Robert Solum (2000) argues for a linguistic approach to thinking about dissent. This probably reflects his own interest in issues like freedom of speech and the legal protection of free speech, and his claim that freedom of speech is valuable because it enables dissent. The downside of this is that Solum is mostly preoccupied with dissent understood only as various kinds of speaking.

This does not quite do justice to the performative character of some kinds of speech or what Austin calls 'illocutionary' speech (or what Bourdieu calls 'performative discourse'). That is, speaking is a kind of practice where a speech act itself become a form of action or calls for action on the part of others, let alone the varieties of other kinds of dissenting expressive and political activity. As a practice, it is inherently relational.

This is suggested when we acknowledge that words like 'dissent' and cognate ideas like 'disagreement', 'heresy', 'dispute', and 'argument' are *deictic* words. There are several important entailments when we say this. First, as Huddlestone and Pullum (2006) note, the category of *deixis* applies to all those 'expressions in which the meaning can be traced directly to features of the act of utterance, when and where it takes place, and who is involved as speaker and as addressee'. To be a 'speaker' implies a relation with a 'listener' or an 'audience'. They offer as simple examples words like 'now' and 'here' that are used *deictically* to refer respectively to the time and place of the utterance. Likewise referring to '*this country* is best interpreted deictically as the country in which the utterance takes place'. As linguists add, 'The referent of a deictic word or expression whether it is spatial, temporal, personal or other, must *be sought in the context of the speech event or in the context of the discourse itself*' (von Bruegel 2014: My stress). As will become clear using a deictic category like 'dissent' or related terms like 'disagreement' or 'dispute' requires that we acknowledge the context of the speech event. That context of the discourse always involves both relations and practices involving speakers and addressees or social actors working in specific fields of action. As I will show soon the language of dissent, and what it is not, all point to a rich field of social relations.

However and to be even more precise, understanding 'dissent' and related ideas as deictic also requires that we understand better some of the complex political and legal meanings and significations circling around the idea of dissent. What precisely this means, however, will not be immediately clear. This has a lot to do with how we understand the 'political', the 'legal' and the relationship between these two fields or sites of collective discursive practice.

As Michael Freeden suggests, this means that we have to ask what it means to think politically as a practice. To engage that question, we will need to ask 'what are the thought patterns to which the adjective 'political' can be allocated in a unique manner?' (Freeden 2013: 3). By extrapolation we will need to ask the same kind of questions about the 'legal'. I leave the important task of establishing what we mean when we talk about the 'political' and the 'legal' and their inter-relationship till a later chapter. Let me focus here on the socio-linguistic aspects of dissent.

If we stick to the semantics of dissent for the moment, then our thinking about 'dissent' is helped when we remember that it is tied conceptually to what it is not, namely 'consent'. The relevant clue here is that semantically 'dissent' and 'consent' are *antonyms*. Dissent is the antonym of consent: the word 'antonym' itself brings together two words 'anti' (or 'opposite') and 'onym' (or 'name'). Philologically both share the same root word *sentire* (Latin) meaning 'to feel'. Putting 'con' ('together') together with *sentire* signifies simply 'feeling together'. This can involve simply being in agreement with someone else about the value of going to the coffee shop together, or it might point to a more formal almost contractual arrangement (like entering into an agreement to do something like forming a coalition of parties so as to form government or it might simply mean that being agreeable is generally a valuable social disposition to have. This then opens up a range of related words like 'consensus' as in 'generally agreed' or 'consensual' signifying the willing agreement of people involved in some activity. As we will also see later, the idea of consent points to an idea that is fundamental to the liberal tradition and the idea that the legitimacy or rightness of modern government rests on the 'consent' of the people. We may also begin to see that there are also emotional and ethical resonances at work here in which 'consent' is favoured over 'dissent'.

In the idea of dissent, the prefix 'dis' simply signifies 'not', so 'dissent' signifies not in agreement. In ordinary language use, dissent has several different meanings. Dissent may simply indicate disagreement. When the antonym of consent, i.e. 'dissent' is looked at, it might just mean 'disagreement' or not being able to agree, or not being able or willing to be agreeable. For example, whatever assertion another person may make, the grammar of English permits me to respond, 'I dissent' as in 'I disagree'. Solum (2000) says we can call this first form of dissent, i.e. 'dissent as disagreement'.

'Dissent' can also refer to a minority point of view. For example, we refer to a judge's minority opinion in a multi-member appeal panel as a 'dissent'. Solum (2000) says we can call this second form of dissent 'dissent as minority viewpoint'.

'Dissent' can also refer to critical responses to the views and actions adopted by or promoted by powerful social/political elite groups whose members dominate business or civil society organizations or may even include the state and its various institutions and agencies. Kaplan (2017: 3–38) makes a very strong case for institutionalizing this kind of dissent in business and state organizations, a point explored in Conclusion.

There is a fourth kind of dissent that Solum calls 'dissent as criticism of established opinion' (Solum 2000: 878). Those who held religious beliefs that were in disagreement with the established Church in England from then middle of the sixteenth century on or in colonial America in colonies like Massachussetts or Pennsylvania were dissenters in this sense.

Yet this focus on forms of minority opinion or belief only begins to catch the many forms of dissent. It also doesn't quite deal with a basic problem, namely the odd relationship between the ubiquity of disagreement as a widespread and normal aspect of any large-scale community and the negativity attached to dissent. Recognizing this disjunction begins to open up at least one core puzzle about disagreement and dissent as well as reminding us of the value of developing a relational account of human practices.

Dissent is disagreement

I propose that we take seriously the idea canvassed in the Introduction, that disagreement is both widespread and normal in many contemporary societies. As evidence for this, I suggest any reader test this by turning to the pages of any major newspaper where letters to the editor are published. This will reveal an extraordinary array of views, on an equally extraordinary array of topics with many correspondents turning on or against both the government of the day, the newspaper itself and the received wisdoms ethical, political, environmental, sexual, religious, medical, economic, cultural, historical and so forth of that community. We humans live in a world characterized by a plurality of knowledge, belief and ideas about that world *and* about how we should live. This is true for any who live in all societies and communities of any scale. That plurality of knowledge, belief and ideas is grounded in practices understood as relations of agreement ← → disagreement.

Philosophers like Elaine Mason (2018) call this 'pluralism'. Pluralism names the circumstances where there just are many things in question like our scientific world-views, theories of reality, modes of discourses and accounts of 'reality'. This pluralism also applies at least as much to our moral/ethical and political ideas. Though this sounds like the start of a joke, this applies to philosophers who have long been split between those who are monists and those who are pluralists.

Pluralism is the opposite of monism. Monists claim that there is just one singular truth, ethical idea or principle. The dominant moral philosophy found in the Anglo-American world called utilitarianism (or 'consequentialism'), e.g. adopts a monistic view arguing that there is – or ought to be – only one fundamental ethical principle, namely well-being, pleasure or happiness, i.e. utility that defines the good. Things get interesting when those promoting this tradition argue that each individual is best placed to work out what will maximize their happiness *and* that governments can and should maximize utility for the greatest possible number of people.

Pluralism goes to claims about big questions about the nature of truth, as well as religious or ethical ideas. Given my interest in the status of dissent in liberal democracies, let me start with Isaiah Berlin, whose commitment to a comprehensive (or foundational) pluralism is well known.[8]

Berlin (1991, 2002), is arguably the greatest of modern liberal theorists. He insisted that we take seriously the idea that, in any human community, there is a non-reducible plurality of 'values' or ethical ideas. This view draws on Berlin's more complex version of epistemic scepticism that began when he rejected 'monism' or the Platonic conception of knowledge-as-truth. By this, Berlin means to highlight the belief central to Western philosophy and much 'modern' scientific thought, that knowledge involves a claim that all genuine questions about our world must have only one true answer, implying that all other responses are errors. Second to arrive at that one true answer, there must be a dependable path or 'method' enabling us to discover those true answers, which is, in principle, knowable, even if currently unknown (Mason 2018: 2). Finally, these true answers, when found, will be compatible with one another, forming a single whole; for one truth cannot be incompatible with another. Each of these propositions, in turn, is based on the assumption that the universe is harmonious and coherent (Cherniss and Hardy 2017).

Berlin's epistemological scepticism about the prospects of a singular truth rests on his argument that our capacity to know reality is constrained by the sheer complexity of that reality. Our experiences of reality are:

> ... too many, too minute, too fleeting, too blurred at the edges. They criss-cross and penetrate each other at many levels simultaneously, and the attempt to prise them apart [...] and pin them down, and classify them, and fit them into their specific compartments turns out to be impossible.
>
> (Berlin 1978: 119)

Berlin's ethical pluralism starts from the parallel premise that our ethical ideas can be both true and deeply important, but are not susceptible to being reduced to a singular truth.[9] That is, there are many true or deeply valuable ethical principles. For example, we might value an idea like fairness as impartiality (treating everyone equally whatever their differences), but that principle sooner or later runs up against the idea that we should also care for and love most those people we are closest to, like our children or family. There are many true or genuine values like these and they simply and frequently conflict with one another. As Cherniss and Hardy (2017: 7) note, the fact that two or more ethical ideas clash does not mean that one of them has been misunderstood or that any one value is always more important than another:

> Liberty can conflict with equality or with public order; mercy with justice; love with impartiality and fairness; social and moral commitment with the disinterested pursuit of truth or beauty knowledge with happiness; spontaneity and free-spiritedness with dependability and responsibility.
>
> (Cherniss and Hardy 2017: 7)

Berlin insisted that the plurality of, and conflicts between, our ethical ideas is 'an intrinsic, irremovable element in human life' and that 'the idea of total human fulfilment is a [...] chimera' (Berlin 2002: 213). 'These collisions of values are of the essence of what they are and what we are'; a world in which such conflicts are resolved is not the world we know or understand (Berlin 1991: 13). Berlin said we will discover this when we encounter our world: our ordinary experience will reveal that 'we are faced with choices between ends equally ultimate, and claims equally absolute, the realization of some of which must inevitably involve the sacrifice of others' (Berlin 2002: 213–14). Joseph Raz (2003) provides a strong basis for agreeing with Berlin in his observations about the sheer range and diversity of social practices in which are found an equally diverse array of values.[10]

Raz sets out to explain the basic features of our evaluative thinking. He does this by arguing that some values exist only if there are (or were) social practices sustaining them (this is his special social dependence thesis). His more general social dependence thesis suggests that all values depend on social practices either by being subject to the special thesis or through their dependence on values that are subject to the special thesis. As he says:

> Regarding any value there is in any population a sustaining practice if people conduct themselves approximately as they would were they to be aware of it, and if they do so out of (an openly avowed) belief that it is worthwhile to conduct themselves as they do (under some description or another).
>
> (Raz 2003: 19)

The affinities between this account and the work of Bourdieu (1977, 1990) and Schatzki (2001) are striking. We need to think of practices as 'embodied, materially mediated arrays of human activity centrally organized around shared practical understanding' (Schatzki, 2001: 2). That is, human practices are grounded in our bodies, habits and social relations. As Raz insists, these practices are oriented to or organized around 'practical', i.e. moral and evaluative concerns. As an example, he locates our aesthetic values and responses to an art form like opera, in 'sustaining practices', like attending operas, music school, listening to CDs, discussing them, writing and reading about them (Raz 2003: 19). Likewise those practices constitute basic relations embracing our friendships, family lives, economic activities, political activities, preferred kinds of relaxation, sport and entertainment and so forth. In these relations of practice, we express an enormous range of ideas about what constitutes a good friend, a good political leader or policy, or a bad boss, a bad film or a bad meal.

Natural law theorists like John Finnis (1980) go further when he argues for a plurality of basic human goods, which he identifies as common or universal human goods essential to leading a human life worth living. Finnis claims that there are at least seven universal goods, albeit goods which can only be specified at a certain level of generality like knowledge, practical (i.e. ethical reasoning), play, beauty, religion, friendship and life itself understood as living a long health and fulfilling life. His subtle yet bracing account of truth reminds us why pluralists are not relativists. Further he claims that his account is not so much a wish list as something descriptively grounded in the actual circumstances of human existence. If we think about our nature, FInnis says we will see that we seem naturally and inevitably confronted by the need to think about our collective lives and to establish the basis of authority for living, acting and choosing to do the things we do and in the ways we do. This is because our nature is so ineluctably social in character: Finnis takes the idea that we are thoroughly social creatures quite seriously. In effect, our human nature as social beings is a fact that compels us time and time again to construct a principled and reasoned specification of valued ends. On this basis, Finnis says every one of our ethical and political theories from Confucianism, Roman Law, Lockean liberalism, Marxism, fascism, or Green politics are examples of this ongoing project, as they debate the various combinations and rank ordering of the human goods. Daniel Chernilo (2013) would add in the various social sciences even when they say they aspire to be or actually are 'value-free'.

Pluralism posits and acknowledges the irreducibility of disagreement, disputes even conflict. We confront choices, not only between particular values in individual cases, but also between different ways of life like living a religious life or a secular life. This is why many liberals have emphasized the importance of choosing freely and without coercion between values, a need especially important in public and political life. Granting that there is no single or right answer either to the ethical question 'how should I live?' or 'what is the good thing I should do?' or to the political versions of these questions framed as questions like 'how should we live?' or 'what do we owe to each other?', it is hardly surprising that liberals like Berlin or others working out of other kinds of natural law traditions like Amartya Sen, Martha Nussbaum or Ronald Dworkin have argued for various conceptions of liberty as a fundamental prerequisite, even though this has also inevitably sponsored vigorous disagreement between them about how to think about liberty.

Equally as anyone who has dipped into the tradition of deliberative democracy (e.g. Habermas (1996) and Gutmann and Thompson (2002)) will know, some liberals are scandalized by disagreement. While Berlin was unfazed by evidence of disagreement, for other liberals, disagreement is a problem, possibly even a scandal. For example, many of those who support a deliberative democratic model, e.g. share with James Bohmann (1996) the 'common demand' that citizens rule their affairs through 'the public use of reason'.[11] This approach holds out the promise that there is a method by which disagreements can be solved. However (and I will return to this question later), this can involve some odd moves indeed by those claiming to be liberals. For example, it seems that this apparently benign proposition involves arguing that certain points of view or moral perspective, like those grounded in religious claims, can never or should never be part of such a 'common ground' because they are not rational enough (cf. Dryzek 2000, 2010). Michael Walzer (1991: 191), e.g. recommends as an antidote to 'dissociated individuals' who are 'easy prey for anti-democratic demagogues', that governments provide the background or framing conditions that can only be provided by state action involving a 'political strategy for mobilizing, organising and if necessary subsidizing the right sort of groups' comprising people who are efficacious and tolerant. Ideas like this prompted Stanley Fish (1999) who shares a good deal with Berlin, Raz et al., to highlight a clear danger in the deliberative democratic theorist's assumption that there has to be a shared or common and preferably rational ground between, e.g. secular democrats and Muslims, such that it would establish rational principles designed to regulate their interactions with one another. As Fish puts it:

> [T]he specification of what a religion is and the identification of the actions that may or may not be taken in its name are entirely internal matters.... What this means ... is that in matters of religion – and I would say in any matter – there is no public space, complete with definitions, standards, norms, criteria, etc. to which one can have recourse in order to separate out the true from the false, the revolutionary from the criminal. And what that means is that there is no common ground, at least no common ground on which a partisan flag has not already been planted, that would allow someone or somebody to render an independent judgment on the legitimacy of the declarations that issue from Bin Laden and his followers about the religious bases of their actions.
>
> (Fish 1999: 35)

To summarize where I have got to go so far. First, I suggested that dissent is *deictic* to the extent that whatever it means it needs to be located in a relational context. If we begin to think about the relational turn then we can discern how semantically 'dissent' is relationally tied to what it is not, namely 'consent': semantically 'dissent' and 'consent' are *antonyms*. Dissent is also embedded in a web of relations and practices which great modern pluralist liberals like Berlin and Raz remind us as a consequence of a world characterized by a non-reducible plurality of ideas about truth and the good life. In effect, agreement//disagreement or consent//dissent are relations embedded in practices. However, we are not done.

Some puzzles

The ubiquity of disagreement as a normal part of our life in common as it is lived in complex, urbanized, multicultural societies requires that we address several large puzzles or questions.

First, if disagreement is as widespread, pervasive and grounded in our normal practices as I have suggested it is, what does this imply for the conventional idea that there is some special quality or characteristic of people who attack, resist, criticize challenge or disobey some conventional idea or institution? This might, e.g. go to the idea that to do these things is either courageous and unconventional, possibly subversive or deeply deviant or evil? Such a view seems to depend heavily on two normative/descriptive ideas. One view long sustained by certain kinds of sociology and psychology and influenced, e.g. by Durkheim, holds that any functional society is a society grounded in basic norms, and that promoting social cohesion is best done by way of promoting moral order by enabling appropriate socialization. The *alter ego* to this view sees modern societies characterized by excessive consent and conformity promoted by fear of freedom (Fromm 1941), a regard for authority (Milgram 1974) or an almost-pathological need to be part of some in-group (Janis 1982).

This thought comes to mind when we consider the slightly cliched idea that to be a critic is to 'speak truth to power' an idea associated, e.g. with the practice of whistleblowing. Weiskopf and Tobias-Mersch (2016) draw on Foucault's (2011) account of 'fearless speech' (*parrhesia*) in social settings shaped by unequal power relations in their discussion of whistleblowing. Foucault thought of fearless speech as a specific 'modality of truth-telling' (2011: 15) that emerges in the context of unequal power relations. Foucault reminded us that in the space of Greek antiquity, the term *parrhesia* was fundamentally a political notion that referred to speaking the truth in public, in front of the assembly. On this account, the '*parrhesiastic* function' is to disrupt and open up established practices rather than reproduce them. In a political context, the *parrhesiastic* function, e.g. is to introduce difference of a truth-telling into the debate (Weiskopf and Tobias-Miersch 2016: 1624) and produce dissensus. Yet if disagreement is normal and widespread, doesn't this pose a prior question, namely under what circumstances does the normal range of disagreement implied by the fact of pluralism get converted into a consensus, even a coerced consensus, which then renders necessary the re-entry or re-emergence of difference and disagreement?

The need to pose this question, e.g. seems inescapable for anyone who has lived through the slow erosion of the normal practices of deliberative democracy that once characterized many Western political cultures (to say nothing of many of their universities) over the past few decades as a mix of neo-liberal policies and managerialist practices, have produced a flattened, dull and often unintelligible consensus augmented by advertising spin, and enforced by low-grade corporate authoritarianism (Watts 2014).

Second, if disagreement is as common as I think it is, why does it have such negative connotations? That it has such a reputation is suggested by one obvious semantic observation. When we use the thesaurus to determine some of the synonyms for 'dissent', we encounter a very wide array of mostly, if not entirely, negative terms. Consider all the synonyms for dissent. These include: discord, dissension, disunity, objection, protest, resistance, schism, dissentient strife, bone, clinker, conflict, denial, flak, hassle, heresy, spat, split, sour note, bone to pick, heretical, dissident, heterodox, iconoclastic, maverick, non-conformist, non-orthodox, out-there, unconventional and unorthodox. Or let us consider words like 'whistleblowing' and 'whistle-blower'. The synonyms for this include canary, stoolie, narc, scab rat, squealer, snake, snitch, tattletale, tipster, stoolpigeon, betrayer, canary [*slang*], deep throat, fink, informant, nark [*British*], rat, rat fink, snitch, snitcher, squealer, pigeon, talebearer, tattler, tattletale and telltale. Then, there are the synonyms for 'protest': these include challenge, demonstration, object, outcry, revolt, riot, turmoil, bellyache, demur, flak grievance, gripe, grouse, holler, howl, kick, knock, march, stink, tumult, big stink and rally. It doesn't take too much effort to establish that dissent and its various forms have long had a bad rap. This goes deep into the very conceptual and semantic field. There are few, if any, positive synonyms.

Finally, if disagreement is as common as I argue that it is, don't we also need to ask why or under what circumstances disagreement becomes 'dissent' and a problem so serious, that governments deem it significant enough it to be criminalized or repressed? As I have already indicated though I have yet to provide the evidence for this claim, the need to address this question is suggested by the abundant evidence of liberal-democratic states engaging in the criminalization of dissent. A more subtle indication of the need to address this question is suggested when we consider the negative assessment of disagreement, some deliberative democratic theorists like Gutmann and Thompson (2002) may well point to the problems liberal-democracies have with dissent or disagreement. This may, in turn, help us understand better how and why disagreement/dissent becomes political dissent and then how it can become potentially or actually susceptible to criminalization. If it is the case as pluralists like Berlin or Raz say it is, that disagreement about what we know and what we value is widespread, then it is possible that we see here a kind of political practice involving the capacity of states to draw a line in the sand linked to a claim that some kinds of beliefs are 'true', 'reasonable' and 'proper' and that contrary views are in some sense 'untrue', 'improper' or 'unreasonable' or worse 'dangerous' and so need to be criminalized.

In short what this brief discussion implies is that there is some kind of relationship between the common practice of disagreement, and the way certain practices become forms of 'dissent', involving at the least some kind of political process and potentially implicating certain kinds of legal and political responses by states. That is, there seems to be something quite political in both deciding to draw a line around certain kinds of disagreement and referring to these by using words like 'dissent', 'protest' or 'civil disobedience', which can be the prelude to some further process that might see the belief or activity criminalized by the state. The word 'heresy', e.g. points to the close connection between those who claim to have established the 'truth' about some important matter like 'knowledge' of some aspect of the world or some important ethical idea that is certain and warranted, and those intent on dissenting. The word 'dissent' has an equally close relationship with the modern liberal-democratic understanding and valuing of the idea of 'consent': 'consent', 'consensus' and 'agreement' are vitally important to modern liberal-democratic politics because of the mythic significance of the claim that the legitimacy of the modern liberal-democratic states depends on consent and not, e.g. on coercion, force, manipulation or outright violence.

In short, there is a significant and highly political and relational process at work when a point of view or a certain kind of action is deemed to be a form of dissent. Dissent involves more than the normal disposition that makes disagreement both normal and ubiquitous. First, then we need to think about the relationship of dissent to whatever we think politics and the political is all about.

Notes

1 Others talk about the 'classical theory of categories', the 'classical theory of definition' (Burek 2004) or the 'classical theory of reference' (Katz 1977).

2 One consequence is the destruction of the traditional literal-figurative distinction, since the idea of 'literal', as used in the traditional distinction itself relies on false assumptions (Lakoff 1993: 206).

3 Natural scientists like to claim they have perceptual experiences of real things. For example, experiential data might be conceived of as being sensations, perceptions, and similar phenomena of immediate experience (Hempel 1942: 674). What this meant is actually more complicated since it typically relies on operationalizing stuff that cannot be directly experienced

> ...such as the coincidence of the pointer of an instrument with a numbered mark on a dial; a change of colour in a test substance or in the skin of a patient; the clicking of an amplifier connected with a Geiger counter; etc.
>
> (Hempel 1942: 674)

4 Not everyone has been persuaded. Michael Burrawoy argues that 'substantialism' is 'a rare and largely mythical creature', suggesting that those advocates for the 'relational turn' have constructed a mythic enemy called 'substantialism' and that 'relational ethnography's' claim to novelty advanced by the likes of Mathew Desmond (2014) is spurious (Burrawoy 2017: 5). I beg to differ.

5 Others like Andrew Benjamin (2015), e.g. acknowledge the work of Descartes, Kant, Fichte, Hegel and Heidegger, while Bertell Ollman (1971) points to the relational perspective at work in Marx's dialectical theory. Donati (2011) points to important work by Mauss, Tarde and Simmel, while Vandenberghe (2018: 39) highlights impressive recent contributions like White's network analysis, Elias' figurational sociology, Bourdieu's sociology of practice, Luhmann's systems theory and Latour's actor-network theory.

6 Not everyone has been persuaded. Michael Burrawoy argues that 'substantialism' is 'a rare and largely mythical creature', suggesting that those advocates for the 'relational turn' have constructed a mythic enemy called 'substantialism' and that 'relational ethnography's' claim to novelty advanced by the likes of Mathew Desmond (2014) are spurious (Burrawoy 2017:5). I beg to differ.

7 Vandenberghe (1999) makes a good case that Bourdieu's work can be treated as an attempt to both systematically translate Bachelard's 'applied rationalism' out of the natural sciences and into the realm of the social sciences, and apply Ernst Cassirer's account of the relational principle in the modern sciences from mathematics to physics and linguistics. Bourdieu acknowledges Bachelard's value in emphasizing the primacy of relations over substances that characterize the modern natural sciences as expressed in his motto: 'In the beginning is the relation' (Bachelard 1985: 65). He also acknowledges Cassirer's work, e.g. his *Substance and Function*, where Cassirer pointed to the displacement of the Aristotelian logic of substances by a functional logic of generating relations which can be found in modern mathematics, physics, geometry and chemistry.

8 There are at least two kinds of ethical pluralism (Chang 2015; Tucker 2016). Foundational pluralism is the view that there are only many moral ideas and principles and that there is no one 'value that subsumes all other values, no one property of goodness,

and no overarching principle of action' (Mason 2018: 2). As I show here, some liberal and some natural law theorists agree about the facts of value pluralism. As a liberal, Joseph Raz (2003) grounds his value pluralism in an ontology of the social, observing that our values reflect a very wide range of social practices. John Finnis (1980) and Alasdair MacIntyre (1981) both natural theorists locate the plurality of human goods in human existence and in MacIntyre's case in communities whose members are engaged in various 'practices' oriented to those goods. Non-foundational pluralism is the claim that in our lives we face the need to choose between plural values, but that these apparently plural values can be understood in terms of their contribution to a single, more fundamental value. As Mason (2018: 1) points out, moral pluralism does not entail relativism, namely the claim that all values or value systems are equally true – or equally untrue – or simply non-rational.

9 As Cherniss and Hardy (2017) note, Berlin rejected both positivisms of all sorts and the nominalist or idealist traditions. Berlin criticized the long-standing premise long central to Western philosophy that all statements, claiming to be true, must be capable of being translated into a single, true knowledge claim and that this belief was both illusory and misleading. He identified two different and opposed approaches based on this erroneous assumption. One was what he called the 'deflationary' approach, which sought to assimilate all propositions to one true type. Thus, empiricism sought to reduce all statements to statements about immediately perceived sense-data. The other was the 'inflationary' approach of idealism/nominalism, which posited entities corresponding to all statements, thus 'creating' or asserting the existence of things that Berlin argued didn't exist at all.

10 It is odd that Raz is both a pluralist and a well-known legal-positivist heavily influenced by H.L.A. Hart. See Muniz-Fraticelli (2014) who attempts to clarify the difficulties set loose by reconciling pluralism and legal positivism.

11 Some important exponents of deliberative democracy like John Dryzek (2000) are entirely comfortable with disagreement and dissent and seem worried by the rush to deliberate it out of existence.

Chapter 2

Thinking relationally

Bringing the political back in

There are plenty of paradoxes at work in how we remember historic dissent and how we think about more contemporary examples of it. Robert Martin (2013: 1) reminds his American readers how they have long celebrated the moment when a handful of protestors deliberately destroyed private property in the form of 342 cases of tea in Boston's cold harbour in December 1773. Today most American barely remember the 'Battle for Seattle' when at least 40,000 protestors determined to prevent the 1999 World Trade Organisation Meeting from taking place, broke windows and battled police who responded with tear gas and concussion grenades to break up the demonstration (Solnit and Solnit 2008). Australians exhibit an equally selective amnesia. They remember the short sharp outbreak of civil rebellion in 1854 when angry miners briefly battled military forces on the Ballarat goldfields at the Eureka stockade as 'the birth of democracy' or as the harbinger of distinctively Australian attitude to authority (Wright 2013). The mobilization of hundreds of thousands of ordinary people attending anti-war Moratorium marches in May 1970 calling for an end to Australia's involvement in the American-led war in Vietnam has still been adequately remembered let alone celebrated (Hamilton 2016). No doubt readers in other liberal-democracies can point to similar cases of selective memory.

It might be thought that this difference simply reflects the effect of the passage of time. As events recede into the past, they achieve a certain golden patina. I think it much more likely that this selective amnesia highlights the puzzling politics of dissent. A central idea in this book is that when states criminalize dissent, they are in important ways criminalizing the political. Working out what this means and why this is the case is my task in this chapter.

To start with there is the basic puzzle implied by Berlin's liberal conception of a pluralist world. The social and political world in which we live is characterized by ubiquitous disagreement about almost everything that matters. It will become clear that other decidedly non-liberal theorists of politics like Hannah Arendt, Chantal Mouffe and Jacques Ranciere share Berlin's premise that we live in communities characterized by diverse opinions and interests and that politics is the 'continual intersection of diverse opinions and perspectives'

(Breen 2016: 135). Indeed pluralism is constitutive of 'the political', since it provides both the basis and the need for politics, which would disappear if this were not so (Breen 2016: 135). Yet this raises a basic problem. Given that politics involves 'the continual intersection of diverse opinions and perspectives', how then is dissent even conceivable let alone discernible? If diversity and difference is as ubiquitous as it appears to be, how, why or under what circumstances does what we can call 'normal' difference or disagreement come to be signified as 'dissent' and then criminalized? Robert Martin helps us to think about this when he says we run the risk of forgetting 'the centrality of dissent to democracy' (Martin 2013: 1).

In a crisp summary of the way this works in liberal political theory, Martin reminds us that liberal-democratic theory since Locke's *Second Treatise on Government* (1689) has assumed that consent is the desired norm, while dissent at best is a marginal activity, more often deviant and at worst criminal. In the course of making a good case for revaluing what 'consent' seems to deny, namely 'dissent', Christopher Nock (1995) makes the point that 'the liberal notion of individual liberty – grounded in the principle of a natural equal right to self-governance – seems to demand a strictly voluntarist account of the relationship between citizen and state'. Nock says this 'explains the adherence of many liberal writers to the consent theory of political obligation' (Nock 1995: 141). Yet as Nock notes, this points to one basic problem of legitimacy. As Nock says, 'it is now widely acknowledged that few people have actually consented to be governed' by the state in which they live. In effect, as Thomas Lewis (1989) puts it, the idea of consent is a metaphor or 'an abstraction that does not correspond to any past or present event' (Lewis 1989: 795). This points to a puzzle: while disagreement is ubiquitous, the core premise that our liberal-democratic order relies on is a story about consent and agreement.

We clearly need to think about 'politics' and 'dissent'. One key problem is that, if we continue to think about 'politics' (or the 'political') and 'dissent' as thing-like entities with certain defining 'properties', we will not get very far. Rather as I argue here, we need to think about 'politics' and 'dissent' in a relational way and do this by understanding the processes or practices at stake. Agreeing or disagreeing with each other, e.g. is a way of relating, just as encouraging or criminalizing disagreement is a way of relating. These relations involve various kinds of action. We express our agreements or disagreements in various speakings, writings and doings. In effect, we can start to think about both 'the political' and 'dissent' as relations of praxis/practice. Let me outline first what taking a relational turn means. This entails paying attention to how we humans act and how we always act in relations with each other. Because the forms of action involved should not be taken for granted, I outline the different but complementary contributions Hannah Arendt and Pierre Bourdieu both made to thinking about human action. I represent this as a unity-in-difference involving *praxis* or action that is free and 'practice' or action that tends to repetition and habit.

Relations are real

The idea of relationality has already been given an outing in the previous chapter. I argued there, that if we are to understand 'the political' or 'dissent', we need to move away from thinking about thing-like entities, and instead start to think relationally. While other modern advocates for the relational turn do not claim that 'relations' are more real than 'things', I argue that the 'relational turn' involves an ontological claim that relations are real.

Frederic Vandenberghe (2018: 48) suggests that relations can be understood in three ways. The first grasps the relations between subjects (i.e. you and me) and the elements that make up the world (i.e. *subjectum relationis*). Then there is the ground that justifies this relationship that conceives of relations in the world as real or *fundamentum relationis*. Finally, there the elements to which the element is connected (i.e. the *terminus relationis*). One very important entailment of this approach needs to be recognized. As Seth Asch (2004: 39) argues, a relational ontology does not require that we trap ourselves into envisioning the world as existing in 'any singular, necessary, and universal way'. The relational perspective implies that an ontological stance 'does not in fact have to be understood as a fundamental account or absolute declaration about our reality, and should not therefore be seen as a project to silence or exclude any other possible standpoint' (Asch 2004: 39) Andrew Benjamin (2015) makes the same point differently when he asks:

> What is a relation? What are relations? The project of developing an understanding of being-in-relation starts with the supposition that the limit of the first question is established by the inevitability of the second – an inevitability to be encountered and then recovered.
>
> (Benjamin 2015: 1)

What this means, says Benjamin, is that the second question is different from the first. 'What the second question holds open is the possibility that the truth of relationality brings a form of plurality into play'. The truth of relationality inheres in what is always at work within relations, namely the effective presence of a founding and irreducible plurality (Benjamin 2015: 2). In short, relationality implies a plurality of possibilities.

This matters deeply, given that, in effect, what we are talking about are some of the most distinctive aspects of how we humans live and act in our world. Central to my approach to both the political and dissent is a preoccupation with action as the distinctive aspect of the human – or the social. This means paying attention to how we humans act and how we always act in relation to each other. As Bourdieu (2017: 42), e.g. notes, 'It is common to speak of a philosophy of history but never of a philosophy of action, that is a theory of what it is to act?' As he then goes on to suggest, this involves asking questions like 'Do we always put intentions into practice when we act for instance? Are all actions necessarily intentional? Is an act which is unintentional automatic or unintelligent?' As Bourdieu indicates, these questions led him to formulating his theory of practice. I will be drawing in that work in conjunction with Arendt's theory of human action-as-*praxis* to think about politics and dissent.

So how and what should we think about the political and dissent? One important argument made outside the Anglophone world insists on distinguishing between 'politics' and 'the political' so as to highlight a fundamental moral paradox in human affairs, a paradox that itself points to the relational nature of politics and dissent.

Preliminary observations: thinking about the political

In his great essay, 'The Political Paradox', Paul Ricoeur (1965) made a distinction between 'politics' (*la politique*) and 'the political' (*le politique*), one which implicates, albeit only tacitly, dissent (the distinction between 'politics' and 'the political' is signified in many languages, like the French by the articles '*la*' and '*le*' *politique*).[1] For Ricoeur, 'politics' refers to the use of power and ultimately violence set loose in the struggle first to establish a political community and state and then to preserve that political community and to continue making decisions on behalf of its members. The implication is that political order is threatened by disagreement. 'The political', however, refers to a domain of human experience and practice different from other spaces of practice (like economic or aesthetic activities) characterized by unique forms of action and evaluated against ethical criteria. 'The political' is the work of rational, free and equal humans. The result however as Ricoeur insists is a paradox: how can (bad) 'politics' give rise to the (good) 'political'?

This question had actually been much discussed in political philosophy ever since Rousseau pointed to the paradox in the eighteenth century. Rousseau (1997) observed that in order for there to be a people well formed or virtuous enough to create a good state capable of good law-making, there must presumably already be a good law, for how else could the people be virtuous? The problem is: where would that good law come from without an already well-formed, virtuous people? (Honig 2008: 119). The result: a chicken-and-egg paradox: which comes first, good people or good law, a paradox much discussed today by writers like Bonnie Honig (2008) and Simon Critchley (2011). (This paradox will be returned to in Chapter 8 when the question of the political legitimacy of the liberal-democratic state is examined.)

For now, it is enough to suggest that the political paradox is one reason why we need to resist the conflation of 'politics' and 'the political' practised by conventional political science and political theory. This is because there are a few problems set loose when a conventional political scientist like Alan Milne (1983: v) declares that 'politics is about governing and being governed'. Milne goes on to

elaborate on this by deploying Proudhon's famously caustic and anarchist definition which starts, 'To be governed is to be watched over, examined, spied upon,
misguided, law-driven imprisoned, indoctrinated, controlled, …admonished,
forbidden, corrected, reformed, chastised, … shot at, executed…' (Cited Milne
1983: v–vi). Here, Milne is simply channelling Max Weber. Again, there is a tacit
acceptance that order and consent are not all that 'normal' or easily 'achieved'
and are threatened by disagreement.

Back in 1919, Max Weber declared in his famous essay *Politics as a Vocation*
that politics is about power, domination and the state. As he said, 'politics' 'means
striving to share power or striving to influence the distribution of power, either
among states or among groups within a state'. As for the state, Weber insists with
Trotsky that 'every state is founded on force': 'Like the political institutions historically preceding it, the state is a relation of men dominating men, a relation supported by means of legitimate (i.e. considered to be legitimate) violence'. Weber
adds that

> If no social institutions existed which knew the use of violence, then the
> concept of 'state' would be eliminated, and a condition would emerge that
> could be designated as 'anarchy'. Ricoeur (1965) whose eye for irony and par-
> adox exceeded even Weber's own inclinations, has had the 'last word' when
> he observes that since 'the political' only emerges through 'politics', and since
> the state is not going anywhere soon, the paradox remains: 'the greatest evil
> adheres to the greatest rationality'.
>
> (Ricoeur 1965: 249)

At least Ricoeur has seen that there is a relationship between 'politics' and 'the
political'.

So too in his own way did Carl Schmitt (1932/2007), one of Weber's last
students – and easily his most infamous. Schmitt also offers a relational account
of the political. He addresses the implied problem at the heart of Ricoeur's 'political paradox' by seeming to conclude that 'the political' has no moral qualities
and so there is no paradox. Schmitt's (1932/2007) 'concept of the political' frames
'the political' as *the relationship* between friends and enemies. Schmitt arrived at
this conclusion by asking what conceptually does a relation of distinction look
like in particular fields like morality, aesthetics or economics. As he puts it, 'Let
us assume that in the realm of morality the final distinction is between good and
evil, in aesthetics between beautiful and ugly, and in economics profitable and
unprofitable' (Schmitt 1932/2007: 26). Schmitt then asks if 'there is also a special
distinction which can serve as a simple criterion in the political and of what it
consists?' (Schmitt 1932/2007: 26). He answers by saying, 'the specific political
distinction … is that between friend and enemy' (Schmitt 1932/2007: 26). That
is, and to be clear, the political is not *about* enmity or conflict *per se*. As he put it
later, 'The essence of the political is not enmity but rather the *distinction* of friend
and enemy' (1963: 93).

Two things need to be noted about Schmitt's account. First, as Márton Szabó (2006: 29) insists, Schmitt's approach is not presented as a timeless Platonic-style definition, but rather as an historically sensitive account 'intended to grasp the special features of late-modern politics'. As both Adam Sitze (2015) and Carlo Galli (2015) add, Schmitt is offering as a 'specifically genealogical' critique of modernity, which treats politics as an originary contradiction which I will deal with in more detail later in the book as a 'unity-of-difference'. Here it is enough to notice that Schmitt is insisting that we contextualize the concept of 'the political' in an historical process. Schmitt (1977: 23) is – unwittingly – caught up in a logic of wanting to able to say in what way the political is distinct from, or as he puts it, is the 'antithesis' of the religious, the cultural, the economic, the legal and the scientific but he cannot do this if his referent for the political is the state. Schmitt says this because he claims the distinction between state and society is becoming less and less relevant. Schmitt says, The equation 'state = politics' becomes problematic at exactly the moment when state and society 'penetrate each other' (Schmitt 1977: 22). This is why older, independent and neutral domains like religion, culture, education or the economy cease to be neutral in the sense that they do not pertain to state and to politics. If the political is to be understood in its own terms, it will require some other approach.

Schmitt adds that the distinction between friend and enemy is an essentially public and not a private distinction. Individuals may have personal enemies, but personal enmity is not a political phenomenon per se. Politics involves groups that face off as mutual enemies (Schmitt 1977: 28–9; Szabó 2006: 30). Two groups will find themselves in a situation of mutual enmity if, and only if, there is a possibility of war and mutual killing between them. The distinction between friend and enemy thus refers to the 'utmost degree of intensity … of an association or dissociation' (Schmitt 1977: 26, 38). As Schmitt makes clear, the relevant degree of intensity of association is signified by the willingness to fight and die for and with other members of one's group, while the ultimate degree of dissociation is the willingness to kill others for the simple reason that they are members of a hostile group (Schmitt 1977: 32–3).

Schmitt has made the point that whatever politics is, it needs to be understood relationally. This at least takes us in the right direction. However, while Schmitt's account has the merit of requiring us to think about the possible kinds of relations and dispositions that, in effect, make 'the political' he also insisted that, 'The essence of the political is not enmity but rather the *distinction of friend and enemy*' (1976: 93). It is not clear why Schmitt should assume that the relationship needs to be grounded in *a relationship of distinction, difference or antagonism*. Schmitt's is a relation of difference, even antagonism. This tends to underplay the possibility that whatever we mean by the political or by dissent, that both involve many more possibilities than a distinction drawn between 'friends' and 'enemies'. We need to acknowledge the centrality of plurality and difference without reducing all difference to enmity as Schmitt does.

We also need a more complex account of 'politics' and 'the political' which incorporates amoral dimension. Schmitt mistakenly imagined he had got rid of the moral dimension, forgetting that the relations of friendship point to deep human goods.

I propose here to draw on the complementary accounts of *praxis*/practice offered by Hannah Arendt and Pierre Bourdieu. I want to twin Arendt's account of *praxis* with Bourdieu's account of practice to create a unity-of-difference. Placed in apposition, they foreground how the political and dissent are relations of *praxis*/practice.

An odd couple: Arendt and Bourdieu on *praxis*/practice

Twinning the two words *praxis*/practice in this way might imply that I am simply highlighting an etymological genealogy which traces our modern understanding of 'practice' back to the classical Greek concept of 'praxis'. Not so. By twinning *praxis*/*practice* in this way, I want to highlight the complementary but contradictory aspects of the political and dissent *and* its criminalization, as relational processes. The twinning of *praxis*/practice grasps the way political *praxis*/practice is both free *and* constrained. *Praxis* is human action, active and free, and 'practice' is entirely habitual and constrained. This is a unity as each depends on the other. In this way, we get a more complete account of human action.

On a first glance, pairing Arendt and Bourdieu might be thought not only an uncommon one, but odd, even eccentric. One of the few commentators who thought about 'bringing their views into dialogue' is Keith Topper (2011: 354) who makes a good case for thinking about pairing these two writers. He says when they are read together, each offer insights that are 'neglected or unthematized by the other' (Topper 2011: 354).

Topper, e.g. says Arendt's account of political speech highlights its status as 'public speech' that links public speech, political action and identity disclosure, while her account of political action stresses its capacity to promote novelty and change. She also stresses the critical connection between speech and power, focussing on those dynamic and 'boundless' forms of political power that simultaneously give birth to new relations and realities and sustain the existence of the public realm. On the other hand, Bourdieu focusses on the ways in which modes of domination and exclusion are enacted and sustained. Bourdieu's is in the fullest sense of the term a 'political economy' understood as an enquiry into how various kinds of powers and resources are both used and (re)produced unequally. Among the ways this is done Bourdieu stresses the way in which symbolic violence is used to shape symbolic orders through and in linguistic exchanges again conceived of in a relational way that stresses the praxis of political speech and action. Bourdieu's account of 'symbolic violence', e.g. treats it as an embodied but noncoercive, linguistic kind of 'violence' that is exercised through misrecognition on the part of the participants of the meanings implicit in their speech. Bourdieu shows us the many ways in which persons lacking the linguistic competences (or symbolic/intellectual capitals valorized in particular social and institutional fields of practice) are effectively excluded from participation in them (Topper 2011: 354). Far from operating as communicative practices or modes of self-disclosure, they become sources of structured inequality that effectively dissolve the political or public realm.

I go further, however, and suggest that Arendt and Bourdieu are sensitive to the claims and challenges of providing a relational account of the social world and of the many side relations between, e.g. the philosophical and the political.[2] Both have valuable and complementary things to say about the political as practice and do so in a relational register. Both approach the political understood as special kinds of 'speakings' and 'doings'. Both offer a relational account of political action and speech as practice/praxis. Their accounts are neither instrumental nor causal. Both stress the politics of recognition in the relations and practices of public life. Although Bourdieu seems to have been subjected to more mis-readings than ought to be expected, like Arendt, he also emphasizes the idea of *agon* as competition: if Bourdieu's fields of action reproduce an order they are also endless sites of struggle over specific kinds of power and using different resources or what he called 'capitals'. Let me start with Arendt.

Arendt on political *praxis*

Arendt offers a bracingly different account of the political. Indeed, as Bikhu Parekh notes, 'It is hardly an exaggeration to say that she is the only philosopher in the history of political thought to undertake extensive investigations into and offer a perceptive analysis of the nature and structure of political action' (Parekh 1981: 125).

On Arendt's account, political action is understood first by what it is not. In ways that can only cause most conventional (liberal) political scientists to experience atrial fibrillation, Arendt suggests that the political is not what the state or state sovereignty makes possible or regulates. Ronald Beiner notes there is no account of the state, or citizenship, or the basic problems modern states deal with in Arendt (Beiner 2014: 2). Nor in spite of criticism by Shapiro (2016), does Arendt think that the political is all about power, or that the power to coerce is what the state is or does naturally and for functional purposes. Indeed, as she puts it, the greater part of political philosophy since Plato could easily be interpreted 'as various attempts to find theoretical foundations for an escape from politics altogether' (Arendt 1958: 222). What she means by this is clear only when we discern her animus against the emphasis on 'order', 'rulership', 'government' and 'sovereignty' which she thinks correctly has for too long been the central preoccupation of Western political theory.

Arendt's take on the political begins with her emphasis on politics as a performance carried out in public in the presence of others. Politics is neither labour nor work but action. As Arendt insisted, it is by being 'in the polis, the space for men's free deeds and living words' that we endow 'life with splendor'. In effect, it is only by acting that we turn a futile, ephemeral and meaningless life into a richly expressive human life (Arendt 1965: 285). In defending her account of action as freedom, Arendt advances three basic propositions: (i) it is only through speech and action in the public realm that a person is able to live a truly human life; (ii) it is only through speech and action in the public realm that an agent is able to reveal her distinctive human identity; and (iii) it is only through the creation and preservation of institutional arrangements that serve as counterweights to the 'machinery of government' by creating diverse spaces for political speech and action as it is possible for ordinary people to live a fully human life and to disclose their distinctive human identities (Topper 2011: 357).

At the heart of Arendt's conception of politics is 'natality'. Central to her concept of natality is the idea that human beings come into the world 'as strangers'. Human action is like a second birth: 'with word and deed we insert ourselves into the human world, and this insertion is like a second birth' (1958: 176). Natality, she says, is 'the central category of political [thought]' because politics has to do with 'the task to provide and preserve the world for, to foresee and reckon with, the constant influx of newcomers who are born into the world as strangers' (1958: 9). In such a world, 'natality' is the source of freedom. Natality is the capacity we have to make a new beginning. Natality is instanced in three ways beginning with the event of biological birth, but includes going on to new beginnings inherent in birth because as 'beginners' we can create something new through 'action', and finally being together with others in a public way who can bear witness to our unique appearance in a political capacity. Understood in these three ways, natality is the capacity to initiate or give birth to something new and unprecedented into a world that is otherwise characterized by natural or historical processes, chains of causes and effects, and normalizing routines.

This is why for Arendt the political is never about power, coercion or violence: politics for her is about the free, unconstrained co-mingling of people in the public space of a polis. For Arendt, politics is about saying and showing who we really are. It is only by acting and speaking in public that citizens 'revealed their unique personal identities and thus made their appearance in the human world' (Arendt 1958: 179). Second, politics was also testimony to human plurality which entailed a mixture of equality and distinction achieved by a competitive display (*agon*) of speech and action in public. As equal citizens, we could rise above any natural inequalities so as to deal with each other in a common world that we made in common together. This implied that politics is less about reproducing order and ruling and more about collaborating with others who are also interested in new beginnings.

In effect, Arendt rejects two of the standard ways political philosophers/theorists have long understood politics. She rejects the state-centric tradition that starts with Plato and Aristotle and includes the Hobbesian-Lockean liberal tradition, that states constitute the political space (which may also involve a 'public sphere') as well as establishing the rules for citizens to engage in civic life enabling the formation of parties, public deliberation or voting for governments.

Arendt is far more interested in how we might best create and preserve institutional arrangements that can be counterweights to the 'machinery of government'. Arendt is committed to disrupting a state-centric view of the political sovereignty and rule, that as Bourdieu (2014) reminds us promotes relationships of domination and an illusory control over what the subjects can do and their environment.

Arendt's account of (political) action is grounded in what action is not: she insists on distinguishing *action* from both *labour* and *work* (Voice 2013). What matters here is her conception of action/praxis with their origins in two Greek ideas: *archein* (Latin: *agere*) and *prattein* (Latin: *gerere*). Arendt says we need to remember

> ... that Greek and Latin, unlike the modern languages, contain two altogether different and yet interrelated words with which to designate the verb 'to act'. To the two Greek verbs *archein* ('to begin', 'to lead', finally 'to rule' and *prattein* ('to pass through', 'to achieve', 'to finish') correspond the two Latin verbs *agere* ('to set into motion', 'to lead') and *gerere* (whose original meaning is 'to bear'). Here it seems as though each action were divided into two parts, the beginning made by a single person and the achievement in which many join by 'bearing' and 'finishing' the enterprise, by seeing it through.[3]
>
> (Arendt 1958: 189)

Action-as-*praxis* appears in 'the web of human relationships which exists wherever men live together' and thus '[t] he disclosure of "who" through speech, and the setting of a new beginning through action, always fall [s] into an already existing web where their immediate consequences can be felt' (1958: 183–4).

Though she is no Aristotelian, neo – or otherwise, Arendt draws on Aristotle's account of *praxis* and *techné/poiesis* and the distinction he drew between them. *Techné* means that an external product is produced by a process that Arendt calls 'work'. Arendt characterizes political action-as-*praxis*. However and unlike *techné* with *praxis*, there is no external product. Instead, *the end of praxis is the activity itself*. As James Knauer (1980) reminds us, Arendt thinks that action is not technical or goal oriented in the way work/*techné* is. As *praxis,* action is informed by *principles* which are not ends. Action, i.e. political action transcends the purely means-end logic of work by orienting to principled, by which means it acquires an additional dimension of significance.

Arendt insists that (political) action is praxis. This means that political action is non-instrumental, fundamentally unplannable and unpredictable and highly vulnerable, if not fragile. Action initiates radically new beginnings that rupture expectations and conventions. Each action 'looks like a miracle' in that it 'break[s] through the commonly accepted and reach[es] into the extraordinary, where whatever is true in common and everyday life no longer applies because everything that exists is unique and *sui generis*' (Arendt 1958: 246, 205). Indeed, Arendt goes as far as to claim that action 'carr[ies] with itself a measure of complete arbitrariness' (Arendt 1965: 198). Arendt always insisted that the political is uncertain and unregulatable: uncertainty plays a central role in Arendt's account of political action. The success of any political action is always uncertain the effects of our political actions remain unpredictable in an agonistic political world of plurality of actors and spectators with conflicting wills and cross-purposes (Tchir 2017: 25). However fervently we express our utopian wishes, there is no 'remedy for the frailty of human affairs' (Arendt 1958: 195).

In effect, Arendt understands both politics and existence as characterized by fragility in a common political world inhabited by a plurality of actors and spectators. Our political lives are characterized by the vulnerability of humans in the face of their 'passive givenness' and in their attempts to actualize their historically situated possibilities from that givenness through action (Tchir 2017: 32).

Relationality is a fundamental characteristic of Arendt's account of political action-as-praxis. Though Arendt seems mostly to equate action with speech, she allows that action involves both speaking and doings. Arendt says that 'in acting and speaking, men show who they are, reveal actively their unique personal identities and thus make their appearance in the human world' (Arendt 1958: 179). This implies that there is no hard and fast separation between the position of the actor and that of the spectator (Tchir 2017: 193).[4] Arendt starts from the premise that the world is made up of a plurality of individuals. Each individual person is 'unique, unexchangeable, and unrepeatable' (Arendt 1958: 97) and each has a narrative that distinguishes her from the manifold of humanity – 'men distinguish themselves instead of being merely distinct' (Arendt 1958: 176). Speech reveals the mind and character of the speaker in the clearest way. Second, speech communicates directly with an audience thus immediately connecting actor and spectator. Third, speech articulates while also challenging the meaning of the life shared by a community. Fourth, speech is connected to reason and judgement, thus humanizing action. A citizen's disclosure of herself is given up for the judgement of others within what she calls the 'space of appearance' action is that it inserts something original and unanticipated into the world. Our individuality is dependent on the witnessing of others. Unlike labour or work, 'action', e.g. must be witnessed because an action involves self-disclosure. It reveals *who* a person is by what they do and say. This notion of revelation and disclosure logically requires a spectator and so there are no strictly 'private' actions, only public ones. This also points to Arendt's agonistic conception of politics as a 'striving for distinction' in a context of radical plurality.

However, the idea of political action as neither instrumental, nor one apparently guided by clear ethical guidelines has persuaded some critics that Arendt's theory of the political is shallow, even amoral (Benhabib 1988). It is true that Arendt refers to action's 'practical purposelessness' (Arendt 1958: 177). Arendt insists that political action is for the sake of itself – i.e. for the sake of maintaining a sphere of plurality in which action can continue to occur (Tchir 2017: 26). Political action contains its own end, rather than occurring 'in order' to achieve instrumental goals (Tchir 2017: 30). Worse Arendt adds that action cannot be judged according to 'moral standards'. On the other hand, the distinction Arendt draws between intrinsically great public action and the kind of merely instrumental fabrication she calls 'work' leads some to worry that her politics is insufficiently attuned to goal-directed or purposive endeavours. Habermas, e.g. claims that Arendt's politics excludes both asocial (i.e. 'instrumental') and social ('strategic') forms of purposive activity and is consequently excessively restricted (Habermas 1977).

Lucy Cane (2015) shows how Arendt's discussion of action written after *The Human Condition* (1958) provides a richer, more complex account (Arendt 1968: 150). Here Arendt allows that political action pursues goals, but that is also oriented to 'principles' of a particular kind (also Knauer 1980). Arendt here corrects her previous claim that political action is characterized by 'practical purposelessness' by claiming that goals are 'important factors in every single act'. (1968: 150). In part, this is because the conditions of political action are such that its goals, unlike the goals of work, are rarely achieved or achieved as the person, who is acting, had in mind. Her point is that while human work can and should have a single technical goal like making a useful chair or growing a decent crop of corn, political action is always a social process involving a plurality of people. For Arendt, the activity of work is 'entirely determined by the categories of means and end'. No such possibility is available to anyone engaged in political action. The sheer mess of our lives lived in common sees to that.

To augment her account of action-as-praxis, Arendt draws on Montesquieu's account of the principles that animate and sustain different forms of government. As Lucy Cane shows, these principles serve as more general and more positive 'springs to action', which come to be reflected in different ways in laws, institutions, culture, and individual deeds (Cane 2015: 62). According to Montesquieu, there are three such principles: honour in monarchies, virtue (or 'love of equality') in republics and fear, in tyrannies (Cane 2015: 62). However, while Arendt draws on Montesquieu, she significantly expands the range of principles. In addition to Montesquieu's trio of honour, virtue and fear, she identifies the principles of 'fame', an Athenian form of 'freedom', 'justice', 'the belief in the innate worth of every human being', 'solidarity', 'public or political freedom', 'public or political happiness', 'the interconnected principle of mutual promise and common deliberation', 'rage', 'charity', 'distrust', and 'hatred' and importantly 'consent and the right to dissent' (Cane 2015: 62).

Second and here, her disposition to *anarche* (i.e. to subvert state-centric conceptions of the political) is richly displayed, and Arendt places less emphasis on attaching principles to particular forms of government and relates principles to the political realm in the broader, less state-centric sense of a public space in which individuals interact and perform. A person who is inspired and guided by 'virtue', e.g. should not be understood as acting in order to bring about virtue. Instead, she should be understood as acting virtuously, or for the sake of a virtue.

Second, Arendt says political action is a performance or a practice that invokes inspiring principles, examples of which might include 'honor, glory, equality, and excellence, but also hatred, fear, and distrust' (Tchir 2017: 29). Through these examples of inspiring principles, it becomes evident that some principles might sustain freedom within the public sphere better than others. These principles are not transcendent metaphysical principles or determined by reason prior to action. They are exhibited in the actions themselves, and, thus, they too must be repeated in narratives to inspire future actions, and in those future actions themselves, in order to sustain their role in the public space. In this manner, political action is for the sake of itself – i.e. for the sake of maintaining 'a sphere of plurality interconnected principles of mutual promise and common deliberation', 'consent and the right to dissent', 'rage', 'charity', 'distrust' and 'hatred'.

Here then is a subtle and rich account of the political. It points to the way that what Arendt calls 'principles' can energize 'praxis' whether these principles involve matters of honour, virtue or fear, a concern to promote 'freedom' or 'justice', by the way of consent or dissent, along with the expression of moral emotions like rage', 'charity', 'distrust' and 'hatred' or a sense that what needs to be expressed is 'solidarity'. This point seems the right time to bring in Bourdieu.

Bourdieu on the political

Bourdieu's work like Arendt's has the virtue of offering a relational account of *practice* and of the political. As Bourdieu observed, the key problem with conventional social science is that:

> … the 'entities' sociologists or criminologist are interested in are presumed to be independent of a social world made up of relations and processes – a perspective reinforced by a language 'better suited to express *things* [rather] than *relations, states* than *processes*' (Bourdieu and Wacquant 1992: 15). Bourdieu's theory of practice replaces 'things' with 'relations'.

Yet it is a different account to Arendt's and valuably so, because it highlights several critical absences or problems in Arendt's account of *praxis*. First, Bourdieu deals with Arendt's unwillingness to allow that the very ubiquity of social inequality, however this might be understood, might compromise the capacity of all citizens to participate equally and effectively in the public or political sphere. This, in turn, would require some address be given to the issue of how, if at all, social 'distinctions' embodied in and expressed through speech can be prevented from corrupting speech and thwarting participation in politics.

Second, while Bourdieu's account of practice (like Arendt's account of *praxis*) stresses its relational character, he also stresses its unconscious and inertial dispositions to reproduce a given order of life rather than propose new ways of doing things – even though that is also going on. Practice itself is both 'unconscious' (i.e. unreflexive and unknowing) and embodied. For Bourdieu, our practice is less a matter of consciousness and intentionality than it is a matter of embodied dispositions. As he stresses, his theory of practice does not emphasize:

> … conscious intentions or premeditations but … dispositions … [this is] a theory which places at the source of actions, not deliberate and explicit intentions but bodily dispositions, schemas that generate practices without requiring access to consciousness in order to function and which can operate below the level of consciousness and will…
>
> (Bourdieu 2017: 43)

This is why he stresses the constant competition in fields of action: the competition for 'what is at stake conceals the collusion regarding the very principles of the game. The struggle for the monopoly of legitimacy helps to reinforce the legitimacy in the name of which it is waged' (Bourdieu 1996: 166–7).

Third, Bourdieu stresses the way the state itself is best understood as a relation of domination in which states exercise symbolic power imposing cognitive structures on agents through which the state itself is thought (Bourdieu 2014: 114–60). In short, if Arendt stresses natality, newness, spontaneity and the leap into freedom characteristic of action-as-praxis, Bourdieu's 'political economy' of practice is a powerful corrective.

Understood relationally, Bourdieu offers a political-economic model of who we are and how we live. Bourdieu's is a *political economy of material, social, political and symbolic goods* including science, art, education along with resources like the number of people we know who have social pull that he calls social capital. As Bourdieu insists we have no choice but to enter into relations of competition with others in order to accumulate different kinds of capital according to the existing disposition of those capitals as well as playing by the rules of the various market places found in the education field, the cultural field, the sporting field or whatever.

On the one hand and in ways that conventional social scientists find hard to swallow, Bourdieu insists that social inequality is not a result of external 'structural' factors: distinction is not 'out there' but is 'in' our bodies. As Michael Burrawoy puts it, 'The social order inscribes itself in bodies, that is to say, we learn bodily, and express our knowledge bodily – all under the organizing power of the habitus, itself largely unconscious… practices and knowledge are bound together by the body' (Burrawoy 2012: 5). *Habitus* refers to embodied 'durable, transposable dispositions'. *Habitus* itself is the product of our history, experience and social location, becoming over time an ethos, a set of flexible and enduring 'mental structures' and 'bodily schemas' that organize, orient and direct one's comportment in private and public space. Again for Bourdieu, practice refers to all those bodily practices that lead to and evolve from the constitution of the *habitus*, the inculcation of dispositions of perception and appreciation.

> The habitus, the durably installed generative principle of regulated improvisations, produce practices which tend to reproduce the regularities immanent in the objective conditions of the production of their generative principle, while adjusting to the demands inscribed as objective potentialities in the situation, as defined by the cognitive and motivating structures making up the habitus.
>
> (Bourdieu 1977 [1972]: 78)

On the other hand, Bourdieu understands human action as relations of practice taking place in 'fields' and 'markets'. For Bourdieu, specific practices and human actions are not the effect of some independent, deterministic external or environmental 'forces' or 'structures', but rather arise as practice in the course of the relation between the *habitus* and specific social fields. These social fields are neither uniform nor homogenous. They are socially structured relations of conflict, with each field or market containing a variety of 'social position' occupied by specific people groups, or institutions. These positions, as well as the relations among them, are determined by the forms and volume of 'capital' that agents possess within each field or market. Importantly, for Bourdieu 'capital' is not just economic capital (material wealth of a type that is 'immediately and directly convertible into money' (Bourdieu 1986: 241). There is also 'social capital' (social connections with prominent or influential persons), 'cultural capital' (cultural knowledge or educational credentials) and 'symbolic capital' (social honour and prestige). Moreover, these forms of capital, while not automatically 'convertible', often can be converted. Bourdieu insists that language is not simply a medium of communication, but is also an instrument of distinction, domination, and violence. As such, the ways in which language is used, the social relations of the speakers, the forms of speech, the setting of speech and the style in which speakers speak are all potentially crucial for understanding the meaning of linguistic exchanges. In. this way, language can be used in what he calls 'classificatory struggles' like the way ideas of 'working-class' or 'middle-class' can be used, a point elaborated on recently by Kwame Appiah (2018) in his discussion of identity politics.

In particular, his account of language practice focusses on how relations of domination and exclusion and of basic inequalities (or 'distinctions') are enacted and sustained through linguistic and symbolic practices that rely on unequal access to various kinds of symbolic and cultural capital. In effect, language is not a neutral medium of communication so much as a site of practice (re)producing distinction, domination and symbolic violence. Bourdieu's account of 'distinction' (or inequalities) focusses on the practices that operate in and through language, namely those distinctions that work as unnoticed conduits of exclusion (Topper 2011: 358).

This raises one important question: how can Bourdieu make sense of or account for the phenomenon of dissent or change given what seems like an inherent structural determinism which privileges domination in his account of how the field reproduces the *habitus* and the *habitus* reproduces the field? Many critics have accused Bourdieu of denying any possibility of change. If practice-as-habitus is all about inertia and the reproduction of domination, how is change or dissent conceivable in such a theory? Collins, e.g. is scathing when, says Bourdieu, it offers 'an abstract picture of invariable domination without the possibility of contradiction or revolution' (Cited Yang 2014: 1537).

Bourdieu on change and dissent

Given his reputation as a dour theorist of reproduction who allows no space for change, Bourdieu offers both a surprising and a satisfying account of change grounded in showing how change comes out of order.

It is true enough that Bourdieu stresses the tendency to order and the *reproduction* of what already is, a disposition shaped as he suggests, by the unequal distribution of all kinds of economic, social, material, symbolic and political resources or capitals. Yet it looks like a serious lack of attention bordering on negligence – or malevolence – on the part of some of his critics, when they represent Bourdieu as unwilling or unable to engage with change or dissent and how it happens (e.g. Alexander 1994; Widick 2003).[5] These criticisms are still made in spite of major books (Bourdieu and Wacquant 1992; Bourdieu 1996) and a series of lectures (Bourdieu 2017) all explicitly framed as an 'attempt to make the very idea of symbolic revolution intelligible' (Bourdieu 2017: 3). As Yang (2014: 1538) insists, Bourdieu both acknowledged how change and conscious deliberation can be achieved and did so more often than many of his critics have recognized and that he offers a clear 'general theory of change' though even Yang has missed out dealing with Bourdieu's sustained interest in and engagement with the relation of continuity-change.[6]

Part of the problem is that many conventional social scientists do not or cannot understand his 'relational turn'. To the chagrin of many conventional social scientists Bourdieu does not rely on a cause-effect logic. As Bourdieu (1990: 90) made perfectly clear, he rejected both determinist structural explanations, in which the outside world is understood to mechanically and directly condition social actors or to 'cause' social activity, as well as more voluntarist or 'agential' accounts of social action which still treats action as the determinate result of conscious even rational ideas or beliefs held by actors. Bourdieu is also alive to the puzzles of change.

As the first Greek philosophers understood, temporal change is very odd. Zeno, e.g. thought that change was an illusion. Zeno argued that an arrow in flight could not really be moving because at any given instant, it would be at a place identical to itself (and not another place); something at just one (self-identical) place could not be described as moving, and an arrow which is motionless at every instant in a temporal interval must be motionless throughout the interval (Mortensen 2007: 2). As Plato records, Heraclitus thought that all was change: 'Heraclitus, I believe, says that all things pass and nothing stays, and comparing existing things to the flow of a river, he says you could not step twice into the same river' (Plato Cratylus 402a=A6). Later writers see in Heraclitus an advocate for the unity of opposites, a position I read as close in spirit to Bourdieu's approach.

Bourdieu is very clear that change comes out of order. Bourdieu insists that:

> We have to move on from the continuous/discontinuous alternative, or rather from the specification of this alternative as a choice between, on the one hand, the myth of the radical break and the uncreated creator, and, on the other, the myth of the absolute continuity of the creator who has discovered nothing.
>
> (Bourdieu 2017: 228)

Bourdieu says there

> is no contradiction between the dichotomous vision that pits two camps or systems against each other…[i.e. the idea of the revolutionary break] which is the dominant perspective of our age, and on the other hand a vision that lays much more stress on continuity and which discovers in an earlier period the seeds, the outline and the prelude of everything that is going to develop at a later time.
>
> (Bourdieu 2017: 235)

For one thing, Bourdieu understood that if the behaviour of actors is *regulated*, it is not *determined* by norms and rules (Bourdieu 1990: 65). Bourdieu certainly understood and valued the role of dissent. As he said to Terry Eagleton: 'What you say about the capacity for dissent is very important; this indeed exists, but not where we look for it – it takes another form' (Bourdieu in Zizek 1994: 1). Yet Bourdieu does not give any ground to a classically romantic interpretation based on talking about 'revolution'. As he says to attribute a

> revolutionary break to a person group or to a single event or date is to ignore the general factors involved and above all else the dynamics at play in a given field … In evoking the revolutionary role of Manet (as well as that of Baudelaire or Flaubert) I would not wish to encourage a naively discontinuous vision of the genesis of the field.
>
> (Bourdieu 1996: 133)

This is why he thought that criticism and dissent were not easy:

> I think the capacity for resistance, as a capacity of consciousness, was overestimated. I fear that what I have to say is shocking for the self-confidence of intellectuals, especially for the more generous, left-wing intellectuals. I am seen as pessimistic, as discouraging the people, and so on. But I think it is better to know the truth, and the fact is that… people living in poor conditions…

are prepared to accept much more than we would have believed.... They put up with a great deal, and this is what I mean by *doxa* – that there are many things people accept without knowing.

(Bourdieu 1994: 268–9)

Rather Bourdieu's is a perspective that sees the unity of conflict and order in any field. Bourdieu argues that any field is itself a field that always contains alternatives. (Here the French word 'champs' from the Latin *campus* has military resonances missing from the English 'field'.) That is, we can see in any field 'contradictory forms in a field, whatever the state of that field' (Bourdieu 2017: 235). Bourdieu says that there 'are internal struggles at work in any field' or what he calls a 'a dynamic at work in this field' (Bourdieu 2017: 253). As he goes on to elaborate:

For example if we take the 1960s French philosophical field, we can see that the seeds of the structuralist period that followed existentialism had already been planted, even as Sartre's towering presence overshadowed them: you'll see that Bachelard, Canguilhem and others – a whole group of social agents – were being overlooked at least in a relative sense.

(Bourdieu 2017: 235)

Put simply, no field is ever completely subordinated to a single symbolic order. The very structure of the field gives rise to change and conflict. As Bourdieu puts it, 'The field of the present is merely another name for the field of struggle' (Bourdieu 1996: 159). For one thing, there is always competition for capitals. As he says:

Arising out of the very structure of the field, that is, from the synchronic oppositions between antagonistic positions (dominant/ dominated, consecrated/novice, orthodox/heretic, old/young, etc.), changes [are] continually taking place at the centre of the field of restricted production.

(Bourdieu 1996: 239)

In effect, Bourdieu's account of the play of capitals in fields of action here points precisely to a built-in dynamic in any field between 'The possessors of specific capital and those who are still deprived of it … [This] constitute[s] the motor of an incessant transformation of the supply of symbolic products' (Bourdieu 1996: 127). This is an account using the idea of *agon* in a way that is different from, but still related to, Arendt's account. As Bourdieu says:

The opposition between the incumbents and the pretenders installs at the very core of the field a tension between those who try to overtake their rivals and those who wish to avoid being overtaken, as if it were a race.

(Bourdieu 1996: 126)

Bourdieu offers a theory of *agon* (competition) without the name. In any field, we will encounter alternative values/practices in *agon*. Though we should not privilege any place of change, it is the case that sometimes young people do promote change. Bourdieu allows that:

> It is true that the initiative for change can be traced back, almost by definition, to new (meaning younger) entrants. These are the ones who are also the most deprived of specific capital, and who (in a universe where to exist is to be different, meaning to occupy a distinct and distinctive position) only exist in so far as … they manage to assert their identity {that is, their difference} and get it known and recognized ['make a name for oneself'] by imposing new modes of thought and expression.
>
> (Bourdieu 1996: 240)

As Bourdieu observes, there is a temporal or historical dimension to this ongoing struggle between the old and the new:

> It is not enough to say that the history of the field is the history of the struggle for a monopoly of the imposition of legitimate categories of perception and appreciation; *it is in the very struggle that the history of the field is made; it is through struggles that it is temporalized.* The ageing of authors, works or schools is something quite different from a mechanical sliding into the past. It is engendered in the fight between those who have already left their mark and are trying to endure, and those who cannot make their own marks in their turn without consigning to the past those who have an interest in stopping time, in eternalizing the present state; between the dominants whose strategy is tied to continuity, identity and reproduction, and the dominated, the new entrants, whose interest is in discontinuity, rupture, difference and revolution.
>
> (Bourdieu 1996: 158)

Bourdieu also points to periods of crisis or transition when the old habitus does not 'fit' the field and is not (yet) adapted to the new Doxa. Bourdieu refers to 'the hysteresis effect' (Bourdieu 1990, 2000). The hysteresis effect means that, in the changed circumstances, we maintain our already-acquired habitus/dispositions even when they are no longer adapted (what Bourdieu, following Marx, calls 'the Don Quixote effect'). Bourdieu (1990: 104–5) refers to 'the presence of the past', where the durable practices are not adapted to the changed context and function *à contre-temps* (Bourdieu, 1990: 105). Bourdieu (1990) draws on the case of Algeria, where Bourdieu himself recorded the 'discordance between the habitus and the structures of the economy (pre-capitalist and capitalist) "at times even within the same individuals" (*"parfois même à l'intérieur des mêmes individus"*)' (Bourdieu 1977: 15).

Finally, change can come out of the very mastery that immersion and success in a field offers. As Bourdieu says, '… you need to know a system very well, to know it from the inside and to be its product or its expression in order to be in a position to tackle it on its own terms, on its own ground'. Bourdieu's delight in being able 'to see both sides of the story at once' is exemplified when he asks:

> How is this possible? If you have so completely absorbed a system that it is in your bones, you feel very comfortable with it, and your only desire is to perpetuate it. So what sort of character manages to be at once completely inside and outside the system? It is the quintessential symbolic revolutionary: it is someone who even as he is completely possessed by the system, mange sot take possession of it by turning his mastery of that system against it. It is a very strange thing. When an autonomous universe, or field has reached an advanced stage of development, this is the only kind or possible form of revolution. There are no self-taught revolutionaries, but there are naïve people who think that there could be.
>
> (Bourdieu 2017: 244)

This understanding informs his insight that in the art field, e.g. parody is a form of critique or dissent. As he notes, 'parody combines things, it brings different things together… we would say it is a *conciliatio oppositorum* – i.e. a marriage of opposites' (Bourdieu 2017: 241). Bourdieu adds that 'the Russian formalist theory of parody [proposes] that that it is a thing that says one thing and its opposite, and which in the process destroys what it professes' (Bourdieu 2017: 242). Further, it is only made possible when the parodist has complete mastery of the thing or form that is being parodied. Bourdieu treats parody as an example of how a person can turn their mastery into critique. Here parody becomes something more a form or practice of critique performed by the 'quintessential symbolic revolutionary'. As Bourdieu says, 'This is someone who even as he is completely possessed by a system, mange to take possession of it by turning his mastery of that system against it' (Bourdieu 2017: 244).

Equally this mastery can also inform the practice of reflexivity-as-critical-practice. Bourdieu clearly allows for the possibility of critical reflexivity, understood as 'the systematic exploration of the unthought categories of thought that delimit the thinkable and predetermine the thought' (Bourdieu and Wacquant 1992: 40). On Bourdieu's account, the reflexive process is itself a practice, a form of habitus and, is often, especially in academic fields, a required and occasionally even valued aspect of a particular field. Scientific and academic fields like sociology tend to value and encourage reflexivity as a habitus-field requirement. Equally reflexivity can potentially emerge anywhere in 'crisis' situations. Understood in this way it is simply a practice and a procedural requirement within a given scientific and academic field and a practice that both relies on and adds to intellectual capita. Bourdieu claims, e.g. in what Geoffrey Mead (2017: 1) calls a 'contentious paradox', namely that if we know the 'laws' that curtail freedom, then *knowing* these laws we are better positioned to labour on subverting them than if they were not known: 'determined… man can know his determinations and work to overcome them' (Bourdieu 2000: 131).

Bourdieu does not underestimate the difficulty that change or dissent involves. Even the act of thinking requires both an epistemological and a social break. Reflecting on the problem of how to use the ready-made objects like official documents or government-produced statistics, Bourdieu suggests a provisional definition of positivism as 'an exercise in in excessive methodological rigour based on objects that have not been subjected to rigorous criticism' (Bourdieu 2017: 57). As he adds:

> There are no self-taught revolutionaries... The naive are far more numerous because you have to be fully conversant with a scholarly system to be able to strike at its heart... It is so onerous to acquire knowledge that those who have become learned no longer wish to destroy that learning, and this is what safeguards the system.
>
> (Bourdieu 2017: 244)

And if that built-in prophylaxis against change does not work, there is always the state.

Dissent and the role of the state

If we accept that diversity (or 'difference') is as ubiquitous as it seems to be, how then is dissent even conceivable, let alone discernible? By this, I mean to highlight the problem that if disagreement over ideas, and politico-moral ideas, is as ubiquitous as they seem to be, how then does the articulation of, or acting out of, some ideas or principles come to be seen as dissent. Bourdieu offers one important answer.

Bourdieu argues that the state is 'the principle of orthodoxy', 'a hidden principle that can be grasped in the manifestation of public order … and the opposite of disorder, anarchy and civil war'. This, says Bourdieu, is because the state ensures as far as is possible both 'logical conformity' and 'moral order'. By 'logical conformity', Bourdieu means that the state tries to ensure that there is some consensus about the categories of thought among people in the society enabling some immediate agreement about perceptions involved in the construction of reality. Moral order involves 'agreement about some basic moral values'. This, in turn, means that because the state is the source of 'logical conformity' and 'moral order', it ensures a fundamental consensus on the meaning of the social world that is the very precondition of politics itself as the site of conflict over the social world.

Central to Bourdieu's account of the politics of order is the state. Bourdieu's account of the state emphasizes its character as a site of order. As he says while political sociologists are 'often struck by the most outwardly striking aspect: rebellions, conspiracies, insurrections, revolutions' 'what is staggering and amazing is the opposite: the fact that order is so frequently observed' (Bourdieu 2014: 163). He draws on his account of symbolic order (as symbolic violence or domination) to argue that states are stable because they exercise symbolic power over their citizens by providing the vocabulary and sense-making through which the state itself is thought to incorporate the categories of the state as implicit background assumptions, a form of preconsciousness rather than false consciousness, which he calls 'doxa' (or opinion/common sense). The citizens then reapply these categories to the social world unconsciously confirming their existence (Bourdieu 2014: 169).

Bourdieu was keen to insist that the state is in one sense an 'unthinkable object'. There is here as Bourdieu (2014: 6) acknowledges a sense that the state is 'as orthodoxy, a collective fiction, a well-founded illusion'. The state as he says exist in one sense because 'people believe it exists'. This is why he says 'we need to be careful when we read sentences that talk about 'the state'': 'we are reading theological sentences – which does not mean that they are false, inasmuch as the state is a theological entity that is an entity that exists by way of belief' (Bourdieu 2014: 10).

Concerned about the ease with which we may become trapped in a web of conventional thinking, Bourdieu warned that we risk applying to the state a kind of 'state thinking', where 'our thinking, the very structure of consciousness by which we construct the social world and the particular object that is the state are very likely the product of the state itself' (Bourdieu 2014: 3). The state, says Bourdieu, needs to be approached first as 'a principle of production of legitimate representation of the social world': this is because the state he says is defined 'by the possession of the monopoly of legitimate physical and symbolic violence'. Bourdieu insists that the monopoly of 'symbolic violence' 'is the condition for possession of the exercise of the monopoly of the physical violence itself' (Bourdieu 2014: 4). In this way, Bourdieu amends Weber's (1978 (Vol 1): 74) famous definition of the state as 'the monopoly of legitimate violence'.

This pursuit of order underpins the 'production and canonization of social categories' (2014: 9). The functions of the state include the quantification and coding of people and the production of legitimate social identity. Having a driver's licence or enrolling to vote means that the categories of 'driver' or 'citizen' are 'legitimate categories' pointing to 'a *nomos*, a principle of division that is universally agreed on within the limits of society about which no discussion is needed' (2014: 10). Equally, this also means that even social behaviours such as rebellion may be determined by the very categories that are rebelled against by those who rebel. And this matters when an authorized person like a teacher declares in some official way like in a school report that a particular child in a school 'is an idiot'.

There are, as Bourdieu shows, two issues. One goes to the construction of categories. The other goes to the way those categories are then employed in the social world. Bourdieu reminds the social sciences quite sharply not to imagine they are responsible for the original constitution of those categories whose logic and necessity they are unaware of. The social sciences only deal with 'pre-named, pre-classified realities which bear proper nouns and common nouns' (Bourdieu 1991: 105). As we have seen, he stresses the role of the state in this 'constitutive process'.

Here, Bourdieu relies on one important criticism. In thinking about the state, e.g. as a source of law, Bourdieu (1977: 814) insists on not falling into one of two habits of mind, one which treats the law as 'an autonomous form' in relation to society and the other which reduces it instrumentally to 'a reflection or tool in the service of dominant groups'. The first tendency ('formalism') includes the tradition of 'legal positivism', which simply treats the law as 'a body of doctrine and rules totally independent of social constraints and pressures, one which finds its foundation entirely within itself' as an effect of government (Bourdieu 1987: 814). (This would include German variants like Kelsen or the English tradition of Austin and Hart.) On the other hand, 'instrumentalism' includes those Marxists who have thought about 'law and jurisprudence as direct reflections of existing social power relations, in which economic determinations and, in particular, the interests of dominant groups are expressed: that is, as an instrument of domination' (Bourdieu 1987: 814).

Bourdieu prefers to focus on the constitutive process closely tied to the performative power of discourse itself where the practice of naming, categorizing or judging someone brings about real actions and changes. The linguistic devices are numerous and include gossip, slander, lies, insults, commendations, criticisms, arguments and praises. They have the magical property of bringing about the things they name and so play a vital part in constructing the social world.

> The authority that underlies the performative efficacy of discourse is a *percipi*, a being-known, which allows a *percipere* to be imposed, or, more precisely, which allows the consensus concerning the meaning of the social world which grounds common sense to be imposed officially, i.e. in front of everyone and in the name of everyone.
>
> (Bourdieu 1991: 106)

This means the social sciences need to be able to develop 'a theory of the theory effect', i.e. the consequences of categorizing and naming people, actions and relationships. Few organizations or institutions possess this capacity to the same extent as the state.

On the power of language to become, as Austin put it, 'performative' (i.e. to 'execute an action'), Bourdieu (1991: 107) is quite clear this power is not contained *within language* so much as it is an *expression* of social and symbolic power:

> The naive question of the power of words is logically implicated in the initial suppression of the question of the uses of language, and therefore of the social conditions in which words are employed. As soon as one treats language as an autonomous object, accepting the radical separation which Saussure made between internal and external linguistics, between the science of language and the science of the social uses of language, one is condemned to looking within words for the power of words, that is, looking for it where it is not to be found.

Categories are employed in the social world via a process of authorization involving 'a series of delegations going back step by step like Aristotle's god: the
state' (2014: 11). This makes Bourdieu's use of the idea of performativity a much
more political and social process that the abstracted linguistic analysis offered by
J.L. Austin (1959) or the Kantian universal-rational analysis offered by Habermas
(1996). As Bourdieu puts it:

> This is the essence of the error which is expressed in its most accomplished
> form by Austin (and after him, Habermas) when he thinks that he has found
> in discourse itself – in the specifically linguistic substance of speech, as it
> were – the key to the efficacy of speech. By trying to understand the power of
> linguistic manifestations linguistically, by looking in language for the princi-
> ple under-lying the logic and effectiveness of the language of institution, one
> forgets that authority comes to language from outside.
>
> (Bourdieu 1991: 109)

When a teacher or a police officer instructs someone to do something, that in-
struction or order calls on the authority of the state which informs and backs up
the categories being used. As we will see, the criminalization of dissent begins
to exemplify the capacity of the state to invest in legal and political categories
important political distinctions.

Conclusion

If we are to grasp the political as a prelude then to grasping the relations between the political, dissent and its criminalization, we will need to bring *praxis*
and practice together as a unity-of-difference. If we start with what appears to be
the case, we can say that Arendt emphasizes the idea of politics as *praxis* as free,
spontaneous and novel action oriented to change, while Bourdieu focusses on
practice involving the reproduction of symbolic order in fields of action. Closer
examination of both points to far more complexity.

From Arendt, we see a unity-of-difference in the political idea which assumes
that consent is the norm, while dissent remains a legitimate activity. On her
account, dissent is tied relationally to consent via her conception of natality.
Arendt says we are to call each new citizen's relationship to law a voluntary consent 'when the child happens to be born into a community in which dissent is a
legal and de-facto possibility once he has grown into a man' (Arendt 1972: 87).
In effect, 'Dissent implies consent, *and is a hallmark of free government*: one who
knows that he may dissent knows also that he somehow consents when he does
not dissent' (Arendt 1972a: 88) (My stress). Each generation of 'newcomers' is
presumed to 'tacitly consent' to the political order until such time as they are
able to dissent.

From Bourdieu, we get an account that emphasizes the ubiquity of order-and-
change within the many fields of action. The very structure of the field itself gives

rise to change and conflict. As Bourdieu puts it, 'The field of the present is merely another name for the field of struggle' (Bourdieu 1996: 159). There is a built-in dynamic in any field between, 'The possessors of specific capital and those who are still deprived of it … [This] constitute[s] the motor of an incessant transformation of the supply of symbolic products' (Bourdieu 1996: 127).

If disagreement over ideas and politico-moral ideas are as ubiquitous as they seem to be, how then do certain kinds of disagreement come to be seen as dissent? Bourdieu in particular helps to address this question when he highlights the central role played by the state. If the idea of political order (*arche*) is always an imaginary more than a given reality, it is still the case that modern states are guardians of the idea of order. Taking a cue from Anderson's famous account of nationhood or national identity as an 'imagined community', we can say that 'political order' is an imagined order and, in the liberal case, one based on the metaphor of consent. This idea is the product of endless communication. Bourdieu's account of the state stresses its capacity for and control of symbolic violence lying in its power to impose its definitions and communication processes on its citizens. The result will be that some forms of action will be defined as dissent, requiring the ultimate political response: its criminalization.

Notes

1 See also in German 'die Politik' and 'das Politische', in Dutch, 'de politiek' and 'het politieke' and so forth.
2 As Bourdieu (1991: 3) insisted *apropos* Heidegger 'we must abandon the opposition between a political reading and a philosophical reading and undertake a simultaneously political and philosophical dual reading dual reading of [Heideggers] writings which are defined by their fundamental ambiguity, that is by reference to two social spaces'. Bourdieu was clear about needing to avoid the equally futile claims that philosophy, e.g. is always autonomous or else it can be explained by reducing it as an expression of the general social setting in which it was created.
3 Arendt follows Heidegger when he said *arche* means both 'beginning and domination … starting and disposition' (Heidegger 2015: 43; also Cesare 2018: 39). More generally, we see in Arendt the central Heideggerian account of Dasein. Heidegger understands the relation of *Dasein* to the world as a relation of mutual dependence (Sandel 2014: 123). *Dasein* is a unity involving a relation of 'thrown-projection', and Heidegger treats Dasein as 'thrown-projection'. Dasein involves 'agency' understood as both entirely passive and entirely active. In Heidegger to be thrown is to be acted upon as when a ball is thrown. To be projected has more to do with acting as when we 'embark on a project'. As Heidegger puts it, 'Being's poem just begun is man' (Heidegger 1971: 4). On the other hand, Being unfolds only through the action of *dasein*. In this sense, 'man is the shepherd of being' (Heidegger 1977: 210).
4 Arendt borrows Kant's idea of an 'original compact' arguing that the inspiring principles of this compact bring the actor and spectator together as one, with the proviso that in this relationship an actor can always become a spectator – and vice versa.
5 The will to misread Bourdieu is sometimes astonishing. Widick, e.g. insists that we see in Bourdieu 'the language of conditioned disposition and environmentally triggered

response … of inculcation and inscription of socially constituted dispositions' (Widick 2003: 688) while Adkins says 'the habitus will always submit to the field'.

6 However, even Yang says that 'it seems difficult to produce convincing evidence that Bourdieu is not a pessimistic determinist' (2014: 1531) and insists that Bourdieu is a determinist who has created a circular theoretical system in which 'social agents are only allowed to move within a predefined circle – certain fields with which their habitus is compatible' (Yang 2014: 1528). Sometimes, we need to be saved from our friends.

Chapter 3

The many faces of dissent

The conventional notion that dissent has a number of important defining qualities or properties that are relatively easily identified informs many an exercise in 'defining' dissent. Robert Martin in his history of the origins of American dissent says that:

> Dissent is any practice – often verbal, but sometimes performative – that challenges the *status quo* (the existing structure of norms, values, customs, traditions and especially authorities that underwrite the present ways of doing things
>
> (Martin 2013: 3)

Joonas Leppanen (2016: 17) says that '[t]o dissent with something is to disagree with a specific feature in society and to articulate this disagreement. It is the articulation of dissent that makes it into a political matter'. He then adds that 'those who dissent in society do it based on demands to correct wrongs in society or to change the state of affairs that are conceived as oppressing'. Gene Sharp who preferred to talk about 'non-violent struggle' rather than dissent understood it as a project oriented to social transformation and social justice (Sharp 1973).

In these and many other exercises, the animating idea is that for dissent to be dissent, it needs to challenge the *status quo* and be designed or intended to bring about change to existing laws, policies or religious, moral or political conventions, practices and beliefs. Roland Bleiker (2000) who is critical of Sharp's theory of dissent points to the problem found in so many social science exercises of looking for a single theoretical framework to 'explain' the dynamics of dissent in all times and places. The point is this: while aiming at complete definitions of dissent, writers like Martin, Leppanen and Sharp paradoxically produce incomplete and partial accounts of dissent. Granting the ubiquity of disagreement, we should expect that dissent will be expressed in complex, odd and divergent ways.

Understood relationally, dissent is always connected to those enduring and orderly elements of social life especially as these are imagined. If the natural and the human world are actually constantly changeful, complex and diverse, many of us are unwilling to deal with this and so we tell stories about eternal life, permanence, order, predictability, persistence, uniformity and consensus. The sense that our lives are orderly and predictable is an important element at work in the discursive practices of any institution: in my parent's family, each day had a particular function (washing on a Monday or going to the football on Saturday afternoon) and a regular menu of food to be cooked and eaten on a particular day. Churches provide a classic case of rule-based ritual, while workplaces design flows of work in mostly predictable ways; order is both imagined and an artefact of practice. Those who work in *and* for the state are a major source of ideas and practices designed to give effect to or to realize an imaginary order that is permanent, stable and secure. The various social sciences have also made a major contribution to this persistent exercise in therapeutic myth-making.

For the most part, conventional social scientists have persisted in thinking about dissent as thing-like and refused to take the 'relational turn'. Dissent and the disposition to dissent are relational. Dissent is a break with 'normal' ways of thinking, feeling and acting. It begins as disagreement or a refusal to agree with someone else's beliefs, opinions, orders, conduct or decisions. To dissent is to disagree and be at variance with other people's ideas and practices: to dissent involves refusing an established order, thinking outside some square, challenging some authority, diverging from an orthodoxy, refusing obedience, opposing, criticizing, quarrelling with and maybe seeking to rearrange the ideas and or to change the conduct of others. It is an expressive activity whether as thinking or doing of a break with a certain order. It is political when the thought or doing specifically breaks with legal rules or authoritatively sanctioned conduct. As a political process, dissent signifies a refusal to accept as legitimate, authoritative/powerful ideas or forms of conduct typically produced by or sanctioned by other powerful people, institutions and organizations.

This is the proposition explored here. I draw on the work of Engin Isin (2002, 2005) whose theory of the political fleshes out the complementary accounts of political action offered by Arendt and Bourdieu. Because I am not able to consider all of the possible forms that disagreement/dissent takes in a shortish book, I highlight the diversity of dissent by considering just two quite different kinds of dissent.

The first is the dramatic case when small but significant numbers of serving Israeli soldiers in the 1980s and 1990s became 'selective resistors' often in highly spontaneous ways. I then turn to the more durable and collective process known as 'squatting', involving large numbers of people occupying abandoned and derelict buildings in large modern cities. Both cases highlight the diversity of dissenting activity.

Thinking about dissent as action: Engin Isin

Dissent is always a political relation. At some point, disagreement slides into dissent as one or both of the parties in the relationship decide that a line needs to be, or has been, crossed. If the specific expression of dissent is against something, it also stands for something. In both cases, that 'something' is always 'political'. The irreducibly political aspect of dissent is because it involves being disagreeable, speaking truth to power, resisting injustice, challenging unequal power relations by pursuing the truth, by exposing lies, denial and deception, abuse and corruption and sometimes even criminality, often on the part of powerful organizations including the state itself.

In this respect, Engin Isin (2002, 2005, 2008) offers a striking relational account of the political as human action that allows for the diverse activities and relations that dissent takes. Isin starts from and restates the basic point made by Arendt that conventional political science is overly preoccupied with an orientation to 'regulation', 'discipline', 'rule' and 'governance' that 'presuppose order' (Isin 2008: 20). Conventional political science privileges describing, explaining or accounting for 'those routines by which humans order their social and political relations', iterating these routines as more important than ruptures or breaks. This is why Isin, like Arendt, focusses on what he calls 'the act' as 'distinct from conduct, practice, behaviour and habit', implying that 'an act is a rupture in the given' (Isin 2008: 25). As he adds, this account is a result of his distancing himself 'from the stale categories of perception that have come to dominate the social sciences in the last few decades' (Isin 2005: 374). He also wants to move the debate on from traditional ideas about citizenship as either *status* or *identity*. As he says, 'These are not fixed identities but fluid subject positions in and out of which subjects move. In other words, being always involves being with others' (Isin 2008: 19).

The result is a fully elaborated and relational account of how being a citizen, implicates all the possible political modes and positions that are constitutively possible in a space that is discernibly political because people in that space are engaging in political *praxis*/practices. Isin argues that it is possible to think about citizenship from the perspective of an account of the formation of groups *as a generalized question of otherness, and of the ways of being political*. He does this in terms of thinking about how we fill up space with our political acts.

Isin's understanding of the political and political space is relational. His relational approach to being a citizen relies on Elias' conception of the 'figuration'. Isin says being political is a spatio-temporal way of being, such that each figuration is constituted as a consequence of the act of interpretation and does not exist as such, but only in consequence of that act of interpretation. As he (2008: 18) also argues:

> The enactment of citizenship is paradoxical because it is dialogical. The moment of the enactment of citizenship, which instantiates constituents, also instantiates other subjects from whom the subject of a claim is differentiated. So an enactment inevitably creates a scene where there are selves and others defined in relation to each other.

His relational approach is represented as a theory of the act which '[i]s neither a practice nor a conduct nor an action, and yet it implies or perhaps makes all those possible' (Isin 2008: 24). To do this, he draws on remarkable accounts of the human act by Adolf Reinach (1913/1983) and Mikhail Bakhtin (1993). Isin notices that Arendt treats the act as the defining capacity of being human. 'Theorizing acts' requires that we focus on 'an assemblage of acts, actions and actors in a historically and geographically concrete situation' (Isin 2008: 24). To flesh out his framing of the political, he provides a theory of the act as well as outlining the possible ways of being political understood as various practices and relations. For Isin, acts produce actors/subjects: 'acts produce actors that do not exist before acts' (Isin 2008: 37). Acts of citizenship, therefore, produce citizens and their 'others', i.e. strangers, outsiders and aliens.

Arguably, Isin over-emphasizes the freedom that he says characterizes 'the act'. As he says:

> When you act you bring something new into being. That is the most fearsome aspect of acting. Bringing something new into being. There is no guarantee of effects or consequences. It requires literally a leap into the unknown with the courage or doubt of one's' own convictions whatever the situation demands. To act is also the core of politics.
>
> (Isin 2018)

This is very like Arendt's account of *praxis*. It expresses an important half-truth but only that as he has left out the responses of others who, e.g. prefer order to freedom.

The value of Isin's work is his insistence on investigating all the ways we can act politically in the everyday life-world. His relational perspective does not offer a simple binary. Unlike Schmitt, who restricts the possibilities of being political to a distinction made between being *friends* or *enemies*, Isin says there are many ways of being political, which include being *citizens, strangers, outsiders* and *aliens*. Isin (2002, 2005) further proposes that we think about these ways of being citizens, strangers, outsiders or aliens less as identities and more as positions that are purposive. As Isin says, categories such as 'citizens', 'strangers', 'outsiders' and 'aliens' are best not understood as beings or things having qualities and engaging in observable acts, but as positions towards which we orient as we *act*. He treats these 'positions' as something irreducible to and different from the attributes of any particular person. He adds that this means treating these ways of being as relational processes in which people 'are [understood as] active producers of the machine [who] derive pleasure and suffer pain from doing so as they invest themselves in its operations' (Isin 2005: 381).

The plurality of ways of being political, brought into being by acts, involve different relations. Thinking about citizenship in this way makes one attentive to the enacting of citizenship, and how it is performed and negotiated. In each case, whether we are *citizens, strangers, outsiders* or *aliens*, we can engage with each other by developing and acting out and using *solidaristic, agonistic* or *alienating relationships* deploying a variety of *orientations, strategies and technologies* as ways of being political.

Finally, and to add what looks initially like a spatial dimension, Isin (2002: 283) suggests that we can conceive of these relationships and the ways of *being political* as occurring in a kind of political space. As he says 'the city is a crucial condition of citizenship in the sense that being a citizen is inextricably associated with being of the city' (Isin 2002: 283). This is why he suggests that to be a citizen requires a city. But this city is not a thing and not even a space. Here Isin's approach is clearly relational. As he says, the city is less a thing or a physical space and more a figuration, or a process:

> The city is neither a background to these struggles against which groups wager, nor is it a foreground for which groups struggle for hegemony. Rather, the city *is* the battleground through which groups define their identity, stake their claims, wage their battles, and Varticulate citizenship rights, obligations, and principles.
>
> (Isin 2002: 283–4)

As a figuration, the city should not be imagined as simply a material or physical place, but more as 'a field that operates as a difference machine' (Isin 2005: 375). The city is a 'difference machine' because:

> … beings are not formed outside the machine and then encounter each other within the city, but the city assembles (groups), generates, distributes, and differentiates differences, incorporates them within strategies and technologies, and elicits, interpellates, adjures, and incites them[1]
>
> (Isin 2005: 375)

Isin understands dissent within this framing of the political as a claim on justice. Isin allows that whatever else can be said, the political is always about some claim to justice. As he says 'Being political means being constituted as a subject of justice' or to put that another way 'an act is interpreted as political only when it constitutes the subject as a claimant of justice' (Isin 2005: 382). What is good about this is the way Isin allows for a large number of ways of dissenting. Being a claimant of justice can take many different forms including dissent, affirmation, resistance and withdrawal. As Isin says:

> Being constituted as a subject of justice means making a claim (solidaristic, agonistic, alienating), articulating it (orientations, strategies and technologies) and making and articulating it from a position (citizens, stranger, outsider, alien).
>
> (Isin 2005: 382)

If we briefly think about the kinds of speakings and doings that are dissenting, we can imagine a spectrum of possibilities. In Figure 3.1, I foreground some of the forms or kinds of action that dissent can take. Ground-breaking work by Rosch

Thinking → writing → images → whistleblowing → expressive → conscientious → strikes → civil → violent → armed

speaking   protest   objection   occupations disobedience protest struggle

Figure 3.1 The spectrum of dissent.

(1975) and Lakoff (1987) reminds us these categories are not and can never be well-bounded: each category or kind tends to bleed readily into other categories. However, if nothing else, this offers a useful way of thinking about dissent metaphorically as a kind of continuous or sine wave.

Granting that dissent is always tied relationally to the enduring and orderly elements of social life, especially as these are imaginatively and discursively constituted by experts, intellectuals and the state, this helps to clarify the basic questions we need to address. First, how and why does disagreement become dissent? Do particular kinds of social settings and relationships enable us to rehearse and act out our disagreements so they become dissent, or do other no-less relational factors block the way to dissent? Is it always the case that dissenters need an audience before whom they practice or act out their dissent? Is it possible that the decision to criminalize disagreement converts it into dissent?

To begin to address these questions in this and later chapters and because I am not able to consider all of the possible forms that disagreement/dissent takes in a shortish book, I highlight the diversity of dissent by considering just two radically different kinds of dissent. The first is the dramatic case involving small, but significant numbers of serving Israeli soldiers who in the 1980s and 1990s became 'selective resistors'. I then turn to another kind of dissent involving a more durable and collective process known as squatting, involving large numbers of people occupying abandoned and derelict buildings in large modern cities.

Like Arendt and Bourdieu, Engin Isin understands that ours is a world exhibiting a complex mix of enduring institutions, habitual conduct, hierarchies of authority *and* irreducible pluralism, difference, criticism disagreement and dissent. That dissent takes many forms is suggested by the contrast between the solitary even isolated character of the refusal by Israelis soldiers to obey orders and the collective and enduring characteristics of people involved in political squatting.

The case of Israel's 'selective resistors', 1982–94

The 'refusers' (or 'Savarnim' in Hebrew) were citizens of Israel who obeyed the legal requirement to serve for between one and two months each year as reservists in the Israeli Defence Forces, but who became 'selective resistors' in the 1980s and 1990s. We know a lot about the conduct and thinking of these serving soldiers who became dissenters whose conduct was criminalized, because Ruth Linn, an Israeli-born moral psychologist who had herself been an army reservist, decided to explore how and why these men took the action they did. What follows draws heavily on Linn's work (Linn 1989, 1996).

When Israel invaded Lebanon between 1982 and 1984, 165 mostly young, male, often well-educated, uniformed Israelis who were serving members of the I Israeli Defence Forces refused orders given by their officers to serve in Lebanon. While happy to do their compulsory military service, these reservists refused on conscientious grounds to serve in Lebanon after Israel mounted what its government declared would be a 'short pre-emptive strike' directed at Palestinian Liberation Organisation (PLO) terrorists' in Lebanon in June 1982. The pre-emptive attack turned into a deeply traumatic, controversial and divisive three-year long invasion and occupation of Lebanon. The political-moral controversy about the occupation was highlighted by the Sabra and Shatila massacre of refugees in September 1982, which led to international condemnation of militarized violence carried out by Israeli troops (MacBride et al. 1983). All the 'refusers' were arrested, tried and sentenced to prison, sometimes repeatedly for periods of between fourteen and thirty-five days.

A few years later in the First Intifada of 1987–93, another 186 Israeli reservists (including nineteen conscripts) refused to obey when ordered to beat up, or to fire on unarmed civilians, including teenagers and women protesting the presence of Israeli troops in the 'occupied territories' of Gaza Strip and the West Bank. Again the 'refusers' were arrested, tried and sentenced to prison. In each case, they were acting in a high stakes situation: their conscientious objection required they disobey the law as a form of resistance to authority. This form of conscientious objection in the military setting clearly parallels other acts of civil disobedience. It involves a non-violent, public form protest against injustice in the sphere of war and normally involves an understanding on the part of the person who is being disobedient that this form of disobedience is illegal. Linn interviewed a total of eighty-four of these 'selective resistors' to illuminate the puzzle posed by the idea of conscience. The result is a very fine nuanced study that raises as many questions as it answers.

In both cases, Linn's 'subjects' were Israeli soldiers who claimed a right to judge their obligation to take part in state-sponsored military action. These Israeli reservists referred to their conscience to justify their selective refusal to obey orders. These men had to stand against both an authoritative political and moral consensus in the broader political community of Israel, as well as resist the requirement normal, in, and perhaps indispensable to any military unit, that members of a unit obey orders given to them by their superiors – and do so unquestioningly.

Linn's research highlights the complexity of the case. Since the inception of the state of Israel in 1948, the belief in the right of Israel to self-defence has been an important part of Israeli national consensus and there has typically been little doubt on the part of the average Israeli male citizen regarding their moral obligation to serve in the Israel Defense Force and the rightness of doing so. As Linn (1996: 4–5) notes, all Israeli men aged between eighteen and fifty years are required to do three years compulsory military service between seventeen and twenty-one years and then be available to serve for up to two months each year. As she adds, this implies that every Israeli citizen 'is a soldier on eleven months annual leave'. There is no general right of conscientious objection and there is no legal status for selective conscientious objection. Only ultra-orthodox citizens have the right to refuse military service for conscientious reasons. At the same time, the Israeli Defense Forces since 1956 have highlighted the rule of personal responsibility for obeying a manifestly illegal order as part of the basic military training all Israeli soldiers get. This means that Israel's defence personnel are aware that they are not obliged to execute a command if they believe that it is inhumane or unconscionable. Individual reservists who choose to act on their 'secular conscience' are legally entitled to be judged by their commanders.

Most of these 'selective resistors' were men in their thirties, were married and had children. Most had participated in previous military service and operations. Importantly, most of these selective resistors sought to return to their unit after their prison sentence. In each case, Linn used a number of different approaches and techniques to explore the way these men made their decisions.[2]

Linn starts from the premise, whatever else these refusers did, it was a deeply social act. However, Linn does not start with a Durkheimian construction of 'the social-as-society' conceived of as a single solidary moral order in which only two practical options are possible either conformity or deviance. Linn offers a highly nuanced account of what is at stake in terms of understanding what in conventional terms appears to be a 'hyper-individualistic' set of processes, revealing in them what she rightly claims is a social process. Here she identifies her acceptance of Mikhail Bakhtin's (1993) and Charles Taylor's (1992) accounts of about the dialogical qualities of ethical practices and self-formation. As Charles Taylor argues, both communities and the self are dialogical:

> This crucial feature of human life is its fundamentally dialogical character. We become full human agents capable of understanding ourselves, and hence of defining our identity, through our acquisition of rich human languages of expression... we learn these modes of expression through exchanges with others.
>
> (Taylor 1992: 32)

Linn frames this approach to the social by focussing on the ways particular organizations like the army or police force have their own morally coercive qualities and sanctions. In Bourdieu's terms, the soldiers who became 'refusers' were members of the Israeli Defence Force who were immersed in a well-defined military field of action by virtue of their training and had acquired a habitus prescribed by training and reinforced by military discipline. They were also part of a larger political and national community in which service in defence of Israel was strongly supported legally and morally by many Israelis *including these resistors*. In fact, it can be added that many of the refusers were dedicated soldiers who had participated in previous military action. They were in effect selective conscientious objectors rather than pacifists as they had in a qualified way agreed with value of military violence while also claiming the right to evaluate each war and their obligation to serve on the merits of each case.

Set in this context, Linn wanted to know how these men came to make their decision to dissent. She usefully distinguishes between two kinds of ways of understanding moral decision-making in relational terms. One, she calls the 'separate moral position'. This represents the decision to dissent as the activities of an isolated, hyper-individual agent engaging in a rational almost philosophical process of deliberation. The 'separate moral position' owes a lot to the Kantian tradition represented in our time by John Rawls' (1971) liberal theory of justice, Lawrence Kohlberg's (1981) account of moral competence as an evolving developmental process and Jurgen Habermas' model of deliberative democracy.

The other position Linn calls a 'connected moral position'. This is exemplified by Michael Walzer's idea that to be a critic or dissident is to express or to live out a relation of connection, or what is called solidarity (Walzer 1970, 1988). As Walzer says to be a critic or a dissident is to take a stand, but they do so because they are already in a position of connection with others such that the only way to understand commitment to moral principles is to view them as 'commitments to other men from whom or with whom the principles s have been learned and by whom they are enforced' (Walzer 1970: 5). In effect, if Rawls and Kohlberg imagine the morally engaged critic or dissident as an isolated individual reasoning their way to a view about their conduct, Walzer treats our disposition to criticize or to dissent as a consequence of being part of a 'community of values'. However, far from making the path to dissent an easy one, Walzer emphasizes the serious tensions this sets loose between, e.g. the citizen who 'is obligated to obey because of his membership of a larger society [and] obligated to disobey (sometimes) because of his/her membership in a smaller one' (Walzer 1970: 14). In this case, Walzer says:

> There is a rough solidarity of men who face a common enemy and endure a common discipline... to disobey is to breach that elemental accord, to claim a moral separateness (or moral superiority) to challenge ones fellows perhaps even to intensify the dangers they face.
>
> (Walzer 1977: 315–16)

As Linn says, the Israeli 'refusers' might be seen either as a form of 'moral selfishness' or as 'the only resort of the principled but lonely man' (Walzer 1970: 14).

Linn decided to start with Kohlberg's well-known account of moral competence. Kohlberg's account of the moral refuser emphasizes how such a person is capable of undergoing a qualitative change in his moral capacities to the point where he is free of personal and societal moral constraints, is independent of culture and is capable of reflecting on conflicting ethical claims in a rational, objective and detached way. As Linn puts it: 'this mode of thinking embodies the premise that when there is a conflict between the legal and moral domains, the moral should almost always take precedence because it represents the more objective and impartial [and universal] solution within and across societies'.

Table 3.1 Kohlberg's stages of moral development model

Level	Stage	Social orientation
Pre-conventional	1	Obedience and punishment
	2	Individualism, instrumentalism, and exchange
Conventional	3	'Good boy/girl'
	4	Law and order
Post-conventional	5	Social contract
	6	Principled conscience

Source: Barger 2000: www5.csudh.edu/dearhabermas/kohlber'01bk.htm

Kohlberg developed what he claimed was a 'culturally universal, invariant sequence of stages of mortal development' (1973: 630) in part by using a Kantian model of moral reasoning as redacted by John Rawls (1971), one of the great modern Kantians and a liberal.[3] Kohlberg argued that human moral development goes through a series of stages. In schematic terms, Kohlberg's Stages of Moral Development model looks like this (Table 3.1):

Kohlberg identified three levels of moral development: pre-conventional, conventional and post-conventional. Each level has two distinct stages. This treats human morality as a 'naturalistic' phenomenon understood as a developmental process with all humans evolving towards the highest stage of capacity, requiring the use of universal principles of reasoning. It also involves the claim that the last stage is 'objectively preferable or more adequate by certain moral criteria' (Kohlberg 1973: 633).

During the pre-conventional level, when we are making moral decisions we accept and believe the rules of authority figures, like parents and teachers, and primarily judge an action based on its consequences like punishment or reward. In this level, people behave according to what they are told to do by some authority figure (e.g. parent or teacher). This obedience is compelled by the threat or application of punishment.

In the conventional period, we look to external and highly social criteria of what is acceptable. Children, e.g. think about moral issues in terms of personal and societal relationships. Children continue to accept the rules of authority figures, but this is now because they believe that this is necessary to ensure positive relationships and societal order and will pay a lot of attention to what is lawful or socially conforming. The first stage of this level (stage 3) is characterized by an attitude, which seeks to do what will gain the approval of others. The second stage is one oriented to abiding by the law and responding to the obligations of duty.

Finally in the post-conventional stages, our sense of morality is defined in terms of our capacity to use universal Kantian-style moral principles of moral reasoning. Stage 5 is an understanding of social mutuality and a genuine interest in the welfare of others. The last stage (Stage 6) is based on respect for universal principles and the demands of individual conscience. This may mean that we decide that some laws are unjust and should be changed or eliminated. While Kohlberg always believed in the existence of Stage 6 and had some nominees for it, he could never get enough subjects to define it, much less observe their longitudinal movement to it. Kohlberg believed that the majority of adults would never make it to the highest stage.

Kohlberg claimed that the stages would be good predictors of the moral maturity or competence of people making decisions in real-life settings. Other studies have made similar claims. A bevy of studies were made at the height of student protests in the USA in the late 1960s and early 1970s. Haan (1972), e.g. argued that students at both extremely high and extremely low levels of moral development were significantly over-represented among the Free Speech Movement student activists, while those at the more modal 'conventional stages of moral reasoning were unlikely to be activists'. Fishkin, Keniston and MacKinnon (1973) drew on Kohlberg's model in a study of university students, suggesting that these students exhibited Stage 5 moral competence, while Stage 4 moral in 1970, a year characterized by significant student protest. Other studies have claimed that Stage 5 moral thinkers are quite often affiliated with left-wing political orientations (Emler 1983; Vine 1983).

So how did Linn's soldiers fare when assessed against Kohlberg's stages of moral competence? Linn found that the moral reasoning of the objecting soldiers in the two groups was tested by Kohlberg's instrument, ranging almost the entire way across from Stage 2 to Stage 5, with a transitional modal stage of 3/4 for both groups. That is, and against the predictions of Kohlberg and others, there was little support for the expectation that the refusers would all be operating at the post-conventional stage. Linn's results further indicated that, using Kohlberg's model, only 22 per cent of the Refusers and 25 per cent of the soldiers who had joined 'Peace Now' were post-conventional, with an additional 22 per cent of the Refusers and 2 per cent of the 'Peace Now' soldiers falling into the transitional Stage 4/5. In effect, only 30 per cent of the Refusers and none of the 'Peace Now' soldiers fell into Stages 4 and 5.

Did anything else suggest that the refusers were different in any way that might point to a disposition to dissent? A few things did stand out though arguably these were not significant. For one thing, nearly eight out of ten had a university education. Linn claimed that other things like being an immigrant from South America (23 per cent) or being ex-Kibbutzim (15 per cent) mattered, but this seems less significant than the general disposition on the part of many refusers to a left-wing political position. Over 31 per cent of the Intifada refusers were supporters of the Communist party, while well over half had joined protest groups or movements opposed to Israel's policy in Lebanon or towards the Palestinians. Again this does not seem all that striking.

The most interesting finding was that in spite of the fact that both groups of refusers had already done at least one tour of reserve duty in the war in Lebanon and/or in the territories prior to their refusal, many of the refusers (around 60 per cent) did not feel strongly attached to their military units. The other thing that seems striking was the speed of their decision to disobey.

Apart from confirming the selectivity of their conscientious objection, it seems that the decision to disobey came most readily for soldiers who were in some sense isolates, soldiers who did not feel closely attached to their unit: only eleven (or 23 per cent) of the refusers felt any strong attachment to their unit. Some refusers from engineer units argued, e.g. that they did not belong to a cohesive group or have a battalion commander who might guide them through military life. For example, the only soldier in the sample who was imprisoned five times in a row served in an engineering unit. In his words, 'This would not have happened if I had had a direct commander, a father-figure, who can sometimes find an alternative solution for you'.

In effect, Linn observes that the selective resistors had apparently distanced themselves from their immediate social and institutional relations. Linn rightly insists that these narratives of moral separateness are better seen as a highly social narrative of 'moral connectedness'. The selective resistor is better seen as being tied to the world, not only by principles but also by moral emotions, moral language and moral action – all deeply social matters – which constitute their sense of self. This is because the conscientious objector, as Michael Walzer (1970: 5) pointed out, is not only morally committed to principles *but also to other people*, '... from whom or with whom the principles have been learned and by whom they are enforced'. The resistor's moral commitment emerges from the conviction and understanding that if injustice is done in the resistor's name '... or it is done to my people, I must speak out against it. Now criticism follows from this conviction' (Walzer 1988: 23).

Linn found among these selective resistors just such a concern. As one of the resistors put it:

> I refused to wear the army uniform and therefore I disobeyed. There are many undemocratic actions done by our soldiers in the territories. They are done by private citizens who wear this uniform. If I wear the uniform, it means that I have come to terms with what they are doing, since all that is being done there is being done in my name as long as I remain silent and obey army orders.

It seems hardly appropriate to call this either a form of 'hyper-individualisation' or 'moral distancing' from the controversy – as Habermas has argued. Even the decision to separate themselves from their military unit is a social matter since they understood all too well that their actions may jeopardize the safety or even the lives of their fellow soldiers.

The second and related discovery Linn made was that the moment of decision was not preceded by any lengthy process of deliberation or analysis. Rather many refusers spoke of a feeling that came to them quickly that the 'right thing to do' was to disobey. In the morally authoritarian settings in which these soldiers found themselves, the moral resistor did not ask himself first what moral principles were being violated – as Kohlberg (1981) has suggested this is the proper course that moral deliberation ought to take – *but rather 'what is the right way to feel?'* As one resistor told her:

> There was no specific reason for my refusal, *I just felt I should not be able to do it* [reserve service in the occupied territories] to disperse demonstrations of kids and women [where] an old person has been killed…
>
> (My stress)

Another resistor told her:

> In the case of refusal *you first feel that you have no option but to act in a certain way. It is a very strong feeling* and you cannot stay calm unless you do it. Only then does one's moral thought become clear.
>
> (My stress)

Here we see a very important clue to the role played by some distinctive moral feelings in the making of practical judgements. It stands in the sharpest possible contradiction to certain philosophical prejudices about the central role played by a style of deliberation that looks a lot like what Bourdieu calls 'the scholastic perspective', which treats the experience of the academic as universalizable. As the philosopher Justin Oakley (1994: 1) notes, this preoccupation reflects in this case '… the predominance of Kantianism, with the devaluation of the emotions which such an approach typically involves, and a preoccupation with moral action'. In Linn's study, the self-narrative of the resistor is not a narrative about adjusting by way of some deliberative process an abstract moral principle to the reality in which the person finds themselves. Rather in the case of the men Linn interviewed, it is experienced in feeling terms, and those moral emotions are rhetorically then turned into a story that draws on the language of justice.

To be clear, these feelings are the same kinds of feelings which the tradition of virtue ethics since Aristotle through to Todorov have insisted mark out the good person engaging in good deeds. As Justin Oakley and Dean Cocking (2002) point out, someone possessed of virtues like courage or care will not have to think either too hard or too long about what to do should they see a person in danger of drowning or being burned to death in a burning dwelling. Such a person we would say will *instinctively* act to prevent harm to that person. What distinguishes such a normal display of 'domestic virtue' from the kind of 'heroic virtues' displayed by Linn's selective resistors has less to do with the degree of physical courage needed to leap into a river or burning building in contrast with the courage needed to resist an order from one's commanding officer and more to do with the need to negotiate the competing imperatives to act set loose in the social setting in which the Israeli resistors acted.

The narrative of the moral resistor is much more a narrative of moral emotion than a highly cognitive or rational-theoretical process. For the experience of these feelings is also a story of emotional struggle as the resistor tries to come to terms with the way the world is. This is as much about a struggle to persuade ourselves as it is an exercise designed to persuade others to address the particular problems which the way the world is *just then* presents to us.

In this respect, squatting too while it is quite different in all sorts of way involves a variety of ways of coming to terms with the way the world is by breaking with the 'order' of the world.

Squatting and occupations

Some might suggest that squatting is not dissent because it is simply a kind of rational response by desperate people trying to cope with the absence of stable, secure housing, squatting. In one myth-breaking account of the global extent and significance of squatting, Robert Neuwirth (2005, 2007) estimates that, in the second decade of the twenty-first century, over one billion people are now occupying abandoned land, or residential or industrial buildings unlawfully.[4] Unlike the solitary 'selective refuser', squatting is a highly collective practice often involving significant numbers of people. Squatting is a collective large-scale activity, and has been an enduring practice in many cities going back at least to the 1960s and 1970s in European liberal democracies like the Netherlands, the UK, Germany and Italy, as well as countries like Canada, Australia and America.

Unlike some other forms of dissent, squatting is often invisibilized. As Kesia Reeve notices, 'squatting is largely absent from policy and academic debate and is rarely conceptualised, as a problem, as a symptom, or as a social or housing movement' (Reeve 2011: 7). In countries like Australia, e.g. squatting rarely attracts much public or academic attention unless it is treated as part of the 'homelessness problem'. In one study of Australian homelessness and using the deathless prose favoured by conventional social science, Flatau et al. (2018: 72) observe those 'that are rough sleeping are inherently more likely to engage in survival behaviour that leads to justice system interaction (e.g. squatting or trespassing)'.[5]

This suggests something of the difficulties involved in understanding squatting. While granting Reeve's point and while there is a large and ever-expanding academic literature on squatting, the social and political history of squatting is not well known. Pioneering research on squatting began in the 1970s (Bailey 1973; Wates and Wolmar 1980) and has since evolved courtesy of major interventions by Corr (1999), van der Walt (2009), Piotrowski (2014), Martínez (2007; 2013) Pruijt (2012, 2014) and Vasudevan (2017). As Bart Steen and colleagues (2014) note, e.g. of the European situation:

> When squatters moved to the city centres in the late 1970s, cities across Western Europe had been in the midst of a prolonged crisis, struggling with a long list of socioeconomic ills … Large urban areas were left empty, thus forming an ideal material basis for squatting. Autonomous activists turned to the inner cities as an arena for experimenting with autonomy and

self – management. However, as squatters brought new life to the inner cities and deindustrialisation led to a definitive turn to service industries, the city centres became popular again and capital returned... As a result, in many cities, squatting moved from the city centres to the outskirts.

(Steen et al. 2014: 16)

Part of the problem seems to do with how squatting is to be understood. For most governments squatting is simply understood: it is a criminal activity because it is a violation of private property rights, and if many politicians are to be believed, it is the work variously of criminals, lazy people who don't want to work, and even foreigners (Dadusc 2017: 1). As for the social scientists who research squatting, there is an equivalent but more diverse response which involves making a number of conventional assumptions about categories, before ascribing or discovering a dominant logic, intentionality or defining characteristic of squatting. Corr (1999: 3), e.g. suggests that squatting is oriented 'to redistribute[ing] economic resources according to a more egalitarian and efficient pattern', while Wates and Wolmar (1980) says squatting is all about addressing housing issues. For McKay (1998), it represents a manifestation of 'Do-It-Yourself culture', while Della Porta and Rucht (1995: 121–23) treat the squatters' movement as a 'left-libertarian' movement. For Reeve, squatting is all about homelessness and it 'typically reflects a lack of other options, a scarcity of provision, and inadequate support and assistance to single homeless people' (Reeve 2011: 4). The social sciences really do need to take some advice from natural scientists like the zoologist Alfred Kinsey, when he advised that the world 'is not to be divided into sheep and goats. It is a fundamental of taxonomy that nature rarely deals with discrete categories... The living world is a continuum in each and every one of its aspects' (Kinsey at al. 1948: 642).

If we approach squatting from a relational perspective we should expect that trying to treating it, e.g. as only a social, economic or a political process misses out on what Reeve (2011: 4) rightly says is the reality that any distinction between people who squat by choice as a form of political protest and those homeless who squat by necessity 'is somewhat blurred'. This emphasizes the highly contingent qualities of squatting.

Pruijt (2012: 4) who adopts a highly instrumental-rational idea of contingency (indicating he has not understood the idea), e.g. argues for five kinds of squatting. This includes deprivation-based squatting involving homeless people because they need housing, squatting as an alternative housing strategy by people not willing to wait on public housing lists, entrepreneurial squatting involving people breaking into buildings to offer a community for cheap bars or clubs, conservational squatting preserving buildings because governments have let them decay and political activists squatting buildings as protests or to set up social squat centres.

It is important to emphasize that whatever else squatting is always a response to patterns of economic deprivation, which have become increasingly prominent since the 1980s and again after 2008 as states embraced various degrees of neoliberal policy and as capital moved to embrace new forms of finance capital reproduction implicating housing markets (Streeck 2016). As Charles Tilly (1995a: 267) has noted, squats and occupations are 'paradigmatic, unconventional dirzct actions', while Lopez adds that they are also part of a 'well-established repertoire of political protest by young people and leftist-anarchist movements' (Lopez 2018: 2). In effect, while many squatters' primary motive is simply to get somewhere to live, even when there is no apparent or obvious connection to politically oriented groups, the practice of squatting should also be treated as a reaction to the normal tendency to economic inequality found in market economies exacerbated by inegalitarian neoliberal government policies. In many cases, squatting may go unnoticed some time until activists run campaigns and establish multiple networks of solidarity to resist evictions supported by social organizations with political agendas of various kinds.

The point is simple: squatting involves diverse groups with diverse dispositions. Unlike the decision to selectively refuse a military order, squatting is an eclectic, collective and often colourful practice that tends to persist over time. Wates and Wolmar (1980), e.g. estimated that the average squat in the UK lasted for several months, though rarely longer than a year Pruijt (2012: 11) estimated that the average squat in Amsterdam lasted several years in the 1980s, but that this declined after 1994. In some cases the squats become permanent homes courtesy of a process of legalization. In Amsterdam, e.g. the city purchased several hundreds of the buildings occupied by squatters. Squatting also persists over time because as Lopez tells us, squatters do many things:

> … they raise flags and banners, write pamphlets and magazines, highlight dereliction and urban speculation, open the doors of the squats to campaigners and speakers of all sorts, claim the right to housing and to the city centre for the homeless, for those on the verge of expulsion or already displaced from their original neighbourhoods, and also for all who are marginalised in the economic, cultural, social and political spheres.
>
> (Lopez 2018: 15)

Historically, we can track the evolution of contemporary squatting in big cities like New York, London and Copenhagen. In each case, we see a convergence between people with serious housing problems interacting with various kinds of countercultural and progressive political projects. In New York in the 1960s, large numbers of black families were living in dilapidated housing. In May 1970, a squatter movement appeared called Operation Move-In (Vasudevan 2017: 25–9). By August, 300 African American or Latino working-class families had occupied abandoned apartments scheduled for demolition by New York City. Eventually Operation Move-In forced the authorities to allow the squatters – who had repaired and renovated their homes – to stay. Nearly a thousand housing units were subsequently added to the urban redevelopment plan on the Upper West Side. In December 1970, the Metropolitan Council on Housing organized the People's

Court Housing Crimes Trial with support from the Black Panther Party, the Young Lords and *I Wor Kuen* (a radical Chinese organization). The event brought together a multiracial and intergenerational group of people working on housing issues in New York City. Tenants, squatters and sympathetic city officials testified to an audience of 1,500 at Columbia University about the poor housing available to low-income residents (New York Times 1970).

In London in the early1970s, squatters including homeless people, artists, musicians and drug-users occupied Freston Road Estate, a dilapidated public housing estate owned by the Greater London Council. In 1977, the Greater London Council announced plans to redevelop the housing. In late October 1977, activists led by Nicholas Albery decided to establish what became known as the Free and Independent Republic of Frestonia and to secede from the UK. Stamps were issued and a national newspaper called the Tribal Messenger began to be published. The squat attracted international attention and the Greater London Council was forced to negotiate leading to the establishment of the Bramley's Housing Cooperative and the estate was subsequently redeveloped as public housing.

Albery was inspired by his experience of Freetown Christiania, a Danish squat that achieved enduring and global fame after it was established by squatters occupying former military barracks in Bådsmandsstræde in Copenhagen on 26 September 1971. The squat began on 17 May 1971 when families in the neighbourhood broke down the fences around the barracks to use parts of the unused area as a junk playground for their children. This particular squat became a demonstration project led by countercultural activists artists and musicians including Jacob Ludvigsen a Provo, a Dutch counter culture movement that practised a form of non-violent civil disobedience. (Provo was a word derived from the Dutch word *provoceren* 'to provoke'.) In a short period of time, Christiania was occupied by several hundred people. As Thomassen (2018) notes, the idea was to create a self-governing society, based on recycling and sustainability, sponsoring a variety of forms of creativity as well as creating a space for the use of drugs. Tom Lunden of the rock group *Bifrost* wrote a protest song *I kan ikke slå os ihjel* (translated: 'You cannot kill us'), which became a kind of anthem for Christiania. Ludvigsen co-authored the mission statement of what became known as Freetown Christiana declaring:

> The objective of Christiania is to create a self-governing society whereby each and every individual holds themselves responsible over the wellbeing of the entire community. Our society is to be economically self-sustaining and, as such, our aspiration is to be steadfast in our conviction that psychological and physical destitution can be averted.
>
> (Cited in Thomassen 2018: 3)

Initially, only the military buildings were used and converted into living quarters. The squatters then brought in mobile workmen's huts a move that was deemed practical in the event that Christiania was reclaimed by the state. Later on, the experimental building followed. In this case, the Danish state decided to live with the experiment. This was signified initially when, on 31 May 1972, a temporary agreement was entered into regarding the squatters' right of use of the state's land and buildings in the area. In June 1989, a broad majority in the Danish Parliament voted for the Christiania Law, whose aim is to allow Christiania's continued use of the area in accordance with a special national planning directive and a district plan. On 22 June 2011, Christiania and the state entered into an agreement concerning the future ownership of the Christiania area. This agreement allowed for the transfer of buildings and land in the Christiania area to a foundation, the Foundation Freetown Christiania in 2012. The government repealed the special law for the Christiania area in July 2013, which ended the autonomous status of Christiania (Thomassen 2018).

The convergence of the need for housing and an increasingly politicized culture becomes especially apparent after the Great Recession of 2008 and especially in southern Europe. The conjunction of urban renewal, redevelopment and gentrification that expelled the poor, precariously employed workers and traditional working-classes from the centre of large European cities combined with spatial segregation and unaffordable housing affecting migrants and refugees seems to have increased the numbers of homeless people and marginalized groups who come to see squatting 'as a feasible and reasonable last resort, regardless of its legal implications' (Lopez 2018: 2). As Lopez (2018) notes, large numbers of unpaid mortgages, foreclosures and home evictions claimed the attention of the media in affluent and increasingly polarized cities especially where homeownership rates and mortgage related indebtedness were on the rise. Multiple networks of solidarity resist evictions supported by social organizations with a specific political agenda.

In some countries like Spain, there was a convergence of anti-Austerity protest movements and squatting: in 2011, Ramon Adell (2011: 135–37) estimated that around 2,500,000 people attended the different Spanish M15 (May 15, 2011) movement marches and occupations of public space between May and November 2011, all over Spain. (Others suggest a much higher number ranging between 6 and 8.5 million people.) Within the same period, at least sixty-seven demonstrations were directly called by the M15M in Madrid and around 500,000 people attended. In Spain, occupations became a feature of the Spanish protests on 15 May 2011 when a group of forty people decided to stay and camp in plaza *Puerta del Sol* in Madrid, after the unexpectedly large demonstration on 15 May 2011. The Sol camp involved setting up of a *temporary city within the city* and became a rallying point in the following month until police dismantled it. Around the Sol camp, some 116 popular/citizen assemblies started to gather weekly, from 28 May on, in the neighbourhoods and municipalities of the Madrid metropolis. Lopez and Bernardos (2015) report that half of the people who pioneered the occupation of Sol had previous connection to what are called Squatted Social Centres. Indeed, people involved in these squats were key players in organizing the first Sol camp and many thought about the Sol camp ads, if it were a squat. Equally, participants made it clear that they thought as one person said that:

> The squatters' movement contributed to the M15's structure and the context in which it emerged by avoiding vicious manipulations in the key assemblies, by trying to decentralise the structure of power, always backing arrested people and being very cautious about mass media.
>
> (Cited Lopez and Bernardos 2015: 166)

The evidence for convergence is seen in the increasing number of squats after May 2011 and increasing support by M15 activists for squatting. As Martínez (2016) notes, Squatted Social Centres, e.g. became the public face of squatters as a protest movement and involved different practices and ideological orientations. They make political demands related to the occupied buildings, the urban areas where they operate and urban policies at large. In addition to their critique of mainstream urban politics and capitalism, squatters active in Squatted Social Centres have developed self-management of their collective resources, direct democracy, non-commercial activities and more egalitarian relationships than in conventional or mainstream daily life.

There is also a long history of political squats in northern Italian cities like Milan, Turin and Florence. Since the mid-1970s, successive waves of mostly young people in the northern Italian city of Turin began occupying buildings like warehouses, shopfronts and apartments as 'squats'. They do so to develop a range of political, social and cultural activities potentially directed to Italy's public sphere. Pruijt (2012: 24) says that 'there is no type of squatting that has subcultural expression as its goal. This is because of the importance of the need for housing by all squatters'. This points to a two- or three-way relation between getting housing, being countercultural and engaging in political activism. Manuel Castells reinforces this point when he adds that squats are new kinds of urban movements doing three things simultaneously: they are addressing the need for adequate housing, they are producing collective identities, generating cultural expressions able to challenge the homogenization of popular culture, and they are claiming the right to imagine and (re)produce urban space in new ways.

This imbrication of different forms of praxis/practice is exemplified in the history of political squats in northern Italy, where groups of young people self-identifying variously as 'autonomous', 'neo-communist', 'libertarians' or 'squatters' have set about providing a roof over their heads as well as promoting various political and cultural projects.

Carlo Genova (2018) argues that the first wave of occupations go back to the *Circoli del proletariato giovanile* in the mid-1970s, when small groups of young people occupied abandoned buildings as places for meeting and to build informal social networks in various northern Italian cities (Genova 2018: 4). The oppositional political dimension of this first wave of squats was already evident in the 1970s when groups loosely associated with *Autonomia Operaia*, a network of

Marxist–Leninist, and/or Maoist groups as well as anarchist and more libertarian groups began using violent protest to provoke state violence as an anticipated stimulus to a popular revolutionary uprising (Wright 2013). Other groups were more interested in cultural experimentation and experimentation with alternative music, creativity and lifestyles. A second wave of squats began in the early 1980s shaped heavily by the rise of punk culture, which spread quickly in Italy in those years. In Turin, e.g. the first squat dates back to 1984, when *Il Diana*, a former cinema was occupied by activists connected to the local punk scene, which had arrived in 1980 in via Artom, a street in the Mirafiori neighbourhood housing Fabbrica Italiana Automobili Torino (FIAT) workers when young punks organized their first street music festival. Semantically important political differences were signified by the way, e.g. Communist occupations adopted and used the label 'centro sociale' (or Squatted Social Centres (Ruggiero 2000; Mudu 2013)), while the libertarian ones referred to what they called 'casa occupata' or 'squat'. In 2017, Genova (2018: 7) estimates that there are eight main political squats in Turin, three identified as Marxist-Communist (Murazzi and Askatasuna identified as an 'autonomous' squat, Gabrio as a 'Neo-Communist' squat) and five as Anarchist squats (El Paso with a 'libertarian' approach, Barocchio, Prinz Eugen, Asilo, Mezcal with a 'squatter' approach).

Carlo Genova (2018: 8) who has interviewed squatters in Turin charts the complex thicket of dispositions and interests that bring people into the squats. In some cases, people with prior experience of social or political engagement including participation in political parties often 'meet the squat' during protests or rallies, while other people with less socio-political experience often meet the squatting movement through concerts or other socio-cultural activities. The complex overlapping of what social scientists call 'youth cultures' with the politics of squats is captured in the account by one young squatter when he recalled

> When I was in the middle school I used to play in a punk band, something like that, then we began sharing records, [...] with a friend of mine, we had a distribution, of records before, and then 291 of books. [...] When I was in the high school there was a publisher 'of the movement', I met them 292 when there was an occupation at school [...] and I distributed their books. [...] Then I used to hang 293 out in occupied houses and then we occupied the house in ***, and also here I had a small distribution 294 of records, books, by mail, stalls, something like that, and then this occupation ... [...] the idea was 295 to live there and have a place for distribution, to carry out activities
> (Cited Genova 2018: 9)

Another squatter tells a story in which squatting begins as a sense of how to lead an autonomous life:

> It's complicated... during my civil service I met a guy [...]who was a DJ in the radio of the squat, [...] I joined him during a broadcast, I went to the

first radio festival of that period [...] and then from there ... one thing leads to another, and it is as a potential energy which [...] when it finds the right push ... all is automatic, you don't need to do or to say anything. When you discover that, in one way or another, you can choose a different life, from A to Z, in which there are no longer circumstances marking out your life path but [...] you understand that you can design a part of your life on your own, you can choose what to do

(Cited Genova 2018: 9)

For another, it was the appeal of alternative music that was the initial attraction

The first thing which attracted me absolutely was the cultural level, [...] the counter-culture, low-price concerts, the level of sociability; [...] the first approach is absolutely the cultural one, [...] the ability of making a non-assimilated culture, outside the market.

(Cited Genova 2018: 9)

For other, it was the very complexity of elements that was attractive. As one activist put it:

Self-management, anti-militarism, anti-clericalism, and then all the aesthetic trends: Musically hard rock, punk core, and many others near these, experimentation, noise, industrial; on the cultural level Dadaism and Surrealism above all. I tell you ... in general [the aim is to] expand the self-management experience as much as possible. [...] The aim is simply to avoid salaried work, to avoid the structure of the family, normal social structures, to avoid the necessity of having money, living on your own....

(Cited Genova 2018: 12)

What is striking in this case is the role played by music. Alternative music and concerts have long been one of the key activities in Turin's political squats and music has always represented an important element of collective identification and distinction. Punk, noise and electronic are the music of choice in Anarchist squats, while reggae and ska predominate the Marxist one (Genova 2018: 13).

This then is the modern squatting movement. It could not be more different from the solitary almost secret moment when a serving soldier decides not to obey. Squatting is loud, highly public colourful and tends to involve large numbers of other people attracting attention to their speakings and doings. If Ruth Linn rightly emphasizes that while the selective refuser's narratives speak to moral separateness, they are still a highly social narrative of 'moral connectedness' we cannot ignore the ways many of them had distanced themselves from their immediate social and institutional setting. As Isin reminds us, there are many relations

The many faces of dissent   85

and other ways of being political and engaging in dissent: solidarity is one of those ways. Squatters seem much more extroverted and far more insistent on the rhetoric and gestures that speak to solidarity.

On squatting, solidarity and dissent

Squatters everywhere have expressed a commitment to solidarity with others who are experiencing deprivation, repression or violence like asylum seekers. Sometimes this is a commitment to a generic solidarity. In Ireland, a Dublin squatter captures this well when describing the motivation to set up a squat in Dublin:

> One obvious way to engage and spread ideas is to create public spaces where ideas flow and hegemonic practices are challenged and debated. Social centres or Solidarity centres have been successful on the continent as one way of providing alternative institutions to the power of the state... together we started off with an ambitious and large project – The Barricade Inn – which was a squatted Anarchist Social Centre on 77 Parnell St. With over 50 rooms to clear out in a former hotel the workload was intense but after 2 months and a lot of help we had the project open to the public.
>
> (Workers Solidarity Movement 2018)

Vaseduvan has described too how, in Berlin, squatters spatialized the processes of anti-authoritarian movements, 'creating a geography of conviction and solidarity' while also serving as an alternative space that re-worked how we might understand urban politics in a context of housing scarcity. As he shows, Berlin's squatters were able to demonstrate an ethos of autonomy, makeshift urbanism and DIY practices to provide a network committed to solidarity. These urban activists were some of the first groups of people to discover the creative, autonomous value in abandoned spaces. Today, these abandoned and interim spaces are often used to represent Berlin as a 'creative city'. Sometimes, the solidarity is more particular.

Since 2016 as the refugee crisis set loose by the war in Syrian deepened, the Greek Solidarity Movement, e.g. opened up squats across Greece to house and support refugees. The Dervenion squat in the Exarcheia district of Athens, e.g. was established as a self-managing squat able to receive and house some 500 Palestinian Afghan and Syrian migrants and refugees. In April 2016, 250 activists and refugees took over the Hotel City Plaza closed for six years and transformed into a Refugee Accommodation and Solidarity Space. Since then the solidarity initiative has, for more than 500 days, provided free and decent housing to over 1700 people in the centre of Athens providing over 385,000 warm meals served by the kitchen group (en-Squat 2017). This commitment to solidarity begins to suggest a different kind of relation than that implied when individuals exercise their conscience.

So how should we think about solidarity? David Featherstone makes a good case for thinking about a version of friendship, which he represents as solidarity. He makes the strong point that while solidarity 'is a central practice of the political left' and a central feature of progressive social and political movements, 'it has rarely been the subject of sustained theorization, reflection or investigation' (2013: 3). He notes, e.g. that, while Laclau and Mouffe (1985) talked a lot about hegemony and socialist struggle, little attention has been given to the conduct or practice of left political activity *per se*.

Featherstone's approach to thinking about solidarity highlights the need to think about the practices which create solidarity rather than assuming it is a given or assuming that it is simply a consequence of a logic of similarity. Featherstone is critical of accounts of solidarity that imply that it is based purely on 'given' attributes such as class, nationality, ethnicity, *and treat it as a natural consequence of* some pre-existing kind of homogeneity or likeness. Featherstone insists that solidarity is all about *making the similarities* needed in order to ground one's commitment to another person, or to a whole group. Further and by definition these categories are relational, i.e. they both include and exclude at the same time. Failure to grasp this relationality can 'trap our understandings of solidarity within a reductive binary of similarity and dissimilarity' (Featherstone 2013: 23).

Thinking through and beyond these binaries is needed if they are not to foster divisiveness rather than fostering connections that go beyond similarity or difference. Certainly the long tradition in sociology of theorizing and researching 'community', e.g. has ostensibly demonstrated that connections and 'belonging' are far stronger in groups when grounded in something shared, be that a characteristic, experience, values, or factors like place, class, or ethnicity. Featherstone's basic premise is that this commonality, which is apparently the basis of togetherness or solidarity, is not a given. Featherstone specifically challenges the notion that for solidarity to occur 'there needs to be a pre-existing commonality for the solidarity to be durable or effective'. (Featherstone 2013: 23). Instead 'practices of solidarity generate or negotiate such questions of difference through political action' (Featherstone 2013: 23). The qualities that make solidarity possible need to be worked at. Solidarity emerges when working together on a common task; it can emerge across space. In short, Featherstone rightly stresses the generative and novel qualities of solidarity as a project. It can be argued as Featherstone does, that solidarity is a transformative relation in that it produces new 'ways of configuring political relations and spaces' while the 'political articulation of solidarity is/are shaped through diverse practices'.

Featherstone uses a number of case studies to make this point while also emphasizing the way solidarity becomes less constrained by parochial space and how, for some centuries now, the politics of solidarity has been developing in a space that is international or global and is created *between* nation-states.

At the heart of Featherstone's thesis about solidarity as having both generative and novel qualities is Richard Rorty's (1989) important argument about the way solidarity involves a relationship between similarity and dissimilarity. Granting that dissent and its antonym consent points to a relational account, Rorty's account of solidarity emphasizes in a provocative way the relation between similarity and dissimilarity.

Rorty starts with the observation that, 'If you were a Jew in the period when the trains were running to Auschwitz, your chances of being hidden by your gentile neighbours were greater if you lived in Denmark or Italy than if you lived in Belgium'. In effect, says Rorty, 'many Danes and Italians showed a sense of human solidarity which many Belgians lacked' (Rorty 1989: 189). He then goes on to say that 'The traditional philosophical way of spelling out what we mean by "human solidarity" is to say that there is something within each of us – our essential humanity – which resonates to the presence of this same thing in other human beings'. As he then says philosophers like himself who deny that there is any such a component, or an essence or that there is anything like a 'core self', are unable to appeal to this idea. As he admits, any account of 'what counts as being a decent human being is relative to historical circumstance, a matter of transient consensus about what attitudes are normal and what practices are just or unjust'. He appeals to the basic idea 'that a belief can still regulate action, can still be thought worth dying for, among people who are quite aware that this belief is caused by nothing deeper than contingent historical circumstance' at the same time as arguing for the claim 'that we have a moral obligation to feel a sense of solidarity with all other human beings'.

This is an important idea and is central to understanding why dissent is a legitimate practice. Rorty's basic claim is that we need to be able to try to extend our sense of 'we' to people whom we have previously thought of as 'they' (Rorty 1989: 192). On this account, solidarity is 'thought of as the ability to see more and more traditional differences (of tribe, religion, race, customs, and the like) as unimportant when compared with similarities with respect to pain and humiliation – the ability to think of people wildly different from ourselves as included in the range of 'us'" (Rorty 1989: 192). This is why he can say 'feelings of solidarity are necessarily a matter of which similarities and dissimilarities strike us as salient, and that such salience is a function of a historically contingent final vocabulary' (Rorty 1989: 192). There is nothing timeless or essential about the way we will identify or respond to similarities and dissimilarities.

These are valuable insights. However, we need to be wary of assuming, as Featherstone does, that solidarity can be treated *essentially and only* as some disposition to be oriented to 'the left', or to be the expression of a (de)limited kind of dissent. Yet this is what Featherstone does. Solidarity says Featherstone (2013: 5) is a political relation (and practice) that challenges oppression and inequalities. Solidarity says Featherstone (2013: 5) is a political relation (and practice) that challenges oppression and inequalities. Solidarity is a transformative relation in that it produces new 'ways of configuring political relations and spaces', while the 'political articulation of solidarity is/are shaped through diverse practices'. Featherstone stresses the generative/novelty of political activism and dissent, but does so in ways that ultimately are too limiting. Featherstone also needs to ac-knowledge that solidarity can be used to (re)produce and reinforce inequality, injustice and oppression.

Conclusion

Selective refusal by serving soldiers to obey orders given to them and squatting represent two radically different kinds of dissent. Each is expressed differently, and presupposes quite different relations: one of separation, and the other of sol-idarity. Each deploys different expressive techniques, in ways that define them as different kinds of *praxis*/practice.

Linn's study reminds us that dissent need not involve large-scale collective exercises in promoting social or policy change. In this case, we see, e.g. that Bourdieu's insistence that dissent is a challenge to symbolic order is not always what dissent is about. We may agree with Bourdieu when he says that dissent or critique aims to:

> ... produce, if not a 'new person', then at least a new 'gaze' and this cannot be done without a genuine conversion, a *metanoia*, a mental revolution, a transformation of one's whole vision of the social world.
>
> (Bourdieu and Wacquant 1992: 251)

However, Linn's soldiers are not all that interested in doing this. Even when Bourdieu suggests that it is sometimes better to do a lot of little things 'because those little things generate changes that generate changes', this still seems to go beyond the expectations of the Israeli 'refusers' (Bourdieu 2000b: 19).

Likewise, the Israeli 'refusers' do not conform with Arendt's account of 'civil disobedience', which she says involves groups of citizens engaging collectively in a political act because they are trying either to bring about new laws and policies or to return to earlier, more acceptable policies. For Arendt, 'civil disobedience' (as distinct from 'conscientious objection') is the paradigm case of political action as participation in democracy. These refusers conform much more with Arendt's ac-count of 'conscientious objection'. Arendt treats conscientious objection as a pri-vate act without political significance: this is because Arendt insists conscience originates in the individual and ought to be exercised only in the private sphere. For her, conscientious objection has little to do with changing government policy and is much more a private statement by the objector distancing themselves from a policy or law because to comply with that law or policy establishes a conflict with that person's conscience.[6] Arendt is on shaky ground when she makes the distinction between 'public/private' and 'civil disobedience'/'conscientious objec-tion' if we take a relational approach seriously. In the case of the Israeli refusers, that distinction seems not to have mattered too much: all of them were making a political point and all were subjected to the full force of Israeli law.

Both selective refusal and squatting challenge an entire way of life and an imaginary order. When a serving soldier says 'no' to an order or command given by her superior and that soldier refuses to obey, there is a direct and dire challenge to an entire and symbolic (and imagined) order, and the imagined orderly way of life that symbolic order exists to legitimate and reproduce. The refusal to obey on this occasion brings into question an order that implicates the state itself that claims a monopoly over legitimate violence through its defence forces as well as certain required attitudes like patriotism and obedience.

Likewise, the occupation of private or public property calls into question the property regime operating in all liberal-democracies beginning with the idea that the right to property is foundational to that order. As Andre van der Walt notes, this 'tension' is especially palpable in many colonial societies, like the US, Canada, Australia, Ireland, South Africa and New Zealand, all of which began with an originary act of eviction or dispossession of the indigenous peoples from their lands by the colonizers (van der Walt 2009). In both cases, we can begin to see why dissent provokes immediate and prolonged reactions by the state.

This is why we need now to turn to the criminalization of dissent by liberal-democratic states.

Notes

1   The indebtedness to structuralism's 'founding father', the Swiss linguist Ferdinand de Saussure and his conclusion that when we look for a sign (significant) that is connected to a referent (signifié), the relation between the two is arbitrary. There is no intrinsic connection between sign and referent. A signifier gets its 'correct' signified, the sign its meaning by means of what Saussure calls the principle of difference. This means that the difference of a sign relative to every other sign within the total system of signs gives the sign the possibility of a singular meaning. We thus give meaning to the sign 'A' because of the fact that A <> B, C, or all other signs. Saussure states on the 'principle of arbitrariness': 'The term implies simply that the signal is unmotivated: that is to say, arbitrary in relation to its signification, with which it has no natural connexion in reality' (Saussure, 1977[1916]: 68–9). This leads him to the famous: 'In the language itself, there are only differences' (Saussure 1977[1916]: 118).
2   This included interviewing and testing the men in their homes. The first part of the interview consisted of Kohlberg's (Test of Moral Development (Form B)). The second half of the session consisted of a semi-clinical open-ended interview in which the subjects' Actual Moral Reasoning (AMR) regarding the specific act of refusal was recorded. The subjects were also asked about the motivation for their actions. Finally, their personal and military histories were explored.
3   Rawls (1971) himself argued that his theory of justice both generalized and carried to a higher level of abstraction the familiar theory of the social contract as found in Locke, Rousseau and Kant.

4 There is a dearth of reliable 'empirical' work on the scale of squatting in most liberal-democracies. In the UK, e.g. while there are no reliable statistics about the prevalence of squatting in England and Wales, credible academic research suggests that squatting is a common way in which homeless people house themselves. Research in the 2000s suggests that as many as 40 per cent of single homeless people squat as a response to homelessness with 6 per cent of the single homeless population squatting on any one night (Reeve 2011: 8).

5 In this lengthy study, squatting is barely referred to at all. Official statistics pick up on trends like the 11,000 university student who were homeless themselves or the 10 per cent of homeless people on Australia's 2016 Census night, some of whom were living in squats.

6 This does not mean that the exercise of conscience is without value. As Arendt (1971: 434) says, apropos Socrates, exercising our conscience is a form of thinking and keeps us from mindless adherence to social conformism: '…thinking inevitably has a destructive, undermining effect on all established criteria, values, measurements for good and evil, in short on those customs and rules of conduct we treat of in morals and ethics'.

Chapter 4

'Protecting democracies from themselves'

How liberal democracies criminalize the political

Notwithstanding some fundamental difficulties involved in trying to define political ideas like 'liberalism', or categories like the 'liberal-democratic state', many political philosophers have claimed that a central, some have said *the* defining characteristic of any liberal-democratic state, is its commitment to upholding the rights and freedoms of its citizens. This is certainly the viewpoint of political philosophers who claim allegiance to the tradition of Western liberalism and who will say liberalism is summed up in the idea of liberty. As Maurice Cranston said, 'By definition a liberal is a man who believes in liberty' (1967: 459).

This idea of liberty has several implications. One is that liberals respect and tolerate opinions and behaviours different from their own. Arguably the best-known version of the liberty principle is the one proposed by J.S Mill (1859/1998) when he said that we should all be free to think and do as we see fit. The only *proviso* is that we do not cause harm to anyone else when we are exercising our freedoms. Another implication is that the primary obligation of a liberal state is to secure and protect the freedom to believe, think and act freely of all its citizens. Again J.S. Mill thought this should be an unconstrained commitment, subject only to the no-harm principle: 'the only purpose for which power can be rightfully exercised over any member of a civilized community, against his will, is to prevent harm to others' (Mill 1859/1998: 21). Finally, understanding 'liberty' as the freedom to think and act as each of us sees fit, requires that the state embed 'the protection of core fundamental rights and the principle of non-intervention by the state' in in relevant constitutional and legal institutions (Carmi 2008: 280). In short on this account we should be confident that a state is liberal to the extent that it acknowledges and tolerates the many divergent opinions and different ways of living of its citizens and does not think difference or dissent a threat to the existence or good order of the state.

If we were to look for an exemplar of a liberal-democratic society, America especially seems to have gone further than many other liberal-democracies in making liberty a core civic idea. It has, e.g. enshrined the right to freedom of speech and assembly in formal legal instruments like the First Amendment to the American Constitution, which declares:

Congress shall make no law respecting an establishment of religion, or pro-hibiting the free exercise thereof; or abridging the freedom of speech, or of the press; or the right of the people peaceably to assemble, and to petition the government for a redress of grievances.

This seems to give an especially clear expression to the core idea of liberty to the point of providing legal protection for that right.

So how then should we think about what in effect amounts to the criminaliza-tion of politics by declaring certain kinds of speakings and doings to be a crime, a political crime? This is the question posed by the case of the Occupy Wall Street movement of September–October 2011, which, in turn, raises some sharp ques-tions about the relationship of liberal-democratic states to dissent.

In what follows, I start by exploring the responses of the American state to the Occupy Wall Street movement, to highlight some of the ways dissent, and the po-litical was criminalized. I then widen the scope of my enquiry to take in two other Western liberal-democracies, Britain and Australia. The task here is essentially descriptive. I survey some of the ways these liberal-democratic states have legis-lated to outlaw dissent by denominating dissent in speech and deed as 'sedition', 'subversion', 'extremism', 'terrorism' or public disorder. I then briefly survey some of the ways in which dissent is then policed using techniques like surveillance, arrest, and harassment.

As I show, it begins to look as if the state, and especially its security and police agencies operate on the premise that liberal democracy needs to be protected from itself even to the extent that the commitment to the 'rule of law' principle may on occasion need to be jettisoned.

The Occupy Wall Street movement in America, 2011

The idea for what was originally thought about as a 'Day of Rage' was the brain-child of Adbusters (2011), a Vancouver-based non-profit Canadian group that used the Wikileaks Central news site in March 2011 to promote the idea. Adbusters put out a call to 'Occupy Wall Street', featuring the image of a ballerina dancing atop the iconic bronze bull sculpture on Wall Street. This collective protest ac-tion ultimately saw activists around the world mobilize, march and in many cases occupy public spaces in 951 cities in some eighty-two countries for varying periods of time.

If we treat Occupy as a case of political *praxis*, we will agree with David Graeber (2013), himself a key player in the Occupy movement, when he said that 'it' expressed a plurality of political positions that escaped easy categorization. The occupation of Zuccotti Park near Wall Street itself became a functioning camp village of ongoing discussion, education, broadcasting, and meetings and even a library with 3000 volumes (Leary 2014: 260). The Occupy movement was established by activists using a cocktail of new digital technologies including

Twitter and smart phones, alongside a more traditional repertoire of colourful rallies, banners and marches, the staging of mock trials of corporations, and the occupation of civic space to get its message out and to attract protestors 'with a smartphone in her pocket, an Occupied activist camping in Zuccotti Park or Chicago or Oakland can become a pan-media outlet, a de-centered knot of video, photographs, and blogging that documents and creates and circulates the Occupied events' (Deluca et al. 2012: 487).

Participants in Occupy wanted to protest against the many banks and financial institutions in both America and Europe, whose reckless, even criminal conduct triggered the Great Recession of 2008 (Tooze 2018). Many also wanted to vent their outrage about the failure of governments anywhere either to prevent the global crisis, or to prosecute any of the key executive bankers and financiers for their negligent and/or criminal conduct. In the build-up to these protests, ideas like 'We are the 99%' were promoted on the Net, a reference to the increasing concentration of wealth among the top 1 per cent of income earners compared to the other 99 per cent in places like Europe and North America. Apart from a clear commitment to non-violence of the kind advocated by Gene Sharp (2005), many of the protestors also wanted to experiment with new forms of participatory democracy involving the use of 'working groups' and 'General Assemblies' in which different speakers addressing the crowd, in turn, to try and achieve a consensus (Graeber 2013).

Given the opening remarks about America as an exemplary liberal democracy, it might not seem all that unusual that in September 2011 elected American officials affirmed the right of Occupy protestors to protest. On 17 September, even as thousand protestors began gathering in Wall Street, New York's billionaire Mayor Michael Bloomberg said at a press conference: 'People have a right to protest, and if they want to protest, we'll be happy to make sure they have locations to do it' (Glass 2013).[1] Equally unsurprisingly, American protestors repeatedly and publicly referred to their right to protest framed in terms of the guarantees to protect free speech in the First Amendment to the American Constitution. The 'Declaration of the Occupation of New York City', passed by the General Assembly on 29 September 2011, e.g. put it simply: 'We have peaceably assembled here, as is our right' before calling on 'the people of the world' to 'exercise your right to peaceably assemble; occupy public space; create a process to address the problems we face, and generate solutions accessible to everyone' (New York General Assembly 2011). This appeal to the rights at stake remained a consistent feature of this movement. As Sarah Kunstler (2012: 1119) noted, the Occupy movement reinvigorated the meaning of the public forum and civic participation in America, and created 'a powerful new form of expression that was worth fighting for'.

Even so, as legal scholars and courts deliberated on the extent of protected First Amendment rights claimed by Occupy protestors, there was mounting evidence that America's courts were actually deeply ambivalent about protecting free speech. Research showed that while federal courts had once decided that overnight sleeping, tent cities and temporary shanties were a form of symbolic communication protected by the First Amendment in the 1980s, by 2011 this was no longer the case (Kunstler 2012: 1007). In 2011, lower courts began finding that camping and sleeping could be distinguished from the First Amendment activity, which Occupy protesters were claiming to be protected. Worse the courts were concluding that local authority bans on sleeping and erecting tents and other structures in a public place were designed to prevent harms to others wishing to use those public places, and were therefore a valid 'time, place and manner' restriction permitting municipalities to promulgate and enforce total bans on Occupy demonstrations.[2]

However and notwithstanding these legal niceties, the Occupy movement had far more to worry about than the preparedness of the courts to protect their right to free speech.

In spite of apparent support by New York's Mayor of the right to protest, we see from the outset a variety of moves to criminalize the Occupy Wall Street movement. This involved as Chris Leary (2015) has shown a mixture of 'soft' tactics like persistent attempts to use media outlets to represent the Occupy Wall Street movement in negative ways, as well as intrusive, even violent practices by government agencies. Even as the Occupy movement gathered momentum in August and September 2011, drawing on the outrage many people felt about the failure of American governments to charge the bankers and financiers responsible for unprecedented levels of criminal fraud and deception with criminal offences, the American government showed no such reluctance when it came to criminalizing dissent. In a pattern repeated wherever the Occupy movement made its presence felt, security agencies like the FBI (moved quickly to initiate 'the process by which "behaviours and individuals are transformed into crime and criminals"' (Michalowski 1985: 6).

Some of the criminalization process was more or less visible when the state used traditional measures to deal with conventional kinds of dissent like rallies, marches and occupation of public space. In New York on the same day that Bloomberg appeared to confirm, even to actively support the right to protest, assemble and speak, New York police were intent on thwarting the protest marchers. At least on this occasion the protestors in New York protestors were only facing police wearing their normal street uniforms: in previous protests like the 2002 anti-International Monetary Fund (IMF) protests in Washington DC, protestors had been confronted by intimidating riot police 'wearing dark Robocop-style uniforms' wearing 'full riot gear including black helmets, batons, and plastic handcuffs' or 'non-lethal' weapons like beanbags, rubber bullet rifles and pepper spray (Fernandez 2008: 1).

This attempt to block passage of the march to occupy Chase Plaza led – ironically – to the protestors deciding to occupy Zuccotti Park near Wall Street, an occupation that lasted from 17 September to 15 November 2011. Zuccotti Park was a privately owned public park owned by Brookfield Properties just blocks away from Goldman Sachs and the Bank of America, two key perpetrators of the systemic financial fraud and deception which had aroused the righteous anger of the Occupy movement.[3] While privately owned, the park had long been open to the public, a fact which initially thwarted police efforts to clear the park as they needed the owner's permission to do so: equally at this point the owners had not drafted rules about the uses to which the park might be put which might have sanctioned the use of police powers of eviction. This would give the Occupy movement a few months of respite.

Conservative lawmakers urged America's media not to glorify Occupy. Republican Congressman Peter King, who represented the Second District of New York, went public on 7 October with a plea to the media to undermine Occupy's credibility. 'It's really important for us not to give any legitimacy to these people in the streets', King said on Laura Ingraham's right-wing radio show, adding, 'I remember what happened in the 1960s when the left-wing took to the streets and somehow the media glorified them and it ended up shaping policy. We can't allow that to happen' (Miller 2011). Media reactions became increasingly hostile in October 2011, as opinion polls suggested that the Occupy message was getting out and was attracting support (Leary 2014: 104). Recognizing the success of the Occupy movement, major media outlets like the *New York Post* (owned by Murdoch's News Corp) campaigned to redefine Occupy in the public mind as dangerous fringe elements, or, in the words of *New York Post* columnist Steve Cuozo, as 'anarchists, vagrants, and zanies' driven 'by a nihilist impulse to disrupt life and commerce' (Cuozo 2011).

Twitter became the technological platform most closely associated with Occupy Wall Street. Apart from its use in mobilizing activists, the Occupy movement used Twitter to document police responses to that dissent by the state. On 1 October 2011, e.g. thousands of protesters marched towards a police barricade in the middle of Brooklyn bridge. Reporters and protestors recorded the resulting mass arrests, as police officers claimed they had warned protesters that marching on the bridge's traffic lanes was illegal and would lead to arrests. Various protesters replied that the police had knowingly allowed them to walk onto the traffic lanes and into a barricade, so that police could eventually make over 700 arrests. In the days immediately following the protests, protestors filed lawsuits claiming First and Fourth Amendment rights violations bringing the conflict between protesters and the police into the courts. Protestors used smart phones repeatedly to record police violence and share the images across social media networks. As Graeber (2013: 255) has said about conflict with police as a protest tactic, 'just as we need to think about what sort of social arrangements would allow us to create a truly democratic society, we need to think about what tactics would best allow us to maintain the democratic nature of the movement'. Ever the optimist Dave Graeber claims that the documentation of conflicts with the police reveal that once state institutions resort to their capacity for violence, critics 'have tilted the field of power in our favor' (Graeber 2013: 257). At the least, this reminds us that surveillance is a relational practice the watcher can easily become the watched as both the protestors and the state made use of digital technologies to watch each other.

However, a 'hard' approach was also evident early on. Police arrested at least eighty people on 24 September, after protesters started marching up Manhattan. Police used a mix of pepper spray and corralling, or 'kettling' protestors, using orange plastic nets to isolate protesters into smaller groups before arresting them. A week later police arrested more than 700 Occupy Wall Street protestors who took to the roadway as they tried to cross the Brooklyn Bridge. (This was the start of a process of arresting protestors which would see in excess of 7,700 protestors arrested in 122 American cities in the weeks after 17 September 2011.)

From the start, the New York Police Department also effectively besieged the Zuccotti Camp using metal barricades while police constantly circled the camp, a manoeuvre clearly designed to intimidate. Police also used their powers to declare certain areas around Zuccotti Park 'soft zones', which was defined as 'public spaces' where First Amendment rights were not fully recognized. This enabled police to arrest activists for using chalk on sidewalks, wearing masks, taking pictures, using a bullhorn or simply displaying a sign (Leary 2014: 108). On one rainy night, police confiscated covers being used to protect Occupy's media equipment from the rain: when a demonstrator sat down on the cover to protect the transmissions that were being made, he was arrested. Authorities also targeted video cameras that documented clashes and bullhorns that augmented speech.

Police also kept the park under constant surveillance. During the Wall Street Occupation, there was a mix of traditional and more sophisticated forms of surveillance carried out by the state (Bernstein 2012). It included the pervasive use of police using video surveillance at protests. New York Police Department 'special ops' officers hovered near Occupy working group meetings at 60 Wall Street, while uniformed 'special ops' officers routinely approached meetings to investigate materials. Plainclothes monitoring and infiltration, and interrogation and intimidation of protestors, all practices that affect the protection of the right to protest, potentially chilling protesters' willingness to engage in lawful activity, and undermining privacy rights (Knuckey at al. 2016: 93). Surveillance also included a 7-m tall mobile 'watch tower' with a two-person observation booth equipped with darkened windows, flood lights, video cameras, a permanent closed-circuit television camera positioned near the park, and a mobile surveillance vehicle with a camera affixed to a 20-foot boom. It also seems that police planted provocateurs who set out to disrupt Occupy meetings (Leary 2014: 132). Surveillance also involved the use of digital surveillance.

As one major retrospective study of the Wall Street Occupation concluded, the state used aggressive, unnecessary and excessive police force (like 'kettling') against peaceful protesters, bystanders, legal observers and journalists, initiating pervasive surveillance of peaceful political activity, carrying out violent late-night raids on peaceful encampments, obstructing press freedoms and independent legal monitoring, and a persistent failure to ensure accountability for those allegedly responsible for abuse of power (Knuckey et al. 2016: v). Though much of this activity by police might be treated simply as a local response by zealous police, there is clear evidence that this police response was part of an intervention by the American state to criminalize activities many Americans thought were free-doms and rights protected by the US Constitution and/or by international law. If many of those Americans involved in the Occupy movement believed that free speech and dissent were protected by the American Constitution, the FBI had other ideas.

The FBI decided that the Occupy movement was a 'domestic terrorist' threat. As early as 19 August 2011, the FBI in New York was meeting with the New York Stock Exchange to discuss the Occupy Wall Street protests describing it as a 'planned Anarchist protest titled Occupy Wall Street'. The result was a na-tional campaign of both surveillance and extensive consultation with banks, stock exchanges, universities and local police that began well before the first Wall Street occupation (Bernstein 2012). Despite acknowledging that Occupy Wall Street organizers 'did not condone the use of violence during their events' and that the organizers had called for peaceful protest, in mid-2011 the FBI initiated surveillance and 'precautionary measures' on the basis that they needed to watch 'notorious domestic terror groups Aryan Nation, Anonymous and Occupy Wall Street'. We know this because repeated Freedom of Information requests from the Partnership for Civil Justice Fund required the FBI to release seventy-seven pages of (redacted) FBI documents, revealing that the FBI and other federal agencies like the Department of Homeland Security deemed the Occupy Movement a 'domestic terrorist threat' and used a nation-wide network of Joint Terrorism Task Forces to co-ordinate a surveillance project.[4] The FBI's Indianapolis division, e.g. released a 'Potential Criminal Activity Alert' on 15 September 2011, even though they acknowledged that no specific protest date had been scheduled in Indiana, while the FBI, the Department of Homeland Security and the private sector, 'discussing the Occupy Wall Street (OWS) protests at West Coast ports to "raise awareness concerning this type of criminal activity"' (InterOccupy.Net 2012).

As many studies have documented, this was not a new approach (Lyon 2007; Shaff 2014; Owen 2017). Ivan Greenberg (2012), e.g. has documented decades of suppression and criminalization of dissent by the Federal Bureau of Investigation across much of the twentieth century. Edward Snowden's revelations in 2013 about a massive, secret and illegal programme of domestic surveillance by the National Security Agency (Greenwald 2014) amply confirmed Greenberg's main claim that key elements of the American 'state [had] actively fought against movements for social change' using 'methods that worked outside the rule of law and the American Constitution' and had done so for many decades (Greenberg 2012: 5).

As we know the Occupy Wall Street protest was overwhelmed by police when they decided finally to evict the occupiers. This became possible after Brookfield Properties, the owners of Zuccotti Park, finally got around, but only after the occupation began, to draft a set of rules prohibiting all the things Occupy had been doing: erect tents, sleep in the park and use amplification. Arguably, the Occupy movement represented a serious symbolic attack on the capitalist imagi-nary. Chris Leary (2014) reports a conversation between a manager of the Brook-field Security team and a middle-aged couple who had stopped to discuss the occupation. Instead of 'banging drums all day', the couple said the demonstrators should have organized a jobs fair. The manager agreed, adding, 'Instead of looking for jobs, they are talking about free food, free health care, free this, free that. That is socialism and it doesn't work'. 'Unfortunately, that is the direction our country seems to be going in', the man replied. 'Well, not in my house', the manager promised (Leary 2014: 136).

On 24 November, protestors appealed to the NY Supreme Court to have their occupation of Zucotti Park affirmed as an exercise of their First Amendment Rights. However, the New York Supreme Court ruled that the claim by Occupy Wall street protestors to a right to free speech by erecting tents and occupying Zucotti Park was not guaranteed under the First Amendment. The Court said that while mindful of the protestors First Amendment rights of freedom of speech and peaceable assembly, it had determined that '[e]ven protected speech is not equally permissible in all places and at all times'. The court decided that the applicants had

> not demonstrated that they had a First Amendment right to remain in Zuccotti Park, along with their tents, structures, generators, and other installations to the exclusion of the owner's reasonable rights and duties to maintain Zuccotti Park, or to the rights to public access of others who might wish to use the space safely.

Police evicted the protestors from Zuccotti Park later that night. Police imposed a ban on media reporting as they cleared the park. Had journalists been able to witness the police action, they would have seen a large force of police in riot gear descend unannounced on the camp around 1 a.m., before turning on klieg lights and loudspeakers. Officers distributed leaflets ordering demonstrators to leave. Those who did not leave by 1:45 a.m. were dragged out. Police arrested over 200 people. Officers in riot gear beat campers with batons, tore apart their tents and littered the floor with their books, tents, medical supplies, food, religious artefacts and personal property. Some journalists were arrested, while other reporters in the park with press passes were forced to leave and restricted to a 'free-press zone' (Gillham et al. 2011: 95–97), where they were unable to document what happened (Leary 2014: 138–40).

Criminalizing dissent

The case of the Occupy Wall Street movement in America suggests how contemporary liberal-democratic states deal with some kinds of dissent. Several features stand out in this case about the way the state responded.

First the ritual liberal affirmation about the right to dissent evaporated quickly. Very few of those Americans who work in and for the American state in 2011 accepted Claude Ake's (1969) proposition that liberal arguments about the obligation to obey the law also entail an obligation to dissent, or Leppänen's (2016) argument that dissent is an irreducible characteristic of any democracy worth having. Despite Farron's (2017) observation that the right to offend and a duty to tolerate offence lies at the heart of liberal-democratic societies, few of those who manage modern liberal-democratic states actually believe this or do this.

Even as New York's Mayor affirmed the right to dissent, the American state was doing two things. Publicly there were concerns flagged about 'getting the balance right' between the right to dissent and the need for order and public safety. As will become clear, the metaphor of 'getting the balance right' is a central trope in liberalism as a political discourse and in the practice of law. It has been noticed how the great majority of liberal lawyers as well as political theorists and scientists either tacitly assume or argue explicitly that in order to 'save' liberal democracy from the scourge of terrorism, a 'balance' must be struck between security and liberty (Michaelson 2006: 1). Critical scholars have riposted that the metaphor of balance and associations of this with the 'scales of justice' is a fundamentally deceptive metaphor. Of the two elements needing to be balanced, i.e. security, and rights, security somehow always trumps freedoms (Neocleous 2000, 2011; Jackson 2011).

Worse the state drew on a vocabulary which emphasized the deviant, even criminal nature of the protestors while amplifying the 'danger', 'risk' and 'harm' set loose by the protest activity. This discursive tactic treated the exercise of peaceful dissent as a criminal activity and was used with no evidentiary basis for doing so as a prelude to initiating extensive surveillance and police measures. Indeed, the state through one of its key security agencies the FBI had drawn a line connecting domestic terrorism/extremism and the Occupy movement. In this way, we see how large is the repertoire of resources that the modern state has at its disposal to suppress dissent. On this occasion, the American state, e.g. did not have to invent new laws: it simply made use of the legal powers it already possessed to achieve a largely non-violent end to the Occupy Wall Street movement even as it covertly connected this peaceful dissent activity to terrorism. It suggests something about the way states can deploy their unparalleled discursive powers, or what Bourdieu calls its capacity for 'symbolic violence' to define situations as real and then acting on that discursive performance, to suppress dissent.

However and this is also a large point, this serves as a reminder that like dissent itself, the criminalization of dissent can take a variety of forms which defy both an easy 'definition' of it, let alone a simple basis for developing a taxonomy of, or some general theoretical explanation or interpretation of it as a political process. In what follows I sketch out some of the key forms that the criminalization of dissent takes in America, Britain and Australia.

Criminalization of dissent takes many forms. One basic response is to make certain conduct illegal by passing a law. In the case of dissent, states can fall back on existing legislation some of which may have a long history. States can also introduce new legislation to define new kinds of dissenting practices as unlawful. In charting the evolution of the criminal codes in America, Britain and Australia, we certainly need to acknowledge the effects of a federated state like America and Australia, which implies that underneath the national legal framework there lurk a whole 'hidden' structure of local and even municipal state legislation, in comparison with the way a unitary state like Britain sets up one national framework.

I will start by focussing on some of the legislation used by the state in America and Britain. However, I do this mindful of the argument made by Luke McNamara et al. (2018) that a focus on legislation, while an important way of making sense of the criminalization process, needs to acknowledge some of the other ways states criminalize dissent. As we have seen in the case of the Occupy Wall Street movement, the state did not rely too much on legislation. Davenport (2007a: 1–20) talks, e.g. about the practice of suppressing dissent through criminalization when it is carried out by state agencies relying on:

> …harassment, surveillance/spying, bans, arrests, torture, and mass killing by government agents and/or affiliates within their territorial jurisdiction… [that] violate First Amendment–type rights, due process in the enforcement and adjudication of law, and personal integrity or security.

In this case, these forms of criminalization may or may not involve the use of lawful and unlawful technologies of policing, surveillance, intimidation and harassment and targets specific social movements, activist groups or individuals. As we begin to see, the question of the lawfulness or otherwise of what states do is often beside the point.

The practice of criminalization: legislation

I focus here on the practice of criminalization that relies on the legislative practices of states. I cannot even begin to pretend that what follows is in any way an exhaustive or definitive account. The number and kinds of legislation that have been used to criminalize, proscribe or suppress dissent are impossibly large. This includes the law of

- sedition
- terrorism
- public disorder
- the use of non-disclosure agreements to prevent disclosure by employees of state, NGO and business organization of corruption, bullying sexual harassment and criminal activities often called 'whistleblowing'
- regulation of fundraising by non-government organizations and political parties affecting their advocacy activities
- the regulation of squatting
- industrial legislation affecting the activities of unions, and legislation suppressing advocacy by NGO's
- the laws affecting libel and defamation
- laws regulating publication in print, performance or electronic media of opinion and information.

For reasons of space, I am not able to deal with the legislative framework in America, Australia or England, regulating and in some case suppressing public interest disclosure by employees of state, NGO and business organizations of malfeasance and criminal conduct, the regulation of non-government advocacy organizations and their fundraising activities, or the activities of unions. Equally I have had to exclude the very large and complex body of common law dealing with the law of libel and defamation that in many cases is used to suppress free speech, to say nothing of the regulation of various kinds of public discussion.

The focus here is on the suppression of dissent, beginning with what is usually referred to as 'sedition' or 'treason'. I then turn to the form of dissent referred to as 'terrorism'. Finally, I examine what is called 'public disorder'. Analytically, we will see in most liberal democracies, the use first of omnibus crimes acts or codes in which dissent involving everything from overt criticism of the sovereign or government, to calling for, or acting to bring about the downfall of a government, is defined as criminal 'sedition', 'seditious libel' or 'treason'. There is more than a hint that historically 'sedition' in most cases simply meant that a government did not like what some of its opponents or critics were saying.

More recently, we also find liberal-democratic states introducing specific legislation apparently designed to 'prevent terrorism' in countries like Australia in staggering numbers. This practice which has taken off since the 9/11 attacks in New York and Washington has done so in ways utterly disproportionate to the level of threat posed by 'terrorism' (Mueller and Stewart 2016a). Apart from the disproportionality of the response, we also see the tendency to by-pass the usual retrospective nature of criminal law which deals with harms *after* they have been committed, by using the criminal law to 'prevent harms' based on a suspicion that somewhere, somehow, some people are up to no good. Indeed, the highly political nature of the criminalization of terrorism is already signified by the decision to go outside the existing criminal law prohibiting murder, conspiracy, violence and so forth.

Finally, I turn to the legislation regulating public protest in the interest of promoting public order. Here again, we see increasingly the disposition in too many cases to treat any kind of public protest as a problem before that problem has actually occurred. In what follows, I offer an overview of each kind of legislation designed to criminalize various kinds of action.

Sedition in Britain

Sedition is a political crime with its origins in Britain's common-law tradition. That tradition was embedded in England's colonies with long-term effects in both America and Australia. As Roger Manning (1980) makes clear, *sedition in effect criminalizes political speech*. Up to the fifteenth century, sedition was talked about as 'treasonable words' involving criticism of the monarch or making prophecies about the death of the King. Alternately, it might be talked about in terms of the doctrine of *scandalum magnatum* if the public criticism was directed at peers or legal officials. Francis Bacon raged against sedition arguing that when 'Libels and licentious discourses against the state, when they are frequent and open' and 'when discords, and quarrels, and factions are carried openly and audaciously', then this surely is 'a sign the reverence of government is lost' (cited Manning 1980: 99). Bacon understood sedition as factionalism or violent party strife and both contributed to an intellectual and a legal animus against dissent, which saw sedition become a political crime. As a political crime, 'sedition' only slowly entered the field of criminal law in England in the late sixteenth century.

Against a backdrop of the tumult, riots and rebellions that characterized the reformation in England after 1530, the Tudor state set about punishing seditious utterances. The Privy Council and the royal judges needed a new formulation of a criminal offence that did not necessitate the cumbersome procedures or extreme penalties of 'constructive treason' (Manning 1980: 101). This they found in the offence of 'sedition', which was defined by the Court of Star Chamber. During the second half of the sixteenth century, that Court defined the crime of sedition as any 'slanders or libels upon the reputations and/or actions, public or private, of public officials, magistrates and prelates, which sought to divide and alienate "the presente governors" from "the sounde and well affected parte of the subiectes"' (Manning 1980: 100). What was at stake then, as now, was an 'imagined' or 'symbolic order'. In the seventeenth century, that 'symbolic order' mingled the divine, the monarchical and the legal order as if they were a single indivisible hierarchy that was never to be questioned. In effect as Manning also makes clear, it was the act of speaking politically that would be punished as 'sedition'. By the end of the sixteenth century, the more 'modern' meaning 'sedition' began to emerge understood as the practice:

> ... of inciting by words or writings disaffection towards the state or constituted authority. Thus, sedition came to be interpreted as words that fell short of treason and did not directly involve – although they might lead to – acts of violence.
>
> (Manning 1980: 101)

After the restoration of Charles II, Britain's Parliament introduced a *Sedition Act 1661* with some provisions reinforced via some of its provisions lingering on in the *Treason Act 1695* and the *Treason Felony Act 1848* until repeal in 1863. However, sedition remained a common law crime until 2009 when it was *apparently* repealed by the Brown Labour government. I say apparently, because Britain's Parliament had already passed the *Security Service Act 1989*, which established a statutory basis for MI5, Britain's domestic counter-intelligence and security agency (which had its origins in 1909 as the Secret Service Bureau) (Northcott 2007; Andrew 2010). The legislation gave MI5 the powers to deal with international counter-terrorism, Irish and domestic counter-terrorism and technical and surveillance operations. Without using words like sedition or subversion, this legislation nonetheless defined a loose yet inclusive objective namely that MI5 was responsible for promoting the 'national security' of the UK and, in particular, to protect it against threats from espionage, terrorism and sabotage, from the activities of agents of foreign powers, and from actions intended to 'overthrow or undermine parliamentary democracy by political, industrial or violent means' (Northcott 2007: 458). The kicker we might say is in the reference to 'political' means being used to undermine parliamentary democracy.

Anti-terrorism in the US

In spite of the fact that many people would probably say 'terrorism' deserves to be criminalized, the fact that terrorism unlike most criminal acts including rape, murder, assault, theft or kidnapping is difficult if not impossible to define remains a basic and inconvenient fact about 'terrorism'. As Anthony Richards has observed '[t]he term terrorism [was] so widely used in many contexts as to become almost meaningless' (Richards 2014: 213: also Golder and Williams 2004). For reasons already outlined, I will not be getting as excited as the many social scientists like Richards who are fussed about the absence of 'a universally agreed definition of terrorism' and who call for 'a more dispassionate and analytical approach' (Richards 2014: 213).

For one thing, the absence of any universal theoretical or legal definition of terrorism has not stopped states from introducing legislation and going to extraordinary lengths to prevent 'it'. While 'terrorism' was hardly a novelty in the twentieth century, after the 9/11 attacks, it took on a new and pervasive even ubiquitous status as *the* sign of insecurity and risk in the new millennium. The lack of clarity about what it was that was being prevented, to say nothing of the inversion of the normal presumption that a criminal act refers to something that has actually happened, has added an extra dimension of surreality to this exercise in criminalizing dissent.

There can be little doubt that the 9/11 attacks in the US triggered an expansion of international and domestic legislation globally directed at the prevention of terrorism. As Rebecca Annina-Welsh and George Williams note, if prior to 9/11 a country like Australia had no national legislation dealing specifically with terrorism, by 2014 the Australian government has enacted more than sixty such laws (Annian-Welsh and Williams 2014: 363). Though this has never reflected the actual risk 'terrorism' posed, e.g. in Australia (Mueller and Stewart 2016), this has not prevented the process of criminalization involved and one paralleled in many countries including all the major liberal democracies. The most worrying feature is how this so much of anti-terrorism legislation is based on the idea of preventive justice involving the recourse to coercive or punitive prevention (Ashworth and Zedner 2014: 2).

At stake here is the (mis)use of the criminal law, which historically has always come into play after a criminal act: the criminal law required that a criminal act has actually been committed before the perpetrator/s end up in a court and face the consequences if the state establishes their guilt. In our time the modern preventive justice model simply requires that the state have a suspicion that some-one is likely to, or is about to commit a terrorist act or a criminal act, a suspicion or belief that may not even be tested in a court. This premise informed the pas-sage of the *Prevention of Terrorism Act* 2005 that saw the invention and use of 'control orders' and 'Terrorism Prevention and Investigation Measures' (TPIMs) in Britain and Australia. If Bernard Harcourt is correct when he says 'the pur-ported need for punitive preventive measures is, on balance, factually overstated and generally unproven' (Harcourt 2012: 6), then there are important questions to be addressed about why liberal-democratic states are so eager to expand their power by adopting preventive punishment measures.

It is perhaps unsurprising that the passage of such a large volume of anti-terrorism legislation since 2001 has highlighted the ease with which governments can target people and organizations engaged in peaceful dissent and categorize them as 'terrorists' or 'extremists': this we saw was the case of the Occupy move-ment in North America. Equally disturbing has been the tendency to avoid com-plying with fundamental liberal legal principles, like *habeas corpus*, evidenced in the way states engage in warrantless searches and mass surveillance, the use of de-tention and control orders, the secret detention and interrogation of non-suspect citizens by security and police agencies without charge or judicial oversight, or the banning of organizations, all measures referred to as 'preventive justice' (Annian-Welsh and Williams 2014: 363). As will become clear, many groups and kinds of dissent have been brought into the harsh spotlight cast by anti-terrorism legislation all sorts of social movement activists, anti-World Trade Organisation (WTO) and animal rights activists, and more recently by activists and groups supporting asylum seekers/refugees in Europe, America and Australia.

So let me briefly outline the introduction of counter-terrorism legislation in America.

Enacted within six weeks after the 9/11 attacks and under the cover of promot-ing 'Homeland Security', the Bush administration introduced sweeping legislative 'anti-terrorism' provisions initially in its USA PATRIOT Act 2001 and its *Home-land Security* Act 2002.[5] These sweeping legislation received little close scrutiny by Congress (Cole and Dempsey 2002: 147–55). A short list of this legislation includes:

   i United States Code Title 18
  ii USA Patriot Act 2001
 iii Homeland Security Act 2002
   v Security and Freedom Ensured Act 2003
   v Intelligence Reform and Terrorism Prevention Act 2004
  vi Protect America Act of 2007
 vii National Defense Authorization Act for Fiscal Year 2012
viii USA Freedom Act 2015.

The Bush Administration insisted this legislation was designed and intended sim-ply to 'protect' America's 'homeland security' by indefinitely suspending principles long deemed to be vital to the rule of law (Cole 2003; Cole and Dempsey 2006; Scheuerman 2006; Tashima 2008).

The legislation introduced or extended powers first granted in the *Anti-Terrorism Act 1996* as well as conferring unprecedented powers to detain, interrogate, conduct surveillance on and search people suspected of terrorism. These powers would seem from a liberal perspective to be deeply objectionable and/or unconstitutional. The USA PATRIOT *Act*, e.g. allowed for the indefinite detention of 'aliens' subject to deportation but which no country was prepared to accept. Section 213 of the USA PATRIOT Act gave FBI officers and law enforcement officers powers to search a home or business without the owner's or the occupant's consent or knowledge for a 'reasonable period thereafter' (Boykoff 2007: 750). It also extended the use of 'National Security letters', which allowed the FBI to search telephone, email, and financial records without a court order (Greenberg 2011). Amnesty International (2003) was not alone in worrying about how a new combination of old and new laws had enabled governments led by the US and Britain to 'sacrifice human rights on the altar of terrorism'.

The authority of law enforcement agencies to investigate and surveil suspects of domestic terrorism was greatly expanded under the USA PATRIOT Act. The FBI and the CIA's investigatory powers were increased again in 2004 when the Bush Administration granted these agencies the power to 'prevent, preempt, and disrupt terrorist threats to and attacks against the United States' (Risen 2006: 44). In the months and years after the 9/11 attacks, the Bush Administration instigated a secret programme of mass electronic surveillance run by the National Security Agency targeting the American people, as well as foreign nationals abrogating basic constitutional and legal rights to privacy and free speech in the process (Greenwald 2014; Fidler 2015).

Anti-terrorism: in the UK

In the 1980s, the Thatcher government introduced its *Prevention of Terrorism (Temporary Provisions) Act* 1984 to deal with Irish Republican Army (IRA) activities. That legislation was extended in 1989 to include the members and supporters of any organization *in the world*, which uses 'violence for political ends' while the legislation was made semi-permanent. The Thatcher government also announced the end of the 300-year-old right to silence in Northern Ireland. Evidence for the idea that the state was emphasizing criminalization, the suppression of dissent and the erosion of the formal norms and values of justice was already becoming clear in cases like the police response to protests at Broadwater Farm in 1986, or the police conspiracies involved in the arrests and trials of IRA activists like Birmingham Six, the Maguire Seven or the Guildford Four (Blom-Cooper 1997).

In 2001, Britain's Home Affairs Committee could observe that Britain 'has more anti-terrorist legislation on its statute books than almost any other developed democracy', possibly reflecting the long running conflict in Northern Ireland that spilled over into IRA attacks in Britain. Since 2001, Britain has introduced a swag of anti-terrorism legislation since 2000 though nothing on the scale of the Australian experience.[6]

Much of this legislation has involved a persistent exercise in enhancing the powers of the state by invoking legislation that had the effect of introducing a permanent 'state of emergency' or what Schmitt called a 'state of exception'. This enables a state to over-ride legal protections and basic liberties enshrined in both Britain's common law and statutes and in international human rights and human-itarian law. The *Terrorism Act 2000*, e.g. widened the definition of terrorism to ap-ply to domestic terrorism and include any 'political, religious or ideological' cause that 'uses or threatens violence against people or property'. Apart from creating new offences like inciting terrorism, it enhanced police powers, providing for stop and search powers and, in a serious breach of *habeas corpus*, enabled police to detain 'suspects' for seven days without laying charges. The *Anti-terrorism, Crime and Security Act 2001* enabled the Home Secretary to arrest foreign nationals who were 'suspected' of terrorism without charge or trial *and to do so indefinitely*. Critics like Clive Walker argue that while the *Terrorism Act 2000* 'represents a worthwhile attempt to fulfil the role of a modern code against terrorism', 'it also failed 'to meet the desired standards in all respects'. There are aspects where rights are probably breached, and its mechanisms to ensure democratic accountability and constitutionalism are even more deficient (Walker 2002).

After that provision was ruled invalid by the House of Lords, the Blair gov-ernment introduced the *Prevention of Terrorism Act 2006*, which introduced ad-ministrative control measures called 'control orders', which allow the government to restrict the activities and freedom of movement of individuals it suspected of 'involvement in terrorist-related activity' where there was insufficient evidence to charge that person. The *Terrorism Act 2006* also extended the pre-charge deten-tion period from fourteen to twenty-eight days. While the maximum period of pre-charge detention in counter-terrorism cases was reduced from twenty-eight to fourteen days following a Home Office review of counter-terrorism and security powers in January 2011, the *Protection of Freedoms Act*, which came into force in May 2012, not only retained the fourteen-day limit (already the longest available to a state in the EU), but it also allowed the maximum period to be increased to twenty-eight days in response to an unspecified 'urgent' situation that could arise in the future.

In December 2011, the government introduced 'TPIMs' which could be applied to UK nationals and foreigners, are limited to two years and allow among other things:

- assigned overnight residence;
- a ban on travel outside the country or outside a specified area within the UK;
- exclusion orders prohibiting a person from entering an area or specific types of places (such as Internet cafes);
- restrictions on access to financial services and the use of mobile phones; and
- restrictions on association with other people.

In 2015, the *Counter-Terrorism and Security* Act became law. It amended previous legislation by re-introducing several of the more stringent administrative restrictions established in the previous control order regime, including the forced relocation of individuals subject to a 'TPIM'. In addition, the threshold for imposing a 'TPIM' was lowered from 'a reasonable belief' to a 'balance of probabilities' that a person has been involved in terrorism-related activities. Phil Edwards (2018) makes the powerful case that much of this legislation exemplifies the use of law to undermine the core features of the liberal 'rule of law' tradition. While he is arguing about Britain, the case applies just as well to America and Australia. What he calls 'counter law', this is what Carl Schmitt and David Dyzenhaus have called 'states of exception'. Either way the point is that 'counter-law' 'erodes or eliminates traditional principles, standards, and procedures of criminal law'. The *Terrorism Acts* of 2000 and 2006 epitomizes the development of 'counter-law' by creating three kinds of new offences, inchoate offences, preparatory offences and situational offences all understood in terms of a discourse of preventive justice. As Edwards notes, these offences all tend to dissociate counter-terrorism from criminal law's standard requirement for 'a clear illegal act that is committed with fault', focussing instead on 'a pattern of behaviour identified as undesirable' or simply suspicious (Edwards 2018: 13). This legislation has been used repeatedly to prosecute and convict people. The Crown Prosecution Service Website lists 155 successful counter-terrorist successful prosecutions between the passage of the Terrorism Act 2006 and the end of calendar year 2016, involving the bringing of 391 charges of which 345 were brought to conviction. The specifically counter-terrorist charges brought in these cases – all of which can be classified as inchoate, preparatory or situational – account for 66 per cent of all charges brought; much of the remainder is accounted for by general inchoate and situational offences (e.g. conspiracy and possession offences (Edwards 2018: 13).

The same impulse to prevent dissent is evident in the ways states regulate public protest by appealing to the idea of public safety. I focus here only on the English experience.

Public disorder: criminalizing protest in Britain

The idea that Britain is a liberal-democratic order in the twenty-first century is supported, e.g. by the fact that the *Human Rights Act* 1998 came into force in Britain incorporating into British law Articles 10 and 11 of the *European Convention on Human Rights*. These human rights instruments appear to enshrine and protect 'the right to freedom of expression' and 'the right to freedom of peaceful assembly'. Yet as many writers have argued, the extent to which these rights are real and protected is open to serious doubt. As Jamie Grace notes in 2009, Her Majesty's Inspectorate of Constabulary released two reports on public order policing that seemed to introduce an explicitly human rights-based approach to the policing of protest by 'defining the starting point for the policing of protest as a presumption in favour of facilitating peaceful protest, reflecting the obligations of the police under [the European Convention on Human Rights]' (Grace 2018; also Gordon 2010). However, as Lockley and Ismail noted recently, at the very least this presumption is heavily qualified:

> The police have powers to place conditions on marches and assemblies, and in certain circumstances, to seek to have a march prohibited. Despite the law's protection of the right to protest, that right is not unqualified. Art 11 of the ECHR – embedded in the law of the United Kingdom by the Human Rights Act 1998 – allows certain restrictions to be placed on freedom of assembly, if necessary in a democratic society (among other circumstances) in the interests of public safety, the prevention of disorder and crime and the protection of the rights and freedoms of others. Additionally, Art 10 protects freedom of expression, and this too is a qualified right, subject to broadly the same restrictions as Art 11.
>
> (Lockley and Ismail 2016: 20)

Others like Mead (2010: 404) would suggest that while it is hard to arrive at definitive picture of the status of the right to protest in England, there has been 'a subtle regressive shift [away from rights to peaceful protest in England and Wales'.

If we start with the British case, we see there has been a clear and persistent move to suppress protest activity. This is evident by the way Britain has regulated public protest over the past three decades beginning with the *Public Order Act* 1986.

As Iain Channing (2015) reminds us, long before the *Public Order Act* 1986 the British state had exercised a wide range of powers to control public disorder including powers to prevent a 'breach of the peace', which went back centuries to the *Justices of the Peace Act* 1361. These powers were 'modernised' in the 1936 *Public Order Act*. These outlined a range of statutory offences of obstruction (of the highway or the police), criminal damage, assault, carrying a weapon, drunk and disorderly, while there were numerous municipal laws prohibiting, obscene language and offensive conduct. Then there was the famous Riot Act with origins in the Tudor's *Riot Act* 1549 which deemed it a crime of 'high treason' for twelve people (or more) to assemble and attempt to kill or imprison any member of the King's council, or change the laws, and refuse to disperse when ordered to do so by a justice of the peace, mayor or sheriff. The *Riot Act* 1714 was introduced as a response to the 'many rebellious riots and tumults [that] have been [taking place of late] in diverse parts of this kingdom' and empowered local authorities to declare any group of twelve or more people to be 'unlawfully, riotously, and tumultuously assembled together' which gave rise to the idea of 'reading the riot act'. (Acts like the Riot Act were transported into British colonies like Australia, Canada and America.) This Act was only repealed in 1967.

However, we see a major shift that began against a backdrop of heightened political dissent after 1979 and the election of the Thatcher government. As

Opposition Leader, Thatcher claimed in 1979 that she wanted 'less tax and more law and order' (Savage 1990: 89). In 1986, the Thatcher government introduced the *Public Disorder Act*. It espoused a tough on 'law and order' agenda, and was justified by the government when it pointed to popular anxiety about what the government said was declining respect for law and order. This anxiety was reflected in opinion polls, indicating large numbers of people said they were anxious about increasing prevalence of riots and disorder and critical of the 'lenient' policing of demonstrations. In this respect, the government could rely on tabloid media editorials about the perceived failure of governments to successfully prosecute unionists and protestors involved in the 1980 Bristol disturbances and the 1984–85 miners' strike.

The 1986 act dispensed with the vague reference to a 'breach of the peace' in the 1936 Act. Section 9 of the *Public Order Act* 1986 also abolished the common law offence of 'unlawful assembly' (Channing 2015: 156–8). This meant there was no longer a legal basis in domestic law for describing a public protest as inherently unlawful. Instead, the 1986 Act (at Section 5), provided a code of public order offences. These started with disorderly conduct. 'Disorderly conduct' involves the use of threatening, abusive or insulting words or behaviour and are penalized if they are 'within the hearing or sight of a person *likely to be* caused harassment, alarm or distress thereby'. It was enough that a police officer could attest to this being the effect of the 'disorderly conduct'. However, the *Public Order Act* introduced a significant shift in declaring that no actual harm needed to be proved and no victim needed to be produced in court. The reference to insulting words was only removed in 2013 while police were being advised that they needed to ensure, they did not apply Section 5 of the *Public Order Act* 1986 in a way which is incompatible with the provisions of the European Convention on Human Rights (ECHR), in particular Article 10, which relates to the freedom of expression, noting that Article 10 is a 'qualified right' (College of Policing 2013).

The 1986 Act then identified a more conventional sequence of increasingly serious offences including affray, violent disorder and riot. The 1986 Legislation Act, e.g. requires that the offensive statements or activity should create fear of, or provoke, violence. Actual, threatened or apprehended violence is a vital element of most of these offences. The exception (at Section 5) provided police with new powers to deal with minor public disorders. At Part 3, the Act also outlined the crime of racial hatred defined as expressions of hatred against a group of persons by reason of the group's colour, race, nationality (including citizenship) or ethnic or national origins.

More alarming was the way the 1986 *Public Order Act* shifted the playing field in regard to civil and political liberties by increasing police powers to restrict and regulate public processions and assemblies. The 1986 Act did not change the procedures and powers for banning processions provided in the 1936 Act. In this respect, the animus against protest remained. If the police expect a procession to result in 'serious public disorder' which cannot be avoided by the imposition of conditions, a ban of up to three months could be imposed on all or 'any class' of processions by the local councillor (in London) by the police commissioners, subject in both cases to Home Office approval (Grace 2018). The organizers of a protest march or procession were now required to provide the police with six days' notice of the proposed date, time and route, and their names and addresses. (Previously insignificant and unenforced municipal laws had required shorter periods of notice.) Organizers were now liable to prosecution and fines if such notice was not given, or if the procession did not conform to the plans notified (unless this was beyond their control). Some provision was made for 'spontaneous' processions which were held close to an event that protestors wished to respond to (Channing 2015). The 1986 Act also extended police powers by the provision of additional grounds on which conditions could be imposed. These included a 'reasonable belief' that the procession was intended to intimidate, or would result in serious damage to property or serious disruption to the life of the community.

In the decades since the introduction of the Act, the number of prosecutions of protestors under its aegis has probably been small (Grace 2018). This is said in the light of the difficulty that the Ministry of Justice does not make it easy to identify the number of arrests, prosecutions or convictions or the kinds of public order offences involved. For the years 2014–18, when total offences going to trial were running at approximately 100,000 cases pa., there were 3,602 public order cases before the courts in 2014, 3585 cases in 2015, and 3023 in 2016, which presumably involved cases where citizen swore at or abused a police officer (as in *Harvey* v *Director of Public Prosecutions* [2011] All ER (D) 143 (Nov)). Sometimes, the activists provide some insight. For example, police made arrests during an anti-Fracking protest in London Road, Balcombe, involving over 1,000 protestors who occupied the site for over two months in late 2013. A Freedom of Information request from protestors elicited advice from Sussex police that they had only arrested three people and that none of these cases had gone to court (Hayhurst 2014).

This is not to deny that on occasion police use the Public Order 1986 to suppress protest activity. There have been regular controversies about the way police have dealt with large protests since 2001. Sometimes this involves pre-emptive arrests. In 2009, police used the Public Order 1986 to allege protestors were engaged in a conspiracy to commit aggravated trespass to frustrate the planned protest at Ratcliffe-On-Soar power station in April 2009 by pre-emptively arresting 114 activists. Ultimately, twenty of those were found guilty. Again in the run-up to the London Olympics in 2012, 182 participants in a regular 'critical mass' bike ride were arrested for breaching a condition imposed on them under s12 of the *Public Order Act* 1986. Occasions like this have led Waddington to argue that police have frequently used pre-emptive arrests to 'selectively disable' and arguably suppress collective dissent. Equally, police have also used heavy handed tactics that have also led to controversy like the G20 protests in the City of London on 1–2 April 2009 where police made 114 arrests and where police violence caused the death of the newspaper vendor, Ian Tomlinson, epitomizing allegations of undue force used by police against protestors.

The use of legislation is not the only or perhaps even the primary form that criminalization takes. I turn NOW to the policing processes that augment the criminalization of dissent.

Criminalization by policing

The practice of treating dissent as threat to the state, national security or social order and then criminalizing it has been firmly entrenched in liberal-democratic states since the eighteenth century. As the case of the Occupy Wall Street movement suggests, a state can draw on a wide array of policing practices to transform people exercising a fundamental human right, i.e. the right to protest into a perceived threat that requires police interventions in effect criminalizing dissent.

Most typically liberal-democratic states like America have commonly used what Jennifer Earl (2011) calls a mix of iron fists, velvet gloves and diffuse controls. This relies on legislation and policing including various kinds of surveillance including the use of undercover agents and agents provocateurs, as well as sophisticated mass digital surveillance along with more straightforward exercises like prosecutions, arrests and injunctions to silence dissidents and suppress dissent (Barkan 1984; Salter 2011).

The use of police to regulate and arrest protestors is the most basic tactic. As some writers have understood, governments facing persistent protest might well come to see they have an interest in representing those protesting as disorderly, violent and even criminal: sending police into protest movements to disperse them has a good chance of diverting attention away from the message of the protestors and instead focussing on them as criminals (El-Anany 2014: 76). Some research referred to as the 'threat-based model of repression' indicates that, as large protest events are threatening because they demonstrate the potential power of an opposing group to the political elite, police are more likely to be asked to suppress the protest (Davenport 2000; Earl et al. 2003). Equally other research sometimes referred to as the 'blue approach' to police action suggests that if the police themselves believe that a large moving protest constitutes a threat, police will move to use force to disperse the protestors (Earl and Soule 2006; Soule and Davenport 2009).

At the same time, we see a persistent discursive exercise in highlighting certain groups of dissidents as more worthy of sustained police attention than others which frequently in the case of America has been colour coded for ease of reception. The relevant colours are red, black and green. The 'red scare' of the 1920s morphed into the long-running preoccupation with reds from the 1940s to the 1980s, while black has been the colour of those the FBI loathes including the civil rights movement and the recent Black Lives Matter movement. Anarchists nicely combined red and black, while the Green movement has helped fill the vacuum left by the fading away of the reds (Carson et al. 2012).

Since the early twentieth century, the US government has persistently prosecuted people and groups represented as 'progressive' or 'left wing' including anarchists, socialists, unionists and labour radicals for crimes of subversion. This project really escalated in the 1940s and 1950s. Since 1940, the US state has used the Smith Act to criminalize advocating for the violent overthrow of the US government and making it illegal to be a member of any organization that espoused such beliefs. This legislation has been used against both anarchists and communists (Siggelakis 1992; Starr et al. 2008). Some 138 individuals were indicted for conspiring to violate the Smith Act: 109 of those were convicted (Siggelakis 1992).

In the late 1940s as the Cold War heated up, Congress established the House Un-American Activities Committee (HUAC) with the goal of investigating Americans suspected of engaging in subversive activities. The Senate Committee, chaired by Senator McCarthy, started dragging prominent Americans before it to investigate their 'communist sympathies'. Congress also introduced the *Subversive Activities Control Act* 1950 designed to prevent the growth of communism. This Act forced communist organizations to register on a member list and prohibited their employment in labour unions and defence plants as well as forbade them from applying for US passports.

Subsequently, the 1960s saw repeated attempts by the FBI and local police to criminalize and harass civil rights activists and anti-war activists (Boyer 2014). Vietnam anti-war protestors were publicly prosecuted as dissidents and, as in the case of Vietnam Veterans against the War, had their organizations infiltrated by FBI informants (Boykoff 2007; Kirkby 2014). During the Montgomery, Alabama bus boycott, police harassed and cited civil rights activists carrying out the boycott and arrested approximately 100 boycott leaders (Barkan 1984). In the state of Georgia alone, over 1,200 activists were arrested for participating in marches, demonstrations and sit-ins in the large-scale effort to desegregate Albany, Georgia. These arrests practically immobilized the entire civil rights movement because of funding bail and court fees incurred by these activist defendants. Martin Luther King Jr., the key leader of the civil rights movement himself, was actively surveilled by the Federal Bureau of Investigations (FBI) for over a decade with the intent of weakening the civil rights movement and discrediting his leadership among his followers by leaking allegations of sexual impropriety (Boykoff 2007).

Suppression also involved the systematic use of surveillance. In the first case of intensive surveillance in modern times, J. Edgar Hoover, the Director of the FBI launched an intensive surveillance programme of social movements in 1956 called Counter Intelligence Program or COINTELPRO (Greenberg 2011). Michael Carley (1997: 153) described COINTELPRO as the 'major domestic counterinsurgency organization operating in America'. Those measure included extensive surveillance operations. COINTELPRO operated until 1971, initiating over 2,300 warrantless wiretaps, nearly 700 cases of bugging, and collecting over 57,000 pieces of correspondence from the CIA during its tenure (Carley 1997). One FBI memo explicitly outlined the function of COINTELPRO:

> The purpose of this new counterintelligence program is to expose, disrupt, misdirect, discredit, or otherwise neutralize the activities of ... organizations and groupings, their leadership, spokesmen, membership, and supporters.
>
> (Cited Carley 1997: 155)

This state-sponsored surveillance programme was used initially to investigate and dismantle the US Communist Party, the Socialist Workers Party and the Young Socialist Alliance (Carley 1997; Greenberg 2011). COINTELPRO then switched to surveillance of leftist social movements like the Student Nonviolent Coordinating Committee, the Southern Christian Leadership Conference and the American Indian Movement (Carley 1997). These organizations were left-leaning dissident groups advocating for civil rights for socially excluded groups like African-Americans and First Nation people. A statement by J. Edgar Hoover, FBI Director at the time, made the following remarks about civil rights demonstrations in 1967:

> Riots and anarchic demonstrations which leave devastation and ruin in their wake place a tremendous burden on law enforcement officers. Already hampered by undermanned staffs, police authorities are forced to marshal their strength in expected trouble spots and leave other neighborhoods without proper police protection. In fact, enforcement officers spend much of their time protecting and guarding marchers and petitioners. However, police officials as well as the general public are becoming weary of persons who, for self-aggrandizement and monetary gain, exploit noble causes and agitate peaceful groups into rioting mobs.
>
> (Cited Leary 2014: 107)

The imaginary conjured up by Hoover treated protestors as 'inauthentic' radicals motivated more by financial motives and self-aggrandizement than by commitment to a good cause who left devastation and ruin in their wake. It was plainly used to justify the measures the FBI took to suppress the civil rights movement.

Suppression also extended occasionally to brutality and the use of lethal force. For example, in 1963 police responded to civil rights activists in Birmingham who participated in marches with the use of firehoses, dogs and baton beatings to repel the marchers. In 1969, two members of the Black Panther Party were murdered during a joint tactical unit raid comprised of FBI agents and the Chicago Police Department (Boykoff 2007; Smith 2008). In 1970, National Guardsmen fired on university students at Kent State, Ohio, who were engaged in anti-war protests, leaving four dead and ten wounded in the aftermath.

As is now increasingly well known, the 9/11 attacks in Washington and New York licenced a major increase in domestic surveillance. Following the 9/11 attacks, the FBI renewed its intensive surveillance efforts against 'dissidents' using the passage of the *Uniting and Strengthening America by Providing Appropriate Tools Required to Intercept and Obstruct Terrorism Act* (USA PATRIOT Act) in 2001. Under the Act, some 1,200 Muslims, most of whom were not American citizens, were detained mostly as the result of 'racial' profiling (Banks 2004) and incarcerated in New York and New Jersey facilities (Shantz 2010). As Cole and Dempsey (2006) point out, there was also concern that the detention process depended on the application of the principle of guilt by association by treating some kind of affiliation with proscribed organizations as the grounds for detaining 'terror suspects'. Some detainees were reportedly 'denied access to their attorneys, proper food, or protection from … physical assault'. Some of them were held in solitary confinement even though they had not been charged with any criminal offense.

At no point did the US government have any evidence linking a single one of these detainees to the 9/11 attacks. On 25 November 2001, the *New York Times* cited a senior law enforcement official who said that just 10–15 of 1,200 detainees were 'suspected' al-Qaeda sympathizers. Some eight months after their detention, the Justice Department still had not identified the remaining detainees. A department spokesman said only that fewer than 400 were still in custody – 74 for immigration violations, 100 who had been criminally charged, 24 held as material witnesses and 175 'awaiting' (sic). They had all been denied legal counsel, access to their families, and details of pending charges, if any. As many have noted this action, taken under the *Patriot Act's* provisions for mandatory detention contravened the Fifth Amendment to the USA Constitution guaranteeing due process of law (Banks and Rudovsky 2011). By denying non-citizens the opportunity for meaningful review of the certification decision, and by authorizing the detention of aliens on substantively inadequate grounds, the *Patriot Act* abrogated both the procedural and substantive aspects of the due process principle afforded by the Fifth Amendment to aliens. The *Patriot Act* vested responsibility in the Secretary of State and US Attorney General to continually redefine what constituted an act of terrorism. It suspended *habeas corpus* and seemed to render protests and other acts of public dissent liable to fall under the definition of terrorism (Congress of the United States of America 2001). The 'Patriot Act II' went further, creating fifteen new crimes attracting the death penalty for acts that intentionally or unintentionally cause death, and declaring martial law.

There can be little doubt that, since 2001, the American state has amplified its classification of people and groups it deems to be extremists or even terrorists. American citizens in their entirety were deeply affected by the *Patriot Act*, though few knew this at the time.

In 2004, the Bush administration gave authorization to the FBI and CIA to 'prevent, preempt, and disrupt terrorist threats' against the US in the 'Further Strengthening Federal Bureau of Investigation Capabilities' memorandum (Greenberg 2011). Empowered to carry out surveillance these federal agencies investigated the ACLU, the American-Arab Anti-Discrimination Committee and United for Peace and Justice. Additionally, in 2005, the *New York Times* reported that the FBI was also surveilling larger, more mainstream organizations such as Greenpeace, the Catholic Worker Movement and People for the Ethical Treatment of Animals (PETA) (Amster 2006). These were all groups including anti-war coalitions, social justice organizations and environmental and animal rights groups, all avowedly peaceful.

The US government, relying on assistance from major telecommunications carriers (including AT&T) and Internet service providers' carriers, initiated massive, illegal dragnet surveillance of the domestic communications and communications records of millions of ordinary Americans beginning in 2001. News reports in December 2005 first revealed that the National Security Agency (NSA) had been intercepting Americans' phone calls and Internet communications (Risen 2006). The full scale of these illegal operations was only revealed in a massive leak of secret government files by Edward Snowden in December 2013 (Greenwald 2014). This confirmed that the NSA was accessing full copies of everything carried along major US fibre optic cable networks. The NSA was not only collecting phone metadata from all US customers under the imprimatur of the *Patriot Act*, but was collecting and analysing the content of communications of foreigners talking to persons inside the US, without any 'probable cause' warrant. All of these surveillance activities were in violation of the privacy safeguards established by Congress and the US Constitution. In 2014–15, NGOs like *Electronic Frontier* began challenging the regime of mass electronic surveillance.

Some researchers have compared the recent levels of surveillance to the heights of the COINTELPRO era (Starr et al. 2008). The implication is that the political climate after the 9/11 attacks has enabled the FBI and agencies like the National Security Agency to engage in levels of surveillance activities that at the least equals if not exceeds the scale of surveillance last seen during Hoover's COIN-TELPRO regime. The FBI can now engage in 'preventive justice' operations as their agents infiltrate organizations in the absence of evidence of illegal activity (Starr et al. 2008: 5).

In 2002, the Joint Task Terrorism Force (JTTF) in Denver, Colorado, was found to be actively surveilling the Denver Justice and Peace Committee, the Human Bean Company, the Colorado Native American Indian Movement, and the Colorado Campaign for Middle East Peace, to name a few (Greenberg 2011). In 2004, the JTTF and the FBI began surveilling members of Food Not Bombs (FNB), a national peace group committed to providing vegan and vegetarian meals to the homeless. One young member, Sarah Bardwell, was put on twenty-four hour surveillance and was visited by FBI agents at her home for questioning. Members of FNB were surveilled from 2002 to 2004: no criminal charges for violent offenses were ever filed against them (Greenberg 2011).

In Britain too, the state has engaged in numerous and repeated exercises in keeping British citizens and groups under surveillance using agents, intercepts of communications or even covert bugging, the last activity requiring a warrant issued by the Home Secretary. It has been revealed that, since the 1960s, police Special Branch and units like the Special Demonstration Squad and the National Public Order Intelligence Unit routinely infiltrated undercover agents into a very large number of mostly left-wing and animal rights organizations locating hundreds of agents inside these groups for long periods of time (Undercover Policing Inquiry 2018b). We know this because the May government set up the Undercover Policing Inquiry in 2015, which is due to report back in 2023 (Undercover Policing Inquiry 2018a). As of April 2018, the enquiry has published the cover names of a hundred such agents and confirmed that undercover police had infiltrated groups and movements including sundry anarchist groups, Animal Liberation Front, AntiFascist Action, Big Flame, Black Power, Brixton Hunt Saboteurs, Colin Roach Center, Dissent, Earth First, Friends of Press Freedom, Globalise

Resistance, the Independent Labour Party, London Greenpeace, Young Liberals, Youth Against Racism in Europe, Vietnam Solidarity Campaign, Militant, London Animal Action, Socialist Workers Party, Red Action, International Socialists, Troops Out Movement and Reclaim the Streets.

We also know that, since the late 1990s, Britain's key intelligence agencies including MI5 and Government Communications Headquarters (GCHQ) have also engaged in mass data collection practices to collect data on millions of citizens since 1998 under Section 94 of the 1984 *Telecommunications Act*. This operation which continues in 2018 involves accessing passports, travel records, financial data, telephone calls, emails and other hidden or open sources. Sedition may no longer be a crime, but the English state continues to criminalize political dissent.

Conclusion

Criminalization of dissent often invokes the idea that the state needs to prevent crime by taking pre-emptive steps. In this chapter, I have examined the worrying tendency to go beyond the traditional and warrantable conception of crime, understood as an actual harm done by a perpetrator to a victim: in too many cases where dissent has been criminalized, nothing has actually been done. On some occasions, this idea can also involve abandoning or ignoring normal legal practices like the principle of *habeas corpus* or juridical oversight, principles designed to secure natural justice. At the same time, too many liberal scholars claim that the liberal-democratic state faces the difficult challenge of 'getting the balance right' between the freedoms that ostensibly define the liberal-democratic order and the need to ensure the safety of all – occasionally done by illiberal means.

Sarah Knuckey and her colleagues note that governments including US federal, state and local authorities are obligated by international law to uphold the rights of individuals to peacefully assemble and to seek to reform their governments. Knuckey and her colleagues add that when the American state suppressed protest and criminalized the Occupy movement, it not only violated international law, but also compromised the basic value of freedom of assembly and expression so essential for promoting democratic participation, enabling the exchange and development of grievances and reforms so as to secure positive social change (Knuckey et al. 2016: vi).The criminalization of dissent reveals the truth of the actual commitments of liberal states: security always trumps liberty.

In this respect, the criminalization of the political makes democratic activists into criminals, and suppresses the political understood as the possibility of the new. When the state criminalizes the political, this needs to be understood as a political crime where the harms done are to the defining and valuable characteristics of democracy itself. This sounds like an explanation but maybe it is only a description. Is it? In the next two chapters, I turn to the simple question invoked by the idea of legitimacy: why do we obey the state and its laws?

As we have seen, the actual commitment of liberal-democratic states like Britain or America to basic freedoms is actually threadbare and has long been that way. This opens up fundamental interpretative questions.

Notes

1 It is a matter of record that Mayor Bloomberg was the eighth wealthiest person in the US and the eleventh wealthiest person in the world with net wealth estimated in excess of $US51 billion in 2018.
2 Kunstler (2012: 993) notes that the US Supreme Court had determined that First Amendment rights were not limited to the communication of ideas through spoken or written words and has afforded First Amendment protection to 'symbolic speech', expressive conduct that conveys messages or ideas. Including expressive activities like demonstrating, marching, leafleting, flying a red flag, staging a sit-in, picketing, wearing armbands and attaching a peace symbol to an American flag. In 1968, that Court set up four tests that included that any restriction of First Amendment rights must (1) be within the constitutional power of the government to enact, (2) further an 'important or substantial government interest' (3) that interest must be 'unrelated to the suppression of free expression; and (4) the infringement 'is no greater than is essential' to further that interest.
3 While no executive or employee has ever faced criminal prosecution let alone be convicted, the US Department of Justice did pursue both Goldman Sachs and the Bank of America as part of a process that eventually saw a total of $US243 billion paid in fines by US banks led by the Bank of America ($US76 billion) and J.P. Morgan Chase ($US44 billion).
4 Those documents are available at https://cdn.muckrock.com/foia_files/2016/11/17/1192185-0_-_Occupy_Wall_Street_-_Section_7.PDF
5 This exercise relied on the delusional premise that the US had been infiltrated by hundreds if not thousands of al-Qaeda agents: not a single al-Qaeda agent was ever found in the USA. It was believed after 9/11 by 'virtually the entire American intelligence community that a second wave of even more devastating terrorist attacks on America was imminent' (Mayer 2008: 3). As Mueller and Stewart (2016:31) note, US intelligence came to imagine by 2002 that the number of trained al-Qaeda operatives in the US was between 2,000 and 5,000. The actual number, as it turns out, was zero.
6 A short list includes: the Terrorism Act 2000, the Anti-terrorism, Crime and Security Act 2001, the Criminal Justice Act, Anti-terrorism, Crime and Security Act 2003, the Civil Contingencies Act 2004, the Prevention of Terrorism Act 2005, the Terrorism Act 2006, the Counter Terrorism Act 2008, The Terrorism (United Nations Measures) Order 2009, the Terrorism Prevention and Investigation Measures Act 2011, the Protection of Freedom Act 2012 and the Counter-Terrorism and Security Act 2015.

Chapter 5

Law against liberty

Making sense of the criminalization of dissent[*]

In 1969, two Danish school teachers, Soren Hansen and Jesper Jensen (1971), wrote a book called *The Little Red Schoolbook*. It looked a bit like an advice book for teenagers, though it is actually a deeply political book. For one thing it looked a bit like the famous *Little Red Book* of *Quotations from Chairman Mao Tse-Tung* which it had become fashionable for student radicals in many Western societies to carry about during the late 1960s. However, apart from being a small format book with red covers, *The Little Red Schoolbook* had little else in common with a book produced during China's 'cultural revolution' to enforce Mao's authority and encourage political conformity. The book's Danish authors said they wanted to encourage young people to think about and challenge the prevailing authoritarianism of schools and the nature of democracy.

   The Little Red Schoolbook was and remains a classic expression of dissent directed against mindless schooling. The overall message was both anti-authoritarian and deeply liberal in a way that owes a lot to J.S. Mills' (1859) defence of liberty. The opening sentences capture the tone and point of the book: 'Grown ups do have a lot of power over you: they are real tigers. But in the long run they can never completely control you; they are paper tigers' (Hansen and Jensen 1971: 13). The big point was to remind young people that schools mostly existed 'to teach you how to obey rather than question things'. The authors said, 'you can only learn about things if you're allowed to think them out for yourself' (Hansen and Jensen 1971: 25). The authors used plain, simple language to make their political points as well as to discuss sex and drugs – briefly. Of the 230 plus pages, just twenty or so were devoted to sex (including masturbation, oral sex and contraception) and illicit drugs. These were the pages that got most of the attention. In short, it was a decidedly liberal book promoting Kant's (1784) enlightenment dictum in his great essay *What is Enlightenment?*: *sapere audere* that loosely translates as 'dare to think for yourself'. Whatever happened to that book exposed some of the basic flaws in the liberal-democratic self-portrait.

   In the years after 1969, the book was translated widely and published in many countries. The reaction in countries ostensibly committed to liberal-democratic principles was entirely symptomatic. *The Little Red Schoolbook* was branded 'obscene' and banned from sale in many countries including Switzerland, France,

Italy and New Zealand. In Australia, the leader of the Country Party, Doug Anthony, e.g. called it a 'Handbook for juvenile revolution and anarchy', while Donald MacKay, the Minister for the Navy, and a Presbyterian declared that, 'The nation was now under siege right now from moral aggression by literature drugs and psycho-political mass communication' (Mullins 2018: 498–99). The Australian Cabinet discussed the book on four occasions, before the Minister for Customs Don Chipp decided that banning the book was unwarranted (Mullins 2018: 498–99). The Literature Board of Review in the Australian state of Queensland banned the book in 1972.

In Britain, the case of *The Little Red Schoolbook* is arguably the most instructive. By the time the Director of Public Prosecutions had got the Metropolitan Police to issue a warrant to seize the book in a police raid on 31 March, 18,800 copies of a total print of 20,000 copies had already been sold, mostly to schools which had placed orders (Sutherland 1983: 11). In spite of employing John Mortimer QC to represent him, the British publisher, Richard Handyside was found to have breached the *Obscene Publications Act* 1964, because the book would 'tend to deprave and corrupt persons who are likely, having regard to all relevant circumstances, to read, see or hear the matter contained or embodied in it'.

Handyside appealed to the Inner London Quarter Sessions. That court rejected the expert evidence that the book was not obscene on the grounds that these experts had been excessively uncritical of the book and had 'been so single-minded in an extreme point of view as to warrant rejecting their evidence' (European Court of Human Rights 1976: 10). That Court also found that 'the Schoolbook was inimical to good teacher/child relationships and was subversive, not only to the authority but to the influence of the trust between children and teachers' as well as being 'completely subordinated to the development of the expression of itself by the child' (European Court of Human Rights 1976: 10). It concluded that, looked at as a whole, *The Little Red Schoolbook* did 'tend to deprave and corrupt a significant number, significant proportion, of the children likely to read it' (European Court of Human Rights 1976: 13).

Handyside then took the case of *The Little Red Schoolbook* to the European Court of Human Rights. He claimed that his right to freedom of thought, conscience and belief, as protected under Article 9 of the European Convention on Human Rights, and his right to freedom of expression under Article 10 of that Convention had been breached. Handyside's appeal was subsequently – and astonishingly – rejected by the European Court of Human Rights. It was astonishing because in its judgement the Court of Human Rights insisted first that 'freedom of expression constitutes one of the essential foundations of [a democratic] society, one of the basic conditions for its progress and for the development of every man' (European Court of Human Rights 1976: 18). It also confirmed that 'Freedom of expression … is applicable not only to "information" or "ideas" that are favourably received or regarded as inoffensive or as a matter of indifference, but also to those that offend, shock or disturb the State or any sector of the population' (European Court of Human Rights 1976: 18). However, the Court then saw fit to reject the appeal by Handyside.

For a scholar like Dinah Shelton (1999), this decision confirmed her description of the European Court of Human Rights as a conservative interpreter of human rights. The Court found that while the Convention indeed protected the right to freedom of expression including the 'freedom to hold opinions and to receive and impart information and ideas without interference by public authority and regardless of frontiers' that this was:

> ... qualified by being subject to such formalities, conditions, restrictions or penalties as are prescribed by law and are necessary in a democratic society, in the interests of national security, territorial integrity or public safety, for the prevention of disorder or crime, for the protection of health or morals, for the protection of the reputation or rights of others, for preventing the disclosure of information received in confidence, or for maintaining the authority and impartiality of the judiciary.
>
> (European Court of Human Rights 1976: 19)

In effect, the Court declared a state of exception. Rather than acknowledge that it is states everywhere including the liberal-democratic ones that are most likely to breach human rights, the Court supported the British state's drive to suppress this case of dissent as free speech. The Court found that Britain's *Public Obscenity Acts* (of 1959/1964) were legitimate under Article 10 because they were intended to 'protect the morals of a democratic society' and that the English courts acted 'reasonably, in good faith and within the limits of the margin of appreciation left to the Contracting States by Article 10' in effect legitimating the idea that the Convention left to 'each Contracting State, in the first place, the task of securing the rights and liberties it enshrines'. The Court seems to have accepted the view of the British government when it offered three reasons for treating *The Little Red School Book* as obscene. First, it was intended to undermine respect for marriage as a social institution. Second, the book passages dealing with 'intercourse and petting' did not advise exercising restraint. Finally, the undesirable effects of the book were amplified by its 'anti-authoritarian' stance and 'hostile attitude' to the teacher/child relationship, which were operating to exaggerate the tendencies likely to deprave and corrupt (European Court of Human Rights 1976: 79). Oddly the Court acknowledged that 'hard core pornography' was freely and widely available in Britain, but chose not to reflect on this. Finally, though the European Court of Human Rights concluded that the book was designed to be 'read by children and adolescents aged from twelve to eighteen', there was no consideration given to the abrogation of the rights of young people entailed by banning the book. The European Court of Human Rights simply decided 'that the Schoolbook would have pernicious effects on the morals of many of the children and adolescents who would read it'.

Thirty eight years later in July 2014 an unexpurgated edition of the book was finally allowed to be published and sold in Britain.

The Little Red Schoolbook: dissent and its criminalization

Faced with a clear choice between upholding the basic liberal idea that all ideas have a right to be expressed, however offensive to some people they might be, and the authoritarian idea that some ideas are simply too dangerous to be allowed to circulate, two British courts upheld the claim that the ideas found in *The Little Red Schoolbook* were likely to 'tend to deprave and corrupt a significant number of young people'. Adding insult to injury, the European Court of Human Rights then failed to uphold anything like the point of the *Universal Declaration of Human Rights* 1948, which recognized that sovereign states should never be allowed to define or adjudicate what is to count as a basic human right, especially when it engages controverted questions of freedom of belief or freedom of expression. In this case, those who detested *The Little Red Schoolbook* had neither truth nor any defensible conception of the good on their side: they could only appeal to various kinds of ignorance in a case about something they believed was likely to happen. This case they made vigorously in various courts. Here *in nuce* is an exemplar of the liberal-democratic state suppressing dissent in this case involving the goods made possible by freedom of expression by criminalizing it.

The Little Red Schoolbook case raises significant interpretative challenges to the self-portrait of liberal democracy. There is first the repeated claim by liberal-democratic states that they value and uphold a variety of liberal freedoms including freedom of expression, of assembly and conduct and so forth. Indeed, sometimes this goes as far as claiming a natural affinity between liberalism and democracy. Both Rawls (1993) and Habermas (1996) have claimed that liberalism is naturally compatible with democracy and even has a certain progressive, i.e. egalitarian political-economic disposition. Then there is the liberal claim of adherence to the rule of law, along with respect for and promotion of human rights. This is presumably what motivates admonitory lectures, directed at authoritarian regimes and 'rogue states' by liberal-democracies like Britain, America and Australia who say they are defending human rights and a 'rules-based international order'. This goes on despite arguments that the 'rule-based international order' has been undone repeatedly by the actions of liberal-democracies like the US acting both hegemonically and unilaterally when deciding, e.g. on illegal invasions of Afghanistan and Iraq (2001–03) (Nardin 2008: 385).[1] These claims are frequently buttressed by appealing to a rich tradition of philosophical liberalism.

Against this highly respectable and redoubtably normative narrative, what we actually see in the case of *The Little Red Schoolbook* in Britain is a commitment to suppressing books and ideas that some people don't like, and more generally persistent moves by liberal-democratic states to suppress dissent by using the criminal justice system.

In this particular instance, Britain's obscenity laws are remarkably like the way the criminalization process works when suppressing other kinds of dissent like 'sedition', 'terrorism' or 'public-order' offences. Like those cases, the British state decided to criminalize the publication of a clearly political text by reconstituting it as 'obscene literature' and did so by adopting a 'preventive' approach. In the case of *The Little Red Schoolbook*, the use of words like 'deprave and corrupt' did not refer to some real effect *arising from* the reading of the publication. The logic of preventive justice does not rest on something having actually happened, nor does the kind of law instituted in preventive justice require that evidence of any actual harm like the moral collapse or degradation of a young person (let alone a 'man's wife or even his servant' be presented for the law prohibiting obscene publications to be invoked. Rather the legislation was intended to refer to materials that *might* 'tend to deprave or corrupt' by, e.g. causing the reader to have 'immoral thoughts'. One attempt by a court to say what the harm was that reading 'immoral literature' might cause could only conclude that the tendency to 'deprave and corrupt' could take various forms, whether it was to 'induce erotic desires of a heterosexual kind, or to promote homosexuality or other sexual perversions or drug-taking or brutal violence' (cited Davidow and O'Boyle 1977: 272). Quite what this is supposed to mean is completely unclear.

After surveying many attempts by judges or policy-makers to clarify what the 'tendency to deprave or corrupt' might mean, Robert Davidow and Michael O'Boyle (1977) concluded that the personal characteristics of the 'ultimate reader are functionally unimportant'. In effect, although the allegedly obscene material has to have a particular tendency relating to the mind of the reader, its harmful qualities can apparently be inferred directly from the nature of the item itself, i.e. its harmful qualities are apparently self-evident. In effect, there is no need for objective evidence of any actual harmful effects 'following from exposure to the allegedly prohibited material' (Davidow and O'Boyle 1977: 272). As Stephen Gillers adds:

> … nothing in [Justice] Cockburn's [single sentence] test for obscenity can pass for legal reasoning, or any other kind of reasoning. Its single sentence seems tossed off. It offers no authority, no analysis, no awareness of the breadth of its declamation.
>
> (Gillers 2007: 220)

Gillers then adds the important observation that criminalizing creative and dissenting literature has a 'chilling effect' on creative work of all kinds. 'The publication of other books, e.g. by Dreiser, Lawrence, and Miller, among others – was delayed or denied, 'plays were not produced. Art was suppressed' and we will never know what was suppressed' (Gillers 2007: 221). The use of the criminal law to define, prohibit and punish books containing dissenting views, or unpopular ideas (at least with some people) is somehow disproportionate or inappropriate especially when then there is no need on the part of the state to make an evidence-based case about the alleged harms such as publication is said to be likely to encourage.

The abuse of the criminal law that took place when Britain's obscenity legislation assumed the legitimacy of a preventive logic has if anything been substantially magnified since 9/11. This is because many liberal-democratic states became obsessed with terrorism, while the explosion of popular protest since the Great Recession of 2008 triggered a heavy-handed response by security and policing agencies. The result has been a security project based on a dragnet to trap people and organizations into an ever-more expansive basket of extremism and terrorism. This requires some kind of sense-making.

In this chapter, I address just two questions. How has the criminalization of dissent been explained and understood so far especially by those working in the field of criminalization studies? What would a relational perspective look like when making sense of a case like The Little Red Schoolbook? To pursue these questions, start by considering how the criminalization process has evolved.

Criminalization studies

Defining certain kinds of human activity as a 'crime' is the product of a process that we can provisionally call 'criminalization'. In a general sense, much of the history of disciplines like sociology and criminology when they engaged with crime were in effect studies of criminalization. I am more interested here in the small but interesting body of work that constitutes a more narrowly defined field of criminalization studies.

Criminalization as a theoretical and research field in the sense explored here is a relatively new project, which takes the role both of the state and of a range of normative claims seriously. Defined in this narrow way, the field of criminalization studies got underway in the past few decades as an 'empirical' and a 'normative' exercise devoted to charting the extent to which governments introduce new criminal legislation. David Brown (2013) has emphasized how this field evolved as a reaction against a body of criminal law scholarship and teaching, practised as a 'heavily doctrinal approach based on elucidating the "general principles" of criminal law [and] drawn from an examination of appellate decisions in homicide, sexual assault and larceny' (Brown 2013: 606). Brown argues that those in the field of criminalization studies have developed a 'contextual, process-oriented and criminologically influenced approach that expanded the field to take in drugs offences, public order offences, criminal process, criminalization and sentencing'. This move also emphasized

> the links between substantive law and process, to focus far more on policing, pre-trial decision-making, and the lower courts, and to draw heavily on socio-legal, criminal justice and criminological materials; in short, to develop a criminologically literate criminal law scholarship, teaching and practice.
>
> (Brown 2013: 606)

As Brown also noted, a key element in the evolution of criminalization studies has been the 'commitment to an analysis of the processes of criminalization prior to any examination of specific offence areas' (Brown 2013: 606). However, Nicola Lacey (2009: 937) points to the work of Douglas Husak (2008), whose account of drug criminalization and its consequences sponsored 'something of a renaissance [of interest in criminalisation] as an object of theoretical interest'. Scholars like Ashworth (2009), Lacey (2009, 2012, 2012a); Duff (2007), Husak (2008) and Zedner 2007) and (Brown et al. 2011: 41–114) have developed a complex account of criminalization. This involves highlighting the historical and cultural 'contingency' of crime, the role of criteria including morality, harm, offensiveness and the 'public/private' distinction as well as social processes like Stan Cohen's (1972) account of 'moral panics', the 'overreach' of the criminal law and the increasing importance of various forms of regulation and governmentality which drew on Foucault's work.

This brief account might imply that the field itself is relatively well-bounded and conceptually clear. This is implied when, e.g. Crofts and Loughnan say that criminalization refers 'to the scope of the criminal law' as well as to identifying 'the basis upon which decisions are made to regulate behaviour through the criminal law' (2015: 1–2). However, this does not mean that it is now a coherent or consensus view about how those involved in criminalization studies ought to study criminalization or indeed what it is that criminalization studies study. Lacey argues, e.g. that the field of criminalization studies does not have any consensus about let alone the conceptual tools and the empirical knowledge which are needed to underpin even the initial assertion about over-criminalization which motivates much of the current scholarly renaissance (Lacey 2009: 941).

There are some quite sharp methodological tensions at work in criminalization studies. These include what Lacey (2004) has highlighted as competing approaches to 'criminal law theory', i.e. 'the philosophy of the criminal law' versus critical theory (Lacey 2004). Lacey takes work by Anthony Duff (e.g. Duff 1998; Duff and Green 2011) as an example of the 'philosophy of criminal law' approach, which emphasizes the rational and 'principled nature of criminal law'. Critical theory, in contrast, represented by scholars like Alan Norrie (2009, 2014) and Henrique Carvalho (2017; also Norrie and Carvalho 2017), questions the assumptions made by those who work with the 'philosophy of criminal law' approach about 'rationality, coherence and systematicity as features of and ideals for both theory itself and criminal law doctrine' (Lacey 2004: 10).

We get some more insight into the problem here when Duff et al. (2014: 2–3) point out that one of the main obstacles to their pursuing the construction of a theoretical 'account of the principles and values that should guide decisions about what to criminalize and how to define offences' was that he and his colleagues could not agree either 'on the structure or the content of such a theory'. As they note, that problem began when they could not even agree about which institutions and practices to include in the study of criminalization. Yet while the major problems they enumerate certainly point to the immense complexity of the sheer range of institutional practices and processes which are to be understood as constituting the criminalization process, there were other, no less basic problems. The institutional complexity concludes: (i) the respective weight to be given to the making of criminal statutes versus non-statutory common law; (ii) the role played by law-enforcement practices involving police, tax inspectors and prosecutors and (iii) the difficulty of treating the criminal law as an isolated institution when it is bound up in the overall institutional structure of the law (this goes to the contrast between 'real' (*mala in se*) criminal law and 'regulatory'.

However, a critical legal theorist, Russell Hogg, has gone some way to resolving that problem when he remarked that there is little point reconstructing the criminal justice system as if it were the product of a philosophy seminar. As he says, 'crime is not external to the practices of criminal justice: we are only enabled to know it through these practices' (Hogg 1983: 9). In one sense, it is this idea that has sustained a research project which sets out to trace the introduction of new legislation as an index of (over)criminalization. This approach has prompted, in turn, an important recent intervention by Luke McNamara and his colleagues (2018). They say there is nothing inherently problematic about asking whether the 'creation of a [new] criminal offence is a sound public policy choice'. Equally, as they rightly insist, 'and against the tendency to equate criminalization with the introduction of new legislation, the creation of new offences is not synonymous with criminalization' (McNamara et al. 2018: 92). I adopted this suggestion in the previous chapter when I bypassed the conventional tendency in criminalization studies to focus heavily, if not exclusively, on the creation of criminal offences and penalty increases, and instead to try to catch the variety of 'criminalization modalities'. Simply put, there are many ways states criminalize conduct, a point highlighted in the previous chapter when I pointed to the modes of suppression that criminalizing dissent can take.

McNamara et al. (2018: 93) make this point about the entirety of the criminal justice system and the variety of forms that criminalization can take. This includes:

> ... the creation and enforcement of offences (and defences) and the setting and imposition of penalties, but also statutes that underpin the operation of allied criminal procedures and the deployment of police powers which can also have coercive and punitive effects (such as a denial of bail resulting in detention on remand). We extend the concept further to legislation concerned with technical arrangements regarding the conduct of criminal trials – such as allowing a sexual assault complainant to give evidence via video link – on the basis that such arrangements are designed to both reduce the risk of further trauma for crime victims and optimise the system's capacity to attribute criminal liability to offenders.

Of special interest are those cases where states expand the criminalization project. As McNamara et al. (2018: 93) point out, this points to cases involving increased punitiveness such as when new offences are created, maximum penalties for existing offences are increased or sentencing regimes are mandated. This is a good start for rethinking the general process of criminalization even though the empirical research process this framework is supporting relies on a conventional set of substantialist assumptions. Equally while this kind of descriptivist approach to mapping the criminalization process is not a major problem, it becomes far more problematic when people start to try to explain *why* criminalization takes the forms it does. This is because any attempt to explain this project cannot avoid engaging with the deep problem at the heart of the criminalization process. That problem simply put is: what is the object of criminalization?

The problem is that the category essential to any discussion of 'legitimacy' and the 'criminal law', i.e. 'crime' itself is neither a 'natural' nor self-evident object. In terms that Ian Hacking (1998) has understood, the criminalization process has the odd effect of creating or constituting the object (i.e. a 'crime') that it then wishes to criminalize. This as I have already shown is problematic when states decide to criminalize dissent.

This thought will not have occurred to many people though it is probably not a problem for many people. Many people doubtless think what the category 'crime' denominates is in Hacking's terms an 'object' that is so 'obvious' that they do not need to think twice about it. Many social scientists agree and have taken the commonsense view that 'of course' crime is real. Wilson and Herrnstein (1985), two well-known conservative criminologists, argued, e.g. that certain activities like homicide, incest, rape, theft and robbery are intrinsically or 'naturally' criminal because all are intrinsically and universally evil, and all are 'condemned in all societies, and in all historical periods, by ancient tradition, moral sentiments and formal law' (Wilson and Herrnstein 1985: 22). Yet historical and anthropological research flatly contradicts this claim. As Wilkins (1965: 46) noted, 'at some time or another, some form of society or another has defined almost all forms of behaviour that we now call criminal as desirable for the functioning of that form of society'.

The uncomfortable fact is that 'crime' is neither obvious, nor objective, nor simple. As David Garland (2009: 118) put it, the problem is that 'criminology's object is not a self-generated theoretical entity or a naturally-occurring phenomenon but instead *a state-defined social problem*' (My stress). There is no privileged, neutral or objective basis for 'defining' 'crime' other than in the terms that states themselves do when they set about criminalizing certain kinds of conduct. Nicola Lacey makes this point too:

> [T]heories of criminal law whether written by or for philosophers or lawyers, are inevitably interpretations of social practices whose practitioners themselves have interpretations *which are an object of the theorization*. The implication is that 'at large' philosophizing which is not addressed to any particular system or practice of criminal law, is, like a map of imaginary terrain, not an exercise in criminal law theory but rather an exercise in philosophizing itself.
> (Lacey 2004: 16). (My stress)

This problem immanent in the very idea or category of 'crime' itself haunts legal studies and legal philosophy, as well as cognate disciplines like criminology, political science and sociology: it points to a basic puzzle found in the relationship between the state as legal arbiter and the legitimacy of that activity. It also highlights the power of the state to define disagreement, which is ubiquitous into dissent.

The reference to legitimacy is typically addressed in the field of criminalization studies in terms of some kind of 'normative' analysis, which some seem to think explains why states criminalize certain conduct referred to, e.g. as 'dissent'. Brown, e.g. asks how do we answer a simple question like why do states criminalize some conduct – and not others? As Brown says:

> It is not self-evident that the answer is a normative approach based on the declared function of criminal law being 'the protection of legal goods/interests', a function that then provides both a guide to statutory interpretation and a limiting principle restricting any criminalization beyond the limits of this principle. This is no more self-evident than a criminologically influenced approach, which describes and unpacks the institutional and political conditions of the existence of the processes and outcomes of criminalization, with a view to arguing in normative fashion how those conditions of existence might be changed to promote specified normative principles.
>
> (Brown 2013: 611)

The reference to 'normative' here when it is used in criminalization studies is generally narrowly construed. As Lacey (2009) notes, the normative elements have chiefly involved discussion initiated by legal philosophers like H.L.A. Hart, Michael Moore and Joel Feinberg who discuss the role played by 'ethical traditions like Benthamite unrestricted utilitarianism' or the constrained utilitarianism represented by J. S. Mill's 'harm principle' or the legal moralism epitomized by James Fitzjames Stephen. In particular and with the criminalization of dissent in mind, what do those normative principles look like and on what basis do these principles claim legitimacy, especially given the way in which this process seems to be so much at odds with basic liberal principles to say nothing of the conventions about criminal law itself? However, David Brown has opened up some other fundamental questions, when he says that it is not self-evident that there are normative principles at stake when a state criminalizes certain conduct which is then driving the process. If normative principles are not shaping the criminalization process, what if anything explains the process?

Against the disposition to privilege a certain (structural) rationality at work in these interpretative schema, we need to acknowledge first a substantial degree of incoherence even irrationality at work in the 'punitive turn'. Pat Carlen (2010) has talked about a 'penal imaginary' sustaining 'risk crazed governance'. This, in turn, points to a more complex and not necessarily rational relationship between liberalism, fear and security. What I offer is not an explanatory theory so much as a relatively simple relational heuristic. This draws on Ian Hacking's (1998, 2001) 'historical ontological' account of how social phenomena (in his case 'mad walkers' and here *The Little Red Schoolbook)* occur in what he calls an 'ecological niche'. This points to the need to treat the modern liberal-democratic state as 'the unity of difference between consent and dissent, and fear and security'.

Explaining criminalization 'risk crazed governance'

Thinking about what has been happening in the criminal justice systems of countries like Australia Britain and America has led Pat Carlen to describe it as a kind of penal imaginary characterized by 'risk crazed governance' (Carlen 2008: 1). By an 'imaginary penality', Carlen points to an essentially irrational discourse (based on a narrative about an 'epidemic of crime spiralling out of control') that has, in turn, become a deranged reality (involving, e.g. the increasing use of prisons tasked with objectives they can never achieve), while those inside the criminal justice system know that the policies they are required to enforce have no chance of working.

Carlen recalls that she first saw this when she interviewed staff in a new Australian prison officially committed to therapeutic rehabilitation just months after it had opened. She found that not one of the staff interviewed would say that the rehabilitation objectives were being met, and none could see any possibility of them ever being met in the future. They were well aware why this was so. For one thing while the new prison had been designed for *sentenced prisoners*, the prison population was made up mostly of *people on remand.* For another, the therapeutic programmes had not been accredited and could not be used in the prison. At the same time, the prisons were part of an 'audit culture' and were expected to provide evidence that the system and its policies were oriented to rehabilitation. The managers charged with the development and/ or implementation of the policy kept on manufacturing an elaborate system of costly institutional practices captured in 'as-if' data. Those managers recognized that the whole system is nothing but smoke and mirrors that can quickly be revealed as imaginary.

The whole criminal justice system becomes a prime example of the power of what she calls a penal imaginary to promote acquiescence in the absurd. The imagined or 'as-if' penality comes to define a criminal justice system when governments try to meet popular demands for tougher, more punitive sentencing at the same time as trying both to justify the increases in imprisonment by promising in-prison programmes directed at recidivism reduction, while also cutting budgets and staff resources. The imaginary serves to cover up the contradictions between the demands of governance and the capacity or willingness of governments to meet those demands even as it serves to exaggerate the contradictions!

Liberalism and security

Another complementary way to highlight the irrational impulses at work in the modern criminalization process is to poke around in the actual mess of contradictory political beliefs or imaginaries found in any contemporary state. While there is a strong case for treating many contemporary political parties and governments as 'neoliberal' and to take the self-portrait of societies like Australia, Britain, Canada, New Zealand and America to talk about 'liberal-democracy' somewhat seriously, this does not imply that modern states have actually embraced a singular or coherent 'ideology' that can be referred to as 'neoliberal', 'liberal-democratic' (or 'New Right', 'Third Way', 'social-democratic' or 'Alt-right' for that matter), and let alone as we have seen that they have consistently set about doing as they say.

There are several considerations that highlight the different kinds and degrees of irrationality at play. First, there is the irrationality occasioned by a patchwork-quilt pattern of agencies found in any state that have 'growed like Topsy'. We need to avoid the tendency seen on the part of many writers who treat 'the state' as a unitary entity possessing a single vision of things or possessing a unitary will or intention to act in a clear and specific and singular fashion and making policy 'as if' 'it' were just like a person. Any close attention to real governments and policy-making shows it to be at best, a messy, unstructured process involving multiple agencies, uncertain information, conflicting expert advice and many unforeseen consequences. In the case of justice policies, there is a crazy-quilt pattern of law-making agencies like parliaments or a Congress, policy-making departments and numerous law-enforcement institutions, a pattern which gets immeasurably more complex in federated states like the US and Australia.

Take the idea that, in a liberal democracy, constitutional authority, and therefore the legitimacy of the liberal-democratic state, depends ultimately both on the democratic idea of 'popular sovereignty' or on some relation to 'we, the people' *and* on the commitment to the rule of law. The power of the hyphen linking 'liberal-democracy' does not mean that the deep contradictions at work between liberalism and democracy have somehow disappeared. Second, we need to acknowledge that the very idea of 'the people' at stake has been and continues to change over the past two centuries because of persistent dissent and changeful advocacy by worker's movements, women's movements, anti-colonial movements, youth movements, anti-racial and other movements. This persistent agitation for basic democratic and civil rights like the right to vote itself or the right to unionize, to receive equal pay for equal work, to be accorded basic dignity irrespective of skin colour, gender, ability, age or sexuality or simply the struggle to have a right to have rights as Arendt (1951) put it, has involved a contested struggle for equality, recognition and what Castoriadis (1993) calls 'effective autonomy'. It also often enough involved bypassing or challenging the law as it stood at the time.

There is here an immanent relational dynamic at work here implicating conflict, solidarity, and co-operation centring around a central contradiction linking fear and freedom. In each case, be it worker's movements, women's movements, anti-colonial movements, youth movements, anti-racial and other movements, the struggle for equality, recognition and 'effective autonomy' has typically invoked fear, itself a moral emotion which can be either deeply rational or deeply irrational. That, of course, cannot be admitted by many working in the modern security state. That is why the usual way of talking about this is to talk about the need to 'balance security and freedom'.

Security and freedom: towards a relational perspective

Defining 'politics', 'dissent' or 'criminalization' or trying to construct some ideal-type of categories like these is neither possible nor desirable. As Ian Shapiro says in his discussion of 'domination', the number of exceptions and fuzzy boundaries involved in making sense of a relational matter like 'domination' as if it were a thing makes the search for watertight definitions not only a fruitless exercise but also a misleading one (Shapiro 2016: 50). Acknowledging that 'politics', 'dissent' or 'criminalization' is a highly contingent relation of praxis/practice, while eschewing bounded definitions and categories as if they are things, requires that we rethink the way we observe and think them so as to avoid being either wrong-headed or useless. So how should we approach the practice of criminalization?

Michael Wilkinson (2018: 10) argues, the state is neither an 'inert container, nor an abstract idea of reason'. Taking a relational view Wolfgang Streeck, who like Wilkinson is interested in the relations between liberal-democratic states and capitalist economies suggests, we should treat the modern neoliberal state as 'the unity of difference between the political and economic' (Streeck 2013: 8). To that, I would add we should also treat the modern liberal-democratic state as 'the unity of difference between fear and freedom'. This formulation is adopted to highlight the deep deceit at work in the utterly conventional formulation that modern liberal-democratic states need to balance 'the need for security with the desire for freedom'.

This the very formulation adopted in a symptomatic text by Ronald Collins and Sam Chaltain (2011: 1). As they put it in terms repeated *ad nauseum* over the past few decades by so many other commentators:

> September 11 challenged our convictions. It defied our resolve for freedom, that dedication to let liberty be the default position in life and law…Times of crisis … pit the need to defend our security against the desire to defend our liberty.
>
> (Collins and Chaltain 2011: 1)

Without for a moment downplaying the horror of the attacks in New York and Washington in September 2001, we need to be clear that the level of fear mobilized in the days and months after those attacks was never proportionate to what had happened, nor were the policing responses that ensued, including the armed invasion of Afghanistan and Iraq, countries whose governments had little to nothing to do with those attacks but that had utterly catastrophic responses creating harm on an unimaginable scale. As John Mueller and Mark Stewart (2012) make clear, the 9/11 attacks were carried out by a tiny group of deluded members of al-Qaeda, 'a fringe group of a fringe group with grandiose visions of its own importance' who managed largely because of luck, to 'pull off a carefully planned risk-laden terrorist act' that became 'by far the most destructive in history' (Mueller and Stewart 2012: 82: also 2016). The American security state insisted that more such attacks were imminent, because of the presence of dozens perhaps hundreds of al-Qaeda agents in the US. None of this was true. As Glenn Carle, the former deputy intelligence officer for transnational threats in the Central Intelligence Agency, said, Americans would become 'victims of delusion', displaying a quality defined as 'a persistent false belief in the face of strong contradictory evidence' (Carle 298–99).

Further and apart from the way Collins and Chaltain conveniently ignore the persistent evidence that this so-called 'default position' has never actually held much sway in the security and police apparatus of the American state (or other similar states), the language is a dead giveaway: the reference to the 'need for security' is pitted against the desire for freedom: the implication is that 'needs' are real and desires are fantasy. Let me suggest a simple inversion: security is the desire even delusion for all sorts of reasons, and the need for freedom is real.

A relational perspective helps to elucidate why the exercises that promote the criminalization of dissent take place. Two relationships stand out: the relation between fear and security and the relational practices occurring in a certain kind of relational space Ian Hacking (1998) calls an 'ecological niche' or what Bourdieu would call a 'field of action'.

Fear and security: an intimate relation

Roger Mathews says we do need to ask why 'neoliberal' governments have taken the 'punitive turn' involving a torrent of new laws that expand the number of crimes that can be committed as well as criminalizing dissent and locking up minor offenders and large numbers of people with mental health issues (Matthews 2005: 187). It becomes clear that this has little to do with neoliberalism *per se* or that it can be understood as a rational response to a real problem.

It is impossible to ignore the way fear has become a central aspect of the public world and popular perceptions. Frank Furedi has made the point that mobilizing fear has long played a key role in both collective and political life especially in liberal-democratic societies (1997; 2005). Though he is concerned only with economic matters within the European Union, Michael Wilkinson catches the larger point to be made about modern liberal-democracies when he says, 'The harnessing of fear can be captured in the new identification of a Schmittian enemy, not external and physical, but rather internal and *ideological*' (Wilkinson 2018: 5). The years since 2001 have seen liberal-democratic states mobilize and harness first a fear of terrorism, and then after 2008 a 'fear' of economic crisis, the latter associated less with the criminal malfeasance of global financial institutions and much more with the possibility that states will not adopt the appropriate 'austerity' measures deemed necessary by the IMF, the World Bank, the OECD, the European Central Bank and so forth. Here the 'internal enemies' include young people as student activists, immigrants as criminals or putative radicals of all kinds including 'Islamist terrorists' and activists associated with all sorts of dissenting social movements of all sorts.[2] This has led some like Mathews to refer to a 'strand of New Right thinking', while Williamson (2018) prefers to call it 'authoritarian liberalism'.

Fear is both a powerful and often a deeply irrational motivation, although it can on occasion be a deeply rational moral emotion. Faced with a speeding rail locomotive rapidly looming up at us as we pause at a rail crossing and wondering whether to cross in its path or not is hopefully a moment when a *frisson* of fear causes us to defer our impulse to do something dangerous. Equally a mass media mobilized generalized fear about 'black people', Jews, immigrants or young Muslims when we may not even know these 'kinds' of people but are persuaded that they pose an existential threat to our lives, safety or well-being are much more likely to be deeply irrational and possibly even to have persistent historical antecedents grounded in prejudices like racism, anti-Semitism or ageism.

It is precisely this kind of fear that regulates the beating of the living heart of our contemporary preoccupation with security. As Michael Ignatieff (1997) reminds us as so many cases of war, genocide and ethnic cleansing in the past century or so involving political regimes of all sorts attest fear is so easily mobilized and harnessed. This is especially the case as he says apropos the ethnic cleansing set loose in the former Yugoslavia in the 1990s, when politicians and the mass media can leverage what Freud called the 'narcissism of minor differences' into a fear that then turns genocidal. I argue that fear sits at the fulcrum when any modern liberal-democratic state is also a security state.

This is to be understood adapting Streeck's (2013) formulation, that the modern liberal-democratic state *is the unity of difference between fear and freedom*. Fear cannot be rendered all that visible: it needs to be transformed into security. To say publicly that 'I am afraid of X' or that we ought to be afraid of x is to expose ourselves to criticisms of cowardice or irrationality. Far better to claim the mantle of being the protector of our security and upholding the great principle proclaimed especially by conservatives and military and security agencies the world over, that the fundamental moral obligation of statesmen and states is to promote the security of the people. Yet to understand what this means and how it works we need to think relationally. We can only understand the criminalization of dissent, as we need to do more generally when thinking politically, relationally. The practices of criminalizing dissent when enacted by liberal-democratic states are grounded in the irrational unity of difference between freedom and fear/security. The 'punitive turn' like the proliferation of counter-terrorism measures and programmes signifies the privileging of 'security'. The criminalization of dissent as criminal reflects the privileging of 'security'. Let me work through this formulation.

(In)security

Security has become the major political cliché of our time linking politicians and parties of all persuasions sometimes silently, often noisily under a tough on law n' order umbrella when terrorism and/or epidemics of crime are invoked. Security involves a relationship with evokes care or worry in us. Etymologically, the word comes to us from the Latin 'se' (without) and 'cura' (care) giving us 'free from care'.[3] Yet as writers like James de Derian (1998) have noticed, one person's security is usually obtained at the cost of increasing someone else's insecurity. 'Security' is a relation and is intimately connected to what it is not, 'insecurity'. All security is defined in relation to insecurity. Hobbes the great, if equivocal liberal whose account of the state is a leviathan, understood that state power exists to pursue security. Not only must any appeal to security involve a specification of the fear which engenders it (as in Hobbes), but this fear (insecurity) demands the counter-measures (security) to neutralize, eliminate or constrain the person, group, object or condition which engenders fear. Securing is therefore what is done to a condition that is insecure. It is only because it is shaped by insecurity that security can secure. This is what Der Derian (1998) describes as the *paradox of security*: 'in security we find insecurity'.

Here, we see the point of the fabulous, indeed mythic invocation of the idea that liberal democracies always have to balance off freedom and security. As Mark Neocleous (2008) argues, we see in (neo)liberalism a deep affinity between the apparent commitment to freedom and the seemingly contradictory commitment to measures designed to promote security that are deeply antagonistic to freedom. The freedom/security antimony is the fault-line that runs deep through liberalism and produces typical patterns of 'crazed governance' (Carlen 2008).

Neocleous reminds us that in 1994 the United Nations *Human Development Report* encouraged 'a new concept of human security' much broader than the older, narrow idea of security focussed on military and territorial issues. The *Report* invited the citizens of the world to move 'from nuclear security to human security' incorporating 'universal' concerns within several broad categories: economic security, food security, health security, environmental security, personal security, community security and political security. Leading New Labour ideologues argued that British social democrats were committed to security for all. Leadbetter argued that at the heart of social democracy is the one economic feature specifically and unashamedly ruled out by the resurgent free market: security. Charles Leadbetter says that 'social democracy offers nothing if it does not offer security' (Leadbetter 1999: 157). Yet Neocleous also reminds us of the deep affinity between the ostensible preoccupation with freedom or liberty in the emergent liberal tradition that begins in the eighteenth century and the far darker interest in security.

Neocleous argues that, by the eighteenth century, the category of security had already developed an intensely political meaning focussed on the state. As with many concepts in this period – such as 'interest', 'independence' and 'security', these ideas underwent a semantic shift while being understood in highly positive ways. Neocleous says that eighteenth-century liberals treated security and liberty as more or less synonymous. Adam Smith, e.g. refers to the 'liberty' and 'security' of individuals as if they were coterminous (Smith 1979: 405, 412, 540). In the 1780s, Bentham suggests that 'a clear idea of liberty will lead us to regard it as a branch of security' (Bentham 1843: 302).

This identification of liberty with security should be understood as a specifically liberal idea of 'security'. For liberals, 'liberty' designated a range of activities which occurred *outside* the political realm shaped by the state. In stark contrast to the state-centred approach embodied in Britain's *Act of Security* 1704 and later revived by the American state in legislation like the 1947 *National Security Act,* as security became the decisive criterion of liberty it came to imply the security of an undisturbed development of the economic lives of citizens. In other words, 'security' for liberalism came to refer to the liberty of secure possession; the liberty, in short of private property. Adam Smith makes plain that government exists 'for the security of property', presenting us with a triad of concepts which are run so closely together that they are almost conflated: 'liberty, security, property' (Smith 1979: 710, 944). It is symptomatic of this shift that by 1861, J.S. Mill could declare that security is 'the most vital of all interests' and that 'security of person and property ... are the first needs of society' (Mill 1859/1998: 355). As Neocleous says:

> Security became the cornerstone of the liberal bourgeois mind. Liberalism's radical recoding of the politics of order in the eighteenth century turned politics into a range of 'security measures' consistent with liberal principles. The concept of security thus became the ideological guarantee of the independent and self-interested pursuit of property within bourgeois society – the guarantee of the egoism of civil society. In doing so, security became *the supreme concept of bourgeois society.*

The preoccupation with security encourages fear of the those who threaten 'our' security be it the 'poor', the unemployed, immigrants, Muslims, young people or coloured people in predominantly white or post-colonial societies. The idea of security becomes one of the principal ideological preoccupations upheld as a distinctly liberal idea one designed to defend the unequal property relations and wealth constituting any society with a capitalist market economy. This is where the specific character of a society like America which has a long dark history of slavery and white racism intersects with the liberal conflation of liberty and security in which 'my' liberty and security is secured by 'your' un-freedom and insecurity.

In the name of promoting security, neoliberal regimes have no problem in 'excluding' those who fail in the marketplace or those who fail to abide by the law – in the latter case typically by means of imprisonment. In one sense, this is no coincidence. Both types of exclusion are associated with the highly liberal *individualistic* social ethos associated with and cultivated by neoliberalism while conversely this kind of competitive economy fosters the belief that individuals are ought to be responsible for looking after themselves.

As is now abundantly clear, the growth of surveillance is now being driven by the preoccupation with security. In the US, it is now known that *at least* 1.2 million Americans have been under surveillance as a potential terrorist threat or a terrorist suspect (Lyon 2015: 5). Since 2015 and post-Snowden, the US Congress passed the USA FREEDOM Act codifying a requirement to publicly report many of the statistics already reported in the *Annual Statistical Transparency Report.* These reports reveal that some 1,437 court orders were granted on some 1337 'suspects' of whom 299 were US citizens (Office of the Director of National Intelligence 2018: 8). More worrying were the numbers of Call Detail Records of mobile phone calls made by American citizens received from Telco providers like Verizon and stored in NSA repositories. In 2016, this amounted to 151.2 million records and in 2017, 534.3 million records (Office of the Director of National Intelligence 2018: 31). (These records of telecom metadata logging identify who contacts whom and when, but not the contents of what they said.) It may also be unsurprising to know following Snowden's revelations contained in a trove of some 58,000 NSA documents handed over to media outlets that the leaders of countries understood to be allies of America like Germany and Brazil have been placed under NSA surveillance or that NSA has routinely hacked into national security agencies of 'friendly countries like the Netherlands' (Lyon 2015: 6).

The strange and unsteady relationship between security and freedom explored here however also needs to be grounded in a far more specific way. We need more than a gestural claim that says we now have a 'security state' preoccupied with security. We need a more specific account of how ubiquitous disagreement becomes specific forms of dissent, warranting its treatment and suppression by or through the criminal justice system. This is very much a relational process. What is needed is a kind of heuristic able to foreground the way certain relational practices occur in and, in effect, constitute specific kinds of relational space that have the capacity to convert disagreement into dissent before then subjecting those engaged in these practices to suppression and criminalization. I offer a relational heuristic based on the idea of an 'ecological niche' first outlined by Ian Hacking (1998).

Ecology of dissent and its criminalization: the case of 'mad travellers'

Hacking (1998) provides a detailed historically inflected account of how a 'mental illness' he calls 'mad travelers disease', and once referred to as 'fugueurs' or 'ambulatory autonomisme' were 'discovered' in France in 1886, before the 'illness' spread to Germany, Italy, and Russia in something like epidemic proportions, before it disappeared completely by the 1920s. Hacking's work is part of his larger project designed to understand 'the interactions between what there is (and what comes into being) and our conceptions of it' or what he calls 'historical ontology'

(Hacking 2001: 2). Courtesy of this 'historical ontology', Hacking says he is able to talk:

> ... about objects in general. Not just things, but whatever we individuate and allow ourselves to talk about. That includes not only 'material' objects but also classes, kinds of people, and, indeed, ideas.
>
> (Hacking 2001: 2)

While Hacking documents an outbreak of compulsive traveling (with amnesia or 'fugue') in France in the late nineteenth century, in order 'to provide a framework in which to understand the very possibility of transient mental illnesses' (1998: 1), I think his heuristic is more broadly applicable, including, to the problem of dissent and its criminalization. To be clear, this is not a theoretical explanation. Rather it says that if you look at particular cases of criminalizing dissent, it might prove useful to look for the 'vectors' as Hacking calls them that are at work.

Hacking argues that 'mad travelers disease' was 'real' in a number of important respects that merit the use of an intellectual framework he calls 'historical ontology'. However, to be clear we should not treat what we call 'mental illness' like 'mad travelers' as real thing-like entities enabling or requiring definitions, diagnosis and treatment. Hacking's is a non-relativist, social constructivist account of a world where some 'things' really exist irrespective of whether we know them or not, alongside what he calls 'artificial phenomena' that come into being because we engage in certain practices involving knowings and doings.[4] Hacking also offers a relational account of the processes grounded in the practices of knowing, ethical deliberation and the usages of power.

Hacking channels Foucault when he says his 'historical ontology' enables us to know the ways 'through which we constitute ourselves as objects of knowledge', because we have the power to 'constitute ourselves as subjects acting on others', and do this cognisant of the 'ethics through which we constitute ourselves as moral agents' (Foucault 1983). What Hacking calls 'axes' of 'knowledge', 'power' and 'ethics' are what, following Bourdieu, I would rather call relations of practice. All are involved in 'all manner of constitutings' as we bring ideas, types of people, institutions and practices *into being* and do this historically (Hacking 2001: 4).[5] Hacking's account of how 'mad travellers' came into being depends on his developing a relational heuristic.

The value of this lies in helping us to foreground the ways in which certain relational practices occurring in a relational space he calls an 'ecological niche' or what Bourdieu calls a 'field of action' allow what comes into being as a mental illness and its diagnosis and treatment to flourish or, as I suggest here, a form of disagreement that becomes dissent. In what follows, I outline Hacking's account before making a small number of amendments to suggest how this makes sense of dissent and its criminalization in cases like *The Little Red Schoolbook* in Britain.

The transition from ubiquitous disagreement to specific forms of dissent warranting its treatment and suppression as dissent is very much a relational process.

It is a result of practices occurring in what Hacking calls vectors or what may be better understood as fields of practice. It needs a small number of practices and dispositions/habitus in place.

Hacking identifies four 'vectors', which he says adds up to an 'ecological niche'. These are the elements that take place, in what following Bourdieu we might refer to as 'fields of practice'. The ecology metaphor is useful up to a point as hacking outlines it. However, he seems to give too much credence to the premise that an 'ecology' implies a bounded space understood as a system of actors contained in a set of locations. This can be dealt with by a few tweaks of the kind suggested by Tilly and Donati when they outline what they call 'relational realism', a tradition of enquiry that treats 'transactions, interactions, social ties and conversations [as] the central stuff of social life' (Tilly 2003: 72). Donati says *pace* Hacking that this means that Society is not a space 'containing' relations, or an arena where relations are played out. Rather we need to grasp the way in which the social is constituted out of the very tissue of relations. This means we need to be able to think society 'as relation' and not as 'having relations' (Donati 2011).

A taxonomy or a classificatory system

The first element is what Hacking calls an existing 'medical taxonomy' or a classificatory system. This vector needs to be in place when in the case he is exploring a 'patient' appears whose presenting symptoms can be fitted into a diagnosis drawing on the prevailing system of classification. In Hacking's case, the first patient, Albert Dadas, was able to be fitted into an existing psychiatric schema that already had categories and syndromes like 'hysteria' and 'epilepsy'. Equally Tissot, his treating doctor went on to identify and name a new syndrome 'ambulatory automatism'. The discursive vocabulary and taxonomy constitute in Bourdieu's terms a 'symbolic order', whose (re)production and validity is grounded in and sustained by iterative practices, even as it can also be subjected to change and modification (Bourdieu 2017). All fields of action are constituted discursively as a symbolic order reliant on practices that deploy a vocabulary of metaphors and categories, which add up to a system of classification, which can then be drawn on by other agents and their practices to deal with processes of arrest incarceration surveillance and so forth. In the case of the criminalization of dissent, this exists in its purest form in the legal and juridical fields and is exemplified though not always exhaustively by legislation that constitutes the criminality of the problem that dissent represents.

Observability

The second element is what Hacking calls 'observability'. As Hacking says, 'In order for a form of behaviour to be deemed a mental disorder, it has to be strange, disturbing, and noticed' (Hacking 1998: 82). In the case of the 'fugueurs', they confronted a 'substantial system of surveillance and detection' both in France and across Europe. This involved a large and extended network of police, customs and border officials on the look-out for deserters, smugglers and draft dodgers, whose officials were willing and able to engage in surveillance so as to detect the 'strange and disturbing conduct'. Observability points to a practice occurring in a field of practice that amounts to a system of surveillance that makes the observation or detection of the problem possible. As Hacking (1998: 82) notes, 'In order for a form of behaviour to be deemed a mental disorder, it has to be strange, disturbing, and noticed'.

In the case of dissent, there is a vast network of 'observers' starting with neighbours, the police, medical practitioners and related welfare professionals, teachers, employers and elements of the modern mass media (especially working in genres like 'current affairs'), whose surveillance can detect, identify and report on people who are different and disagreeable in ways that warrant reporting to the authorities. Being different and/or disagreeable can lead to being identified as a form of dissent. There is all too frequently at the least a powerful elective affinity often amounting to a synergy between economic and political elites and the large corporate mass media about what constitutes a problematic expression of disagreement and a consensus about the ideas and actions that constitute dissent. This, in turn, can be harnessed by the state and its security agencies to propose actions from surveillance to arrest, interrogation and other processes that warrants suppression through a large and ever expanding apparatus of state-sponsored policing and increasingly sophisticated and large-scale surveillance. In the state itself, there is an extensive network of police and security agencies whose job is to carry out surveillance and to prevent or discover criminal conduct.

'Cultural polarity'

The third element is what Hacking calls 'cultural polarity'. Hacking proposes that the behaviours associated with a transient mental illness like 'mad travellers disease' tend to fall between 'two social phenomena … one virtuous, one vicious' that preoccupy the society in which what becomes an illness like 'mad walker's disease' arises. In the case of the 'mad travellers', the problematic behaviour lay between 'romantic tourism and criminal vagrancy' (Hacking 1998: 81) As Hacking (1998: 81) notes

> fugue perfectly fitted between two social phenomena romantic tourism and criminal vagrancy: one virtuous, one vicious. Both were deeply important to the middle classes because one stood for leisure, pleasure and fantasy escape, while the other stood for the fear of the underworld.

Tourism was becoming an admired practice, fuelled by the rise of tourist companies like Thomas Cook and Baedekkers guide books and the growth of a hospitality industry in the mid-nineteenth century and was already becoming a preoccupation of those with the means to indulge in tourism. Vagrancy, on the other hand, was a feared long stigmatized activity associated with 'the poor' and the 'criminal classes' and had been criminalized in most European countries.

In effect and understood relationally, the sayings and doings that become dissent bear an uncommonly close relationship to ideas and behaviour that are already valued and/or practised by others especially though not always by the elites. Dissent is a relation of difference-as-polarity. In effect, dissent is the *alter ego* to beliefs or practices that when done by 'us' is valuable, virtuous, admirable and important, but when done by 'them' is wicked, subversive of order and morality even depraved and criminal and deserves suppression.

Release

Finally, there is the activity itself which Hacking says offers some kind of existential release, freedom of expression or escape. In the case of the 'mad walkers', Hacking says walking was 'an inviting escape … it offered release' Walking 'was a space in which dysfunctional men, on the edge of freedom, yet trapped could escape' (Hacking 1998: 82). Read literally this is the least satisfactory part of Hacking's heuristic. Applied to the many forms that dissent can take, Hacking seems to be inviting us back to the trivializing proposition long advanced by conservative sociologists that dissenters were or are 'just' deviants, madmen, criminals or sociopaths, who cannot cope with their assigned role or position assigned to them. This idea further does not make much sense, given Hacking's own moving suggestion-cum-extrapolation that modern 'mad walkers' are today more likely to be illegal immigrants or asylum seekers. Hacking says the hills around the Franco-Spanish border town of Le Boulou:

> …is great fugue country. There on a flowery slope you may still encounter a nervous man who was hoping not to be seen. Today he is more likely to be a confused Moroccan making his way gingerly through to France … Today he is just a mixed up illegal immigrant.
>
> (Hacking 1998: 79)

Notwithstanding the merits of Carlen's notion of 'risk crazed governance', the many forms that dissent take are best not treated as a pathological form of 'escapism' on the part of 'dysfunctional people'. Rather it involves rich and complex forms of expression taken by solitary people like serving Israeli soldiers, or by small groups of courageous journalists, satirists or hacktivists, or by larger collectives of squatters or by vast gatherings of colourful noisy protestors gathering in great public squares. I have, e.g. already said enough to point to quite complex moral and emotional motivations at work among the Israeli selective resistors discussed by Ruth Linn. These serving soldiers pointed to rich and complex actions, implicating complex moral emotions like patriotism, pride, love, righteous anger or simply a deep sense of justice these are the dispositions that are more likely to illuminate the path way to dissent. Hacking's account of 'mad travellers' also points to the kinds of social relations and practices that are already in place that begin to explain the reactions of the state to signs of difference or dissent.

Let me 'apply' Hacking's ecological niche heuristic to the case of *The Little Red Schoolbook*.

Taxonomy

By the 1960s, the British state had a long history of a concern with 'obscenity', 'pornography' and 'indecency'. It had a legal tradition committed to regulating 'obscenity', 'indecency', 'attempts to corrupt public morals' and activities likely to cause 'outrages to public decency' (Klugg et al. 2003). Arguably, the first conviction for obscenity in Britain occurred in 1727 when a well-known publisher Edmund Curll was found guilty of 'disturbing the King's peace' when he published a book entitled *Venus in the Cloister or The Nun in her Smock* (Baines and Rogers 2007). Regulation of stage play has an even longer history with an official called the 'Master of the Revels' responsible for censoring stage plays after 1600. Parliament passed the *Licensing Act 1737* creating a position called 'The Examiner of the Stage' located in the Lord Chamberlain's office (itself responsible for managing both the Royal household and the House of Lords) to look out for sexual impropriety, blasphemy and foul language on the stage. This legislation while modestly amended by the *Theaters Act 1843* effectively established a framework for censoring plays by licencing plays, a system that stayed in place until 1968 (Handley et al. 2004).

In the 1960s, a series of high profile legal cases spotlighted the British state's ongoing preoccupation with 'obscenity'. British law had long had an offence called 'obscene libel' established in common law since 1727 and first enacted in statute by the *Obscene Publications Act 1857*. The 1960s had already seen the publishers of both D.H. Lawrence's *Lady Chatterley's Lover* and Hubert Selby Jr.'s *Last Exit to Brooklyn* engaged in high profile cases facing charges of publishing 'obscene literature' – with mixed results. Britain had introduced the *Obscene Publications Act 1959* (amended subsequently by the *Obscene Publications Act 1962*). Lawrence's novel first published privately in1928 was only published in the UK in 1960 by Penguin. The court found Lawrence's book was not obscene, though Selby's book was judged to be obscene in 1966, a finding overturned on appeal. In each case, the Courts were bound to apply the so-called 'Hicklin test' first spelled out by Chief Justice Cockburn in 1867 in R v Hicklin. This 'test' held that a publication was 'obscene' under these statutes if taken as a whole, it is 'such as to tend to deprave and corrupt persons who are likely, having regard to all relevant circumstances, to read, see or hear the matter contained or embodied in it'.

In 1965, John Osborne's play *A Patriot for Me* was denied a licence by the Lord Chamberlain. Lord Cobbold argued that the play needed major script changes cuts to get his approval. Ostensibly, the Lord Chamberlain objected to the depiction of homosexuality in the play: homosexual acts would remain illegal in England until 1968. He objected to lines like 'He was born with a silver saber up his whatnot' while he also took exception to a scene in the play centring on a Drag Ball, in which aristocratic members of Viennese society appear in drag. As the Lord Chamberlain noted, this presented 'homosexuals in their most attractive guise, dressed as pretty women' and thus 'will to some degree cause the congregation of homosexuals (sic) and provide the means whereby the vice may be acquired' (Gilleman 2014: 144). As Luc Gilleman 2014) notes, it probably mattered more that Osborne had been in the forefront of major playwrights pushing for the abolition of theatre censorship: he had called the Lord Chamberlains role as a censor 'ridiculous and infamous' (Gilleman 2014: 144). The Royal Court Theater was forced to stage the play in a private club and the Lord Chamberlain unsuccessfully urged the Wilson Labour government to prosecute the theatre company. (Oddly other plays like Orton's *The Entertaining Mr Sloane* or Dyers *Staircase* with explicitly homosexual themes were passed for performance.) The Department of Public Prosecutions suggested that prosecution would not be prudent (Whitebrook 2015: 145).

Observability

By the 1960s, Britain already had a well-established system of surveillance involving a thicket of 'obscenity' legislation and a network of agencies dedicated to watching and regulating the work of publishers, writers' playwrights and theatrical production. That surveillance was committed to both legislate against obscenity and police it. Obscenity was a much observed matter.

Britain had introduced a range of legislation and common law offences like blasphemy, or libel as well as a host of laws regulating public entertainment like the *Cinematograph Act 1952*, the *Theatre's Act 1843*, the *Obscene Publications Act 1959*, the *Obscene Publications Act 1964*, the *Theatre's Act 1965*, *Criminal Justice & Public Order Act 1994 Pornography* and so forth.

Observability was a function of the system of courts, police and security agencies. In 1932, London's Metropolitan Police established the 'C' Division Clubs and Vice Unit, the unit later became better known as the 'Clubs Office' or colloquially as the 'Dirty Squad'. The unit was responsible for policing prostitution, and later nightclubs, gaming and casinos. After the introduction of the *Obscene Publications Act* 1964, it took on responsibility for pornographic publications. When it moved into its West End location in 1941, it looked after the Soho area famous as London's 'Redlight' district. This unit continued on until 2014 when it was restructured and merged into London's Metropolitan Police Human trafficking unit.

There was plenty to be seen and done in the run up to the charges brought against Richard Handley in 1971. In 1970 Eugene Schuster's London Arts Gallery on New Bond Street, Mayfair was raided by the Obscene Publications Squad, barely open two days. Schuster elected to open with The Bag One exhibition – fourteen 'intimate and erotic' lithographs by John Lennon of himself and his wife, Yoko Ono, doing sexual things to each other. The gallery was immediately closed down and Schuster was charged. The case went to court several months later in April 1970. While the warrant had originally been issued under the *Obscene Publications Act* 1964, police used an older law. The police alleged that the gallery had 'exhibited to public view eight indecent prints to the annoyance of passengers, contrary to Section 54(12) of the *Metropolitan Police Act, 1839*'. Police later decided to proceed under the Act of 1839 which meant that the defence of artistic merit or public interest could not be used. During the case, the police introduced one witness a grey-haired accountant from Wandsworth Common who testified that he had 'felt a bit sick that a man should draw himself and his wife in such positions'. It had been a shock, he said, to see a picture of 'Yoko in the nude with rather exaggerated bosom with apparently somebody sucking a nipple'. The magistrate dismissed the case.

One month later OZ magazine produced its famous Schoolkids issue drawing on contributions from some twenty schoolchildren. Fifteen-year-old Islington schoolboy Vivian Berger produced a raunchy parody of Rupert Bear fucking a large woman using a cartoon by Robert Crum. In July 1970, the magazine was raided by the Obscene Publications Squad in July 1970 and the three Oz editors – Richard Neville, Jim Anderson and Felix Dennis – were charged with producing a magazine which would 'debauch and corrupt the morals of children and other young persons within the realm and to arouse and implant in the minds of those young people lustful and perverted desires'. This charge came from the Obscene Publications Act 1857 and was intended as a way of avoiding the 'public good' defence that had saved Penguin in the *Lady Chatterley* case in 1963. The defendants were tried in 1971 and were represented by John Mortimer and Geoffrey Roberston before Judge Michael Argyle who 'from the outset seemed to think Oz magazine threatened the fate of western civilisation' (Soreen 2016). It would become the longest obscenity trial and end in the conviction and jailing of the OZ editors.

If obscenity was a much observed matter, it was also lucrative especially to the 'Dirty Squad'. There is more than a little irony in the consequence of allegations made by tabloid newspapers of a 'connexion' between James Humphreys, a leading publisher of pornographic photos and magazines, and Commander Kenneth Drury, head of the Flying Squad (Soreen 2016). Those allegations included claims that both men had enjoyed a luxurious holiday in Cyprus accompanied by their wives, and paid for by the Soho pornographer. Humphreys turned informant and handed over details of the payments to police from himself and other porn shop owners made through the 1960s. As Barry Cox and colleagues document, those allegations led to the resignation and dismissal of twenty senior police officers including DCI George Fenwick, head of the obscene publications squad, his superior Bill Moody, Commander Wallace Virgo, head of the Serious Crime Squad, in overall charge of the unit, and Commander Kenneth Drury, head of the Flying Squad. Subsequent criminal prosecution of the corrupt police revealed that DCS Bill Moody who headed the unit from 1964 to 1972 received over 40,000 pounds a year from the owners of porn shops in Soho part of kickbacks worth over 100,000 pounds (Gillard and Flynn 2012). This situation points to the third important aspect at work: cultural polarity.

Cultural polarity

Richard Handyside, the publisher of *The Little Red Schoolbook*, was caught in a cross fire of cultural polarity. He fell between 'two social phenomena … one virtuous, one vicious' that preoccupy a community. This means that what becomes a problem like obscene literature represented by *The Little Red Schoolbook* or the 'Schoolkids' issue of OZ arises sit cheek by jowl with activities which enjoy social approval or are approved of. Handyside fell into a space occupied by a fear-driven preoccupation to regulate and censor overt expressions of sex and the actual explosion in the availability of pornography and public expressions of sexuality that marked out the 1960s and 1970s.

Some sense of that polarity is suggested by a conversation between DCI George Fenwick, head of the 'Dirty squad' and the Home Secretary, Reginald Maudling in the Heath Conservative government. As Paul Soreen tells it, Fenwick informed Maudling that:

> In this country at the minute there are somewhere in the region of 80 publications which advocate what in the current idiom is called the alternative society. Of these about 25 can be termed 'underground' press and a number of them contain articles which can be described as indecent. However, by far the worst of these are *Oz, Frendz and IT*, in that order. These in fact are the only ones against whom action has been taken or indeed contemplated in the last 12 months.

Maudling then asked Fenwick why the sex shops of Soho were operating with something close to impunity. Fenwick replied: 'It is an unfortunate fact of life that pornography has existed for centuries and it is unlikely that it can ever be stamped out'. It seems that combination of police venality and public demand for porn drove the increase in Soho's sex shops from a handful in the early 1960s to over sixty by the early 1970s. On one interpretation, the *Dirty Squad* needed to raid exhibitions like John Lennon's Bag One or charge 'alternative' magazines like *Oz* and *Little Red Schoolbook* so as to look like they were doing something.

Another sign of the cultural polarity at work in 1971 is suggested by the way Heath's Conservative government (1970–74) presided over an extended debate in the public sphere about *The Little Red Schoolbook* beginning in March 1971 (Limond 2012). On the one hand, progressive opinion was strongly supportive of the book including media outlets like the *Times Education Supplement*, progressive educators (including A.S. Neill) and groups like the National Council for Civil Liberties, Gay Liberation Front, the Society of Teachers Opposed to Physical Punishment, and the Schools Action Union. Even the purse-lipped Trotskyite newspaper *Socialist Worker* concluded that there was some merit in the book (Limond 2012: 525–6). The Defence of Literature and the Arts Society would publicly support the publisher after the police began prosecution case.

On the other side, various Churches expressed their outrage, as did some members of the House of Lords who huffed and puffed about the threat to moral and social order. The trial of Penguin, the publishers of *Lady Chatterley's Lover* in 1961, had highlighted the volatile mix of class and sexuality that bothered some conservatives. In the trial of Lawrence's novel, the prosecutor had asked 'Would you approve of your young sons, young daughters – because girls can read as well as boys – reading this book? Is it a book that you would have lying around in your own house? Is it a book that you would even wish your wife or your servants to read?' In 1971, Parliament Conservative MP Gerald Nabarro demanded to know whether or not the Home Secretary, Reginald Maudling would ban the book. Maudling demurred and aided he would refer the matter to the police. The British tabloid press like the *Daily Telegraph* demanded that the Director of Public Prosecutions ban the book on 29 and 30 March 1971. Leading 'moral campaigners' like Mary Whitehouse, the organizer of the Clean Up TV Campaign added her weight to those seeking a ban on the book arguing the book was a 'a political and sexual revolutionary primer'. She would claim that she had been invited to a meeting at the headquarters of the Metropolitan Police, where, as she later reported, the then head of the vice squad: 'told me that he and his colleagues were "frankly appalled" by the book and said they were going to raid [the offices of the UK publisher] Stage 1' (Limond 2012: 527).

Habitus/release

Hacking says we see in the actions of 'fugueurs' an experience of release or freedom of expression. We can ask what was it that the Danish school teachers, Soren Hansen and Jesper Jensen (1971), and the British publisher, Richard Handyside, respectively the authors and the publisher of *The Little Red Schoolbook* were doing. For Handyside, the publication of *The Little Red Schoolbook* was part of a wider commitment to publishing radical or revolutionary literature. His company called Stage 1 had already published books by Che Guevara and Fidel Castro. He seems to haver thought that publishing the book would appeal to young people and in the spirit of the time shaped by the ideas of Wilhelm Reich, imagined too that open discussion of sexuality was a progressive thing to do. The small number of pages that attracted all the attention was the discussion of adolescent sexuality. The book's commitment to plain speaking included advice on masturbation ('When boys get sexually excited, their prick gets stiff. This is called having an erection or "getting a hard on". If a boy rubs his stiff prick it starts feeling good and this leads to orgasm') and contraception ('If a boy and girl fuck they may have children. To avoid this contraceptives are used') (Hansen and Jensen 1971: 130).

His commitment to revolutionary politics also inclined him to treat the high-handed police raid of his office as a provocation to seek justice under the protection he imagined Europe's human rights court might offer him (Sutherland 115). It is not clear if he knew as we now know of the hypocritical commitment on the part of police to prosecute his book for obscenity when they were part of lucrative project designed to protect the porn industry in Soho.

Conclusion

Apart from noting that criminalization studies have been unwilling to pay much attention to the criminalization of political dissent, I also offered a relational heuristic that makes sense of the process of criminalization of dissent. Along the way I observed we cannot evade the problem provoked by Garland's observation that crime itself is not 'a self-generated theoretical entity or a naturally-occurring phenomenon but instead *a state-defined social problem*' (Garland 2009: 115). This highlights the significant disinclination to attend to the ethical (or normative) dimensions that ought to be raised when we ask on what basis, and with what kinds of legitimacy do states embark on the criminalization process? This seems to open up some very deep problems about the kind of legitimacy attending the criminalization of dissent process. Implicitly at least, there seem to be some fundamental moral, and normative issues are involved when states begin to the criminalize dissent. Assuming that there is some sort of interdependence between basic moral issues and political ideas that go to issues about the relationships between power, legitimacy dissent and justice, what precisely do these look like? It is to the question of legitimacy raised by the problem of dissent that I now turn.

Notes

* I gratefully acknowledge Jeff Shantz who called his 2011 edited book *Law Against Liberty*.
1 A 'rules based international order' is best understood as a shorthand for the UN-centred system that imposes limits on what states can do and which provides a wide array of rules governing matters like international economic relations (Bisley 2018).
2 At the time of writing and in the course of an election, one Australian political party (the Aussie Battler party) has called for all new immigrants to be put on a 'ten year good behaviour bond' with deportation as punishment for breaching it (The *Age* 16 November 2018: 5).
3 'Cura' was the name of a divine being in Rome whose name means 'care'. It segues out to include ideas like 'caring' and 'curing' and implicates the priest (cura) and the 'curator' of art and collections.
4 Hacking makes a clear distinction between objects (of scientific enquiry), which are really there, like atoms and bacteria and 'objects or their effects which do not exist in any recognizable form until they are objects of scientific study' (Hacking 2002: 11).
5 It is worth adding that Hacking also relied on Erving Goffman's complementary though smaller-scale accounts of the same kind of processes occurring in institutions like hospitals and prisons.

Chapter 6

Liberalism, law and the problem of legitimacy

The time is 1944, the place Nazi Germany. What in many other countries would be a minor and private act of dissent threatens catastrophe for one German man who had served as a conscript in the Wehrmacht since 1940. His wife, known only as 'Mrs X', denounced her husband to the local leader of the National Socialist German Workers' (Nazi) Party responsible for her area. She alleged that while, on leave from the army, her husband had made 'insulting' remarks about Adolf Hitler, the Fuhrer of Germany. The man had said he regretted 'that Hitler did not go to the devil on the 20th of July 1944' a reference to the failed plot by army officers to kill Hitler (Sanson et al. 2009: 148). She claimed the cloak Samuel Johnson said all scoundrels wore, when they declared themselves patriots, because it seems she simply wanted to get rid of her husband. As a Bamberg Court later put it, 'she had turned toward other men and had conceived the desire to divorce him'. The wife demonstrated that she was an obedient citizen of Germany. Her allegation however mattered because it fell under German law introduced after 1934. This included *A Law Against Malicious Attacks on the State and the Party and for the Protection of the Party Uniform Law* of 20 December 1934, and Article 5 of *A Statute Creating a Particular Criminal Law in War Time* Law of 1 August 1938. Both of these laws look a lot like American and British anti-sedition legislation. Under the 1934 legislation, e.g. it was unlawful to make 'spiteful, rabble rousing statements, or statements that generate base attitudes about the leading personalities of the state or the Nazi Party' or that 'undermine the trust of the people in the political leadership' (Gaydosh 2017: 185).

Because he was a soldier, the husband was tried and found guilty by a military tribunal and sentenced to death. After a week in custody, he was placed on probation and sent back to the Russian front. Miraculously he survived the war and on his return instituted proceedings against his wife. The woman was prosecuted for the offense of illegally depriving her husband of his liberty in 1949 in the West German court of Bamberg. In her defence, Mrs X argued that she had not committed a crime because a court had sentenced her husband in accordance with the law of the time, i.e. the Nazi statutes of 1934 and 1938. The court agreed. However when her ex-husband appealed that decision, the Bamberg Court of Appeal found that Mrs X had 'illegally depriv[ed] another of his freedom', a crime under the *Penal Code* 1871, and a code which had remained in force throughout the Nazi period. The Bamberg court said the Nazi laws were 'contrary to the sound conscience and sense of justice of all decent human beings'.

Here in essence are some of the central issues at stake in the criminalization of dissent. In this case, a man makes a critical observation about the German head of state. Making that statement was an offence under the existing laws of the German state. His wife demonstrated that she was a good citizen by complying with the law, as did the military tribunal that sentenced him to death. Isn't this a good example of justice at work?

Notwithstanding the fact that the Nazi state was a decidedly non-liberal-democratic state, what has become known as the 'Grudge Informer' case has become a central element in an ongoing debate involving important Western legal philosophers about what it is that renders law legitimate. That debate began in 1958 when Herbert Hart and Lon Fuller debated that question at Harvard University (Hart 1958; Fuller 1958). Fuller and Hart addressed the questions raised by Gustav Radbruch's (1946/2006) claim that Germany's culture of 'legal positivism' had contributed to the inability, or refusal, by German lawyers to respond adequately to the Nazis' abuse of the legal order after 1933. Given that legal positivists say that the fact a state has enacted a given law is enough to ensure that the law is legitimate, did the fact that the actions of the woman and the judgements of the various German tribunals and courts (up until the Bamberg Court of Appeal judgement) were compliant with the *Law Against Malicious Attacks on the State and the Party and for the Protection of the Party Uniform* Law 1934 render those actions and judgements legitimate? Or did the fact that the Nazi state was generally understood to have been a 'wicked' or 'criminal state' affect the legitimacy of its law-making and law-enforcing processes illegitimate, and if so, how and why? (It is important to note that another question this debate raises was what if anything made the husband's act of dissent legitimate? For reasons which are revealing, this question has never become part of this ongoing debate. I address that question later in the book.)

In thinking about the 'Grudge Informer' case, Hart (1958) provided the quintessential modern statement of the legal-positivist conception of law adumbrated later in his *The Concept of Law* (1961). Hart denies that there is any necessary connection between law and morality. This implies that the fact that a state has enacted a given law means it is legitimate. As an advocate for natural law, Fuller countered that law is only legitimate when it rests on a solid moral foundation, a view outlined in his *The Morality of Law* (1964).

The key questions

There are just a few questions I will address here. What is legitimacy, and how has it been understood? On what basis does the legitimacy of state power, domination, lawfulness and enforcement actually rest? The answer we give to the question as to what makes law 'lawful' or 'legitimate' addresses the question of legitimacy: why ought I, or we, obey a state – and its laws and policies? Our answers to this question have a fundamental effect on how we think about dissent when it involves a breach of the law, or when states decide to criminalize that dissent.

To be clear I am not going to get trapped into assessing whether Hart or Fuller 'won' the debate. Nor do I want to be constrained by a narrow legal philosophical frame. There is no good reason to distinguish sharply between legal philosophy and political philosophy (or political theory) for reasons that begin to be clear when we encounter Carl Schmitt's critique of liberalism: legal philosophers treat Schmitt as a juridical philosopher, while political theorists treat him as a political theorist. The very open question I am addressing here is how well do the analytic legal-positivist accounts of the law, or various natural law accounts of the law account for the way liberal-democratic states and their legal systems actually work, or are legitimate, especially when they criminalize dissent. As I will argue here, we confront a very basic problem to do with the relationship between state sovereignty (or power) and legitimacy as this is understood by liberals.

The liberal tradition treats the liberal-democratic state as a state committed to protecting freedoms and rights and justice, and to preventing the exercise of arbitrary power. On this account, the kind of liberalism traced back to John Locke envisages that substantial limitations will be placed on sovereign power embodied in the state. Locke, e.g. denies that the sovereign has arbitrary power over the lives of the citizenry. Any authority the sovereign has is limited to the public good served by the exercise of that authority. As Locke puts it, 'that power hath no other end but preservation, and therefore can never have a right to destroy enslave or designedly to impoverish the subjects' (Locke 2002: 67). Second, the supreme authority in the State 'cannot assume to itself a power to rule by extemporary arbitrary decrees, but is bound to dispense justice and decide the rights of the subject by promulgated standing laws and known authorised judges' (Locke 2002: 68). Here is the appearance of the liberal idea of the 'rule of law', and of the idea that the rule of law provides a fundamental check on arbitrary power. Likewise, Locke outlines the idea that sovereignty is not indivisible but can and should precisely involve a separation of powers between the legislative and executive branches which includes rejecting any delegation of legislative power, e.g. to the executive or to the judiciary: 'The legislative cannot transfer the power of making laws to any other hands; for it being but a delegated power from the people, they who have it cannot pass it over to others' (Locke 2002: 71). I have said enough in previous chapters when detailing the many forms that criminalizing dissent takes to cast serious doubt on the idea that Locke's account serves as a portrait of actually existing liberal-democratic states.

Here I want to show why this is so, by exploring the way some key liberal legal theorists have understood the legitimacy of the state. If legitimacy is best framed as a question, that question is why are we obligated to obey the state? I survey some of the answers given by some of the key figures in the liberal tradition, like Hobbes, Bentham and Austin before arriving at the debate between Hart and Fuller.

We will see after a lot of twisting and turning, a surprising and frank admission that states secure obedience to laws and policies by imperative means. Imperative theories of law conceive of law as a command enforced by some coercive power. In a very important statement of what is at stake here, Bernard Schwartz (1950) pointed to certain self-reinforcing dispositions set loose by imperative theories of law. On this account the state 'is taken as the source of both the command *and the coercion*' (Schwartz 1950: 442: my stress). One entailment of this is that other social and economic institutions, either as competing or countervailing power-structures tend to be minimized. Worse is the way a certain kind of intellectual framework can then facilitate this political effect. Citing the first explicit 'legal positivist' John Austin, Schwartz notes how the science of jurisprudence Austin claimed to have formulated, insists on a rigid separation of law from all ethical elements. As Austin said, 'The science of jurisprudence … is concerned with positive laws, or with laws strictly so called, as considered without regard to their goodness or badness'. Given the way the self-portrait of the law comes to incorporate the legal-positivist frame with its trademark separation between law and moral principles or conceptions of justice, then it becomes 'difficult to think of the State as subject to any limitations except self-limitations'.

One implication of this is that there is not a lot of difference between the way a significant strand of liberal political-legal theory has developed a legal-positivist imperative theory of the law, and Carl Schmitt's explicitly anti-liberal description of state sovereignty at work in his declaration: 'Souverän ist derjenige, der über die Ausnahme entscheidet' (sovereign is he who decides on the exception) (Schmitt 1976: 5). This, in turn, suggests what Simon Lavis (2015) is getting at when he says an historically nuanced, rigorous study of the Nazi legal system can highlight the 'possibility of continuities and similarities between Nazi law and other modern legal systems' to say nothing of 'the relevance of Nazi law for some pressing jurisprudential issues'.

What is legitimacy?

'Legitimacy' is a slippery category. Both as an adjective or as a verb 'legitimate' comes from the Latin *Lex* (law), which migrated from the verb *legitimare*, (from Latin *legitimus* ('lawful') to the medieval Latin *legitimatus* ('made legal'). If it initially meant anything, it meant what was prescribed – or proscribed – by law like a 'legitimate' male heir, or a marriage. It has since broadened out to embrace the more general idea of being 'right' or 'good', like when we offer a legitimate excuse for lateness, or carry out a 'legitimate', i.e. 'correct' logical deduction. This slipperiness has long characterized the ways philosophers have thought about legitimacy. As Adam Sitze (2015: 144) notes, Cicero in his commentary on Plato's *Laws* treated 'law' (*lex*) as the written expression of a universal kind of 'right reason' common to all humans that binds the entire universe into a single commonwealth (*civitas*). This natural law tradition underpins the modern global liberal dream of order progress and affluence for all epitomized by the United Nations *Universal Declaration of Human*

Rights (1948) and numerous human rights treaties and conventions. Another approach was spelled out by Carl Schmitt (2003) when he thought about law as 'nomos' drawing on the ambiguity of the Greek word *nomos* as both 'walls' and 'laws':

> … a law is a law only and precisely to the extent that it inscribes itself on the ground – dividing and distinguishing, including and excluding, carving out relations between inside and outside, producing boundaries
>
> (Sitze 2015: 145)

This is like some influential 'modern' accounts of legitimacy that claim to eschew any 'moral point of view' and prefer a kind of objectivist, descriptive account grounded in the idea that states understood to have sovereignty also possess legitimacy (Bartelson 1993, 2014).

Mostly, we will see that when the question of legitimacy is addressed in the twentieth century, liberals like Hart and Fuller get stuck on the question whether the legitimacy – or authority – of law is a matter of compliance with legal principles and procedures (Hart's view), or whether the legitimacy of the enacted law depends on its correspondence with higher moral rules or *justice* (Fuller's view). This squeamish liberal view shares little with the older liberal idea that legitimacy relies on a system of commands issued by a sovereign entity, like a monarchy or a liberal-democratic state, based on and requiring a habit of obedience backed up by an entirely realistic and predictable threat of punishment. This is an answer which says that because states have power or sovereignty, they also get to tell their citizens what to do.

A close reading of major philosophical enquiries into the grounds said to constitute the legitimacy of law demonstrates that the distinction between 'legitimate' and 'illegitimate' authority leads a fugitive existence. As Richard Tuck (1999) and Eric Wilson (2008) point out, the origin of modern international law and political theory will be found in Grotius *Des Indis* (1617), Hobbes *De Cive* (1641) and Austin's *The Province of Jurisprudence Determined* (1832). How do Grotius, Hobbes and Austin address the basic question of legitimacy, i.e. 'why are we obligated to obey the law'? The answer is grounded not in any normative or moral idea but in some alleged 'facts'. For Grotius, law is a command that relies on habituated obedience by people naturally constituted as 'slaves' (Grotius 1960: 62). For Hobbes and Austin, it is the fear of punishment that obligates us. Hobbes says 'law comes from one who has power over those whom he instructs' (Hobbes 1998: 154). As Hobbes puts it:

> The obligation to obey individual civil laws is derived from the force of the agreement by which individual citizens are obligated to each other to offer absolute and universal obedience… to the commonwealth i.e., to the sovereign whether that is one man or one council.
>
> (Hobbes 1998: 165)

This approach would be developed in the eighteenth and nineteenth centuries by people like Jeremy Bentham and John Austin. Each of these writers claims that law is nothing but a system of commands issued by sovereign power, vested in a monarch or in a democratically elected head of state or government. The threat that disobedience would lead to great evil, i.e. punishment being visited upon the disobedient, seemed to these writers to provide the minimum basis for answering the question of legitimacy, i.e. why should I obey the laws or the regulations and other commands issued by a state? The idea is simple if brutal: legitimacy relies on a habit of obedience backed up by an entirely realistic – and predictable – threat of punishment. Hobbes seems to be suggesting that 'law is a matter of duty' requiring only the practice of instilling a fear of punishment in all citizens based on the principle that there is always 'a penalty attached to every civil law' (Hobbes 1998: 158). Two centuries later, Austin says that when a law is made or promulgated, we need to understand that it constitutes a command which *obligates* those subject to the law to obey it (Austin 1995: 21–22). Austin says simply this obligation exists because the lawmaker will cause an evil to be done to you in the form of punishment should you go ahead and disobey the law. At the end of the day, the lawmaker's threat to punish or hurt is the only obligation to obey that matters. Not only do Hobbes and Austin agree they also end up anticipating the claim made by Jacques Derrida when he reminded us that law is a 'violence without ground' (Derrida 1992: 14). There are many good reasons for thinking that this is an accurate account of why legitimacy rests on the power to coerce – and why dissent becomes a 'bad' thing to do.

Thomas Hobbes: the imperative theory of law/state

Apart from acknowledging the pre-eminent role of Thomas Hobbes in creating modern political philosophy, it has long been conventional to treat Hobbes as both the 'father of liberalism' (Strauss 1936; MacPherson 1962) and as Michael Cuffaro suggests as 'the father of legal positivism' (Cuffaro 2011: 175). Others, less kind like Sheldon Wolin, have described Hobbes as the father of despotism (Wolin 1990). However, while Hobbes clearly accepted what we can call the 'imperative theory of law' and has often been seen as a legal positivist, careful commentators have also noticed that he was also a natural lawyer allowing a role for certain moral ideas like the idea of legitimate resistance to the power of the state!

Hobbes was clearly committed to an imperative theory of law/state. In *On the Citizen (De Cive)*, Thomas Hobbes declares that 'law comes from one who has power over those whom he instructs' (Hobbes 1998: 154). In his *Leviathan*, Hobbes says bluntly 'Sed Authoritas non Veritas facit Legem' ('Authority not truth makes law'). Hobbes thus defines law:

> [L]aws are obeyed not because of their content but because of the will of the instructor, law is not advice but command and is defined thus: LAW is a command of that person (whether man or council) whose instruction is the reason for obedience.
>
> (Hobbes 1998: 154)

This claim is supported in two ways. One involves Hobbes' seemingly benign story about a social contract that was negotiated when humans moved out of a 'state of nature' and into a civil or political state. According to Hobbes, humans agreed to surrender all of their natural rights and freedoms in return for that state guaranteeing them civil order. As Hobbes puts it:

> The obligation to obey individual civil laws is derived from the force of the agreement by which individual citizens are obligated to each other to offer absolute and universal obedience… to the commonwealth i.e., to the sovereign whether that is one man or one council.
>
> (Hobbes 1998: 165)

The other involves the simpler proposition that 'law is a matter of duty' requiring only the practice of instilling a fear of punishment in all citizens in the idea that there is always 'a penalty attached to every civil law' (Hobbes 1998: 158). In his *Leviathan*, Hobbes put this point quite crisply:

> [I]t is manifest, that Law in generall, is not Counsell, but Command; not a Command of any man to any man; but only of him, whose Command is addressed to one formerly obliged to obey him. And as for Civill Law, it addeth only the name of the person Commanding, which is Persona Civitatis, the Person of the Commonwealth.
>
> (1985: 137)

This is why some commentators treat Hobbes as a proto legal positivist. Hampton concluded, e.g. that '[Hobbes's] is a positivist position, because law is understood to depend on the sovereign's will. No matter what's a law content, no matter how unjust it seems, if it has been commanded by the sovereign, then and only then is it a law' (Hampton 1986: 107). Riley (2009: 25) too has argued that Hobbes is the father of modern 'legal positivism'. Yet Cuffaro (2011: 178) argues that Hobbes is not a legal positivist as that is now understood. For Hobbes, a law of nature is

> a Precept, or generall Rule, found out by Reason, by which a man is forbidden to do, that, which is destructive of his life, or taketh away the means of preserving the same; and to omit, that, by which he thinketh it may best be preserved.
>
> (Hobbes 1985: 64)

Hobbes thought that natural law is actually more binding than civil law. Unlike the civil law that binds only subjects, natural law 'ought to be Obeyed, both by King and Subjects' (Hobbes 1971 [1681]: 10). Further Hobbes insists that natural law includes more abstract commands like the first law of nature (that one should endeavour to preserve the peace where peace is possible), the second law of nature (that one should be willing to lay down one's right to all things where others are also willing), and the third law of nature (that one should keep one's covenants or promises). It also includes more determinate commands like the fifteenth law of nature that mediators are to be granted safe passage throughout the realm (Hobbes 1985: 64–65).

This seems to set up a deep contradiction: how can the natural law be law, if law depends for its validity on the sovereign. The contradiction set loose here by Hobbes is apparently resolved by his 'mutual containment thesis':

> The Law of Nature, and the Civill Law, contain each other, and are of equall extent. For the Lawes of Nature, which consist in Equity, Justice, Gratitude, and other morall Vertues on these depending, in the condition of meer Nature... are not properly Lawes, but qualities that dispose men to peace, and to obedience. When a Commonwealth is once settled, then are they actually Lawes, and not before; as being then the commands of the Common-wealth; and therefore also Civill Lawes: For it is the Soveraign Power that obliges men to obey them
>
> (Hobbes 1985: 138)

What Hobbes is getting at is that to say that the laws of nature are valid insofar as they have been commanded by the sovereign does not entail that the sovereign is the author of the laws of nature. That authorship lies with God, and the 'precept, or general rule' exists, with or without the sovereign. In effect, as natural laws, these are innate moral virtues which exist before the constitution of a state or as he calls it a commonwealth. After the state has been set up, they can become civil laws and so become binding law. Hobbes complements that attempt to resolve the contradiction by adding the second part of the mutual containment thesis:

> Reciprocally also, the Civill Law is a part of the Dictates of Nature. For Justice, that is to say, Performance of Covenant, and giving to everyman his own, is a Dictate of the Law of Nature. But every subject in a Common-wealth, hath covenanted to obey the Civill Law.... And therefore Obedience to the Civill Law is part also of the Law of Nature. Civill, and Naturall Law are not different kinds, but different parts of Law.
>
> (Hobbes 1985: 138)

Even so Hobbes somewhat undermines this apparent solution of the contradiction when he then goes on to allow that any subject of the sovereign does not have the freedom to interpret the commands of the sovereign as they see fit. That right to interpret is the prerogative of the sovereign. Hobbes is clear on this point:

> ... the Interpretation of all Lawes dependeth on the Authority Soveraign; and the Interpreters can be none but those, which the Soveraign, (to whom only the Subject oweth obedience) shall appoint
>
> (Hobbes 1985: 143)

As Hampton says, Hobbes here is clearly not endorsing the natural-law frame. This would imply that the ruler's power is limited by natural moral rules, 'which would make them the source of law, rather than the sovereign' (Hampton 1986: 107). It is the sovereign alone who has the authority to interpret both the civil *and* natural law. Hobbes was less a proto-legal positivist and more a natural lawyer who continued to think that natural law provided principles which the sovereign (or officials like judges deputed by the sovereign to execute the law) would need to take into account. However, after apparently allowing a place for morality in the law, Hobbes falls back onto an imperative theory of law. As Hobbes says, 'The Judge is to take notice, that his Sentence ought to be according to the reason of his Soveraign, which being alwaies understood to be Equity, he is bound to it by the Law of Nature' (Hobbes 1985: 145). In effect, as Sharon Lloyd put it, Hobbes remains a natural lawyer, albeit one committed to a self-effacing natural law which *informs* but does not obligate sovereign power: sovereign power is all that matters not least of all because natural law requires that all of us accept that 'the judgement of the sovereign judge as authoritatively and properly adjudicating all disputes, including those over what does or does not conflict with natural law'. Hobbes's position retains:

> … a strongly positivistic element. Natural law has supreme authority; but it directs us, first and foremost, to act as if legal positivism were true. Natural law is thus self-effacing.
>
> (Lloyd 2001: 295)

The legitimacy of the law lies in its status as the obligation that sovereign command are to be obeyed because that is what subjects owe to the sovereign. (However and to anticipate, the ever-surprising Hobbes also allows a space for serious dissent as outlined in Chapter 8.)

If we move into the eighteenth century, we encounter Jeremy Bentham, a figure claimed by liberals and the Anglo-American legal tradition as both a legal positivist and a utilitarian. What does Bentham have to say about the problem of legitimacy?

Jeremy Bentham

Bentham's modern reputation as a philosopher, reformer and gadfly rest on just a few published works like his *Introduction to The Principles of Morals and Legislation* and *A Fragment on Government*. His passionate production of ideas and restless advocacy for law reform are buried in a vast and sprawling mass of manuscripts still being edited and published in the twenty-first century. Apart from making major contributions to economics, law, political science, and public policy administration he did much to shape the ethical tradition of utilitarianism (Martin 1997). Courtesy of major figures like J.S Mill, Herbert Spencer, Karl Popper and Bertrand Russel through to modern philosophers like Peter Singer utilitarianism has become the dominant tradition in the legal and economic cultures of Anglo-American societies to say nothing of the role in shaping the consumerist culture in these societies. Bentham's ambition was to develop a science of human behaviour based on the principle of 'utility': utility is the idea that humans naturally pursue what makes them happy and avoid whatever causes them pain. The ethical idea he derived from this is that the good is whatever makes us happy and the bad is what causes us pain. The public policy idea he derived from the utility principle is that governments should work to promote the greatest happiness of the greatest possible number of people. We should therefore expect that the principle of utility would underpin Bentham's engagement with the problem of what makes a state legitimate.

However, it proves to be very hard to work out what Bentham thought. Or to put it another way, Bentham is wonderfully, even radically confused. There are at least three ways in which this confusion, or more benignly a lack of clarity, is displayed – if it can ever be said that a confusion can be clear. First, he is a utilitarian offering a monistic theory of the good. This means that, both descriptively and as an ethical idea, Bentham insists that people cannot help but seek to increase their happiness or well-being: it is simply our natural disposition. Bentham thinks this principle can be used both by individual persons and by the policy- and law-making activities of a community: if it promotes utility, do it, because it is good.

Yet Bentham also proposes a legal-positivist account of the law, i.e. law is whatever a sovereign (state) declares to be law and is therefore devoid of moral significance: law ought not to be oriented to promoting any particular moral views or ideas. Finally, he also outlines a command or imperative theory of the law that looks a lot like the Hobbesian account of the state and why we ought to obey it. Let me try to unpack this mess, starting with his highly problematic account of the utility principle.

Bentham offers a radically monistic ethical theory: whatever causes us pleasure is good, whatever causes us pain is bad. As Bentham put it: 'Nature has placed mankind under the governance of two sovereign masters, pain and pleasure. It is for them alone to point out what we ought to do as well as to determine what we shall do' (Bentham 1948: 125). This is Bentham's principle of utility:

> By the principle of utility is meant that principle which approves or disapproves of every action whatsoever, according to the tendency which it appears to have to augment or diminish the happiness of the party whose interest is in question.
>
> (Bentham 1948: 126)

This principle says Bentham is the foundation of human morality. On this account pleasure (utility) and pain serve a basic normative function and will in some manner dictate our moral attitudes and conduct. The principle of utility sustains a theory of the good and then claims to explain how that principle will shape our actual behaviour.

Bentham believed that this 'principle of self-preference' was at once axiomatic, self-evident and irrefutable. As Bentham puts it:

> By the principle of self-preference, understand that propensity in human nature, by which, on the occasion of every act he exercises, every human being is led to pursue that line of conduct which according to his view of the case, taken by him at the moment, will be in the highest degree contributory to his own greatest happiness, whatsoever be the effect of it, in relation to the happiness of other similar beings, any or all of them taken together.
>
> (Bentham 1954: 421)

Many critics have pointed to overwhelming problems with Benthamite utilitarianism sponsoring an array of attempts to defend it (Williams and Smart 1973; Williams 1985). (Since Bentham various kinds of utilitarianism. have evolved to deal with these criticisms including act utilitarianism, consequentialism, and rule utilitarianism.) As Sicker (1978) argues, one basic problem with Bentham's principle of utility is that Bentham is 'racked by ambiguity and contradiction in his effort to base utilitarianism on egoistic hedonism'. This kind of critique was first made by Kant and, since then, has inspired many of the savage critiques of Bentham by the likes of Rawls (1971) and Finnis (1980).

Here the basic problem with the principle of utility is this: if all of us are busily pursuing and maximizing our utility, why would we ever need a state? Bentham has an answer and it is a very Hobbesian answer: 'In their competition for limited resources men inevitably enter into conflict with one another' (Bentham 1931: 109). Bentham says that:

> ...it is only necessary to consider the condition of savages. They strive incessantly against famine... Rivalry for subsistence produces among them the most cruel wars. And like beasts of prey, men pursue men as means of sustenance (Bentham 1931: 109)

(This is odd: even Hobbes never went so far as to say 'man' entered into civil society to pre-empt self-cannibalization!).

As many critics have noticed, and especially in these conditions of scarcity and conflict, the principle of utility is actually not at all helpful in resolving such conflicts: I want to eat your pet sheep because I am hungry, while you want to look after it because it gives you pleasure to do so. Diametrically opposed actions or wants may each be equally expressive of the utility principle. Sicker demonstrates how the many conflicts between utilitarianism and egoistic hedonism can only be resolved initially by calling on a social contract story in which individuals renounce their hedonism in favour of the security offered by the state enacting as the system of law. As Sicker says, 'By refusing to openly acknowledge this, the utilitarian foundation erected by Bentham for his system of jurisprudence becomes extremely fragile' (Sicker 1978: 284). As Sicker (1978) also shows, Bentham makes use of a fiction to get out of this logical conundrum. Bentham makes use of a fictitious notion 'as-if' it were true. Bentham postulates the existence of a phenomenon called a 'community', which he defines as 'a fictitious body, composed of the individual persons who are considered as constituting as it were its members. The interest of the community then is, what? – the sum of the interests of the several members who compose it' (Ogden 1959: XXXI–XXXII). Given that this interest cannot be the expression of each person's desire to maximize their utility, we are entitled to ask: what is that interest?

As Mark Neocleous (2008) argues, one answer is security. The regard for security is the dark secret of Bentham's liberalism. It depends on the fiction that 'things' like 'the community' or 'the people' can be talked about as if they are real. (As Hans Vaihinger (1935) and Charles Ogden (1959) knew, Bentham understood too well all of our basic categories, like 'community', are 'as-if fictions'.) By providing security to 'the community' the interests of its individual members will automatically be taken into account and this becomes the actual rationality of law:

> Law alone has done that which all the natural sentiments united have not the power to do. Law alone is able to create a fixed and durable possession which merits the name of property... Law does not say to man, Labour and I will reward you; but it says: Labour, and I will assure to you the enjoyment of the fruits of your labour – that natural and sufficient recompense which without me you cannot preserve; I will insure it by arresting the hand which may seek to ravish it from you (Bentham 1948: 126).

Bentham squares the relationship between the universal rule of utility and the rule of law, rather like a magician pulling a rabbit out of the hat when he says:

> The only difference between politics and morals is, that one directs the operations of governments, and the other the actions of individuals. But their object is common; it is happiness. That which is politically good cannot be morally bad, unless we suppose that the rules of arithmetic, true for large numbers, are false for small ones.
>
> (Bentham 1931: 63)

As many critics have noticed, this answer is nonsense: if anything it merely reinstates the central problem, namely that 'the rules of arithmetic, true for large numbers, are indeed false for small ones'. Worse by making laws or policies that ostensibly claim to promote the greatest happiness of the greatest number, it may involve the promulgation of restrictive laws that are inherently antagonistic to, even destructive of the utilitarian idea that governments promote the 'greatest possible quantity of happiness, on the part of those whose interest is in view'. This magic trick is put to use by modern liberal-democratic states when they claim to defend the interests of 'the people' or 'the community': sometimes this is true, but sometimes this is more a defence of the interest of elites.

However, Bentham is even more confused than this. Bentham has argued that 'the business of government is to promote the happiness of the society, by punishing and rewarding' (Bentham 1948: 147). Yet he also wants to argue that:

> Law exists to prevent mutual harm and as a general rule the greatest possible latitude should be left to individuals, in all cases in which they can injure none but themselves, for they are the best judges of their own interest … The power of the law need interfere only to prevent them from injuring each other.
> (Bentham 1948: 147)

Here, we also encounter a very odd hole in a theory ostensibly devoted to leave people free to do whatever maximizes their utility. That hole is Bentham's refusal to think about rights or to take the idea of rights at all seriously. For Bentham as a legal positivist, it is a given that the state is both a reality (and not an 'as-if' fiction) *and* the source of all law. Put bluntly without the state and its laws, there can be no talk of rights (Ogden 1959: cxxviii):

> Rights, are, then, the fruits of the law, and of the law alone. There are no rights without law-no rights contrary to the law-no rights anterior to the law … Rights, are, then, the fruits of the law, and of the law alone. There are no rights without law-no rights contrary to the law-no rights anterior to the law.
> (Bentham 1931: 83–7)

This all has a lot to do with the other very basic problem that Bentham set up for himself.

Bentham defines the law as the will of the Sovereign who declares what the rules are, which are issued exclusively from the commands of a sovereign state (Bentham 1970: 27–8). For Bentham, a sovereign is the highest superior body in a political society (i.e. a 'state') and, therefore, an entity that does not owe any obedience to any other body. Bentham treats 'the sovereign in a state' as the 'source' of all its laws, at least in the sense of 'adopting' laws, which may actually be laid down by lawmakers. The sovereign is understood as 'any person or assemblage of persons to whose will a whole political community are (no matter on what account) supposed to pay…to pay obedience' (Bentham 1970: 18). Why this might be so is suggested when Bentham refers to the motivational element of law as its 'force', and that this suggests the use of coercion or, to speak frankly, the use of violence to enforce the law. The sovereign does not owe any allegiance to any other body or group. It is the will of this sovereign body which is known as law. That is, 'there must be some person or persons who are bound or in other words coerced by any law' (Bentham 1970: 54). In case he is misunderstood, Bentham adds:

> A law by which nobody is bound, a law by which nobody is coerced, a law by which nobody's liberty is curtailed, all these phrases which come to the same thing would be so many contradictions in terms.
> (Bentham 1970: 54)

He also adds that the anticipation or fear of being punished confirms the coercive character of law and that law is 'a necessary evil': as he says there is always a risk entailed by any law, namely 'that, some person or persons… are exposed at least to suffer by it' (Bentham 1970: 54). This looks a lot like an imperative theory of the law, a conclusion reinforced by Bentham's own use of the word 'imperative'. However, as many before me have noticed, Bentham is a one-man bundle of contradictions.

This becomes clear when Bentham having claimed that law is coercive, and then adds that law is 'unimperative, unobligative…[and] uncoercive' (emphasis in original: Bentham 1970: 96). Bentham provides examples of what he means when he says, 'The law which prohibits the mother from starving her child commands her to take care that it be fed. The one may be at pleasure translated or *converted* into the other'. That is, the law may be issued either as a command to 'Do', (i.e. feed the child) or 'Do not do' (i.e. do not starve the child). In this sense, the law can express what might be called 'contrary attitudes' towards the conduct it wishes to suppress or to promote. Bentham adds another example:

> 'Every householder shall carry arms': this is an example of a command: 'No householder shall carry arms': this of a prohibition: 'Any householder may forbear to carry arms': this, of a non-command: 'Any householder may carry arms': this, of a non-prohibition or permission.
>
> (Bentham 1970: 95)

Kept in isolation, this is a shrewd insight on Bentham's part, but does not offer a coherent account of the law. David Lyons (1972) trying heroically to defend Bentham from charges of radical confusion ends up merely amplifying the confusion. On the one hand, as Lyons argues, Bentham's basic concept of law should not be treated as a proto-Austinian imperative theory even though he allows that it is true that 'Austin shared Bentham's approach to understanding law and that their conclusions about the nature of a legal system were similar' (Lyons 1972: 362). Lyons tries to show that Bentham added to the idea that law is imperative and coercive by pointing to laws that were also permissive laws, even as he concedes that all 'efficient' laws-all laws for directing behaviour – are *essentially* coercive (?!?) (Lyons 1972: 362).

We have followed Bentham in his attempt to show how and why his account of the liberal-democratic state was legitimate when grounded in his principle of utility. He demonstrated no such thing. What we have is a magic show reliant on a lot of smoke and many mirrors, but at the heart of it is one basic idea: law is both coercive and in that respect law is 'a necessary evil' (Bentham 1970: 54).

John Austin: law as imperative command

John Austin does not have the kind of reputation that his achievement warrants. Austin can be credited with formulating the modern theory of 'legal positivism', which argues that there is no necessary connection between law and morality

(Bix 2004). A neighbour and protégé of Bentham (and of fellow utilitarians like James and John Stuart Mill – and of vehement critics of utilitarianism like Thomas Carlyle), Austin was appointed professor of jurisprudence at the newly founded University of London in 1826. His one book, *The Province of Jurisprudence Determined* (1832), sank without trace in his lifetime and only achieved posthumous recognition. Austin put the legal-positivist account simply:

> The existence of law is one thing; its merit or demerit is another. Whether it be or be not is one enquiry; whether it be or be not conformable to an assumed standard, is a different enquiry. A law, which actually exists, is a law, though we happen to dislike it, or though it vary from the text, by which we regulate our approbation and disapprobation
>
> (Austin 1995: 157)

Unlike later liberal theorists, Austin put a great deal of faith in the idea that the legitimacy of a state and its legal system rests on its capacity to compel obedience. Indeed for Austin the cultivation of a habit of obedience seems a fundamental prerequisite in any liberal order. This does not bode well for the conventional idea that liberals value both freedom and even dissent based on a rules-based order.

The idea of obedience is a prominent motif in Austin's account of sovereignty. By 'sovereignty', Austin means to refer to a person, or a collective entity like a government that is independent, i.e. not in the habit of obeying any other power or entity. Sovereignty is also defined as the power or capacity to issue commands that are generally obeyed because of the sovereign's capacity to threaten and impose punishment for disobedience: the sovereign imposes legal 'obligations' on his subjects. In effect, sovereignty defines a circumstance in which every law made by a sovereign person or body of persons is then imposed on those inferior people who are subject to that law. For Austin, it was enough that when a law is made or promulgated, we only need to understand that it constitutes a command which *obligates* those subject to the law to obey it (Austin 1995: 21–22). As Austin put it, we obey the law because it is an imperative command:

> Every positive law or every law simply and strictly so called, is set by a sovereign person, or a sovereign body of persons to a member or members of the independent political society wherein that person or body is sovereign or supreme.

Why is that? Austin says simply, this obligation exists because the lawmaker will cause an evil to be done to you in the form of a punishment should you go ahead and disobey the law. That threat of evil being done to you says Austin is the only obligation to obey that matters.

Austin argues that 'in order that a society may form a political society, the generality or bulk of its members must be in a habit of obedience to a determinate and common superior' (Austin 1995: 167). This is central to his theory of the law as an imperative system. John Austin (1995) adds that the law can be reduced to those commands and prohibitions issuing from the 'sovereign'. This is why Austin regarded individual laws as coercive commands. Austin says that laws ('properly so called') are the commands of a sovereign. He clarifies the concept of positive law (i.e. man-made law) by analysing the constituent concepts of his definition, and by distinguishing law from other concepts that are similar: 'Commands' involve an expressed wish that something be done, combined with a willingness and ability to impose 'an evil' if that wish is not complied with. Rules are general commands (applying generally to a class), as contrasted with specific or individual commands (like 'drink wine today'). Positive law consists of those commands laid down by a sovereign (or its agents), as distinct from other law-givers, like God's general commands, and the general commands of an employer to an employee. The 'sovereign' is defined as a person (or determinate body of persons) who receives habitual obedience from the bulk of the population, but who does not habitually obey any other (earthly) person or institution. Austin thought that all independent political societies, by their nature, have a sovereign.

On this account, positive law should be contrasted with other 'laws by a close analogy' (which includes positive morality, laws of honour, international law, customary law, and constitutional law) and 'laws by remote analogy' (e.g. the laws of physics). For Austin, this means that we have a state that looks a lot like Hobbes' state: it has no intrinsic limitation:

> It follows from the essential difference of a positive law and from the nature of sovereignty and independent political society, that the power of a monarch properly so called or of the power of a sovereign member in its collegiate and sovereign capacity is incapable of legal limitation …
>
> (1998: 212) …

This implies among other things that 'The immediate author of a law of any kind or any of the sovereign successor to that immediate author, may abrogate the law at pleasure' (1995: 212). It also implies that 'every political society must have a sovereign (one or a number) freed from legal restraints'.

Austin unlike his many liberal successors is not shy in spelling out what this means. Austin says that the preoccupation with rights and liberties found in liberal societies '[h]as been erected into an idol and extolled with extravagant praises by doting and fanatical worshipers'. In effect, says Austin, any state, even a liberal-democratic state, can choose to protect political or civil liberty – or not. Political or civil liberty is merely a gift granted to its citizens by the state:

> … political or civil liberty… is left or granted by a sovereign government to any of its own subjects; and… since the power of the government is incapable of legal limitation, the government is legally free to abridge their political liberty, at its own pleasure or discretion.
>
> (Austin 1995: 159)

This as we will see is hardly different in any way that matters from the critiques of liberalism and its 'rule of law' model offered implicitly by Max Weber who says legitimacy is what citizens confer on a state when they *believe* it is legitimate, irrespective of whether that belief is warranted and when Carl Schmitt more explicitly argues that legitimacy is irrelevant since state sovereignty rests on its use of coercion. Before I get to that part of the argument, I want to see how well modern liberals like Hart and Fuller do in rising to the challenge of showing that the authority of law, or its legitimacy, rests on law's capacity to justify coercion by grounding itself in something other than the ability of the state to use coercion.

The Hart-Fuller debate

Nicola Lacey (2010: 41) says correctly the Hart-Fuller debate 'continues to shape contemporary jurisprudence to a quite remarkable degree'. Lacey (2008) has also pointed out the effect of this when she notes:

> The fact is that the exchange between Hart and Fuller really did set the agenda for modern jurisprudence: the separation of law and morality, the place of values in interpretation, and the relation between the concept of law and the values associated with the rule of law.
>
> (Lacey 2008: 996)

This might not be a good thing. Thomas Mertens gets closer to the real significance of the Hart-Fuller debate when he says:

> In the Anglo-Saxon world, the discussion on the 'legality' of Nazi Germany or the lack thereof took place primarily within the confines of the Hart/Fuller debate for a very long time. This means that it could safely be isolated, and that legal theory could restrict itself to the rule of law as something primarily 'good'
>
> (Mertens 2007: 539)

Jeremy Waldron has also acknowledged that 'some jurists have suggested that the Hart-Fuller debate actually skewed the agenda for jurisprudence in unfortunate ways, which we are only now beginning to correct...' (Waldron 2010: 135). I agree.

This is because both Hart and Fuller take the debate about what makes law lawful or authoritative to some unfortunate places with serious consequences for the status of dissent. This was very much a consequence of their commitment to defend their respective traditions. Worse it also meant that they failed to address the question of legitimacy altogether. At its most basic, it is all very well and good for everyone, including David Dyzenhaus (2016: 3) to say that 'Legal authorities have or at least claim the right ... to tell subjects what to do', but the question needing to be asked but likely to be begged is this: on what basis does that authority rest? At stake is the idea that the philosophy of law (represented by Hart, Fuller, Dworkin or Dyzenhaus) is able to explain law's legitimacy or, as we might say, its authority. Neither Hart or Fuller can identify why the rules that Hart says make law what it is, or Fuller's claim that certain moral ideas make law what it is, show why we ought to obey the law or why the use of coercion to enforce the law is justified. Indeed their debate has the effect of privileging the liberal legal and political tradition especially when set beside a 'criminal' political-legal regime like the Nazi state, while obscuring some real and uncomfortable affinities even parallels at work in liberal-democratic legal systems like the use of preventive justice to suppress dissent. So how do Hart (and Fuller) explain law's authority?

Hart on the separation of law and morality

Hart used the 'Grudge Informer' case as an excuse to lay out his legal-positivist view of the law. Like Hart I am not interested too much here in the German case *per se*. That case gave Hart an excuse to strengthen the legal-positivist case by apparently getting rid of Austin's command theory of the law. Hart does this on the premise that if legal positivism can be differentiated from the command theory, then critics of legal positivism will be unable to rely on the rejection of the command theory to justify rejecting legal positivism.

Hart rejects the command model of law, i.e. law is comprised of the commands of a legally unlimited sovereign backed by threats' in a striking way: 'Law is surely not the gunman situation writ large, and legal order is surely not to be thus simply identified with compulsion'. He then sets about buttressing the fundamental legal-positivist claim, i.e. 'the separation of the law that is from the law that ought to be' (Hart 1958: 606), while restating the claim that it was useful and possible to carry out 'a purely analytical study of legal concepts' (Hart 1958: 601). This is supposed – presumably – to identify the basis of legitimacy (or authority) on which the law rests. I think it can be said he fails to do this. Having got rid of the unseemly idea, especially for a twentieth-century liberal like Hart that the only obligation to obey the law is that if you don't, you will be punished till you do, Hart is strangely bereft of any other idea. This is odd especially for a positivist who one would think would be inclined to follow the facts and who indeed is required to generate the 'ought' of legal authority from the 'is' of social facts.

Hart tries to sidestep the fundamental question of legitimacy by saying that any claim of legal authority presupposes the existence of some set of legal rules that confer that authority. For hart, law is just a social fact validated by its promulgation according to procedures laid down by higher (primary) legal rules (Hart 1961). For Hart, law has at its centre a stable core of purely legal interpretations that does not require recourse to external factors like messy moral principles to determine what is lawful or not. As a system the law to be law is dependent only on very minimal and contingent principles of morality for its functional existence. As Charles Olney (2016) notes, Hart (1961) argues that the law is a 'self-contained apparatus of positive rules with no referent to any outside values' (Olney 2016: 52). There is a sort of implied hint of an appeal to a hierarchy, but this is really just the idea that there are higher-order rules and lower-order rules. The lower-order rules obey the higher-order rules. Law is law. This is why laws remain valid long after both the issuer and subjects of the rules have died: this is because law stems from a sovereign source, where that sovereign is sustained only by the persistent collective affirmation of the legal order itself (Olney 2016: 52).

As Olney (2016) notes, Hart's evasion sets loose a red herring by suggesting that, for the most part, law is 'settled law', i.e. a 'hard core of settled meaning' in law' (Hart 1958: 601). This helps define the substance of the law – i.e. what law is. Outside of that hard core is 'a penumbra of debatable cases', those gaps in the law that require judicial creativity to fill. This Hart says does not rely on the judge discovering something that is already 'latent' within the law, i.e. an inherent morality (Hart 1958: 601). Hart's intention is clear: he is not interested in the question of authority or legitimacy. Rather, he simply wants to defend the separability thesis:

> To assert mysteriously that there is some fused identity between law as it is and as it ought to be, is to suggest that all legal questions are fundamentally like those of the penumbra. It is to assert that there is no central element of actual law to be seen in the core of central meaning which rules have, that there is nothing in the nature of a legal rule inconsistent with all questions being open to reconsideration in the light of social policy.
>
> (Hart 1958: 615)

It seems that for the same reason Hart makes a crucial strategic adjustment to the separability thesis by allowing for a minimum, necessary requirement of natural law, i.e. moral principles within any 'positive', i.e. actually existing legal system, in the form of certain principles that make it possible for the legal system and, indeed, the society itself to function at all. These include a prohibition on violence, a minimum protection of property rights, and claims to promote principles like objectivity and neutrality in the administration of the law like the utilitarian principle of treating like cases alike (Hart 1958: 623–24). Hart suggests these 'moral ideas' are vital for the operation of a legal system, but are strictly limited in their scope, to the extent that only 'some parts of society need to fall within these principles (i.e. to be treated equally under the law, be protected from violence and have their property safeguarded) in order for these criteria to be considered met' (Hart 1958: 624). In all other cases, Hart argued that moral factors remain external to the law.

Even here, Hart's argument is problematic. Hart's argument implies that in order for a rule to qualify as a law for a society, it must be one of the rules enumerated in a particular document, like the 'constitution' for that nation-state, which reflects certain social norms (Hart 1961: 92). Hart has smuggled in the idea that laws reflect social norms. This is a decidedly 'sociological' idea even though it is incoherent. It is incoherent given the pluralism of actually existing societies, which requires that we ask 'whose norms'? It is incoherent because it confuses the idea of social 'norms' with a moral account of the basic human goods. Hart surely cannot think that we should take seriously the idea that those societies in which a dominant group establishes a vicious social 'norm' are an example of the moral authority of law? What e.g. should we think about a case like the way white racist norms operating in the American south sustained cultural and political practices like lynching, persistent physical brutality or voter suppression. How should we understand misogynist norms in countries like Bangladesh which underpin widespread physical, even murderous violence and emotional abuse of women?

Hart's answer to the question of what renders the law lawful, and therefore, to be obeyed merely says that the law is lawful when those working in the law determine cases by applying lower-order interpretative rules informed by higher-order rules to their cases. On Hart's account, purely legal interpretations do not require recourse to external and messy (because contestable) 'moral' principles to determine what is lawful or not. Yet Hart's account of what counts as a 'moral' idea is extraordinary in the way it refuses to say anything specific about our moral ideas as defensible accounts of how we ought to live oriented to the goods that our conduct brings about for ourselves and our community (cf. Finnis 1980; MacIntyre 1981). For Hart, it is enough that moral norms be characterized by qualities like (i) 'importance', (ii) 'immunity from deliberate change', (iii) the 'voluntary character of moral offences' and (iv) the 'forms of moral pressure' surrounding them (Hart 1961: 164).

However, Hart's claim that law to be lawful and/or legitimate needs only a stable core of purely legal interpretations is subject to one basic and quite devastating objection. Hart's account, unlike say Bentham or Austin's account, fails to say why we ought to obey the law, or the state. Charles Olney (2016: 52) observes that Hart has not resolved the legitimacy problem: 'If law enables sovereign authority, then what sustains the law itself?' Answering that question by proposing a distinction between 'first order' and 'second order' rules doesn't work even when, as Hart (1961: 100) claims, it is possible to follow a chain or rules that ends up in the ultimate rule, the 'rule of recognition' upon which all authority to validate the entire legal system rests. Olney's point, while it seems subtle, is sharp and to the point. The ultimate rule, i.e. 'the rule of recognition' 'is not subject to questions of legality, but itself is an *exception to these normal requirements of law*' (Olney 2016: 52: My stress). The idea of validity depends on the difference between 'internal' and 'external' justification. From inside a legal system, the rules are judged by an 'internal statement of validity', while on the outside observers only look for 'external statements of fact that the rule exists in the actual practice of the system' (Hart 1961: 108). As Olney notes, 'the rule of recognition implies a basic gap at the heart of law – a point of singularity where the normal terms of law are reversed' (Olney 2016: 53).

In effect, there are no legal constraints on the decision to affirm a particular rule of recognition. Paradoxically, the rule of recognition is the 'exceptional core of law', a proposition that brings Hart close to the political theory proposed by Carl Schmitt that claims that, when we examine the liberal state as a lawmaker, we encounter the essence of 'the political', namely the sovereignty of the state and its capacity to declare 'an exception'. This exceptionality is doubly so. Apart from being able to declare a legal exception, the authority of the law is found outside both the law, and if Schmitt is to be believed, outside of any moral or 'normative' framework. To put this simply: on Hart's account, the system of legal norms or rules is only possible because a power exterior to legal and moral norms secures legitimacy for the exercise of legal authority. 'Without the idea of a space beyond law, there could be no law at all. Law, then, does not just *include* the exception; it is *founded upon it*. This concept of something *outside* law that is the founding point *of* law' is remarkably close to Schmitt's 'decisionist' account of sovereignty and 'the political' (Olney 2016: 53). I will return to this point later in the book

Worse as Scott Shapiro points out, Hart cannot escape a self-created contradiction to do with his account of the authority of legal rules:

> ... some source invested with legal authority must exist to create them. Legal rules after all are the products of legal authority. Who then is the legal authority responsible for the existence of the authorising rules. Surely the source of the rules cannot be identical with the subject of the rules, because the subject does not have legal authority before the rules confer it. Conversely if the source is different from the subject of the rules then it must have secured its legal authority from another set of rules. But then we are forced to ask the same questions again...
>
> (Shapiro 2001: 150)

Shapiro tries to excuse Hart by suggesting that this means there is a 'self-reflexivity at work in law'. Hart and Shapiro may think this, but if legal authority can only be created by rules, who makes the rule that creates the authority in the first place? (Shapiro 2001: 152). As Shapiro admits, it seems we are condemned to ask the same questions 'chicken or egg, vicious circle or infinite regress', again, and again, and again.

The hard answer given by John Austin to the question of legitimacy does not go away: if 'every political society must have a sovereign (one or a number) freed from legal restraints', then the obligation to obey is found in sovereign power. In short, Hart fails to provide us with a warranted answer to a question, why ought we obey the law?, grounded in terms of either the conventional approach adopted by legal positivists or in his acknowledgement of the role played by legal norms. How well does Lon Fuller deal with this problem?

Lon Fuller on the moral basis of law

Unlike Hart, Fuller at least intuits that engaging the question of lawfulness, i.e. what makes law lawful, requires an answer couched in terms of *why* we might be obligated to obey the law. As Fuller puts it:

> I do not think it is unfair to the positivistic philosophy to say that it never gives any coherent meaning to the moral obligation of fidelity to law. This obligation seems to be conceived as *sui generis*, wholly unrelated to any of

the ordinary, extra-legal ends of human life. The fundamental postulate of
positivism – that law must be strictly severed from morality – seems to deny
the possibility of any bridge between the obligation to obey law and other
moral obligations.

(Fuller 1958: 656)

Fuller resists the ideas that the lawfulness of law rests on either 'a simple fiat of
power or a repetitive pattern discernible in the behaviour of state officials' (Fuller
1958: 632). Fuller accordingly sets out the key claim made by those who belong
to the natural law tradition that, for law to be lawful, it must be based on moral
grounds. To make this case, he treats 'order' as what the law supplies, and good
order as 'law that corresponds to the demands of justice, or morality, or men's
notions of what ought to be' (Fuller 1958: 644). He adds the odd idea that law has
its own 'inner morality'. As he puts it:

> … law, considered merely as order, contains… its own implicit morality. This
> morality of order must be respected if we are to create anything that can be
> called law, even bad law.
>
> (Fuller 1958: 645)

In 1958, Fuller did not say what these moral ideas that constituted the 'inner
morality of law' were. Six years later, he (1964) would spell out that these moral
ideas include the proposition that laws should: (i) be general; (ii) be publicly
promulgated; (iii) not be retroactive; (iv) be understandable; (v) be consistent
with one another; (vi) not require conduct beyond the abilities of those affected;
(vii) remain relatively constant and (viii) be administered in a manner consistent
with their wording.

It could be argued that these 'moral ideas' are hardly different from Hart's
grudging acknowledgement that basic moral principles like objectivity and neutrality in the administration of the law actually do matter. Equally and more substantively, the problem with Fuller's list is that it is not quite clear why these are
goods that matter. It is perfectly easy to ask how these eight principles 'apply' to
laws like the Nazi informer statutes and conclude that those statutes conform to
those principles, but are still deeply bad legislation. Fuller's list looks a lot like the
kind of abstractedly Kantian principles Fuller's Harvard colleague John Rawls
was developing to buttress his account of justice. This approach treats rules *per
se* as moral without saying clearly why these are accounts of human goods that
matter. Fuller's moral principles like efficiency or the rational alignment of our
means and ends look a lot like instrumental values. That is, it is not clear why
a general, perfectly understandable and well-publicized law requiring parents to
circumcise all their children or the one requiring every citizen to report about
people they hear criticizing the current government or its leader meets some test
of human good. Equally, as Dyzenhaus (2016) has pointed out, we really would
need to think about the moral basis of any legal system in which, e.g. one law

conscripts eighteen-year-olds into the military forces, while another denies them the right to vote.

Fuller seemed to think that his moral rules were well able to be treated as legal rules, which seems to his mind at least to point to a 'merger' between law and morality. On the question of whether admitting moral ideas into the very heart of the law posed any dangers – as Hart argued it did – Fuller thought it did not. Fuller made the case that morally good ideas or intentions are intrinsically 'more coherent' than evil aims. He added that the best protection against Hart's concern that morally bad ideas might insinuate themselves into the law is not to insist on the legal-positivist separation thesis, but rather to strengthen the connection between law and morality. He made this case by asking a rhetorical question: would a judge intent on evil objectives:

> ...[b]e likely to suspend the letter of the statute by openly invoking a 'higher law'? Or would he be more likely to take refuge behind the maxim that 'law is law' and explain his decision in such a way that it would appear to be demanded by the law itself?
>
> (Fuller 1958: 637)

The larger issue, however, is what does this mean? And is it sufficient to claim that the authority of law is grounded in moral facts or appeals made to some moral principle? The problem is this. As Simon Lavis (2015: 87) notes, the Hart-Fuller debate conflated the possibility that laws can be used as an instrument of power with the idea that law can be treated as an explanation for this. As David Dyzenhaus notes, this 'has had an unfortunate impact on philosophy of law', in particular on the way in which Fuller's challenge to legal positivism somehow became a debate between legal positivists and natural lawyers about how to understand the judicial interpretation of the law (Dyzenhaus 2006: 224).

We can see the tangles people can get into when trying to ground legitimacy in 'morality'. This is what Ronald Dworkin (1978) did when he took on the challenge of defending Fuller's natural law position by deciding, given Hart's distinction between 'settled law' and the 'penumbra of difficult cases', that this is only a question about how to understand the judicial interpretation of 'difficult cases'. As Dyzenhaus notes, Dworkin's 'interpretivist' model claims that, in a 'hard case', the judge decides the case by extracting a theory from the relevant positive law (i.e. the law as it is in a given legal system) in ways 'that reveals the law, and the whole legal order as whole, in its best moral light' (Dyzenhaus 2016: 131). In effect any answer the theory supplies in response to the legal question posed by the case is the 'right answer', because it is 'the answer that the judge is under a legal and moral duty to give' (Dyzenhaus 2016: 131). Yet this won't do as Dyzenhaus (2016: 131) points out, especially given the widespread and 'sheer facticity of unjust laws and illegitimate legal systems' I have highlighted in earlier chapters.

The problem – or dilemma – is an artefact of Dworkin's own natural law interpretivist perspective, which rejects the Separation Thesis of legal positivism, i.e. that there is no necessary connection between law and morality. To use the classical formula, Dworkin has to be committed in some important sense to the proposition, *lex injusta non est lex* – 'an unjust law is not law'. However, he is then faced with the problem of establishing whether the moral basis of an unjust legal system is a 'morally repugnant ideology', a step he really doesn't want to take. Efforts by later theorists like David Dyzenhaus (2016) to deal with this problem end up adopting what looks like a political argument that says we will only make law work towards the ends of justice by political means, which may, e.g. mean using a legal framework of human rights politically to hold the coercive powers of the state accountable.

The more basic problem is that factually there are unjust laws and illegitimate legal systems. For example, it is estimated that eight million African-Americans were denied the right to vote in the Presidential election of 2016.

Some twenty-one states denied their right to vote that was established under the *Voting Rights Act* 1965 by using legislation to impose restrictions, purging voters, like voter-ID laws, or restricting the hours that polling places were open or by preventing felons from voting: 1.7 million felons, e.g. were not allowed to vote in Florida – representing about a fifth of possible black voters. As Dyzenhaus notes, faced with an illegitimate legal system, one dedicated overall to extreme injustice, or simply with a small number of laws like those used to prevent African-Americans from voting, the best explanation of this will 'surely be that it is the product of a morally repugnant ideology'. However, when a natural lawyer like Dworkin addresses this problem, he faces a self-created dilemma between the natural law position that very unjust laws are invalid, and the legal-positivist position that, if they are valid, we should simply decide that the laws are so unjust that they should be disobeyed. In either case, we are left with the insight that something external to both the law and to a range of moral principles is determinative of how states make policies and laws: that 'something' seems to have to do with power and politics.

Conclusion

In this chapter, I have confronted the liberal tradition's claim to say why a liberal-democratic state is entitled to insist on obedience. This tradition developed across a distinctive genealogy of legal philosophy is split between those who say just look at the (legal) facts, and those who say consider the moral grounds upon which the law they claim is said to rest.

Legal positivists seem, in general, to be agreed first that the law either has nothing to do with morality or that it *ought not*. As Gardner puts it, all we need to know is that 'at some relevant time and place some relevant agent or agents announced it, practiced it, invoked it, enforced it, endorsed it, or otherwise engaged with it' (Gardner 2001: 200). I explored Harts attempt to avoid relying on Austin's command theory, by suggesting that the authority of law rests on following rules. This does not work. Hart's clever arguments do not quite get rid of the elephant in the room: even liberal-democratic states rely on sovereign power to ensure obedience to the law, i.e. the 'imperative' or 'command theory' of the state/law. Hart actually relies on a decisionist account of law's authority, where the system of legal norms or rules is only possible because a political power exterior to or prior to legal and moral norms secures legitimacy for the exercise of legal authority.

What of the idea that there are distinctively moral obligations that secure legitimacy? A variety of philosophers of law or political theorists have looked for 'ethically' good reasons for why we should obey the law and the state. Natural lawyers like Fuller (1958, 1964) argued that law to be legitimate needs to conform to formal or procedural standards such as generality, publicity, comprehensibility, consistency and so on. This thin account of moral ideas is hardly adequate to the task.

This is so because somehow – and mysteriously – the liberal imaginary has evolved into Schmitt's world of walls. As Elizabeth Vallet (2014: 1) reminds us, if the fall of the Berlin Wall in 1989 seemed to promise a 'world without borders', the rush to build walls in Iraq, Israel, Saudi Arabia, France, Hungary, Bulgaria, Tunisia and even America tell us otherwise. As she notes even ostensibly, liberal-democratic states now rely on ever-more:

> … sophisticated and domineering systems of checkpoints, surveillance, and data collection … enforced by increasingly militarized police forces … that reproduce the nationalism and xenophobia of the populations they at once enclose, protect, and suffocate.
>
> (Vallet 2014: 1)

Much of this wall building is dedicated to promoting security, one consequence of which has enabled the suppression of dissent (Sitze 2015: 145; Brown 2010). In effect, the liberal-democratic tradition has undermined the conditions for its 'own coherence and effectiveness' (Sitze 2015: 145) both in a legal sense and as I will now suggest politically.

We begin to see how this has happened when we turn to the other way liberal-democracies have set about claiming legitimacy, the idea that there are political foundations upon which democracies and the authority of liberal-democratic states rests, namely the consent of their people.

Chapter 7

The political legitimacy of the liberal-democratic state

Alex Jones is a multi-millionaire radio talk-show host, blogger and film-maker in America. He is the host of *The Alex Jones Show*, nationally syndicated on some sixty radio stations, and claiming an audience of seventy million listeners. He self-describes variously as 'right wing', 'conservative', 'paleo-conservative', 'alt-right' and 'libertarian'. On the afternoon of 11 September 2001, and just hours after the attack on the World Trade Center in New York City, Jones went to air in Austin, Texas, saying to his audience, 'I'll tell you bottom line. Ninety-eight per cent chance this was a government-orchestrated controlled bombing'. Years later he was still insisting that the 9/11 attacks were 'controlled demolitions... You just watched the government blow up the World Trade Center' (Zaitchik 2011). Apart from videos and his radio show, Jones runs two conspiracy-themed websites, InfoWars.com and PrisonPlanet.com, to promote the 9/11 Truth Movement whose supporters are usually referred to as 'Truthers'.[1]

Alex Jones is someone who normal people would describe as 'delusional' at best, who is encouraging too many other Americans to believe palpable nonsense. Jones has persistently claimed, e.g. that the 1996 bombing of the Oklahoma FBI building by Timothy McVeigh was actually carried out by the American government. He has claimed to have:

> ... interviewed people who said they'd seen Timothy McVeigh planting explosives with a military escort and cops who mysteriously died after telling him the government did it. Just like the Reichstag! And there was a bombing drill that morning!
>
> (Richardson 2015)

In December 2012, he would claim the Sandy Hook Bay School mass shooting was a hoax, sponsored by the Obama administration and was 'completely faked with actors', to provide a rationale for tougher firearms legislation. Jones promoted the idea that President 'Obama is hardcore Wahhabist; he is al-Qaeda', and that the Boston Marathon bombing was really a 'false flag' operation instigated by the American government or by secret evil 'globalist' forces planning to establish a 'New World Order' that would replace sovereign nation-states and undermine

'Judeo-Christian civilization'. According to Jones, the New World Order is promoted by a mixture of governments, corporations and a secret order called the Illuminati. Sometimes Jones likes to add that this is all a front for 'lizard people' who are mounting what he has called an 'intergalactic invasion':

> Just like the Bible says, it's basically an intergalactic invasion into this space through people. I'm telling you, it's what all the ancients said. It's what they warned of. It's what we're dealing with. They're demons! They're frickin' interdimensional invaders OK?
>
> (Sommerlad 2018)

The Southern Poverty Law Center, a not-for-profit human rights and legal advocacy agency located in Montgomery, Alabama, e.g. has described Jones as 'almost certainly the most prolific conspiracy theorist in contemporary America' and may be the conspiracy theorist 'with the most far-reaching influence in the nation's history' (Southern Poverty Law Center 2018). Jones can arguably claim some of the credit for survey-based evidence suggesting that 28 per cent of American voters now believe that there is a global conspiracy to subvert American sovereignty. (Those surveys suggest that 34 per cent of Republicans and 35 per cent of independents believe in the New World Order threat compared to just 15 per cent of Democrats. Other research suggests that perhaps half of the American public believe in one or more conspiracy theories (Oliver and Woods 2014). Unsurprisingly perhaps, during the last years of the Obama presidency, 44 per cent of Republicans had come to the view that 'an armed revolution in order to protect liberties might be necessary' (Public Policy Polling 2013).

This might suggest why someone like Alex Jones highlights some fundamental questions about dissent. Don't his bizarre beliefs and the level of popular support for those beliefs highlight the dangers to any liberal democracy of allowing the free exchange of outrageous ideas and dangerous beliefs? Doesn't his case indicate why liberal democracies might need to restrict the classical liberal support for the right to free speech, because it runs the risk of allowing extremists to destroy the very fabric of a liberal democracy?

I think not. In this chapter, I want to suggest that Alex Jones' claim to speak for 'The People' against elites and outsiders is not only an exemplary expression of populism, but also points to certain intrinsic problems with the political idea that popular sovereignty secures the legitimacy of liberal democracy states. There are some basic and unresolvable contradictions that are embedded in the seemingly rock-solid foundations of liberal democracy which the rise of populism of the kind Jones speaks for and helps to foreground.

Populism and The People

David Niewert (2017) argues that Jones' conspiracy theories are but a small part of a long-standing streak of right-wing racism and populist sentiment which

American populism has directed against African-Americans, immigrants, Jews, and Hispanic Americans, especially Muslims of late. Since the Trump Presidential campaign in 2016, we have learned to talk about the Alt-Right. Paralleling Arlie Hochschild's research on the Tea Party movement, Niewert argues that the latest version of this strand of populism relies on a narrative about how hard-working, mostly white Americans are under siege, even assault from a combination of greedy power-hungry elites from above and a parasitic class of immigrants, blacks, Hispanics, Muslims and welfare recipients from below (also Hochschild 2016).

There are many things to be said about the recrudescence of populism. From the perspective of this book, it is plainly one of the many contemporary expressions of dissent. Jan-Werner Mueller (2016) argues this kind of populism is hardly unique to America: there are local versions of this in most advanced Western liberal-democracies today. As Muller sees it, populists always claim that they, and they alone, represent The People and their true interests. The various global expressions of nationalist and xenophobic populism all tell a story based on an imaginary. The story is about The People who are under assault from enemies both within and external to the national community. The enemies of The People are always Other who can include Jews, Catholics, Muslims, coloured people, immigrants, unionists, gays and lesbians, feminist women, young people, liberals, people on welfare and so on. Muller treats the construction of a narrative about The People as the clue to the monistic politics of right-wing populism. Populists hate the implied pluralism of democracy. The essential irony is that when considered as a form of dissent which I understand as the sign of pluralism, populism is both anti-pluralist and anti-democratic. This kind of dissent promotes the abolition of difference and pluralism. Most importantly, it points to two key problems with how we think about the idea of democracy and The People.

For one thing, the way in which contemporary populists use a combination of traditional mass media and new social media to influence public opinion raises important questions about the legitimacy of liberal-democratic states. The kind of public opinion represented by Alex Jones' combination of ignorance and hate-filled prejudice serves to highlight problems with the idea that liberal-democratic regimes are legitimate when the public engages in rational, truth-oriented deliberative processes to arrive at public opinion. What does the level of influence achieved by right-wing populism of the kind represented by Alex Jones say about the premise that liberal-democratic polities secure their political legitimacy by engaging in rational deliberative processes? What if the deliberative processes involved in public opinion making aren't all that rational?

This matters because ultimately liberal democracy claims its legitimacy rests on the consent of The People. This is why in one sense dissent is such a problem. The democratic idea of The People seems to imply that The People will need to achieve a substantial, if not perfect degree of unanimity if democracy is to thrive: Rousseau thought he had made a major contribution to democratic theory when he gave us the idea that The People can make a 'social contract' and then somehow generate a 'general will', thereby making democratic government possible. Equally, the very idea of a 'general will' is just one of the several ways liberal-democratic theorists since Rousseau have privileged consent over dissent. Dissent of any kind subverts any simple idea about the point and value of popular consent or the virtues said to inhere in The People. This is true when liberal elites begin to express a deep distrust of the masses especially when this involves advancing loopy conspiracy theories like Alex Jones' account of 'lizard people' invading earth. It is equally true when making left intellectuals make well-argued and robustly evidenced claims about how neoliberal policies state and elite interests have generated systemic economic inequality since the 1980s on a scale not seen since the 1890s (e.g. Picketty 2014).

Here we encounter a deep political paradox even riddle. On the face of it, as Geoff Mann notes, much of the left wants democracy without populism (2017: 21). Equally it might be added much of the right wants populism without democracy. Either way there is a deeper, grittier question to be addressed: what are the political grounds for securing the legitimacy of liberal-democratic states? In particular, what role does the idea of popular consent play in securing the legitimacy of liberal-democratic states? And what, if anything, does this imply for the practice of dissent – and its criminalization?

Political legitimacy: framing the questions and an argument

Peter Singer is a modern moral philosopher, widely acknowledged as the 'inventor' of the Animal Liberation movement. Philosophically, Singer has long identified as a utilitarian. Singer has usefully highlighted the political grounds upon which a liberal-democratic state claims legitimacy. This is because to his credit, Singer (1973) wanted to think hard about when, if ever, it is legitimate to disobey a democratic government? (That question I return to in the following chapters). To engage that question, he says we need first to work through when we are required or obliged to obey a government. By 'obligation', I understand Singer to mean the idea that we have a duty or a responsibility to obey a government: this is the question of legitimacy.

As we saw in the previous chapter, a tradition of legal philosophy associated with the liberal tradition claims we are obliged to obey the laws of the country in which we live. Singer calls this a 'legal obligation':

> I am under the laws of the United Kingdom legally obliged to refrain from assaulting other people. This is a valid law, which says I must not do so, a law certain to be upheld by the highest court of the United Kingdom if I should be misguided enough to challenge it.
>
> (Singer 1973: 2)

For many liberal legal theorists and philosophers, legitimacy begins with the *fact* that states with sovereign power have the power to make law. However when asked the obvious question, 'what precisely obligates us to obey the laws of a state?' we get several kinds of answers. The answer given by legal positivists like Hart says that we should obey the law, and the state that issues them, because the rules and modes of reasoning that characterize the law requires that we do. The other answer given by natural lawyers says we obey the state and its laws because there are good moral reasons for doing so. The answer given by the first legal positivists seems more honest: Bentham and Austin accepted that the fact of state sovereignty explains why we are obligated to obey the law. Close examination of the more recent arguments suggest why modern legal philosophers have not been able to get around the 'imperative' or 'command theory' of the state/law: the obligation to obey actually rests on the likelihood that we will be punished if we don't.

Alongside the idea of legal obligation, Singer (1973) points to a different, and distinctly political kind of obligation grounded in the fact of democracy itself, and in the idea of 'popular sovereignty'. As Singer observes, the idea of 'popular sovereignty' says we ought to obey any government elected by the people because 'we are the people'. This points to a conventional liberal-democratic argument, which says democratic governments derive their authority from the consent of the people. This answer was crafted initially by seventeenth- and eighteenth-century political philosophers like John Locke and Jean-Jacques Rousseau, before it was popularized in American political culture by way of things like the Declaration of Independence of 1775. In effect, as Singer puts it, the obligation to obey a government occurs because 'Its citizens ought to obey it because they have consented to its rule' (Singer 1973: 24).

This argument has even been used to argue that we are obliged to obey even a palpably bad law made by a democratic government precisely because of the principle of popular sovereignty. So does political philosophy (or theory) do a better job than legal philosophy in explicating the grounds upon which the legitimacy, or authority of a liberal-democratic state rests?[2] What are the political grounds that indicate why we ought to obey a democratic state? On what basis if ever, or at all, does popular sovereignty provide the answer to this question? How are the people to assert their sovereignty? To address these questions, we need clarity about the nature of 'the political': what do we mean when we talk about politics or 'the political'?

On politics

We saw in Chapter 2 that while there are good reasons for distinguishing between 'politics' and 'the political', this has not been the usual approach taken by conventional political science. The 'political' of 'political science' has long been defined in a small number of ways. Some insist that politics is about the exercise of power or legitimate domination, others the making of collective decisions or the business of government or what states do, while others talk about the management of conflict and so forth. Many have agreed with Max Weber's influential account when he said 'politics' 'means striving to share power or striving to influence the distribution of power, either among states or among groups within a state'. It was not a big step for the 'black prince' of German legal philosophy Carl Schmitt to insist that politics is the relation between 'friends and enemies'.

There are several reasons for taking Schmitt seriously. One is that he offers a relational account of political action, albeit one framed in terms of an adversarial or antagonistic relation. Another is that his critique of liberalism calls out the complacency of so much liberal legal and political theory. That said Adam Sitze notes this has sponsored a tug of war over Schmitt by his critics unable to decide whether to praise or blame, accuse or apologize for him (Sitze 2015: xvii). When Schmitt (1976) argued that the condition of possibility for legality and legitimacy is always susceptible to being undone by the political act that suspends it, Schmitt subverted the central claim of the liberal tradition that it renders the state subject to law. Schmitt reminds us that the state is both the source of law *and* above the law. Schmitt goes further when he argues that a truly political decision breaks free from any norm, and from any normative justification and becomes the expression of 'pure political will'. This points albeit tacitly to another merit of Schmitt's work. The apparent absence of any normative basis of Schmitt's account of the political poses a question: is there really no normative basis for politics? This re-quires some thinking given the premise that political theory like its object politics is a normative practice: see writers like John Dryzek (2000), Bonnie Honig (2008) and Ronald Beiner (2014). As Dryzek et al. (2011: 1) puts it:

> Most of political theory has an irreducibly normative component – regardless of whether the theory is systematic or diagnostic in its approach, textual or cultural in its focus, analytic, critical, genealogical, or deconstructive in its method, ideal or piecemeal in its procedures, socialist, liberal, or conservative in its politics.

I want to suggest that his own argument there is a normative basis in Schmitt's account of the political, not least of all when a sovereign power declares a state of exception. If Schmitt has admitted that there is one normative basis, I will go on to show that there are other arguably more important norms like the value of dissent (a task left to the next chapter).

Here I begin by examining the claim that popular sovereignty does a better job when democratic states claim to be legitimate.[3] The essential claim is epitomized by the English liberal philosopher T.H. Green when he argued that we should obey the law even if we disagree with it. Green supposes a case where a person has:

> … decided that some command of a 'political superior' is not for the common good, how ought he to act in regard to it? In a country like ours, with a popular government and settled methods of enacting and repealing laws, the answer of common sense is simple and sufficient. He should do all he can by legal methods to get the command cancelled, but till it is cancelled he should conform to it?
>
> (Green 1907: 111)

Apart from appealing to 'common sense', Green seems to repose a good deal of faith in the idea that a popular government will somehow make things right. This is a nice idea, but again falls apart on the obdurate rocks of the real. As many cases like the voter suppression project in the southern American states suggest today, when a majority of people want to oppress the most basic human rights and freedoms like voting, they can and will get away with it and do so by appealing to the majoritarian logic of democracy.

This then opens up the point of examining what we have called the 'political paradox' (Ricoeur (1965), a paradox at the heart of the idea of popular sovereignty. This is the political version of the 'legal paradox' that Scott Shapiro (2001) highlighted when he asked how law ever to constitute its own authority is. The political version of this, says Kevin Olson, is that 'democratic lawmaking becomes paradoxical when it must establish the very conditions for its own institutionalization' (Olson 2007). But how is that that be done?

As will become clear, that paradox is resolved by the political means, and Carl Schmitt has provided one compelling account of how this works. As Schmitt says, 'Sovereign is he who decides on the exception' (Schmitt 1976: 5). In Schmitt's view, even though the sovereign 'stands outside the normally valid legal system, he nevertheless belongs to it' (Schmitt 1976: 5). The sovereign belongs to it precisely in virtue of the sovereign's capacity to decide on the exception. Tracy Strong says that, for Schmitt, 'it is the essence of sovereignty both to decide what is an exception and to make the decisions appropriate to that exception' (Strong in Schmitt 1976: xii). This, in turn, poses a second question. What enables the sovereign to decide on the exception and thus be sovereign? The answer offered by Walter Benjamin is unflinching and chilling: the answer is violence, a violence always 'implicated in the problematic nature of the law itself' (1978: 287). What all this adds up to indicate both why dissent is so valuable and why it is so readily criminalized by liberal-democratic states.

Legitimacy and popular sovereignty

Let me turn to the claim that we obey governments and their laws because they are the expression of popular sovereignty. As Kevin Olson suggests, in Western liberal-democracies, this is a kind of ready-made narrative that conjures up an immensely attractive:

> … idea of a democratically self-constituting people … A new nation boldly asserts its independence from a dominating dictator, colonial power, or occupying force. It declares itself sovereign and performatively constitutes itself as such by democratically ratifying a constitution.[4]
>
> (Olson 2007: 330)

Yet as Olson points out immediately, this idea of a people constituting a democratic state through democratic means points to an inherent 'bootstrapping problem'.

'Democracy is both a necessary feature of such a project and its intended result. This reveals a circularity at the heart of constitutional democracy' (Olson 2007: 330).

There are clear parallels between those legal philosophers who claim that the 'rule of law' secures the legitimacy of the legal system of a liberal-democratic state and those political philosophers who claim that popular sovereignty secures the legitimacy of the political order. Legitimate procedures structuring democracy cannot be the pre-requisite for legitimate procedures structuring democracy. So on what basis then does popular sovereignty become legitimate? Why ought we to obey a democratic state? Second, how are the people to assert their sovereignty? Could the answer be that they are not to assert their sovereignty, or at least not too often, or too insistently? I address these issues first by engaging with one of the greatest theorists of democracy Jean-Jacques Rousseau.

Rousseau on popular sovereignty

A central figure in the eighteenth-century European Enlightenment, yet radically unconvinced of the virtues of philosophy practised by fellow *philosophes* like Voltaire, Hume or Diderot, Rousseau is a central figure in modern political philosophy. Chris Bertram (2004) argues that the central political question of politics for Rousseau is how to reconcile the freedom of the individual with the authority of the state. Bertram says Rousseau makes the case in *The Social Contract* (1762) that each person can enjoy the protection of the state, while remaining as free as they were in the state of nature. What achieves this reconciliation is the idea of the 'general will', that is, the collective will of the citizen body taken as a whole. The 'general will' is itself the source of law and is willed by each and every citizen. In obeying the law, each citizen is thus subject to his or her own will, and consequently, according to Rousseau, remains free. This also seems to solve the problem of legitimacy, i.e. the idea that a state is legitimately entitled to require its citizens to obey it only when it is guided by the 'general will' of its citizens.

However, the question of popular sovereignty bedevilled Rousseau. As close readers of Rousseau like Bonnie Honig (2008) and Simon Critchley (2011) have noticed, Rousseau's pursuit of legitimacy depends on a version of what has been called 'the political paradox', which haunts the relationship between legitimacy and sovereignty. As Honig puts it, paraphrasing Rousseau:

> In order for there to be a people well-formed enough for good lawmaking, there must be good law for how else will the people be well-formed? The problem is: where would that good law come from absent an already well- formed, virtuous people?
>
> (Honig 2008: 119)

She adds that while Rousseau seemed to imply that the paradox was at work in the origins of a regime, it is more than that, because that paradox is alive at every moment of political life.

This paradox literally can only be resolved magically. Critchley argues that Rousseau sought to elucidate the nature of 'the political', understood by Rousseau as the act by which a people became a people able to exercise sovereignty and so give birth to a democratic order. This process sets loose a paradox of sovereignty. Critchley in making this case, notes that Louis Althusser (2006: 175–200) had already observed that, in Rousseau, the conditions of the possibility for Rousseau's account of the political are the conditions of its impossibility. This paradox runs through Rousseau's (1762/1997) *The Social Contract*, a book devoted to answering two questions: why is a political order required? and how may individuals come to agree that each person has an interest in being just and agree to constitute a political order?

For Rousseau, this involves establishing first that men have grown away from a state of nature towards a Hobbesian-like circumstance characterized by violence and disorder. Second, he assumes that it will be possible by some philosophical argument to supply good reasons which will enable the 'average man … capable of deriving his rules of conduct to arrive at justice … from this manner of reasoning' (Rousseau 1994: 80). Rousseau expected that this would mean using the very reason which had initially led humans astray. By using reason, man could

> … learn to prefer his interests rightly understood to his apparent interests … he will become good, virtuous, sensitive, and in sum, finally, instead of the ferocious brigand he wanted to be, the most solid bulwark of a well-ordered society

(As Critchley (2011: 33) puts it the 'poison of reason' would in Rousseau's hands also be 'the antidote'.)

Rousseau set out to tackle head-on the question of the legitimacy of the political order, which he said needed to pass one test namely the need to create a 'general will':

> … a form of association that will defend and protect the person and goods of each associate with the full common force, and by means of which each, uniting with all, nevertheless obey only himself and remain as free as before.
> (Rousseau 1997: 49–50)

Rousseau's answer is his idea of the 'social contract', 'which is the act by which a people becomes a people which is the true foundation of society'. Having established the civic order, Rousseau then turns to the next question: 'By the social pact we have given the body politic existence and life: the task is now to give it motion and will by legislation' (Rousseau 1997: 69). By law Rousseau means to identify the special role of the general will. As he puts it:

> But when the whole people enacts statutes (*statue*) for the whole people it considers only itself, and if a relation is then formed, it is between the entire

object… Then the matter with regard to which the statute is being enacted is general, as is the enacting will. It is this act which I call law.

(Rousseau 1997: 67)

But Critchley rightly captures the paradox at work:

How can humans live according to a law that they recognize as equally binding on all citizens, as legitimate for the collective as a whole, and yet at the same time a law to which they freely submit because they see it as the expression of their own freedom?

(Critchley 2011: 37)

For one thing, Rousseau argues that, in order for the general will to be truly general, it must come from every citizen and apply to every citizen. This is in the nature of law itself. The law cannot identify particular individuals and it must apply to every citizen. Rousseau thought that this might lead citizens, to be guided by a consideration of what was in their own private interest, and so favour laws that secured the common interest. However, if this were to work, the situation of citizens would need to be substantially equal, a clear problem in any society like eighteenth-century France marked by radical inequalities of wealth, education, culture or opportunity. In such a society, it is unlikely that a citizen will take on the standpoint of the general will merely by imagining the impact of general and universal laws on his or her own circumstances. This implies further that, while under the right conditions citizens will agree on the laws that correspond to the common interest, in any unequal society, the state will lack legitimacy.

Rousseau's attempt to wiggle-waggle his way around this problem by talking about the 'general will' simply abolishes any idea that the 'general will' involves or 'contains' the expression of private interest. The general will does not seek to promote private interest, but only the public good: the citizen is 'free' to choose to do what will promote the public good because that is what civil liberty as distinct from natural liberty promotes.

Frank Michelman (1997) and Charles Olson (2007) canvas the problems set loose when political processes or groups create constitutions for themselves. While Rousseau followed Hobbes and Locke in talking up the idea of social contract, Michelman (1997) suggests this contract is unlike any normal contract which relies on existing rules and laws of contract to enforce the contract. In the state of nature, there is no existing system of rules or procedures to establish the founding contract. Rather as Rousseau argues, there is an originary moment of creation-as-alienation when all of the putative citizens surrender their freedoms and rights to a new political entity 'the people':

These clauses [of the social contract] rightly understood all come down to just one, namely the total alienation of each associate with all of his rights to the whole community.

(Rousseau 1997: 50)

As Critchley notes, this is a magical moment:

> The so-called social contract begins with the fact of the total alienation which is overcome by an act of total alienation whereby I give myself to the community an imagined community, to an imagined generality to a people which does not in fact exist
>
> (Critchley 2011: 49)

That magic moment dissolves quickly into paradox. First, there is the paradox revealed when we consider the hint of circularity in Gimmler's (2001: 23) argument, that the legitimacy of modern liberal states is the 'result *of* a discursive practice that provides the framework for solving political conflicts rationally', where the 'validity of the justification is apparently produced by recourse to rational discourse'.

The problem is always there in the liberal drive to find a rational or procedural basis at the heart of the originary founding moment. There is, of course, no problem in creating a polity, or a system of laws or a constitution or a political order by simply declaring that it be brought into being by force: 'obey these laws or suffer the consequences'. Such decisionism of the kind Schmitt advocated simply reflects the unilateral political will of a personal dictatorship, or a collectivity like an army, or the moment as in East Germany in 1989 when the people simply withdrew their support for the Communist regime in the space of days.

However, given the liberal wish to ground legitimacy in something other than violence or a unilateral political will, any such unilateral decisionism is deemed to be procedurally valid because it is not procedurally regulated, i.e. it is not the fruit of the rule.

Liberals want people who want to found a political or legal order to engage in a ground-clearing task of establishing a consensus about how to proceed. Their deliberations must themselves be guided by some idea about what is to be decided and by whom. Yet this liberal disposition dissolves into something quite odd. For those seeking such procedural legitimacy, a legitimate first step in founding a constitution based on procedure is not possible. As Olson (2007: 331) puts it:

> A legitimate first step would need to be formed through normatively acceptable procedures. Such procedures cannot exist however because by definition the first step in lawmaking is not proceeded by a normatively acceptable procedure.

In practice, any democratic attempt to create a constitution, e.g. requires a previous constitution that has already established democratic procedures. There is an infinite regression of procedures presupposing procedures each necessary to form the procedures following it.

One way the paradox can be dealt with is to bind people to the state which Rousseau says forcing people to be free. As Critchley suggests, the state may, e.g. construct and use a form of civil religion complete with uplifting and emotionally engaging ceremonies to create the kind of appropriate political will among citizens: this is a version of Dahlgren's account of 'civic culture', where the state takes on the task of socializing its citizens and creating the kind of emotional dispositions, which will enable the individual citizen to want to conform to the general will. Another option, as William Connolly (1995) suggests, is simply to acknowledge that violence is the source of the obligation to obey. That violence as John Austin said is carried out daily in the name of law, which claims to be nonviolent by representing itself as purely self-grounding or of popular sovereignty (which claims to be nonviolent by representing itself as the true and total will of the people (Honig 2008: 119).

This is precisely the problem that dissent becomes to any liberal-democratic regime. It reveals that the 'general will' is a chimaera. It reveals that there is a plurality of beliefs and competing ideas about the goods of human life. It reveals the deep fear that those who work in and for the state have of dissent. And it reveals courtesy of the criminalization of dissent that the fear drives the violence carried out daily in the name of law.

We also see how magic is involved in the way 'sovereignty' reworked to become 'popular sovereignty'. In monarchies, 'sovereignty' is literally inscribed in the body of the monarch or in dictatorships in the person of the Leader. The magic of this lies in the way there can be no external manifestation of sovereignty, e.g., in the body of a monarch or even in a parliament. Popular sovereignty means that 'sovereignty is the pure presence to itself of the body politic, animated by the general will' (Critchley 2011: 56). As Rousseau insists:

> Sovereignty cannot be represented for the same reason it cannot be alienated: it consists essentially in the general will, and the will does not admit of being represented either as it is the same or it is different: there is no middle ground.
>
> (Rousseau 1997: 114)

This is the basis of Rousseau's rejection of any idea of representative democracy. Morgan has argued that the liberal idea of parliamentary representation is a fiction and we might add arguably at least as much a fiction as Rousseau's idea of the general will. Political representation which is the dominant model of liberal democracy requires that the few represent the people. The truth as Critchley (2011: 57) says is that 'the spurious legitimacy of representative government rests on the fiction of the few *believing* that they represent the many and if the fiction is believed, vice versa'.

On sovereignty and legitimacy: Weber and Schmitt

As Giorgio Agamben (1998, 2005) has reminded us, there is an answer. Carl Schmitt (1985, 2005) argued that the condition of possibility for legality and legitimacy is always open to being rendered suspect by the political act that suspends it. This is Schmitt's account of sovereignty. Sovereignty is revealed in the state of exception (*iustitium*) it makes possible: 'sovereign is he who decides on the state of exception'. What Roman law called *iustitium* is the 'state of exception', that circumstance when the operation of the law, or the constitution is suspended by the state. This answer did not come out of nowhere.

Unlike the Anglo-American liberal tradition, a nineteenth-century German tradition of *Staatslehre* (or 'political theory') had conceived of the political in a state-centric way: states are the legitimate source of domination, which possess the power to coerce. This was the tradition which von Gerber drew on when declared 'the legal nature of the power of the state, that is the state's power of will [resides] in the concept of domination' (Cited Vollrath 1995: 51). In the early twentieth century, Max Weber likewise affirmed that *Herrschaft* is the 'authoritative power of command' (*authoritare Befehlsgewalt* – where the suffix *gewalt* can mean both *unlawful violence* and *legal force* (Cited Vollrath 1995: 51). This implied that legitimation-as-authority is based on rule or domination (*Herrschaft*).

But what did this imply for some conception of normative legitimacy which is normally understood as Alex Levitov (2016) says to mean that a given state is legitimate because its public officials enjoy 'a moral permission' to use or threaten force to apply the law within its jurisdiction. The corollary as Levitov notes is that 'the subjects of this state fall under a general (if not exceptionless) moral duty *at the very least* to refrain from engaging in violence or coercion in that state's jurisdiction except as explicitly licensed by the state itself (sic)' (Levitov 2016: 1).

The twentieth-century tradition of German political theory represented especially by Weber and Schmitt was quite prepared to ditch the idea of 'moral permission' when thinking about legitimacy.

Max Weber on legitimacy

As Wolfgang Mommsen (1989) pointed out, e.g. Max Weber's account of legitimacy appears to refuse any recourse to normative or ethical criteria. This is not surprising given that Weber was also a persistent advocate for the idea that scholars *should* be value-free (Mommsen 1989: 20). Weber's approach to the idea of political legitimacy is important if only in an exemplary way: Weber consistently begs the question of whether legitimacy is in some sense real, or something that like 'beauty' really belongs to the eye of the beholder.

The question of legitimacy arose for Weber because as he argued states enjoy a legitimate monopoly of violence. Weber insisted in his famous speech, 'Politics as a Vocation' that if we ask what is the state, he said 'Today, however, we have to say that a state is a human community that (successfully) claims the *monopoly of the legitimate use of physical violence* (*das Monopol legitimer physische Gewaltsamkeit*) within a given territory' (Weber 2011). What then confers legitimacy?

Max Weber argued while a state might secure at least temporarily compliance 'from motives of pure expediency' or 'on a purely customary basis through the fact that the corresponding behavior has become habitual', state institutions upheld on these bases are 'much less stable than an order which enjoys the prestige of being considered binding, or, as it may be expressed, the prestige of 'legitimacy" ([1922] 1978, 31). As Alex Levitov (2016) notes, Weber's approach to legitimacy describes the belief that those subject to the directives of a state widely believe it to enjoy the moral right to rule. According to Weber, to claim that a state or its laws are legitimate simply means that the citizens of that state *believe in the rightness of that state* (*legitimitätsglaube*) in regard to it: 'the basis of every system of authority, and correspondingly of every kind of willingness to obey, is a belief, a belief by virtue of which persons exercising authority are lent prestige' (Weber 1964: 382), that is, it is enough that if those subject to the commands of a state simply and widely believe that the state enjoys the moral right to rule.

Levitov (2016) is not alone in thinking that the question of legitimacy involves asking whether states are morally entitled to wield political power over their subjects, specifically by issuing legal commands and the being prepared to enforce those commands with the threat or use of physical force. Yet what the reference to being 'morally entitled' means is unclear.

Classical liberal social contract theories have tried all sorts of manoeuvres to say what this means and have done it badly. One tactic in the hands of liberal theorists like John Locke was to argue that we freely handed over our rights and freedoms to the state in a kind of social contract. The appeal of the social contract idea as Levitov (2016) puts it is that our freely given consent or agreement is normally thought necessary for us to incur enforceable obligations to other persons or organizations. Locke's version of the social contract model argued that:

> Men being... by nature, all free, equal and independent, no one can be put out of this estate and subjected to the political power of another, *without his own consent.* The only way whereby any one divests himself of his natural liberty, and puts on the bonds of civil society is by agreeing with other men to join and unite into a community.... This any number of men may do, because it injures not the freedom of the rest; they are left as they were in the liberty of the state of nature.
>
> (Locke 2002 [1689], 330–331)

Even so this formulation still left the problem of what to do if and when states behave badly: if we have consented to be governed by a tyrannical state, for example, does the social contract still oblige us to obey its commands? (In Locke's case, the answer was that we could not lose or cede all of our natural rights so we preserved a capacity to disobey a tyrannical government.)

The alternative account proposed by natural law theorists like Kant and Rawls starts from the premise that we cannot hope for justice without some common legal authority, i.e. a state to designate what justice looks like and then enforce it. Like Hobbes, Kant, e.g. thought we cannot talk about rights and freedoms until there is a common political authority (i.e. a state) prepared to spell out what this means. The value of establishing a state is that it can be charged with issuing and enforcing a single specification of its subjects' rights, freedoms and duties. For Kant, it followed that we are obliged to recognize certain natural moral duties that require we support such an authority so long as it is 'reasonably just'. What this curious phrase might mean is never made clear. The contradictions set loose when we recall how Kant himself systematically espoused deeply racist and anti-Semitic sentiments completely at odds with his espousal of the universalizability premise are truly staggering.

More recently, John Simmons seems to think that for any state to be legitimate all that is required is that the state properly 'define and enforce the basic rights of its subjects, thereby enabling them to discharge their duty of justice through its institutions' (Simmons 2001: 140). Or as Rawls puts it:

> ... our natural duty of justice, requires us to support and comply with just institutions that exist and apply to us. It also constrains us to further just arrangements not yet established, at least when this can be done without too much cost to ourselves. Thus if the basic structure of society is just, or *as just as is reasonable to expect in the circumstances,* everyone has a natural duty to do his part in the existing scheme.
>
> (Rawls 1999: 99) (My emphasis)

When Rawls says everyone has a natural duty to do his part in the existing scheme when the basic structure of society 'is just, or *as just as is reasonable to expect in the circumstance's*' (Rawls 1999: 99) we must surely ask him to clarify what he means by what must otherwise be dismissed as a bad case of weasel words. At the least referring to a notion of justice opens up another version of the political paradox we've already discussed: how can a deeply, unjust because unequal, society enable or obligate the state regulating such a society to start to promote social justice by challenging the very fabric of such an unjust society?

No such paradox is evident in Weber's common-sense realism. On the one hand, Weber's account of legitimacy only requires that enough people believe in the legitimacy of the state irrespective of whether there are any compelling or reasonable moral reasons to do so. The implication of Weber's account of legitimacy is that legitimacy understood as the normative connection between people and the political order they live in really doesn't matter. It may either be a chimera, a *mythos* or a device enabling people to sleep easy at night. As Joseph Raz (1979: 109–110) points out, when a state perceived to be legitimate has issued a law or a regulation, this does not by itself give those subjects of the state any compelling normative reasons whatsoever to comply with that directive, that is, it remains quite unclear what, if any, compelling moral reasons there are that obligate citizens to obey the state – apart from the brute fact that functioning states, especially liberal-democratic ones, typically have a monopoly of physical violence which can draw on as a last resort when all else has failed.

This is not to deny, of course, that, on some occasions, the citizens may agree that the state has good reasons for introducing laws requiring the compulsory wearing of seat belts or avoiding drinking alcohol before driving and so conferring legitimacy on that specific legislation or policy. (The fact that many citizens may go on not wearing seat belts or abstaining from alcohol does not alter the legitimacy at stake in these cases.) However, this does not imply that we ought to make acceptance of, or agreement with, the reasons a state has for introducing a law as the basis of according legitimacy to the state as a whole: the implication of this is that wholesale rejection of the reasons offered by a state for introducing a whole range of policies and laws has an equal and opposite effect of denying legitimacy *en tout court*.

Weber is a lot like John Austin. Weber wanted us to agree with him when he says that we obey the law because it is a fact that the law exists: he is a legal positivist who says our moral ideas about law being just or good has nothing to do with our being obligated to obey the law. Yet even this seemed to go too far for Carl Schmitt, the most redoubtable of the great critics of liberal democracy, whose account of the political and the nature of sovereignty forces us to the ultimate showdown.

Carl Schmitt on the political

Schmitt's decisionist conception of 'the political' and his account of sovereignty was developed in response to his own time, a time characterized after 1918 first by the collapse of the German Empire followed by a period of intense violent struggle characterized involving left and right militia-led coups (ca 1919–20) and then by a long period of political struggle going on within the Weimar republic before Adolf Hitler was offered the Chancellorship of Germany in January 1933. Schmitt set out imbued with a deeply conservative disposition or *habitus* to make the point that liberalism was unable, or unwilling to theorize the true nature of the state and the political. This meant that he even rounded on Max Weber.

Schmitt claimed that in the landscape dominated by pluralist democracies informed by liberal-individualist theories, 'one seldom finds a clear definition of the political'. Liberalism itself in Schmitt's view simply did not understand the state or politics. Liberalism had no positive theory of the state or the political. Rather liberalism has only:

> ...attempted to tie the political to the ethical and to subjugate it to economics. It has produced a doctrine of the separation of and balance of powers, but this cannot be characterized as a theory of the state or of basic political principle.
>
> (Schmitt 1988: 61)

Schmitt also thought that Weber had failed to grasp the autonomous and objective essence of the political. As Schmitt (1988: 20) saw it, Weber had defined the political using the concept of power as the decisive factor, yet power appears mostly as state power. Accordingly, we get from Weber a circularity which is unhelpful: 'The state thus appears as something political, the political as something pertaining to the state – obviously an unsatisfactory circle' (Schmitt 1988: 20).

Schmitt rejected the legal positivist tradition which evolved during the Wilhelminian Empire producing a highly rationalist, formalist and relativist theory of jurisprudence. Schmitt also rejected the liberal constitutional theory of the state, which treated the state as both subordinate to law and subject to the will of a representative parliamentary assembly. Schmitt disliked the reliance on abstract rationality and was sceptical about the consequences of the liberal-individualist conception of a private sphere inhabited by rights bearing individuals protected from state interference. He also rejected the parliamentary conception of politics grounded in discussion made possible by the free deliberation of elected representatives meeting in assemblies.

Schmitt's approach to the political is frequently identified as 'decisionism'. This is because the political requires not deliberation but decision. Why does he say this? Schmitt's 'decisionistic' formulation depends on his radical reduction of the 'political' to the ways we deal with our friends and our enemies. Equally, sovereignty is revealed as a purely political act exemplified in

the decision to suspend the rule of law:

> ... the decision on the state of exception, the moment of the suspension of the operation of law, brings the subject 'who'? into being. To put it into a slogan, *the subject is the consequence of a decision.*

Ironically given his criticism of Weber, the core of Schmitt's theory of the political is the idea that the true subject of the political is the state, and that the state must always stand higher than the law (Critchley 2011: 105). As Schmitt (1976: 19) put it bluntly, Weber thought that 'The concept of the state presupposes the concept of the political'. Yet Schmitt's attempt to escape the circularity he was so critical of in Weber when he tried to ground the substantive foundations of law and politics in certain existential situations like war, or in the conceptual distinction between friend and enemy when conceptualising the political, does not work.

Thomas Moore (2010: 722) notes that while Schmitt argued for the autonomy of the political, his account of the political is actually highly dependent on the state. Having set out to de-couple the identity between 'the state' and 'the political', Schmitt almost immediately reinstates the identity.

For one thing having declared that the political is the relationship between 'friend and enemy', he instantiates this by talking about war and then talking up the state as the 'decisive political entity': 'The state as the decisive political entity possesses an enormous power: the possibility of waging war and thereby publicly disposing of the lives of men' (Schmitt 1976: 44). Killing thus becomes the concretization of the concept of the political. It functions as a way of determining whether the enemy is a real enemy: 'If there really are enemies in the existential sense as meant here, then it is justified, but only politically, to repel and fight them physically' (Schmitt 1976: 47). As Moore notices, by linking killing to the political, Schmitt undermines his claim that politics is autonomous. Even more unaccountably, Schmitt subverts his own case when he argued that the condition of possibility for legality and legitimacy is always susceptible to being undone by the political act that suspends it. In effect, the political is instantiated by the power of the sovereign/state to declare an exception. Perhaps Schmitt was so delighted by the beauty of his aphorism that he neglected to grasp how it subverted the fundamental claim that politics is autonomous of everything else – including the state!

Assuming that the political could be grasped as something both 'autonomous' and 'objective', Schmitt's existentialist account stressed the adversarial even violent nature of politics. The political is born out of struggle. For Schmitt politics itself was conceived of as a friend-enemy relationship in a world best understood as a battlefield. For Schmitt both the state and the political have a deep and basic existential quality which liberalism and its valorization of the individual have simply failed to acknowledge.

The political acknowledges the fact that humans in groups confront each other as enemies. Any entity involved in friend-enemy relations is by definition 'political', whatever its origin or the origin of the differences leading to enmity. As Schmitt insisted even, 'A religious community which wages wars against other members of other religious communities or engages in wars is already more than a religious community: it is a political entity' (Schmitt 1976: 37). Politics is an existential state of affairs informed neither by rational motives nor bound by law: the political is prior to and emerges before law. 'Every religious, moral, economic, or ethical or other antithesis transforms itself into a political one, if it is sufficiently strong to group humans beings effectively according to friends and enemies' (Schmitt 1976: 37). Politics exists when I can conceive of or act to physically liquidate my enemy by killing him. Only where there is a real possibility of physical killing, can politics be said to exist.

It is political struggle which gives rise to political order. States arise as a means of continuing, organizing and channelling political struggle. As Hirst (1988: 9) notes, for Schmitt, struggle and conflict are so much part of our natural condition that 'No amount of discussion, compromise or exhortation can settle issues between enemies. There can be no genuine agreement because in the end there is nothing to agree about'. For Schmitt, the political was all about the need to defend the nation-state with the blood of its own citizens. Schmitt argued that 'In case of need, the political entity must demand the sacrifice of the life. Such a demand is in no way justifiable by the individualism of the liberal thought' (Schmitt 1988: 60).

As various commentators have noticed Schmitt offers a devastating critique of democracy and liberalism and the 'conjuring trick which is law'. Paul Hirst (1988: 73) notes that:

> Schmitt's analysis cuts through three hundred years of political theory and public law doctrine to define sovereignty in a way that renders irrelevant the endless debates about principles of political obligation or the formal constitutional powers of different bodies.

As Schmitt puts it:

> About an abstract concept there will be no argument ... What is argued
> about is the concrete application and that means who decides in a situation
> of conflict what constitutes the public interest or interest of the state, public
> safety and order ...The exception which is not codified in the existing legal
> order, can at best be characterized as a case of extreme peril, a danger to the
> existence of the state ... But it cannot be circumscribed factually and made
> to conform to a preformed law....
>
> (Schmitt 1988: 7)

As others have noted, Schmitt's (1957/2003) account of the law-as-*nomos* is complementary in the extreme.

On the moral dimension of 'the political'

It is time to draw this lengthy discussion to its point. We have already seen that
despite his attempt to overcome what he saw as Weber's tautological conflation of
the state and the political he failed to avoid doing this himself. We can now ask
if Schmitt is right when he claims to have got rid of all moral or normative considerations by reducing the political to the struggle between friends and enemies.
After all, Schmitt is very clear when he says, e.g. that:

> ... the friend and enemy concepts are to be understood in their concrete and
> existential sense, not as metaphors or symbols, not mixed or weakened by eco-
> nomic, moral, and other conceptions, least of all in a private – individualistic
> sense as a psychological expression of private emotions and tendencies. *They
> are neither normative nor pure spiritual antitheses.*
>
> (Schmitt 1976: 28 (My stress))

Yet Schmitt cannot get rid of moral or normative ideas so easily. There are a
number of basic problems. First, Schmitt could not have missed out on the fundamental idea first articulated by Aristotle that friendship is an inherently moral
idea-cum-relation. As András Körösényi (2005: 1) notes, 'the concept of friendship belongs to the core of Aristotle's political philosophy'. The concept-cum-
relation of friendship is fundamentally a moral conception and one with many
intriguing and important qualities. In Aristotle's hands, 'Friendship, as a moral
code and a civic ethos, becomes a *normative* concept, which lays the foundation of
the concord in the city. It is idealized as a relation between good men' (Körösényi
2005: 1). The capacity for friendship is understood as a virtue because it arises
among people who become friends out of a shared concern for basic human goods.
Alasdair MacIntyre (1984: 158) has made the point more recently, e.g. that it is
the shared concern for basic human goods that enables 'genuine friendship and
which provides the paradigm for the relationship between husband and wife in
the household as well as for that between citizen and citizen in the *polis*'.

Aristotle did understand that friendship could also be problematic. In his *Nichomachean Ethics* (1155a: 22–7), Aristotle highlighted the crucial role of friendship in politics in the following way:

> Friendship also seems to keep cities together, and lawgivers seem to pay more attention to it than to *justice*. For like-mindedness seems to be similar, in a way, to friendship, and it is this that they aim most at achieving, while they aim most to eliminate faction, faction being enmity; and that is no need for rules of justice between people who are friends, whereas if they are just they still need friendship – and of what is just is thought to be what belongs to friendship.

We now understand that, for Aristotle, there was only one possible Good. This meant that Aristotle could not acknowledge the possibility of conflict within the *polis* arising from the existence of rival concepts of the Good. He unhelpfully assumed that the virtues that matter are all in harmony with each other and the harmony of individual character is reproduced or reflected in the harmony of the state. On McIntyre's account, Aristotle's belief in the unity of the virtues led him to disavow the impossibility let alone the value of conflict either in the life of the good man or the good city (*polis*). In this way, a deep and abiding prejudice about the value of disagreement and dissent was set loose. As MacIntyre puts it, '(C)onflict is simply the result either of flaws of character in individuals or of un-intelligent political arrangements' (MacIntyre 1984: 157).

In fact on a closer reading of Aristotle, we will also see how the relationship between friend and enemy which is so central to Schmitt is also present in Aristotle. In stark contrast to the soppy sentimentality with which the idea of community has been sprayed around neoliberal polities by welfare workers and community development workers to disguise the rotting smell of inequality and exclusionary practices (Sassen 2016), Francois Dubet (1994) pointed out that logic of community has always been imbued with the logic of the friend-enemy relationship: community works on the principle of excluding the enemy/the Other. In this respect, Dubet merely channels Aristotle. The ideal of the just *polis* as a community of friends, i.e. that of good men, could only be maintained by the *exclusion* of those citizens who would threaten its cohesion, or by the exclusion of the morally inferior (i.e. the large majority of the population, including slaves, craftsmen, tradesmen, manual labourers and women) (Blum 1980; MacIntyre 1984: 159; Lynch 2002: 107).

Second, if we take the relational perspective seriously, as I have suggested we need to, then we also see that the category of the enemy as a relation also makes the category of friend possible. Recall that Schmitt insists that, 'The specific political distinction to which political actions and motives can be reduced is that between *friend* and *enemy*'. Schmitt says that 'the distinction of friend and enemy denotes the utmost degree of intensity of a union or separation, of an association or dissociation' (Schmitt 1988: 26). Aurel Kolnai argues, 'It is clear that the more fundamental idea here is not friendship but enmity, since the latter phenomenon is regarded as constitutive for friendship itself in the strongest sense, for the political unity of human beings' (Kolnai 2004: 19). In this respect, the normative character of the friend-enemy distinction is reinforced. For a virtue ethicist like MacIntyre, '(I)t is through conflict and sometimes only through conflict that we learn what our ends and purposes are' (MacIntyre 1984: 164). In a similar fashion, Gabriela Slomp (2003) argues that the concept of friend/enemy distinction is crucial for our identity. First, the consciousness of the self emerges from the comparison with the 'other', and second, identity emerges 'through psychological and physical confrontation with the enemy and, conversely, through the psychological and physical collaboration with friends', as Slomp (2003) puts it. We realize 'who we are' in a conflict with the other, and establish our identity through conflict.

A third and no less significant problem arises when Schmitt claims that he is offering a political theory without a normative foundation in his account of sovereignty and the capacity of sovereign power to declare an exception.

András Körösényi (2005: 9) gets it wrong when he seems to accept at face value Schmitt's claim that the 'enemy is given by nature, they are the *different* people' and so are either neutral in ethical terms or do not have any ethical meaning. Körösényi may have been better advised to treat political-cum-military conflicts as involving political considerations and processes. On Schmitt's account, the definition of a group as an enemy is a political decision. The enemy may be imagined as different or it may really be different. It may pose no threat or it may pose an existential threat.

It is true enough that Aristotle thought that the politics of friendship would or should lead to a transcendence of, or avoidance of, conflict. On that score, achieving unity in a civic community certainly has a moral quality. Yet it does not follow in spite of arguments made by Aristotle and Korosenyi (2005) that conflict, strife and violence within a state or between warring states, are devoid of moral qualities.

In such conflicts, a number of moral or normative considerations matter. For one thing, Stephen Buckle (2013) claims that the first law of politics is epitomised in the Latin tag *Salus popula suprema lex* ('the safety of the people is the first law'). Buckle (2013: 68) insists that:

> The most plausible understanding of the task of politics and of social policy is that they operate within the bounds of at least one constraint: that public safety be protected and preserved, now and into the future.

If nothing else, the *salience* of this proposition – as distinct from its *truth* – seems 'obvious' given that we live in an era with abundant evidence, suggesting that the executives of many declared liberal-democratic constitutional states believe they are in an extended episode of *Game of Thrones*, surrounded by insidious terrorist Islamist 'enemies' who can only be dealt with by 'blood and power'.

As previous chapters have documented, the executives of states including those in Australia, Britain and America have used their sovereign power to variously suspend the normal 'rule of law', create new laws and apply existing laws to crimi-nalize and to limit certain political rights and practices – like the rights to privacy, protest and free speech. Suspending the normal rule of law has had the effect of rendering actions that were previously illegal, like the invasion of states themselves deemed to be havens sponsoring terrorism, torture, detention without legal pro-cess, political assassination or unrestrained surveillance of citizens, legal. It also has other effects some that would be laughable except no-one is laughing. Yet it cannot be denied that rightly or wrongly there has been a normative cast to the decisions by states to declare exceptions and wage a 'war on terror'. The task of assessing the truth claims about the degree of threat actually posed by Islamist terrorism has been carried out but so far with precious little effect (Mueller and Stewart 2016a).

Third, and more generally, when civil strife or war between states erupts, there are always moral emotions involved. At least since Homer's *The Iliad*, we can have no illusions about the potency of, or the role played by, a range of moral emotions. These can involve the love of country, righteous anger provoked by some real or imagined hurt or harm, a desire for honour or renown, or the desire to display courage in the face of mortal threat. In each case, we are confronted with a distinctive set of moral characteristics that inevitably are implicated in conflict between friends and enemies. This cannot be gainsaid. Schmitt in his eagerness to prove his point has overlooked something quite important.

Finally, we can be assured that, in most such conflicts, the enemy becomes a moral enemy, and the war against it becomes a 'just war'. By this last phrase, I mean only that there are now well understood normative criteria articulated at least since the fourth century CE by St Augustine of Hippo for determining whether states have identified and or can meet certain criteria either justifying initiating war or for governing the conduct of that violence. It can here be noted without further discussion in this chapter that Schmitt did acknowledge the idea of the 'just war'. In his (1991) last great work, *The Nomos of the Earth*, Schmitt conceded that, in the centuries after Grotius and Puffendorf developed a body of 'international law', and following the establishment in 1645 of the Westphalian system in Europe, an idea of *jus publicum Europaeum* prevailed. This presupposed that every state-qua-enemy could be considered just, and as defending a just cause, and this signalled rationalization and humanization of war for three or more centuries (Schmitt 1991: 91). This era of enmity was based on the presump-tion of equal rights conferred by the laws of war (*jus belli*) agreed to by sovereign states. Schmitt claimed that, by the start of the twentieth century, however, a newer conception that envisaged the moralization of enmity produced a new type of absolute enmity, in which the enemy state was outlawed before it was to be annihilated/exterminated.

The point of all this is simple. Schmitt subverts the liberal tradition that ren-ders the state subject to law by reminding us that the state is both the source of the law and above the law. In this respect, we cannot, nor should we, be taken in by the promise of liberalism. Its claim to legitimacy is tricky. As Derrida (1992) and others have shown, any critical attention given to the idea of legitimacy reveals a basic problem: 'legitimacy', as Derrida has noticed, is a self-defeating idea. While some who use it seem to think that it refers to some kind of extra-legal moral quality, etymologically the idea of 'legitimacy' refers simply to the quality or authority attributed to a practice imparted by *lex/leg* (i.e. law). In effect, the 'legitimacy of law' or the legitimacy of the state as lawmaker refers to a system of discourses and practices said to constitute the law and renders it obligatory and desirable by claiming that 'the law is the law'. In effect, the legitimacy of the law relies on the fact that 'law is law' a claim long attributed to the legal positivist tradition.

This view is entirely unsympathetic to and unwelcomed by modern liberals and/or to democratic theorists who want to locate the authority/legitimacy of the law in everything but violence, legitimate or otherwise.

They prefer to rest the claims for legitimacy made by liberal democracies on theories of social contract, or on the principles associated with democratic sovereignty, deliberative rationality, discourse ethics, utility maximization or simply on Kelsen's (1945) idea of a ground norm, i.e. in the fact that there is a constitution or a legal system with rules. Any or all of these have seemed to liberals and legal positivists like Hart to supply to supply the reasons why we ought to obey the law. These answers are generally understood to possess some normative ground i.e. they appeal to some minimal ethical grounds: those who ground the legitimacy of the law in democratic sovereignty, e.g. appeal to the idea that the sovereignty of the people supplies grounds enough for us to obey what are after all rules 'we the people' have apparently made. Likewise, those who appeal to the story of a social contract appeal to the idea that reason we left a state of nature that was in Hobbes' phrase a state where life was 'short, nasty and brutish' did so in order that, by surrendering all our natural rights and freedoms to an all-powerful state, we might at least secure the kind of collective security and civic order that allowed us to get on with our lives in a civil space characterized by some degree of peace and good order.

Yet as it has become increasingly clear, much of this defence of legitimacy of liberal-democratic states understood as the search for the implied ethical or normative basis of liberal democracy does not stand too much close scrutiny.

If liberal-democratic theorists have so far failed to identify the relevant normative framework that sustains the legitimacy of liberal-democratic states, does this mean that Schmitt's case that there are no such norms hold good? I think not. Schmitt wants to deny a normative basis for the political. He has failed to do so. The implications of this are dealt with in the next chapter.

Notes

1 *Infowars.com* has an Alexa rank of 890 in America (2018), while *PrisonPlanet.com* has an Alexa rank of 19,190 in the US (2018). An Alexa ranking of around 100,000 suggests significant popularity and a score of 890 extreme popularity.

2 We see a tendency on the part of political philosophy (e.g. Rosenblatt 2018) to have little to do with legal philosophy (e.g. Lacey 2016) and vice versa. This mutual aversion doubtless has explanations grounded in disciplinary habitus as well as more substantive explanations.

3   While I was tempted to examine Habermas' claim that political legitimacy is secured
    by processes of rational public deliberation, I decided that little good would be derived
    by starting from the premise that treating political processes as if they were – or ought
    to be – a philosophy seminar presided over by Professor Jurgen Habermas, which is
    even remotely sensible. This really is an exemplary case of what Bourdieu (2000) calls
    the scholastic fallacy.
4   Julian Jackson provides a compelling account of the vertiginous nature of such a con-
    stitutive process in his historical account of how Charles de Gaulle stepped into a
    power vacuum in post-liberation France after June 1944 to 'found' the modern French
    state (Jackson 2011: 310–68).

Chapter 8

The legitimacy of political violence

The difficulty liberal-democratic governments have with dissent was illuminated starkly in August 2018 when British Prime Minister Therese May travelled to South Africa. Questioned by one journalist about what she had done personally in the 1970s and 1980s to secure Nelson Mandela's release from prison, she replied indignantly that she had not taken part in anti-apartheid protests but that she was proud of 'what the British government had done'. Another journalist wondered if this meant May had supported Conservative backbencher's call to hang Nelson Mandela or whether she thought that the then Prime Minister Thatcher was right to call Mandela a terrorist (Sarkar 2018).

One way of grasping that difficulty is captured in the cliché that one man's freedom fighter is another's terrorist. While some may point to figures like George Washington, Eamon de Valera, Menachem Begin or Jomo Kenyatta, or more controversially someone like Ulrike Meinhof, Nelson Mandela is the usual go-to-example for this cliché.

Here I focus on Mandela and the hard case of political violence as dissent. While all sorts of elaborate and frequently heated controversies have swirled around Mandela, the African National Congress and its armed militia *Umkhonto we Sizwe* centring on the question of whether they were – or were not – terrorists, there is no point in beating around the bush. After a period of advocating for peaceful political struggle including civil disobedience in the Gandhian tradition, Mandela became a clear and forceful advocate for armed violence.

The case of Nelson Mandela forces us to address a hard question: when, if ever is political violence justified? Naomi Sussman would add that the hard case of political violence – or terrorism – raises cognate questions like what is just or even, merely justifiable political violence? What particular forms or uses of violence may be just, or justifiable in political contexts or to political purposes? What distinguishes just political violence from unjust [political] violence? (Sussman 2013: 426). Is it enough, as state-centric theorists have argued, that states are always justified when using violence while non-state actors are never justified?

Certainly Mandela was the key leader of the struggle to end apartheid in South Africa, a struggle that began in the 1950s. Built on centuries of racialized government that had begun in South Africa when it was a Dutch colony, apartheid

(The Afrikaans word means 'separateness') was a system of racial segregation legally installed in South Africa when D.F. Malan's National Party was elected to government in 1948 by white South African Boers. At this time, whites made up barely 20 per cent of the population of South Africa. In the 1980s, using the population categories legally in force, there were 4.9 million 'whites', 24.9 million 'blacks', 2.8 million 'coloureds' and 0.8 million 'Asians' (South African Institute of Race Relations 1986). The effect of new laws like the *Population Registration Act 1950* was to institutionalize white minority rule politically and ensure widespread and increasingly violent control of most black South Africans.

Trained first as a lawyer, Mandela became an activist and, from the 1940s, became a key leader of the African National Congress (ANC) established in 1912. He was also a member of the South African Communist Party from around 1960 (Landau 2012: 548). As Elleke Boehmer (2005) observes, from the time when Mandela first became politically active until his arrest and imprisonment in 1962, he was an anti-imperialist, a nationalist and a democrat. He faced repeated arrest and trial on charges including sedition, treason and armed violence in the 1950s and 1960s. In 1961, following the Sharpeville massacre of 1960, when police killed at least sixty-nine protestors outside the Sharpeville police station, he became the founding leader of *Umkhonto we Sezwe* ('Spear of the Nation') (MK), the armed wing of the African National Congress. The establishment of MK initiated the turn to violent struggle initially taking the form of sabotage against the white apartheid regime. The South African state consistently revealed its willingness to repeatedly resort to extreme violence to crush the ANC's campaign to promote black majority rule in South Africa.

Following the Rivonia trial in 1963–64, Mandela, already serving a five-year prison sentence, escaped the death sentence along with seven other ANC leaders: all were given lengthy prison sentences in 1964. For much of the 1980s, while Mandela was imprisoned, the ANC waged war on the apartheid regime just as the white South African state waged war on the ANC state. Between 1985 and 1989, serious political violence erupted in South Africa initially as black townships became the focus of the struggle between anti-apartheid organizations and Botha's Nationalist government. On 20 July 1985, President Botha declared a State of Emergency that lasted for several years. This act gave police and the military sweeping powers, anti-apartheid organizations were banned or had restrictions placed on their activities, 2,436 activists were detained under the *Internal Security Act*, while other many activists had restrictions like house arrest imposed on them. This exercise simply expanded the scope of the violence as the ANC triggered insurgencies in Angola, Mozambique, Zimbabwe and Lesotho putting even more pressure on the South African state.

After twenty-seven years in prison having been convicted of sabotage, Mandela was freed from prison in 1990. He then worked with F.W. de Klerk's Nationalist government to dismantle the apartheid regime beginning with the repeal of the *Population Registration Act 1950* in 1991. Mandela was subsequently elected the first black president of a fully democratic South Africa serving between 1994 and 1999. In the twenty-first century and until his death in 2013, he would be globally acclaimed as a moral hero of global stature – though the US government kept Mandela on its FBI terrorist watch lists until 2008 nearly a decade after he had retired from the Presidency of South Africa. As will be clear, Mandela was not a terrorist, though like many other revolutionary leaders (including Washington and de Valera) he used political violence against the military and security forces of the state he was seeking to overthrow.

This chapter is the first of two forays into the legitimacy of dissent. As will become clear, some philosophers have not shied away from the challenge of thinking about the legitimacy of dissent. Some of this has involved a defence of civil disobedience (e.g. Arendt 1972a; Simmons 2001; Brownlee 2012). As Susan Brownlee's (2012) work testifies, much of this discussion involves an elaborate and somewhat abstracted discussion about the properties said to define 'proper' civil disobedience like the presence of a conscientious or principled outlook, the communication of both condemnation, a desire for change in law or policy, publicity, non-violence and fidelity to law. Peter Singer provided a much admired answer to the hard question: what if anything renders various forms of dissent like civil disobedience legitimate, especially when that dissent is targeting a law or policy made by a democratically elected government? It is characteristic that his approach, while it avoided the then-conventional Oxford analytic philosophical method of picking at the words and meanings, set up the case for conscientious objection and civil disobedience by setting up a hypothetical dispute in an Oxford college whose Master was elected by his peers. This is surely open to Bourdieu's polemic against the scholastic fallacy, i.e. the practice of generalizing from the often highly limited experience or insights of scholars.

The case of Mandela raises a series of 'hard' questions especially in a context dominated by a 'common sense' view of terrorism promoted by political leaders in many liberal democracies. As Uwe Steinhoff observes, that commonsense view treats terrorism as 'the paradigm of senseless… downright illegitimate and detestable violence' on the premise that terrorism is the work of amoral, utterly irrational and fanatical insurgents and, therefore, beyond dialogue, negotiation and certainly lacking all legitimacy (Steinhoff 2007: 1). This view is a consequence of what modern political leaders like to call 'moral clarity', a euphemism actually embracing what Steinhoff calls 'perverted and ignorant ideas' 'grounded in unconditional solidarity' (Steinhoff 2007: 1). As I show there is a good case made by philosophers like Honderich (2003, 2006), Held (2008), Steinhoff (2007) and Nathanson (2010) that deploying a form of enlightened liberal philosophical analysis to conclude that 'political violence' or 'terrorism' is a legitimate activity although this conclusion depends on how they understand 'terrorism'.

The legitimacy of dissent: the case of political violence

As philosophers like Stephen Nathanson (2010: 94–103) acknowledge, justifying state-sponsored violence has long been understood to require a better justification than the simple claim that as a state 'we' are entitled to do these things – while no-one else is. This introduces the long and complex history of the development of a tradition of 'just war' theory in the West. It also poses an obvious question: if just war theory warrants states using violence, does it also provide a legitimate basis for non-state actors to use violence? As I will show, philosophers like Jason Brennan (2016, 2019) go further and argue that we need to resist the temptation to assume that, in liberal democracies, only non-violent resistance to state injustice is permissible, and that 'we must defer to democratic government agents, even when these agents act in deeply unjust, harmful, and destructive ways' (Brennan 2016: 40). Let me work my way through this argument. I will start by considering the issue of whether the use by liberal-democratic states of just war theory also applies to non-state actors like the ANC in South Africa. I will then turn to the harder question of whether we are ever warranted in employing political violence like assassinating a leader of an unjust and tyrannical government, or a military or law enforcement officer enforcing the policies of such a government.

I begin by briefly defending using the case of Mandela and the ANC in South Africa under apartheid.

Apartheid South Africa?

The recourse to armed violence by Mandela and *Umkhonto we Sezwe* was clearly a form of political dissent. The burden of this chapter is to consider the hard case of armed violence. While it is arguable whether South Africa before 1994 was really a liberal-democratic state, I want to use this case because it does exemplify some of the important features of dissent and the criminalization of dissent in liberal-democratic states. While it might be (too) easy to treat apartheid South Africa as an abject (i.e. as disgusting), and so dismiss it because it has nothing to offer us by way of insights into the ways 'we' do things, several things need to be remembered.

First, there were South Africans like the idealist-liberal philosopher Rudolf Hoernlé who thought of South Africa as a liberal polity where the liberal 'rule of law' mattered: hence his objections to apartheid were exceeded only by his rejection of revolutionary violence and civil disobedience (Sweet 2013). As William Sweet observes, Hoernlé faced the challenge of how to respond ethically, to the challenges of living in a deeply unequal multi-ethnic, multi-cultural state, while maintaining a liberal commitment to freedom and equality (2013: 178). Hoernlé was a social liberal in the tradition of T.H. Green. For Hoernlé, this meant that a liberal state should aim to 'free human beings from whatever stands in the way of their realizing the best that their nature is capable of' (Hoernlé 1945: 9). It also meant that he ended up arguing for the integration of Black Africans into 'the orbit of Western Civilization' though he added that, 'It is probable that, in making Western civilization their own, the African peoples will retain elements of their own traditional culture, and, combining them with what they adopt, create new nuances of Western civilization' (Hoernlé 1945: 111). Oddly, Hoernlé's liberalism meant what it has meant for so many other liberals: 'there is no such thing as freedom of conscience, if by this phrase is meant that society should guarantee to every one of its members the power to disobey any law of which his conscience disapproves' (Hoernlé 1945: 4). Hoernlé's liberalism also meant obedience to the law: 'we must accept them [the laws]' (Hoernlé 1945: 115). As Sitze observes, this was because 'For Hoernlé, the law was the law: self-identical with itself, rationally constituted in form if not in content, the law demanded obedience no matter how repugnant to the liberal spirit its particular provisions may be'. On this view, any theory of disobedience, whether in the name of Gandhian nonviolence or Marxist revolutionary violence, would be an opening to anomie and for that same reason illegitimate, unreasonable and immoral (Sitze 2015: 149).

However, Sitze makes the more interesting case that even if apartheid South Africa was not a pure example of a liberal state, neither was it a pure example of a Schmittian 'state of exception'. Sitze (2015: 144) proposes that if we set Schmitt's account of law-as-*nomos* against Cicero's natural law account of law-as-*lex*, as universal 'right reason' that underpins the liberal rule of law idea we will see something quite important in South Africa. Schmitt drew on the polysemic and relational qualities of *nomos* (where nomos means 'walls' *and* 'laws') to treat law as local and constituted in specific spaces (*polis* or *civitas*) where law is law 'only and precisely to the extent that it inscribes itself on the ground' (Sitze 2015: 144). Law-as-*nomos* works like a wall to divide and distinguish, include and exclude, by 'carving out relations between inside and outside, producing boundaries' very much in the way that apartheid law set racial categories and racialized communities against each other (Sitze 2015: 144). Yet as Sitze points out, the history of South Africa after 1948 shows how the apparent commitment to a liberal rule of law principle can also sit comfortably alongside deeply antiliberal laws and policies. In a brilliant account of Mandela's legal thought, Sitze shows how Mandela understood that the law in the Union of South Africa 'was defined by an irreducible incoherence: it not only coexisted with but also demanded the very arbitrary violence that the "rule of law," this concept so treasured by white South African jurists, was supposed to constrain'. As Sitze notes,

> South African law already hosted within itself the very anomie that Hoernlé seemed to fear. Instead of the rule of law, it was governed by dictatorship; instead of peacetime norms, it was ordered according to the exceptions of martial law; instead of health, welfare, and safety, its administrative apparatus produced conditions for the extermination of African populations.
>
> (Sitze 2015: 153)

The ways the South African state criminalized and suppressed the ANC and anti-apartheid activists have too many uncomfortable affinities with the way more 'obviously' liberal-democratic states have done, and continue to do the same sorts of things. For example, the way the South African government 'banned' Mandela, e.g. looks a lot like the way liberal-democratic states engage in the same exclusionary practices. Adam Sitze (2018) notes that as early as December 1952, Mandela was subjected to 'one of the strangest and most brutal forms of legal persecution invented by the apartheid government': Mandela was subjected to a 'banning order'. This meant the South African state could:

> ... forbid a person, for a period of up to five years and sometimes longer, from (a) being a member of specific organizations (which were mostly communist or antiapartheid in orientation), (b) being in or leaving a specified place or area, (c) receiving visitors (Mandela would be prohibited from speaking with more than one person at a time), (d) performing any act as specified by the minister of justice, and (e) having one's speech or writing quoted. At its most powerful, the banning order produced a deprivation of public space so extreme that it amounted to the wide-open confinement of the banned person at his or her own expense.
>
> (Sitze 2015: 154)

South Africa's apartheid state suggests how two apparently antagonistic juridical traditions, the liberal universalist notion of law-as-*lex* and the place-specific conception of law-as-*nomos*, enabling the declaration of exceptions, are neither always nor necessarily antithetical, but can indeed coexist quite comfortably. This, it might be said, is equally true of other Western liberal-democratic states like Britain, America and Australia – as the criminalization of dissent reminds us all too forcefully.

At the least, this suggests why liberal-democratic states have felt impelled to justify their actions by appealing to some part of the just war tradition. It also indicates why we should not simply accept any presumption that is central to the legitimacy/authority claimed by states that they are somehow permitted to do things that are harmful even murderous that no-one else can do, or that they should not be stopped from doing these things. This is what Jason Brennan (2019: 4) calls the 'special immunity thesis', which he describes as 'a special magic moral force field that both removes their normal moral obligations and at the same time requires the rest of us to let them act unjustly'. As we will see the point of what Brenna calls the moral parity principle suggests that we may do to the state officials whatever we may do to each other, just as individuals and non-state actors can call on the same legitimations used by states when they appeal to just war principles.

I start by considering the case of Mandela's decision to use armed violence.

Mandela, apartheid and armed violence

Two points stand out. First, the long and hard-fought struggle to end apartheid reminds us that politics and the politics of dissent are relational. Second, the decision by Mandela and the recourse by *Umkhonto we Sezwe* to violence were clearly thought out from the outset in terms of a tradition of moral justification long available in Western philosophy and international law and referred to as 'just war'. Both aspects are clearly evidenced in a famous three-hour speech, usually referred to as his 'I am prepared to die' speech. The speech was made during Mandela's trial in 1964 in Rivonia.

Criminalization of dissent and political violence

At various points in this book, I have argued for talking the relational perspective more seriously when thinking about dissent and its criminalization: this point is reinforced, when we think about the turn to political violence. Political violence generally involves a mix of physical injury or harm to others as well as inducing fear, insecurity or violations of rights and personal integrity. It is not like other forms of violence, because it typically invokes public claims to some special moral or legal legitimation for any injury and harm done to others. Equally, it usually has some collective manifestations: both its perpetrators and victims are understood to be representatives, respectively, of the state and of oppositional or dissenting groups (du Toit and Manganyi 1990). In South Africa, political violence was polarized between violent state oppression oriented to preserving domination and order, and violent insurrection oriented to promote equality and change. As Andre du Toit and Manganyi (1990) puts it:

> ... the violence of apartheid was generally understood as part of the pathology of apartheid; the problem, at root, was not so much the violence engendered by it, but apartheid itself. Similarly, the turn to political violence in the struggle against apartheid was justified and criticized from moral, political and strategic points of view, but precisely for those reasons it was also conceived as embedded in, and subservient to, these larger concerns.

Using Elias' vocabulary, we can say that political violence in South Africa formed a figuration. That is to say that the people working in South Africa's state agencies who fought to maintain apartheid and those political and communal groups working to destroy apartheid constituted a 'web' or 'network' of relations and processes. In that 'network', no-one controlled the whole figuration which nonetheless both constrained and made possible various kinds of *praxis*. Andre du Toit and Manganyi (1990: 8) claims the election victory of the National Party and inauguration of apartheid in 1948 could only generate increasingly violent and racially polarized conflict over the following decades. As Mandela made clear in 1964, the South African state had already resorted to violence all through the 1960s:

> There had been violence in 1957 when the women of Zeerust were ordered to carry passes; there was violence in 1958 with the enforcement of cattle culling in Sekhukhuniland; there was violence in 1959 when the people of Cato Manor protested against pass raids; there was violence in 1960 when

the Government attempted to impose Bantu Authorities in Pondoland. Thirty-nine Africans died in these disturbances. In 1961 there had been riots in Warmbaths, and all this time the Transkei had been a seething mass of unrest.

(Mandela 1964)

In the 1960s, the National Party government increasingly relied on coercive measures to maintain the apartheid regime. The security forces were expanded and given extensive and discretionary powers by statute. A renewal of opposi-tional campaigns culminated in major student revolts in Soweto in 1976 that were met with savage repression by the state, culminating in the death of the young black leader Steve Biko at the hands of the state and the banning of a range of anti-apartheid organizations in 1977. The early 1980s saw another cycle of anti-apartheid resistance sponsoring the formation of the United Democratic Front followed by country-wide popular insurrections of 1984–87 (Cobbett and Cohen 1988). The National Party-controlled state saw this in terms of a 'total onslaught' which needed to be met by a 'total strategy' involving an increasing militarization of (white) South African society. The 'executive presidency' of P.W. Botha, relied heavily on the South African Defence Force and security forces saw the National Security Council usurp key functions from the cabinet, while Parliament itself became increasingly marginalized (Swilling and Phillips, 1988; cf. Frankel et al. 1988). By the second half of the 1980s, the ANC, historically long committed to non-violent and constitutional methods, was giving prominence to the 'armed struggle' in conjunction with internationally imposed sanctions and popular mobilization aimed at making the country 'ungovernable' as a prelude to taking power. The National Party (NP)-controlled state responded by the imposition of successive states of emergency, deploying troops in the townships and the con-struction of a national network of Security Management Centres. The Security Management Centres were supposed to co-ordinate policy and security action under military control and potentially provided an alternative to the existing structures of civilian rule.

We know a lot about the violence of the state – and of the ANC – because of the decision taken by President de Klerk and Mandela in 1993 to establish the South African Truth and Reconciliation Commission. As Sam Garkawe (2003: 347) observes, the National Party government had agreed to relinquish power on the basis of the negotiated 1993 *Interim Constitution* (subsequently replaced by the *Constitution of the Republic of South Africa* 1996). The granting of am-nesty to members of the ANC and the security agencies of the former apartheid regime and of ANC personnel testifies to the relational qualities of political vio-lence: state violence and revolutionary violence were precisely linked in the way Schmitt's account of the political as the *relation* of friends and enemies implies.

What we can call the internal or relational logic of political violence was instantiated in a *cyclical process* of increasingly violent confrontation in South Africa. The predominantly Boer white minority entrusted the defence of their power and privilege to a reactionary and militarized 'garrison state' explicitly based on the use of coercive violence (du Toit and Manganyi 1990: 7). In his evidence to the TRC, Former President de Klerk, e.g. tried to draw a distinction between the moral wrongs of apartheid, and any suggestion that the South African state had engaged in 'crimes against humanity' as maintained by the United Nations. That said, de Klerk admitted at the Truth and Reconciliation Commission, this included assassination, murder, torture, rape and assault, though De Klerk emphatically denied that his government had been involved in or had authorized or had knowledge of the violations for which police and military personnel were now claiming amnesty (Pigou 2003: 211). Equally, he acknowledged that he had authorized some actions such as cross-border raids against legitimate military targets (Amnesty International 1992).

De Klerk's testimony indicated that apart from the usual tactics of arrests, assassinations, torture and capital punishment for political crimes, the South African state had relied on secret operations (Amnesty International 1992). These operations targeted activist lawyers like Albie Sachs who lost an arm and an eye to a bomb planted by security agents in his car in Mozambique: Mandela subsequently appointed Sachs to the Constitutional Court in 1996. One former police and military intelligence agent in his evidence to the Commission argued, e.g. that 'that secret, violent and other actions against the revolutionary enemy were accepted and approved procedure in our overall arsenal of counter-insurgency weapons'. Citing a report delivered to a National Intelligence Symposium held at the National Intelligence Services (NIS) headquarters in June 1982, he added that 'when survival is important it is often necessary for a service to resort to secret actions which does not comply with the laws, morality, norms and values… Secrecy both offensive and defensive is important'. The state also relied on a form of ethnic cleansing. In the 1950s, 60,000 people were forcibly moved out of Johannesburg to a new township called Soweto. In. the 1960s, 1970s and early 1980s, the government implemented a policy of 'resettlement', to force people to move to their designated 'group areas'.

Just as the state ramped up its legitimate violence, so too did the ANC. After decades of preaching non-violence, the ANC switched course in 1961. The white-dominated South African state had long relied on state power and violence to repeatedly declare 'states of emergency' to justify criminalizing the ANC and other opposition groups. It relied on heavy-handed police and military violence including lethal force. After 1961 the ANC would turn increasingly to violence in its fight against apartheid. As Landau puts it, 'the transformation of the ANC at the leadership level must be reimagined within this other, encompassing transformation' of the South African state. By this, Landau means that, while the South African state had been relying in increasingly violent suppression of opposition to apartheid, it was also relying 'on the persistent belief in the rule of law among even ANC and South African Communist Party (SACP) leaders, so as to catch them unawares at home and imprison them' (Landau 2012: 540). Equally popular opposition to apartheid played its part.

Violent conflict broke out after Sharpeville in 1960–61 at places like Zeerust, Sekhukhuniland, Pondoland, and the big sugar estates in Natal. Mandela and Slovo initiated a co-ordinated response to the Sharpeville killings. First, Mandela and President Lutuli publicly burnt their internal passbooks, inviting immediate arrest. The government began arresting other people, and entering African people's homes and beating them in Langa and in other townships, and on 30 March 1960, it declared a 'State of Emergency'. Philip Kgosana, a twenty-three-year-old PAC leader, then led more than 30,000 people in an unprecedented mass assembly, through the streets of Cape Town. Mandela, Duma Nokwe and many other Transvaalers were arrested and jailed again. On 8 April, the government banned the ANC and the Communist Party declaring them illegal. As Paul Landau shows, it was most likely, in April or May 1960, that the jailed activists took the decision to favour violence (Landau 2012: 546). The leaders of MK like Mandela, Nokwe, Sisulu, Slovo and their allies embraced sabotage as a first response to the state: this was not just 'armed propaganda', but was a prelude to, or a part of, guerrilla war. One set of MK notes observed that 'Sabotage is an invaluable arm of people who fight a guerrilla war. In the initial stages it fulfils the strategic task of creating the conditions necessary for the formation of guerrilla units from among the people'. The ANC and later the United Democratic Front in the 1980s devised a narrative about the insurrection framed as a (quasi-)revolutionary project to take power and control of the state, end apartheid and ensure majority rule.

As the Commander of the MK, Mandela drew on his extensive reading of revolutionary texts like Che Guevara's *Guerilla Warfare* (1961) as well as accounts of revolution and peasant uprisings like the Malay conflict, the anti-French war in Algeria, the Chinese Revolution (1912–48) and the American War of Independence (1775–83). Mandela seems to have been impressed especially by Menachem Begin's account of how the ultra-radical Zionist group called Irgun waged war against Britain to secure Palestine as a Jewish homeland after 1944. Mandela noted with approval Irgun's claim to justice: 'in this battle we shall break the enemy and bring salvation to our people, tried in the furnace of persecution, thirsting only for freedom, for righteousness and for Justice …' Mandela also embraced organisational insights from Begin taking accounts of ideas about 'Regional Command' and 'High Command' into the MK from Irgun terminology. Mandela noted, e.g. that:

> The High Command of Irgun controlled all the activities of the Irgun, both military and political. It considered general principles, strategy and tactics, information and training, relations with other bodies and negotiations with their representatives. It took decisions, and orders were given as in all military organizations; but there were never any decisions by an individual. There was always discussion.
>
> (Cited Landau 2012: 556)

According to the South African Truth and Reconciliation Commission in 2003, the ANC staged about 190 attacks on government buildings in Cape town

Johannesburg and Durban between 1961 and 1963. Between 1976 and 1984, there were over 265 armed attacks involving assassinations, and attacks on police stations. In 1985–88, the number of attacks increased with 300 attacks in 1988 alone. The Truth and Reconciliation Commission estimated that seventy-seven people died in these attacks including fifty-two civilians and nineteen security force personnel. Ironically, the release of Mandela from prison in 1990 did not lead immediately to any quietus as tensions flared within the African community: during 1990 and 1991, more than 6000 people were killed in incidents of political violence (Cooper et al. 1993). The months following the release of Mandela saw a sharp escalation of violent conflicts in the Natal Midlands, as factions of Inkatha fought groups allied to the United Democratic Front (UDF)/ANC and which saw the ANC engage in shoot-outs, killings, petrol-bombings, abductions and the use of 'necklaces' (burning tyres placed around the necks of political opponents) (du Toit and Manganyi 1990: 10–11). So how did Mandela and the MK understand and legitimate their turn to violence.

Mandela and the legitimacy of armed violence

The relational nature of political violence in South Africa is reinforced by the way each side justified its recourse to violence. In both cases, the Augustinian tradition of just war theory was available and was used. For those committed to white supremacy and the defence of apartheid, the apartheid system was itself a 'just war'. Lara Johnstone (2018: 1) observes, e.g. that:

> If we impartially and unemotionally examine the motivations for implementing Apartheid it meets all the requirements for a Just War of self-defence: It was a just cause to ensure Afrikaner demographic survival; it was a last resort; it was declared by proper authority; it possessed morally right intention; it had a reasonable chance of success; and the end was proportional to the means used.

On this account, it was important to secure the legitimacy of apartheid because the survival of the Afrikaner community was at stake and this was understood in terms of a 'liberation' theology albeit one that was skewed by a belief in white supremacy. Terreblanche (2002: 299) writes: 'the ideologies of Afrikaner nationalism was really a means to an end, namely the mobilisation of ethnic power to attain political power, and especially greater wealth'.

There is a view that the very point of just war theory is to privilege states as the legitimate source of law and the legitimate use of force and to delegitimate insurrectionary and revolutionary movements. The just war principles require that only the rightful authority with a just cause may wage a war.

As David Dyzenhaus (1997) demonstrates in his insightful account of the way South African courts dealt with apartheid-based legal cases between 1948 and 1994, there was another line of defence. As is well known, South Africa's judges refused to give evidence at the TRC, where they might have been required to give an account of their negligent judicial conduct. Like Australia's High Court judges, South Africa's judges claimed that they could not overturn parliamentary legislation because they were just vehicles for the legislative branch: the legal order of apartheid was based on parliamentary supremacy. Adjudication was confined largely to a process of statutory interpretation. In fact, South African law was a hybrid system combining elements of English common law and Roman (Dutch) law. The result was a system that had the resources that could have been used to combat statutory tyranny of the kind enacted by the 'apartheid state'. As Dyzenhaus (1997: 151) notes that the courts could have imposed judicial constraints on the criminalization of dissent involving suppression of political opposition or the lengthy detention of people suspected of political crimes. However, the judges opted to cleave to an Austinian notion of the rule of law as 'the embodiment of the legislative will' rather than as an expression of legal tradition or normative principles (Dyzenhaus 1997: 19).

Mandela almost certainly understood that the law in South Africa had become part of the apparatus of oppression rather than a guarantor of freedom. Mandela spelled out his thinking at length and with great clarity. Mandela had already made his position on political violence very clear in January 1962 in a very important speech entitled 'A Land Ruled by the Gun', in Addis Ababa in his capacity as the leader of the ANC delegation to the Pan-African Freedom Movement of East and Central Africa. There he declared that: '[I]t is first and foremost by our own struggle and sacrifice inside South Africa itself that victory over White domination and apartheid can be won'.

> The freedom movement in South Africa believes that hard and swift blows should be delivered with the full weight of the masses of the people, who alone furnish us with one absolute guarantee that the freedom flames now burning in the country shall never be extinguished.
>
> (Mandela 1962)

As he later made clear at his trial in Rivonia in 1964, Mandela had no intention of denying:

> … that I planned sabotage. I did not plan it in a spirit of recklessness, nor because I have any love for violence. I planned it as a result of a calm and sober assessment of the political situation that had arisen after many years of tyranny, exploitation, and oppression of my people by the whites.
>
> (Mandela 1964)

He also set out clearly his judgement that what he was doing was not terrorism but a kind of 'just war':

> …we believed that as a result of Government policy, violence by the African people had become inevitable, and that unless responsible leadership was given

to canalise and control the feelings of our people, there would be outbreaks of terrorism which would produce an intensity of bitterness and hostility between the various races of the country which is not produced even by war.

Mandela described how he had made the move away from peaceful opposition:

At the beginning of June 1961, after a long and anxious assessment of the South African situation, I, and some colleagues, came to the conclusion that as violence in this country was inevitable, it would be unrealistic and wrong for African leaders to continue preaching peace and non-violence at a time when the government met our peaceful demands with force.

As he put it 'We first broke the law in a way which avoided any recourse to violence; when this form was legislated against, and when the Government resorted to a show of force to crush opposition to its policies, only then did we decide to answer violence with violence'. Mandela added that:

This conclusion was not easily arrived at. It was only when all else had failed, when all channels of peaceful protest had been barred to us, that the decision was made to embark on violent forms of political struggle, and to form *Umkhonto we Sizwe*. We did so not because we desired such a course, but solely because the government had left us with no other choice.

As Paul Landau notes, the decision taken in 1961 to use sabotage in cities, suburbs and train-yards was to be the first phase of a 'planned, wider campaign which was to involve the taking of lives, and which had as its *telos* a general insurrection against the state' (Landau 2012: 540). That insurrection was conceived in distinctly political, and so moral, terms. In effect, Nelson Mandela assumed the lead in the effort because:

…he grasped the need for directing, controlling, and monopolizing violence. His models for doing so were Israel, Algeria, Cuba, and China, as well as France, 1789: anti-colonial and revolutionary situations.

(Landau 2012: 540)

In spelling out his justification, Mandela emphasized that he wanted to avoid terrorism: 'the violence which we chose to adopt was not terrorism'.
    As Mandela put it:

Firstly, we believed that as a result of Government policy, violence by the African people had become inevitable, and that unless responsible leadership was given to canalise and control the feelings of our people, there would be outbreaks of terrorism which would produce an intensity of bitterness and hostility between the various races of this country which is not produced even by war. Secondly, we felt that without violence there would be no way open to the African people to succeed in their struggle against the principle of white supremacy. All lawful modes of expressing opposition to this principle had been closed by legislation, and we were placed in a position in which we had either to accept a permanent state of inferiority, or take over the Government. We chose to defy the law. We first broke the law in a way which avoided any recourse to violence; when this form was legislated against, and then the Government resorted to a show of force to crush opposition to its policies, only then did we decide to answer with violence.

(Mandela 1964)

The decision to create MK reflected two propositions. On the one hand, 'The ANC was a mass political organization with a political function to fulfil. Its members had joined on the express policy of non-violence it could not and would not undertake violence'. On the other hand, 'the ANC was prepared to depart from its fifty-year-old policy of non-violence to this extent that it would no longer disapprove of properly controlled violence'. The decision to create the MK therefore reflected the need for a small, closely knit organization required for sabotage (Mandela 1964). The same clarity informed the idea that sabotage would be the weapon of first choice As Mandela explained:

Four forms of violence were possible. There is sabotage, there is guerrilla warfare, there is terrorism, and there is open revolution. We chose to adopt the first method and to exhaust it before taking any other decision. In the light of our political background the choice was a logical one

(Mandela 1964)

Mandela added that 'Umkhonto was to perform sabotage, and strict instructions were given to its members right from the start, that on no account were they to injure or kill people in planning or carrying out operations' (Mandela 1964).

It is noteworthy that, in this respect, the Truth and Reconciliation Commission later endorsed Mandela's implied claim to be waging a legitimate struggle because, under international law, the policy of apartheid was a crime against humanity rendering the ANC internationally recognized liberation movements conducting a legitimate struggle against the former South African government and its policy of apartheid. Ironically, however, the Commission then drew a distinction between a 'just war' and 'just means' and found that, in terms of international convention:

both the ANC, its organs NEC, the NWC, the RC, the Secretariat, and its armed wing MK, and the PAC and its armed formations Poqo and APLA, had all committed gross violations of human rights in the course of their political activities and armed struggles, acts for which they are morally and politically accountable.

(TRC 1998, vol. 2, ch. 4: 235)

While this doubtless opens up many lines of enquiry I follow just one here: on what basis does any claim that the use of political violence (or terrorism) carried out by states and non-state actors is legitimate rest? As we will see the claim by states that they and they alone have and enjoy a legitimate monopoly of violence does not wash. This is the why the long history of just war theory in the West is so important – if ultimately self-negating.

Just war theory

As many philosophers like Michael Walzer (1977) to Uwe Steinhoff (2007) point out, states have long engaged in organized violence calling it everything from 'police action', 'counter-terrorism' 'total war' – or even the 'Third Way of War' when the extermination of whole peoples and the spoliation of their livestock crops and the denial of access to their land is envisaged. The question of whether political violence of any kind can be justified, or rendered legitimate is therefore already foregrounded by the long history of state-sponsored violence evident in both intrastate conflict (or 'war') and more pointedly in colonial exercises after 1492 involving the conquest of lands and peoples involving slavery, land-clearance and a combination of active and passive genocide (Todorov 1980). This exercise as Eric Wilson shows in a bravura piece of scholarship was implicated in the creation of a framework of international law by the likes of Hugo Grotius in the early seventeenth century. As Wilson notes:

> It is not the least of the ironies of the history of western jurisprudence that one of the seminal texts of international public law Grotius' *de Indis* should be a legal defence of privateering... pointing to the juridical legitimation of state sponsored organised violence as the normative – and normalizing – keystone of international relations.
>
> (Wilson 2008: 17)

There is now a significant and growing body of philosophical work from major philosophers like Barradori (2004), Honderich (2003), Goodin (2006), Walzer (2006), Steinhoff (2007), McMahan (2009) and Nathanson (2010) who do not validate the exercise of legitimating state violence just because states claim legitimacy. Much of this work takes issue with the long history of attempts to justify state violence evident in a tradition centred on the idea of 'just war' going back to Imperial Rome and to Christian theologians like St. Augustine and St. Thomas Aquinas. (Ironically, Augustine only tackles the subject of the justifications for war in one chapter of his twenty-two written chapters in his *City of God* (in Book XIX, Chapter 7). Other key early modern philosophers like Hugo Grotius, Francisco de Vitoria and Francisco Suarez played a major role in formalizing the doctrine in the seventeenth century.)

Much of this exercise in outlining the principles of 'just war' has been devoted to showing why and when it was morally acceptable for states to wage war on each other. As Jeff McMahan notes, just war theory 'is unique in contemporary practical ethics in two respects: it is widely and uncritically accepted and differs very little in content from what Western religious thinkers have believed from the Middle Ages to the present'. This has been used to justify the condemnation of political violence like insurrection or terrorism when groups carry out a collective political exercise that involves sabotage, armed attacks on security and police personnel or even attacks on civilians. Philosophers like Anthony Coates (1997) don't like terrorism or other philosophers like Tony Coady (2008: 172; also 1985) who think that terrorism is a defensible political activity so long as it conforms to some principles derived from just war theory. Coates himself relies heavily on the idea that just war theory should only apply to states since states are the primary example of legitimate authority and any other violent activity by non-state actors is 'terrorism' and so by virtue of its provenance illegitimate.

As McMahan and other modern philosophers now point out, even the justification of state-sponsored violence has long been understood to require a better story than the simple claim that because 'we' are a state, 'we' are morally (and legally) entitled to do these things, but no one else is.

These philosophers engage general questions about when and if political violence of any kind carried out by state actors and non-state actors can ever be justified. Since states have drawn on centuries of 'just war' doctrine, e.g. we are reminded that there is a long and rich history of attempts to justify political violence. Kai Nielsen who is a consequentialist in ethics and a socialist in politics, e.g. has argued that there can be a moral value in political violence. This might include achieving morally and politically worthwhile objectives like 'a truly socialist society' or liberation from colonial rule. 'When and where [either] should be employed is a tactical question that must be decided ... on a case-by-case basis ... like the choice of weapon in a war' (Nielsen 1981: 435). He argues that:

> ... terrorist acts must be justified by their political effects and their moral consequences. They are justified (1) when they are politically effective weapons in the revolutionary struggle and (2) when, everything considered, there are sound reasons for believing that, by the use of that type of violence rather than no violence at all or violence of some other type, there will be less injustice, suffering and degradation in the world than would otherwise have been the case.
>
> (Nielsen 1981: 446)

Other philosophers who are not utilitarians or 'consequentialists' (e.g. Coady 1985; Coady and O'Keefe 2002; Honderich 2006; Steinhoff 2007) have interrogated the claims of just war doctrine to outline some of the moral considerations at stake. Here I draw on Steinhoff (2007) who engages the question of when, if ever, is terrorism (political violence) legitimate?[1] He traverses the qualities of legitimate authority, just cause, innocence and non-innocence among targets, and the ethics of terrorism. He argues that those who seek to legitimize terror, and those claiming that it is never just, both need to make their case. In effect, he is making the case for moral parity and rejecting the 'double standards', used by states which imply that state-perpetrated violence is less morally objectionable than the violent acts of 'subnational or underground organizations' (Steinhoff 2007: 2).

Just war theory has two sets of criteria, the first establishing *jus ad bellum* (i.e. when is it right to go to war), and the second establishing *jus in bello* (i.e. what is the right way to wage war). There is general agreement about the key elements of the relevant considerations for going to war (or *Jus ad bellum*).

The legitimacy of the competent authority?

Charles Guthrie and Michael Quinlan (2007) claim that just war theorists have conventionally argued or assumed that only duly constituted public authorities, i.e. states or institutions or persons possessing sovereignty like monarchs, elected presidents or parliaments can wage war and do so legitimately (2007: 11–15: also Walzer 1977). When asked to say why this is so, one premise relied on is that 'there needs to be a political authority within a political system that acknowledges distinctions of justice'. It then takes but a little hop, skip and jump to claim that some states, usually referred to as 'rogue states' run as dictatorships violate this criterion as do all non-state actors. On one reading, this is question begging on a grand scale: the question being begged is whether any entity or person automatically possesses the capacity to acknowledge 'distinctions of justice' simply by virtue of being either a state or more narrowly, e.g. a liberal democracy, or else and alternately lacks that capacity because it is not a state or is just a totalitarian state. (Gerry Simpson (2004) has brilliantly critiqued the premises underlying the way some states ('Great Powers') get to call other states 'rogue' or 'outlaw states'.) On another reading, the premise has the merit of opening up a good question: is there a matter of justice involved when a person, group or state contemplates political violence and do those involved have the moral and/or political capacity to discern and then to act on that principle.

Just cause

The reason for going to war needs to be just and cannot therefore be solely for recapturing things taken or punishing people who have done wrong. Typically, the concept of a just war relies on the idea that it is waged defensively against an aggressor and that innocent life must be in imminent danger and any violence used to protect life.

Proportionality

The anticipated benefits of waging a war must be proportionate to its expected evils or harms. This principle is also known as the principle of macro-proportionality, so as to distinguish it from the *jus in bello* principle of proportionality.

Comparative justice

While there may be rights and wrongs on all sides of a conflict, to overcome the presumption against the use of force, the injustice suffered by one party must significantly outweigh that suffered by the other.

Right intention

Force may be used only in a truly just cause and solely for that purpose – correcting a suffered wrong is considered a right intention, while material gain or maintaining economies is not.

Probability of success

Arms may not be used in a futile cause or in a case where disproportionate measures are required to achieve success.

Last resort

Force may be used only after all peaceful and viable alternatives have been seriously tried and exhausted or are clearly not practical. It may be clear that the other side is using negotiations as a delaying tactic and will not make meaningful concessions.

As might be guessed, the weakest part of the whole 'just war' tradition is the claim that states are legitimately entitled to use violence because they are states. This simply takes us back to the fundamental question already discussed at length in previous chapters: on what basis does that claim to legitimacy rest? As might be anticipated, those philosophers committed to the idea of a clear distinction between 'legitimate' and 'illegitimate' violence based simply on whether a ('legitimate') state does it, or an ('illegitimate') non-state actor entity does it, ends up in an incoherent mess quickly.

Some philosophers like Anthony Coates (1997) who try to make the case that terrorism is illegitimate, because it is not carried out by a legitimate authority, rely heavily on the implicit assumption that a state is able to wage a just war, while no other entity can do so. This is the implication when Coates, e.g. says apropos the idea of non-combatant immunity used to condemn terrorism is valid, insists that this is so because this distinction, i.e. between 'combatants' and 'non-combatants', 'only applies to a state of war' – and wars can only be waged by legitimate authorities (Coates 1997: 123). When forced to say what this means Coates can only suggest that 'Legitimate authority is not to be taken for granted. The state's *right* to [wage] war derives not from its *de facto* or coercive sovereignty...' (Coates 1997: 126). This would be to simply retreat to the Austinian or Schmittian idea that states have legitimacy because they can enforce the law with violence which becomes both tautological and not very nice: the moral claim to legitimacy has gone up in smoke. Coates claims that legitimacy is grounded in that state's 'membership of an international community to the common good of which the state is ordered and to the law to which it is subject' (Coates 1997: 126). This is to put it mildly incoherent. As Steinhoff puts it, this means that legitimacy is the quality possessed by a legitimate authority, i.e. some quality which a legitimate representative of a community has (whatever that means) confirmed by the way it abides by the law (whatever that law may actually be) that is valid for inter-state or international community relations (Steinhoff 2007: 12).

Steinhoff in an equally brusque way, dispatches Janna Thompson's parallel effort to argue the case for a distinction between 'legitimate' and 'illegitimate' political violence based on the principle that a legitimate organization is defined as one that represents others: 'The leaders of the state or organisation should be acting as agents of their people' (Thompson 2004: 155). Since it is doubtful that many democratic states can ever meet this criterion (instance Britain's Blair government when it invaded Iraq in 2003), it is difficult to see why this should become the norm conferring legitimacy on non-state actors like the IRA or Hamas. This clears the way for Steinhoff to go well beyond the state-centric tradition, by claiming that legitimate authority may be exercised by individuals and small groups:

> Contrary to the tradition of just war theory ... every single individual is a legitimate authority and has the right to declare war on others or the state, provided only that the individual proceed responsibly in his or her decision process
>
> (Steinhoff 2007: 3)

Resistance and the liberal tradition: Locke and Hobbes

Steinhoff concludes that political violence terrorism is justified when a group of people face a threat from a more powerful group in a situation where it can deter perceived acts of aggression by the more powerful society. The object is to protect the lives of a large number of innocents in their own society (Steinhoff 2007: 135). Steinhoff stresses that these life or death judgements always have to be made in the light of specific cases. Steinhoff (2007) also makes a convincing case that classic liberals like Locke did not think that people lost the right to resist unjust state power even after, or especially if, they had entered into a social contract to surrender their rights and powers to the state in return for its protection.

John Locke and the right of resistance

As Steinhoff notes, Locke was well able to conceive of an inalienable right to oppose unjust state power when he posed the question: 'May the commands then of a Prince be opposed? May he be resisted as often as anyone shall find himself aggrieved?' As Locke himself conceded, the idea that the people held executive power as individuals in the state of nature, and could resume and exercise that power against a tyrant was 'a very Strange Doctrine' (Locke 2002: 7–9). It also marked a remarkably original move, as scholars who have studied Locke's use of writers (i.e. Cicero, the Bible, Filmer Hooker, Pufendorf, Barclay, Machiavelli and Calvin) have noted: none of the sources Locke engaged with supported a right of resistance (Tuck 1978; Skinner 1978; 1988; 2002; Pocock 1992).

Locke starts from the premise that the move out of a 'state of nature' and into civil or political society began when people experienced differences and conflict concerning the ownership and distribution of property, including the fruits of their labour (Marshall 1994). Locke assumed that we have the freedom, and thus the right, to dispose of, within the bounds of the laws of nature, those properties which are intrinsic to our personalities, and in particular our lives and liberties (Skinner 1978). To that Locke added the symmetrical assumption that the fundamental justification of government consists in its ability to preserve the natural rights of its citizens and, especially their enjoyment of life, liberty and property. On the one hand, this means that when the members of a society establish a government through mutual agreement, then all of those people are bound by duty to obey the authorized governors, because an agreement is not an agreement if its terms and conditions are fluid, and therefore, subject to change at any time. This entailed that the constitution of government may not be changed by the will of society and, for the same reason, the allegiance of the individual may not be dissolved at will, because that allegiance is based on the principle that consent, once freely given, is binding and cannot be retracted. Equally the legislators may not of their own volition change or amend the nature of the legislative power, because that power is a trust. The legislators do not own that power – they are not its proprietors – and therefore it is not theirs to give away (Locke 2002: 141). On the basis of that proviso, Locke identifies an absolute right of resistance.

Locke's constitutional theory privileges a 'mixed government' in which the executive and legislative share power on an equal basis (Locke 2002: 151). Locke claims that legitimate government is properly based on the idea of separation of powers. First and foremost of these is the legislative power. Locke describes the legislative power as supreme (Locke 2002: 149) in having ultimate authority over 'how the force for the commonwealth shall be employed' (Locke 2002: 151, 143). This means that neither the executive nor legislative entity is authorized to change the constitution from which they jointly derive their power and authority. This is because the source of all legitimate authority is to be found only in the consent of men who are by nature free. This indicates why the established lawmaking state were to be displaced, and replaced by a new and unauthorized legislative power, then this is synonymous with the unauthorized use of force, and hence brings in to being what amounts to a state of war.

In the *Two Treatises of Government*, Locke vindicates the lawfulness of resistance, in the language of rights and natural rights. As Locke put it:

> Man being born, as has been proved, with a Title to perfect Freedom, and an uncontrouled enjoyment of all the Rights and Priviledges of the Law of Nature, equally with any other Man, or number of Men in the World, hath by Nature a Power, not only to preserve his Property, that is, his Life, Liberty and Estate, against the Injuries and Attempts of other Men; but to judge of, and punish the breaches of that Law in others, as he is perswaded the Offence deserves, even with Death it self, in Crimes where the heinousness of the Fact, in his Opinion, requires it
>
> (Locke 2002: 187)

Finally, Locke goes on to locate the authority to resist not only with the body of the people even with 'any single man, if deprived of their right' (Skinner, 1978: 328, 329, 338, 347). That idea follows from his privileging of natural law that is 'as intelligible and plain to a rational Creature, and a Studier of that Law, as the positive Laws of Commonwealths, nay possibly plainer' (Locke 2002: 3). Under this law, the individual, 'has not liberty to destroy himself', indeed is 'bound to preserve himself, and not to quit his Station wilfully'.

This means that each person has a right to defend themselves and their property. Locke understood the right to property as a natural right upon which self-preservation depended. This had important consequences for his idea about self-defence and resistance. Locke understood an attack on one's property as always equivalent to an attack on one's person. In Locke's argument for the right of resistance to tyrants, he frequently compared the tyrant to 'an Aggressor', 'a Thief and a Robber', a 'Pirate' and 'the common enemy and Pest of Mankind... to be treated accordingly' (Locke 2002: 16, 202, 228, 239). Tyrants are like animals and private criminals. they live by passion, compulsion and plunder. This is also why 'whenever the *Legislators endeavour to take away, and destroy the Property of the People,* or to reduce them to Slavery under Arbitrary Power, they put themselves in a state of War with the People, who are thereupon absolved from any farther Obedience' (Locke 2002: 412).

Finally, as Steinhoff notes, Locke disposed of the argument that acknowledging the legitimacy of resistance or rebellion did not give ground to those who feared that accepting this principle implied a persistent threat of anarchy (Locke 2002: 401ff). To that supposition Locke replied, 'That Force is to be oppose to nothing, but to unjust and unlawful force: whoever makes any opposition in any other case, draws on himself a just condemnation'.

Locke offers a remarkable defence of the right to resistance. It is remarkable because it runs so hard up against the general disposition in early modern Europe to counsel obedience at all times to legitimate authority. Certainly, this is what his near-contemporary Thomas Hobbes is generally understood to have argued.

Thomas Hobbes and the right to resistance

The conventional reading of Hobbes emphasizes the way he treats the sovereign as all powerful and committed to suppress all resistance and revolution. We have long understood Hobbes to prize stability in the state above all else. To have a sovereign in place – even a tyrannical sovereign – is apparently better than the alternative, 'a war of all against all'.

On this reading, while Hobbes accepts that the state is the product of a social contract based on consent, the conventional reading of Hobbes has it that because he believes that man's natural state is one of a 'war of all against all', then the sovereign must remain independent and autonomous in order for him to be able to enforce the laws of the land. In such a state, there needs to be a sovereign who can readily correct the natural tendency to conflict and violence. Without supreme, unconditional power, any society will disintegrate. Hobbes' political theory has conventionally been read as an endorsement of state power and a prescription for unconditional obedience to the sovereign's will. The result is what looks to be and has long been understood to be the idea that rebellion and indeed lesser forms of dissent are at the least foolish and imprudent if not wrong and deserving of punishment. This is an odd legacy for a philosopher understood to be a liberal though as I have been arguing we should not be too surprised at the many puzzles and contradictions liberal-democratic states generate.

As Susan Sreedhar (2010) points out in a close-reading of what Hobbes actually says, Hobbes, the apparent absolutist, in fact has a theory of resistance rights. Indeed, Hobbes has a veritable arsenal of resistance rights retained by individuals, including the right to rebel. This is said mindful as she also says that Hobbes' objective in writing *Leviathan* was not to produce a rebel's catechism, but to generate arguments intended in general to stabilize the state.

Sreedhar argues, e.g. that Hobbes clearly countenances that when

> the sovereign issues a life-threatening command, according to Hobbes, the subject is justified in disobeying. The subject must retain the right to private judgment in such cases since it is up to the subject to *judge* whether her life is in danger.
>
> (Sreedhar 2010: 118)

Sreedhar makes a strong case against writers like Jean Hampton who accuse Hobbes of incoherence. According to Hampton, Hobbes gets himself into a muddle when he demands that subjects give up their right of judgement to the sovereign while simultaneously allowing subjects to retain their judgement regarding when they are in danger or when their interests are threatened. Hampton says this is a fatal flaw in Hobbes' theory of sovereignty. However, Sreedhar notes that

Hampton has misread Hobbes. Hampton suggests that when Hobbes says that subjects must 'submit... their Judgements, to his Judgement' (*Leviathan*, chap. 17), it meant surrendering one's faculty of judgement altogether and acquiescing in the sovereign's judgement in all cases except those in which one's life or interests are directly threatened. Sreedhar says read correctly that all that Hobbes is saying is that no man can give up his judgement (in chap. 7 and 8 of *Leviathan* and elsewhere). The notion that Hobbes thought man could give up his judgement as Hampton suggests is untenable (*Leviathan*, chap. 7). Hobbes' position is clear, e.g. his discussion of counsellors, whom he states the sovereign will need: 'he that hath the most experience in that particular kind of businesse, has therein the best Judgement, and is the best Counsellour' (*Leviathan*, chap. 25).

The 'standard interpretation' of Hobbes has acknowledged that he allowed a small basis for resistance because it is impossible to alienate the right to defend oneself against life-threatening attacks because death, as the greatest possible evil, cannot be rationally willed. Any transfer of right is a voluntary act, 'and of the voluntary acts of every man the object is some good to himself'. Sreedhar disposes of this arguing that the right of self-defence is inalienable within the specific conditions of social contract, not 'because death is the worst evil'. Rather, she says:

> ... the right is retained ... first, because there is no assurance that parties would fulfil a promise not to resist death; second, because such a promise would undermine the purpose of the social contract; and third, because the Hobbesian commonwealth does not require such a promise
>
> (Sreedhar 2010: 51)

Sreedhar observes that, on Hobbes' own account, the conditions for the validity of covenants mean that the implied transfer of the right of self-defence in the covenant that creates the commonwealth would violate all three principles of covenants: those principles include:

i   The reasonable expectations principle: a covenant is valid only if each party can reasonably expect every other party to perform their part of the covenant.
ii The fidelity principle: the transfer of a right has to be faithful to the purpose of the covenant, i.e. one cannot transfer a right when the transfer contradicts (or undermines) the purpose for which that right is transferred.
iii The necessity principle: one only transfers those rights that are necessary to achieve the purpose of the covenant.

> (Sreedhar 2010: 5)

Having highlighted these three principles (i.e. reasonable expectation, fidelity and necessity), she then shows how this works when set against the traditional interpretations of Hobbes' views on the preservation of a right to self-defence in the creation of the Leviathan where those interpretations highlighted the conceptual impossibility or the psychological implausibility of transferring this right.

How can Hobbes hold that it is conceptually or psychologically impossible to transfer the right to self-defence if he also argues that this is precisely what soldiers do when they enlist in the army? One way out of the apparent muddle is to insist Hobbes was inconsistent on this issue. Sreedhar's solution is that the right to self-defence is not alienated in the creation of the commonwealth, but is also not, strictly speaking, inalienable. It is neither psychologically nor conceptually impossible for soldiers in their particular covenant to transfer their right to self-defence in exchange for money.

On the problem that the Hobbesian sovereign right to expect obedience is greater than the subjects' right to disobey that sovereign Sreedhar seems to err on the side of philosophical consistency – and caution. She draws on Joseph Raz (1979) to argue that the commands of a sovereign are well-understood as 'exclusionary reasons', a term that refers to a reason that is to be understood as ruling out the consideration of other reasons. On Sreedhar's reading, when a 'sovereign'/state's command does not concern an action within the scope of the subject's rights, this is an exclusionary reason. Accordingly, we are not entitled to use our own judgement to decide whether that command is just or good. However, when a 'sovereign'/state's command does impinge upon the subject's rights, the sovereign is still just, but the sovereign's command is now understood as an ordinary reason. We may in those cases weigh the threat to my life and well-being presented by my disobedience against other hazards and benefits that in our judgement we guess will occur. Sreedhar (2010: 121) says that the vast majority of sovereign commands are not life-threatening and therefore the vast majority of laws and commands are exclusionary reasons. The result is a small list of rights derived from the right to self-defence, including the rights to resist 'wounds' and 'confinement' (i.e. imprisonment), the right to refuse incriminating testimony against oneself or a loved one, to disobey 'dishonourable' or 'dangerous' commands, and, finally, to 'join' in insurrection or rebellion if one's sovereign poses a threat to our survival.

Sreedhar again errs on the side of caution when she emphasizes that the right from which these rights are supposed to derive, the right to self-defence, must be substantial. She argues that what she calls ideological rebellions like those founded on religious conviction are excluded by sovereign command and are therefore illegitimate. The moot point I guess is the extent of the dissent, given the nature of the states' actions that are provoking dissent.

When Sreedhar gives us an example of a specific case of rightful rebellion Sreedhar similarly emphasizes cases, in which rebels acted against what they perceived as certain death; if they obeyed the relevant state like the Warsaw Ghetto Uprising of 1944, we get the point (Sreedhar 2010: 144, 147). To these, we might add other cases like the case of the ANC facing a brutal even violent racial state intent on preserving the power and privilege of a white minority.

On Sreedhar's reading, Hobbes argues that 'If [a subject] judges that obeying the command will threaten her life, she is permitted to disobey – 'If I obey this command, I will die' is a nonexcludable reason on Hobbes' account' (Sreedhar 2010: 121). On this basis, Hobbes, e.g. even goes so far as to argue that every subject of the state preserves the right of self-defence including even those who have been found guilty of a capital offence and are facing execution: these people have a right to try to escape death at the hands of the state irrespective of their guilt or the lawfulness of the punishment! Sreedhar concludes by suggesting that, in light of Hobbes' wide-ranging rights to resist, '*we* are not prepared to allow liberties that he was' and that Hobbes should therefore serve as 'a mirror in which we may somewhat uncomfortably look upon some of our own (perhaps unjustifiable) illiberal tendencies' (Sreedhar 2010: 175). Indeed.

Conclusion

It may well be concluded that the chances of any real liberal democracy becoming so tyrannical and violent such as to justify armed resistance are highly unlikely and so the case of apartheid South Africa with which I began this chapter has limited or little practical value or suasive power. This may well be the case.

One difficulty in using a case like South Africa is that it was so extreme an example of a 'racial' minority brutally oppressing a very large number of people, that the merits of the case for insurrection being what they were and that it hardly seems to require too much detailed attention. Certainly, the more usual circumstances obtaining in too many liberal democracies typically involve a large number of people using their democratic majority to oppress sexual, gender, religious, ethnic, or 'racial' 'minorities' and often doing it legally. This is the point of voter suppression of black voters in the southern states of America. It is the way the passage of equal employment opportunity legislation then authorizes various groups to legally discriminate against minorities as is the case in Australia. Occasionally as in the case of the so-called Federal intervention, a state may first suspend anti-racial discrimination legislation, so it can then lawfully introduce overtly racist legislation to penalize indigenous groups as happened in Australia after 2007. The trashing of the clearly defined international legal rights of asylum seekers as liberal-democratic governments close their borders in the name of 'national security' is an even more egregious example. It is these more normal circumstances that raise the difficult question as to how far those groups should go in protesting against or resisting policies and legislation that may enjoy both the protection of the law and even majority support.

Yet as I have also argued, the disposition of modern liberal-democratic states to criminalize dissent ought to be both better understood and a matter of public concern. In the following chapter, I turn to the more general question of the legitimacy or value of dissent itself. Why should I dissent and when and why might this be a good thing to do? By implication if the case *for dissent* is strong, this will indicate why suppressing it or criminalizing it is a bad idea.

For reasons that may seem self-evident, there is far less evidence of much interest historically in making the case that dissent is a good and legitimate thing to do. For one thing, the legitimacy of dissent is not self-evident simply because it is dissent. Any claim that dissent in general or in its various forms presumably will depend on the success of appeals to various grounds said to make an action legitimate... like the idea that as citizens we have rights to freedom of speech, association and movement (given to us by states) or that we have natural rights, e.g. to freedom of speech, association and movement... or that there are consequential benefits for some or many people.

Note

1 I have not addressed the work of Michael Walzer (1978) who addresses the main issues of contemporary just war theory, including the Civil War, secession, intervention and terrorism, but unaccountably deals only with states as the agents possessing 'legitimate authority'. His treatment of self-determination, e.g. represents non-state actors as undiscovered or unrecognized states and strips them of any real legitimacy (1977: 86–90). Andrew Valls notes correctly that Walzer 'never considers the possibility that stateless communities might confront the same 'supreme emergency' that justified, in his view, the bombing of innocent German civilians [in World War II]' (Valls 2000:66).

Chapter 9

Why dissent is good for us

It is entirely apposite that Bayard Rustin, a gay, African-American Quaker and civil rights activist, should be credited with formulating the idea of 'speaking the truth to power' in 1942. Rustin later co-authored the famous Quaker pamphlet *Speak Truth to Power: a Quaker Search for an Alternative to Violence* published in 1955 (American Friends Services Committee 1955). The idea itself was far older. As Michel Foucault argued in his American lectures just before he died, the idea of speaking the truth to powerful people was well understood in Classical Athens as the practice of *parrhesia* which is ordinarily translated into English as 'free speech' (Foucault 1983). Foucault notes that the *parrhesiastes* is the one who uses *parrhesia*, i.e. the one who speaks the truth. As Foucault adds when Plato confronted the tyrant Dionysius, he became a *parrhesiastes*:

> Someone is said to use parrhesia and merits consideration as a parrhesiastes only if there is a risk or danger for him or her in telling the truth … when a philosopher addresses himself to a sovereign, to a tyrant, and tells him that his tyranny is disturbing and unpleasant because tyranny is in compatible with justice, then the philosopher speaks the truth, believes he is speaking the truth, and, more than that, also takes a risk (since the tyrant may become angry, may punish him, may exile him, may kill him
>
> (Foucault 1983; also Foucault 2011)

In this chapter, I make the case that if and when dissent involves speaking truth to power, it is a good and legitimate practice. This is because the pursuit of truth, however uncomfortable this is, helps to dispel ignorance in all of its many forms: dissent is something we all need. This is well illustrated by William Kaplan (2017) in his book dedicated to showing why dissent is valuable when he shows why ignorance can lead whole nations to ward catastrophe.

Yom Kippur (or Day of Atonement) is the holiest day of the Jewish calendar and falls each year on the tenth day of the Jewish month of Tishrei. In 1973, Yom Kippur fell on October 6. Around 2.00 p.m. that day, Egypt and Syria invaded Israel. Code-named 'Operation Badr', five Syrian army divisions invaded Israel attacking two under-strength Israeli Defence Force brigades on the Golan Heights.

Simultaneously, five Egyptian infantry divisions crossed the Suez Canal to fight 450 Israeli soldiers in sixteen small forts (Reidel 2017). Israel would lose over 3,000 of its troops and 500 of its tanks before it won the war and under pressure from America, agreed to begin negotiations with Egypt.

The Yom Kippur War is generally treated by those working in the field of security studies like Uri Bar-Joseph (1995a, 2005) as a study in 'surprise attacks' and 'intelligence failure' (also Hughes 1976; Handel 1977, 1984, 1987; Levite 1987; Hulnick 1991). If we break with this framework, which assumes that 'surprise attack' like the Yom Kippur War (or the 'unforeseen' collapse of major banks and financial institutions in America and Europe in 2007–08) is a pathology, then we see two things more clearly.[1] The failure to use available evidence to work out what is actually happening testifies to the normal role played not by knowledge but by ignorance. Second and even more to the point, these kinds of cases go directly to the question addressed in this chapter: why is dissent, when it involves some matter of truth, a good.

William Kaplan (2017) reminds us that Israel's Directorate of Military Intelligence Branch had promised through 1973 that it would give at least forty-eight hours notice of any Arab attack. It failed to do this, in spite of its having evidence that meant it could have done far better than just giving two days notice. As Kaplan (2017) and other writers have shown, Israel's intelligence services had plenty of evidence about a looming attack. Just eleven days before the invasion, King Hussein of Jordan had flown secretly to a meeting at a guesthouse run by the Israeli Institute for Intelligence and Special Projects (Mossad) in Tel Aviv to meet Israel's Prime Minister Golda Meier and the head of Mossad Zvi Zamir. Jordan had been part of an anti-Israeli coalition since 1948, but Hussein had begun having clandestine meetings with Israeli officials some years before (Ashton 2008) when he came to warn Meir about the pending invasion – though he did not know the precise date as it had not then been set. Hussein told the Israeli Prime Minister that he had attended a summit meeting between 10 and 12 September between President Anwar Sadat of Egypt as the host and President Hafez al-Assad of Syria. Hussein said war with Egypt and Syria was coming – and soon (Reidel 2017). He also wanted to try and persuade Meier to move quickly to re-start a peace process with the Arabs (Bar-Joseph 2005: 192).

Meier immediately contacted the head of Israel's army General Moshe Dayan. Dayan reassured Meier that he would strengthen Israel's positions (Bar-Joseph 2005: 90). However, the following day when Dayan discussed the warning with the Israel Defence Forces (IDF) chief intelligence officer, Major-General Eliyahu Zeira, his deputy Aryeh Shalev, and other key security officials all dismissed the idea of any imminent invasion. Dayan and his colleagues were in the grip of what has become known as the 'concept': the Israeli's 'knew' that the Arabs would not go to war because they would lose (Parker 2001: 144).

This 'concept' was a long-standing political narrative recycled by senior Israeli political and military figures after the Six-Day War in 1967 that Egypt (or Syria) would never attack Israel. This view was maintained in spite of intelligence coming in from Mossad intelligence agents close to Sadat in November 1972 and January 1973 that Egypt was preparing to invade Israel (Kaplan 2017: 6). Worse as Ben-Joseph (1997: 590) argues, in late September, Zeira, the director of military intelligence who promoted the 'concept', refused suggestions by his subordinates, to activate 'special means' of gathering intelligence evidence, which would have confirmed Hussein's warning. At the same time, he was reporting to his military and political superiors, when asked about the operational status of these 'special means' that they had already been activated: here Zeira was resorting to one of the forms that ignorance takes: lies. This deception reinforced the Israeli belief that there was no evidence supporting the idea of Arab War preparations. All evidence of war preparations and any warnings of war were fed into the 'concept' and then explained away (Morris and Black 1991: 291: also Reidel 2017). Here we see a concatenation of deception, denial and presumed knowledge, some of the more common forms of ignorance.

Among the few dissenters was Lieutenant Colonel Zusia Keniezer. He believed the king should be taken seriously. He knew the Syrians were in pre-attack position, and their preparations were being coordinated with Egypt. Keniezer sought the security of his community from surprise attack. However, Keniezer's commanding officer in charge of research and analysis in military intelligence, General Aryeh Shalev, called Keniezer an 'alarmist' and rejected his assessment (Bar-Joseph 2005: 91–2). King Hussein too was a dissenter though for somewhat different reasons and motivations who promoted the good of truth. Hussein wanted a negotiated peace and Both Keniezer and King Hussein spoke truth to power, and as is all too often the case, power preferred some of the many forms ignorance takes, and preserving the *status quo* over truth and its unruly effects.

Bar-Joseph (1995a) claims that there are any number of explanations or what he calls 'pathologies' that lead to surprise attacks. With Margaret Heffernan (2011), I beg to differ: these 'pathologies' are not the exception but the norm. The tremendous capacity for self-deception, delusion and irrationality manifested by most of the leading Israeli politicians, its military leaders and the professional intelligence officers points to a more general problem: most of us seem too often to prefer not to know what is actually happening. As Margaret Heffernan (2011) argues, there are many cognitive mechanisms and social practices which combine to induce a condition she calls 'wilful blindness'. She describes it this way: we all face circumstances where 'we could know, and should know, but don't know because it makes us feel better not to know'. (Heffernan notes that the category of 'wilful blindness' itself comes from the law and has played a significant role in American criminal law.)

As Heffernan's survey of an array of social science research indicates, we know a lot about why we have trouble working out what is actually happening even or especially when the evidence is pointing clearly in one way. Leon Festinger's (1957) theory of cognitive dissonance, e.g. explains why intelligence analysts tend to ignore evidence of looming danger when that evidence contradicts their belief that any surprise attack is unlikely. (Festinger's famous research studied the case of a religious cult convinced they had received a warning from God about the imminent destruction of earth and how they would all be rescued by a space ship he would send: Festinger wanted to see how they dealt with the failure of their prediction.)

Daniel Kahneman's and Amos Tversky's (1972, 1979) 'prospect theory' shows how many of us prefer a 'good' story to a 'bad' story. Their research tested the claim made by neoclassical economists that people make invariantly rational decisions when doing economic things like investing money. They set out to find out how people actually made decisions about economic questions like whether to buy insurance or not and choose between alternatives that involve risk where the probabilities of outcomes are uncertain. Kahneman and Tversky argue that people make decisions based on heuristic judgements or mental shortcuts when confronting complex situations. They showed, e.g. how people prefer to make decisions based on expected gains rather than losses and this privileging of expected gain is often deeply irrational. In complementary fashion, Irving Janis's (1972, 1982) account of the role played by 'groupthink' in producing a string of American foreign policy disasters like the Bay of Pigs invasion of Cuba in 1961 highlights the way small and cohesive groups favour conformity over dissent. This disposition is especially prominent when there is a hierarchy of power either inside or around the group. The dynamics at work in the relations of hierarchy reward consensus and conformity and punish dissent: the result as any history of an intelligence agency like the Central Intelligence Agency (Weiner 2007) or of foreign policy failures like Britain's appeasement polices of the 1930s or its decision to go to war in Iraq (Chilcot 2016) are policy disasters based on an unwillingness to acknowledge reality.

In short, notwithstanding the temptation to treat 'military intelligence' as an oxymoron, the more serious point is that we need to treat the refusal of Israeli intelligence to take the evidence it was getting seriously, not as pathology but as a normal example of the role played by ignorance. This also highlights the role and value of dissent. In effect, there is a complex relation between knowledge-ignorance mediated by dissent.

The case for dissent

In what follows I make the case for 'dissent'. Like Steven Schiffrin (1999), I will restrict the idea of dissent to the practice of free speech even though some kinds of dissent go well beyond speaking and include – as we have seen – many kinds of actions, both peaceful and violent, legal and illegal. My point here is simple: the value of dissent is undeniable since it promotes basic human goods and our capacity to live out our lives in the pursuit of those goods both 'individually' and collectively. To that end, we need to acknowledge the value of truth. In turn, the value of dissent lies in its capacity to promote truth. The difficulty is that the good of knowledge so frequently encounters the many forms that ignorance takes: the pursuit of truth is what we may call knowledge, but knowledge leads a fugitive existence given the ubiquity of ignorance. Dissent when carried out with the aim of promoting the truth is a good. Let me say why.

The good of knowledge

For too long, the social sciences have claimed to be value free. For many social scientists the difference between factual claims and ethical claims is absolute. That this proposition itself depends on a self-negating proposition (i.e. we *ought* not conflate factual claims and ethical claims) suggests a degree of muddle best avoided. Rather we might better understand the relation between factual claims and ethical claims as a unity of difference. I want to argue that dissent is part of a practice of discerning and living out the goods that make our lives good and fulfilling and worth living. *Praxis* since Aristotle, and as somewhat reaffirmed by Arendt, is oriented to a range of goods: so what are the goods which define or enable a human life to be understood and lived as a good life?

John Finnis (1980) provides a strong answer to this question. John Finnis offers an uncompromising account of the fundamental human goods. It says something about Finnis' courage, if nothing else, that he is writing at a time when all manner of 'post-modernist' and more recently identity-political relativist claims have flourished which deny that truth matters or even that reality is real. As Finnis announces from the start, he wants to identify both the human goods and the requirements of practical reasonableness, which help to constitute a sense of what we might mean by a good human life. It is an unfashionable book since Finnis is neither a relativist, nor a classical liberal. Finnis is a natural lawyer who grounds his claims about the good life initially in a naturalistic anthropology and then in a religious account of an order of things established by a God.[2]

Finnis offers us a profound and relationally inflected enquiry into the kinds of goods which support human flourishing and what practical reasonableness looks like. As he says for this enquiry to be possible, the theorist has to find a point of 'reflective equilibrium' between description and evaluation. His account is grounded in the capacity of a theorist like himself to develop a *non-value neutral descriptive* account of the goods, which accepts that such a theorist necessarily participates in the work of *evaluation*. Finnis proposes a kind of relational dialectic which moves backwards and forwards between assessments of human good and its practical requirements *and* explanatory descriptions using historical, experimental and sociological materials and methods. This says Finnis requires both a descriptive-evaluative anthropology of the goods which support a flourishing life, or inform the good life, conjoined with a capacity to understand what is really good for human persons and what is really required by practical reasonableness.

Finnis makes the ambitious claim that we are able to identify certain universal human goods. These goods however can only be specified at a certain level of generality. He discounts any notion that this is a 'wish-list' insisting it is grounded in the actual circumstances of human existence. His enquiry relies on the descriptive social sciences which seek to tell us how people in different societies engage their pursuit of the good life. His enquiry is not deflated by the inevitable discovery that people in different times and places are not equally devoted to or united in their conception of what justice or the human goods may look like.

As Finnis notes, Leo Strauss (1959: 10) treated the fact that there is an indefinitely large variety of notions of right and wrong, as not so much 'incompatible with the idea of natural right, [and more as] the essential condition for the emergence of that idea'. Equally pursuing those basic human goods needs to be informed by some well-justified judgements about all aspects of genuine human flourishing and what 'authentic practical reasonableness' looks like. Let me consider his claim that knowledge of truth is a basic human good.

Finnis defends the proposition that the first great human good is knowledge conceived of as knowledge of truth. This good he (1980: 60) says is grounded in a very common human activity, namely the 'activity of trying to find out, to understand and to judge matters correctly'. As he (1980: 61) puts it:

> In explaining, to oneself and others, what one is up to, one finds oneself able and ready to refer to *finding out, knowledge, truth* as sufficient explanations of the point of one's activity, project or commitment. One finds oneself reflecting that ignorance and muddle are to be avoided ... 'it's good to find out...' now seems to be applicable not merely in relation to oneself ... but at large ... and for anyone.

Finnis says this idea of knowledge of truth – as a good is not limited.[3] Saying that knowledge is a valuable activity is simply to say that the pursuit of knowledge 'makes intelligible any particular instance of the human activity and commitment involved in such a pursuit' (Finnis 1980: 65).

Knowledge or perhaps *knowing as an activity* (or praxis) is good, and there are no sufficient reasons for doubting that this is the case.[4] While Finnis accepts that the truth of this claim 'cannot be demonstrated', 'it needs no demonstration'. Put simply, while it is not possible to demonstrate the basic good of knowledge if we make the claim that knowledge is a basic good, we propose a self-refuting claim if we claim that it is not. This is because to ask the question 'is knowledge is a basic good?', one has demonstrated, by the very pursuit of the issue, that one wishes to know. Claiming that the knowledge is not a good is to self-refute. [5]

When Finnis claims that the basic goods are self-evident, he does not mean we know this innately, nor is he claiming that there is unanimous agreement that the basic goods are in fact the basic goods. Nor does he mean that 'self-evidence' is simply some experience of a *feeling* of certitude.

Rather the basic goods are described by Finnis as activities and states that are worthwhile for their own sake. As activities and states that are worthwhile in themselves, they are ends of human activity. As ends of human activity, there is no need for any recourse to a further reason to explain their value. The basic goods as ends are the fundamental reasons for action. As fundamental reasons for action they cannot be inferred from more fundamental reasons or ends for they are the first and fundamental reasons for action. They are self-evident as they are the first and fundamental reasons for action. It is of the very nature of ends that they are self-evident, for if they are not self-evident, they are not basic goods or ends.

If Finnis has established the reasons why knowledge is a fundamental human good, I want now to ask how we might think about the relationship between knowledge and the forms that ignorance takes before making the case for dissent. How common is it that we get it right? It is far less common than we might like to believe, because ignorance plays a large, persistent and complex role in the things we claim to know. Ignorance is the absence of or negation of knowledge. Sometimes we don't know, and we may not even know we don't know. US Secretary of Defence Donald Rumsfeld made the point in 2002 – and a year away from the disastrous invasion of Iraq – when he answered a simple question: 'In regard to Iraq weapons of mass destruction and terrorists, is there any evidence to indicate that Iraq has attempted to or is willing to supply terrorists with weapons of mass destruction?' Rumsfeld replied:

> … as we know, there are known knowns; there are things we know we know. We also know there are known unknowns; that is to say we know there are some things we do not know. But there are also unknown unknowns – the ones we don't know we don't know. And if one looks throughout the history of our country and other free countries, it is the latter category that tend to be the difficult ones.
>
> (Rumsfeld 2002)

When he said this, it was treated as a joke. It was no joke. The real problem as it turned out was his complacent claim that 'there are things we know we know'. The Bush administration claimed it knew that Iraq possessed weapons of mass destruction. Given that Iraq had no weapons of mass destruction, the only question we should be asking is what kind of ignorance was Rumsfeld gripped by?

Seven kinds of ignorance

The 'recent' invention of the field of 'ignorance studies', sometimes unhappily referred to as 'agnotology' (Proctor and Schiebinger 2008), suggests why we need to avoid any complacency. The relations between knowledge and ignorance is what we need to pay attention to.

To be clear as Mathias Gross and Linsey McGoey suggest, even to raise this point by acknowledging and observing 'what is not known is often a challenging and unpopular field of research and teaching' (Gross and McGoey 2015: 7). Both the challenge and the antagonism it may arouse is presumably amplified when the object of scrutiny is the very place deemed central to the banishment of ignorance, the university. We need, however, as Joseph Schumpeter argued apropos the work of neoclassical economists, to remind ourselves how 'how near to each other … dwell truth and error' (Schumpeter 1951: 17).

The modern (research) university is supposed to be the only institution bearing witness to the Enlightenment belief 'that knowledge when systematically produced through adherence to reliable methods of data collection or extraction will inevitably trump superstition?' This as Mathias Gross and Linsey McGoey note is 'a conceit that dominates the social or physical science to this day' (Gross and McGoey 2015: 3). That something had gone wrong was suggested in 2005 when John Ioannidis published his famous paper in which he announced that 'There is increasing concern that in modern [bio-medical] research, false findings may be the majority or even the vast majority of published research claims… It can be proven that most claimed research findings are false' (Ioannidis 2005). Some of the sciences implicated are still struggling to get the relationship between knowledge and ignorance right.

Jens Haas and Katja Vogt start by proposing that 'ignorance is the absence of knowledge' (2015: 19). They also note that philosophers have said far less about ignorance than knowledge. This bad habit arguably started after Plato saw the trouble Socrates got into by his pursuit of others' ignorance courtesy of the *elenchic* irony Socrates put to such stunning use in his dialogic enquiry (Vlastos 1991). They note helpfully that 'ignorance' as absence of knowledge is etymologically based on 'I' (a negator preface) attached to '-gnorance' (from the Greek *Gnosis*). While this is the common Greek noun for 'knowledge' bit also points back to a special kind of religious or mystical 'insight'. This does not, of course, go very far in specifying the kinds of ignorance.

Haas and Vogt point to four kinds of ignorance. First, there is the ignorance based on choice or preference which they call 'preferred ignorance'. This is based on a simple desire not to know anything about things like Jane Austen's novels, the calculus, French cooking, Bitcoin or the Armenian genocide of 1916 …. The second kind of ignorance is what they call 'investigative ignorance'. This is the kind of fruitful ignorance that starts with the discovery that we don't know something. This discovery can trigger our curiosity which once aroused means that we have to follow it up and resolve. In physics Einstein's puzzlement about the lack of fit between Newton's classical mechanics and Maxwell's laws of electromagnetics was fired by Michelson and Morley's measurements of the speed of light. The third and most complicated kind of ignorance is what they call 'presumed knowledge'. This is a special and widespread kind of ignorance based on thorough going ignorance but masked by the certainty that we know. Harry Frankfurt's (2005) best-selling book *On Bullshit* addresses the problem created when people talk as if they know something – when they don't. This is another kind of ignorance worth following up. Finally, there is 'complete ignorance', the kind of ignorance that is so profound that we don't even know that we don't know. Sometimes this may reflect the complete absence of anything which we might even know by discovering evidence that might give us clues to something like the origins of human language. Sometimes this complete ignorance may simply reflect the role played by dominant assumptions that serves as a thick impenetrable veil of ignorance.

This analytic offers a heuristic for thinking about the relation between knowledge and different kinds of ignorance. In what follows, I extend the model of ignorance proposed by Haas and Vogt (2015) and suggest there are a number of important kinds of ignorance as well as different descriptions.[6] Table 9.1 highlights seven kinds of ignorance:

Table 9.1 Seven kinds of ignorance

Investigative ignorance	Lies	Deception	Delusion	Error	Denial	Presumed knowledge
The discernment that we don't know something or that some kind of ignorance is at work and requires investigation and enquiry is a vital spur to knowing-as-praxis.	Claiming to know something that is not the case.	Partial accounts that are true but, leave out important facts.	Serious sustained misbelief.	Reliance on techniques that do not work.	Uncomfortable facts/painful reality that are ignored or repressed.	Conventional belief systems supported by powerful incentives and sanctions that prevent refutation.

Knowledge and investigative ignorance

The premise in what follows is that knowledge is what we are after and that knowledge is having well-justified reasons and or good evidence upon which we make claims that such and such is actually the case. Knowledge as the praxis of enquiry is properly driven by investigative ignorance informed by a persistent and niggling sense that any claim to know is always and ought to be, as Popper (1963) argued, amenable to critique and refutation.

First, we can say with John Finnis (1980) that we know something because we have a well-justified basis for claiming that x is the case. This can only be the case because we have engaged in practices like thinking, judging and enquiry: it is not enough that we have found an authority like the *Encyclopedia Britannica* or Wikipedia to back up a claim we want to make. As Finnis notes, this brings every 'controverted question of epistemology to a focus'. In mitigation, he presents a number of basic considerations as a guide to what might be well-justified reasons for thinking we have got it right. He appeals (i) to the principles of logic like good deductive inference – allowing, of course, that 'no non-circular proof of the validity of these principles is possible since any proof would use them'; (ii) the principle that self-defeating or self-negating theses are to be rejected; (iii) phenomena are to be treated as real unless there is some reason not to; (iv) a full description of data is to be preferred to a partial description; (v) a successful method of interpretation is to be relied on in all similar cases until contrary reason appears; (vi) successful theoretical accounts which are simple, predictively successful and explanatorily powerful are to be accepted in preference to other accounts (Finnis 1980: 67). As he says, none of these principles are demonstrable. They can even be denied. 'But to deny them is to disqualify oneself from the pursuit of knowledge and to deny them is as straightforwardly unreasonable as anything can be'.

Here we see a perfect example of the imbrication of knowledge and ignorance. Conceiving of relational ignorance understood as 'investigative ignorance' is a powerful and vital spur to enquiry. This is the kind of fruitful ignorance that begins when we discover that we don't know something, or that something doesn't quite add up. This discovery ought to almost always be the default position from which any useful process of enquiry should start. As Karl Popper (1963) properly insisted, every 'science' (*wissenschaft*) ought to be a project committed to offering *provisional conjectures* which can then be subjected to rigorous enquiry and testing oriented to *refutation*. Popper argued in effect for a practice of science-as-dissent when he argued against the prevailing inductive model of science arguing instead that what distinguished sciences from pseudo-sciences is not that sciences are verified by evidence, but rather that makes risky predictions or questionable descriptions that are capable of being refuted. As Steve Fuller has argued, Popper set out to liberate science from the dictates of the prevailing symbolic order (as Bourdieu would call it) or, as Kuhn called it, the 'ruling paradigm', by relentlessly exposing scientific theories to the test of falsification (Fuller 2000, 2004). For reasons that will become clear, this important idea while it is routinely applauded is equally routinely ignored: the factors that we will call 'ignorance' are generally far more important in everyday life and even in many, though not all scientific fields of practice.

Just as knowing ultimately has to be an activity based on practices like thinking, judging and enquiry, so too we will see that a lot of effort is put into upholding and (re)producing ignorance. In what follows, I briefly outline the forms that ignorance takes in ascending order of importance. We are all familiar with lies.

Lies

Ignorance can be a consequence of our own lies or the lies of another. Lying is a knowing act: we know something to be the case – or believe it to be so – and choose to mislead someone who has an interest in knowing the truth. White lies are little versions of this: even though I knew I would be late because I chose to sleep in and so miss the 7.30 a.m. train, I tell my colleagues the train was delayed. It is common enough and provides many instances of what Midgley (2001) calls 'ordinary wickedness'. The black lie goes to cases like Bernie Madoff's career as an investor. Madoff was a billionaire financier who ran a Ponzi scheme over decades that eventually crashed in late 2008 owing his creditors $69 billion. Madoff relied on the ignorance created by his and his co-conspirator's persistent and deliberate lies (Henriques 2012). Those lies 'made sense' partly because his lies were legitimized by the belief system sustained and reproduced by neoclassical economists and by neo-liberal policymakers.

In the case of white and black lies, we, or they know better but we, or they, decide for any number of reasons to intentionally deceive. This is to say that an intention to deceive creates ignorance. I will not say much about this kind of ignorance.

Deception

Deception is a kind of lying one that involves a mixture of truth and concealment of something that needs to be known if we are to have the full picture. It can take many forms. The Nazi state's turn to genocide which began in the second half of 1941 after the invasion of the Soviet Union was accompanied by systematic deception withholding information about the killing of Jews, Slavs and Communist officials while reminding their own citizens about the false atrocity stories spread by the Allies during the Great War. Equally, the deception extended to the use of euphemisms like 'resettlement' to persuade the Jewish victims that they were merely being shipped off to ghettoes in the east. Deception may be as simple as a politician addressing some allegation of misconduct by answering a question truthfully but omitting some important additional information. It may be that the omission is justified on the grounds that the truth doesn't fit the categories used in the allegation of impropriety. President Clinton's answer to the question of whether he had had 'sex' with Monica Lewinsky is a classic case of this kind of deception: he answered by treating the category of 'sex' as synonymous with 'sexual intercourse' and so could say he hadn't had 'sex' with Lewinsky because she had only fellated him – mostly inconclusively.

Error

Another kind of ignorance is a consequence of errors which have entered into some claim to knowledge that is variously technical, technological, conceptual or even logical in nature. The ecological fallacy at work when a statistically large problem (like unemployment) is used to explain a statistically small problem (like youth suicide) is a kind of error that encourages ignorance of this kind. In one respect making a category mistake is another example of this kind of ignorance. This is the kind of error that Ryle says we make when we attribute a property to a thing that it can't possibly have or mistake a thing for something else or even misattribute something to a whole class. For example, one might say that 'the movie had too much salt in it' (Ryle 1949: 16–17). However, this opens up many large issues again which point to the complex relationship between 'knowledge' and 'ignorance' which too frequently 'fly under our radar'.

This is evident, e.g. when social scientists and administrators try to create or deploy 'categories of people' (like 'the unemployed', 'the poor', 'the homeless', 'the obese'…). Creating categories of people is a practice often used to manage people as part of the normal work of government, charged with running everything from registries of births, deaths and marriages to passports, waging war or managing people seen as a threat, or to 'help' individuals seen as needing support. Ian Hacking (1998) has shed light on the way government officials, scientific experts and professionals generate classifications of people, and how those categories affect those deemed to be named by them as well as how those people can work back on the classifications being applied to them.

Crucially the practice of 'making up people' entails identifying, describing and 'explaining' (often in scientific or administrative ways) certain kinds of people *based on the premise that to be in that category the people must possess certain traits or characteristics in common*. This, in turn, reveals at least one fascinating and mistaken assumption. This is the assumption that there is some 'essence' which the definition of a thing like a 'cat', a political institution like 'democracy' or a 'generation' can and ought to express. Here we see the persistence of a conventional background theory of language that is still dominant in both popular culture and in the social sciences.

The philosopher Ludwig Wittgenstein did much to highlight what this 'theory' assumes and the ignorance it sustains. Wittgenstein introduced his *Philosophical Investigations* by discussing St Augustine's *Confessions* in which Augustine describes how he remembers learning to use language (Wittgenstein 1958). Wittgenstein saw here a conventional idea about human language: namely, that (i) words name objects, and (ii) sentences are combinations of words. Wittgenstein argues this is the naïve basis of a lot of subsequent philosophical accounts of reality, language and truth. Not so much a 'theory of language', or a 'theory of meaning', it is more a common still conventional and widely admired framework of thought. This conception of language holds that every word has a single meaning, that this meaning is correlated with the word, and that the meaning of a word is the object it stands for. A further extension of this is that if the meaning of a word is the object it stands for, then a sentence is a collection of names entailing that the essential function of sentences is to describe how things are. One further implication of this is a simple theory of truth, which holds that when we match up a sentence with the way things are we will have truth.

None of these assumptions actually hold true. Wittgenstein, e.g. demonstrated that 'vagueness' and the way a word can have multiple meanings are entrenched and pervasive aspects of all languages (1953: 104–08). In this way Wittgenstein punched the first big hole into the classical theory of categories (1958: 66–71). The classical theory says a category has *clear boundaries,* which are defined by *common properties.* Wittgenstein pointed out that a category like *game* does not meet this criterion, since there are no common properties shared by all games. Games, like any other category (like 'animal', 'species' or 'fruit'), are similar to one another in a wide variety of ways. That, and not a single, well-defined collection of common properties is what makes *game or fruit* a category.

Delusion

Notwithstanding the tendency to equate delusion with some sort of mental illness (like delusional disorder or psychosis), the more substantial problem occurs when large numbers of people have unshakable beliefs in something untrue or which is not susceptible to any kind of evidentiary verification. The more common kind of ignorance-as-delusion occurs as a consequence of people often in large numbers who believe in things that are in no way real and for which evidence can never be produced or used without relying on some large and precarious assumptions. This includes the kinds of systemic beliefs that are upheld by great religious traditions.

We can, e.g. bundle up and talk about contemporary traditions like 'creationism' or 'Intelligent design' as an example of this kind of delusion. There has been a marked revival of creationism in some countries sponsored by a mix of postmodernist relativism and intellectual defences of 'scriptural literalism' mounted by writers like Phillip Johnson (1991, 1995). In 2017, four out of ten Americans claimed adherence to a fundamentalist Christian creationism holding that God created humans in their present form at some time within the last 10,000 years or so (Swift 2017). Michael Ruse (2018) argues that while 'creationism' is 'scientifically worthless, philosophically confused, and theologically blinkered beyond repair'], its social and political power is undoubted. Ruse also makes the point that the very success of science and technology in delivering economic goods and services may have impelled the alarming rise of creationism in the twenty-first century in countries that are host to significant numbers of both Christian and Muslim communities.

Delusion is also a key part of political processes. The resurgence of right-wing populism in erstwhile liberal-democracies provides a good example of the political role of delusion explored at length by writers like Jacqueline Rose (1996) and Cornelius Castoriadis (1993, 1997). Jan Werner-Mueller (2016), e.g. argues that populism is a degraded form of democracy that relies on a narrative about 'The People'. The 'People' is an imaginary 'community', made up of ethnically and culturally coherent and single-minded people who are under attack from 'elites' and/or 'outsiders'. This imaginary is put to work when right-wing populists claim 'The People' are being undermined or victimized by various elites ('big money', 'big government', the EU or the UN, the Illuminati, or just 'cosmopolitan intellectuals') and/or by 'outsiders' usually foreigners, asylum seekers and immigrants. Populists from Trump, Orban, Marin Le Pen, to Duterte or movements like the Brexiteers, the Tea Party or Fidesz all claim that in leading the fight against various elites they alone represent the people: 'We are the people. Who are you?'

The slide into denouncing certain groups as enemies of the people is but a small one: regimes on the left and the right can mobilize mass sentiment against enemies of 'The People' like the 'Jews' (Nazi Germany), 'Kulaks' and 'Trotskyites' (Soviet Union) or 'Reds' and 'Communists' (America in the 1940s and 1950s).

Denial

Denial or 'preferred ignorance' can be innocent as Haas and Vogt (2015) suggest simply because we are not interested in things others may well be. We may miss out on something beautiful or curious, but that's our loss. However, it also goes to far darker possibilities. One version of denial has been illuminated by Stan Cohen's (2001) great study of how states consistently deny the damage they wreak on the lives of their own citizens or of other states when they engage in various security operations or economic policy processes like the great Chinese famines of the 1960s (Dikötter 2010). This involves him in an intricate study of both the processes of denial and the questions citizens and scholars need to ask when they suspect denial is going on. Drawing on cases from his native South Africa and his adopted home in Israel, Cohen shows how 'statements of denial Involve blatant assertions that something did not happen, does not exist, is not true, or is not known about' (Cohen 2001: 3). Cohen also points to the kinds of questions we need to ask: what is the 'content of denial'? pointing as he suggests to possibilities: 'literal denial' ('it did not happen'), 'interpretive denial' ('it happened, but its meaning is different that it appears') or 'implicatory denial', what is happening when we witness ('it happened, but its significance is different than it appears'). A second question goes to questions whether the denial is personal, or (collective) in that it reflects some official, or cultural belief. Again Cohen is clear that the forms that denial can take include everything from outright lies to those processes in human consciousness by which truths are hidden, repressed, obfuscated or distorted by us by virtue of our own mechanisms of denial as repression or by virtue of some process like 'groupthink'. In. one sense, however, as he notes denial almost always involves lies: in order to use the term 'denial' to describe a person's statement 'I did not know', one has to assume that she knew or knows about what it is that she claims not to know? Otherwise the term 'denial' is inappropriate. Strictly speaking, this is the only legitimate use of the term 'denial' (Cohen 2001: 6).

Denial can also take on a systemic quality in many sciences. As economists like Thomas Picketty and Tony Atkinson have noted, neoclassical economists were simply not interested in studying either poverty or inequality. As Atkinson notes for much of the twentieth century, the topic of economic inequality had become marginalized before adding that, 'some economists hold the view that the economics profession should not concern itself at all with inequality' (Atkinson 2015: 14–15). This denial in part reflected certain deep prejudices fundamental to neoclassical or micro-economics. One of those was an effect of 'the micro-foundation' of macro-economics because 'the aggregate functions may have different properties from those at the individual level'. This means that 'the macro-economy behaves like some "representative" individual'. It is indeed optimistic to suppose that we could derive properties of the aggregate demand functions without specifying anything about the distribution of tastes and income across the population (Atkinson 1987: 27). Another was the problem that Atkinson's pioneering efforts to measure inequality assumed that underlying any measure of income inequality was 'some concept of social welfare and it is with this concept that we should be concerned', which affronted the conventional premise of value freedom held to by most economists.

Presumed knowledge

Arguably the single most significant kind of ignorance is the belief that we know something when a large body of evidence and/or rational analysis suggests otherwise. We think we know that x is the case or we may even think we know why x is the case, when we actually don't. This is most likely to occur because those working within a given social field of practice (e.g. academic disciplines like economics, psychology, sociology and so forth) work within an authoritative symbolic order presumed to be true. The relevant symbolic order or intellectual tradition has prestige because it is assumed to be true, enabling some part of the world to be both described or explained in a particular way. The fact that, on almost every point, available evidence suggests that this is not true is suppressed or simply ignored. For outsiders, this looks like an ongoing scandal.

This is possibly the most widespread kind of ignorance both historically and in the present time. In our time, neoclassical economics provide a clear-cut example of presumed knowledge. In spite of decades of devastating criticism and/or profoundly disconfirming events like the Great Recession of 2008, the ship of conventional economics sails on, its adherents like any cult deploying to the full the rich resources of cognitive dissonance (see Mirowski 1989; Nelson 2001; Varoufakis 2005; Keen 2015).

The problem of ignorance

The various kinds of ignorance outlined here are not tight, seamlessly or well bounded. They can be practices or involve states of mind that are porous. It remains an open question, e.g. whether the 'ignorance' which characterized claims after 2001 that the Bush Presidency and the Blair New Labour governments had 'hard evidence' that the Hussein regime in Iraq possessed 'weapons of mass destruction' was a result of delusion, error, presumed knowledge or lying – or some mix of all these.

The big point here is that whatever knowledge is, its relationship to ignorance is persistent, deep and complex. At the least, the argument made here suggests that knowledge is not some kind of box of truths or 'information' able to be transmitted and memorized (which is an idea set loose by encyclopaedias, some textbooks or TV quiz shows), rather knowing as a praxis begins with problems and issues yet to be resolved and includes developing a capacity to identify which of the various kinds of ignorance we might be gripped by. This is because all of the forms of ignorance outlined above are wrapped like tendrils of seaweed around our efforts to know what is actually happening. As I want to indicate this, also goes to questions of a 'practical' or ethical kind.

At issue then are important epistemic issue about the imbrication of what we know and what we don't. There is a no less complex relationship between what we know and what we don't know when faced with the many practical (i.e. ethical) issues involved in deciding what we ought to be doing. This if anything only highlights further the vital epistemic and practical role played by dissent in overcoming ignorance. As philosophers from Socrates to Gregory Vlastos (1991) and Mary Midgley (2001) have understood, ignorance can and will get in the way of answering the essential practical question 'how ought I (or we) live?' The point is simple: we are far more likely to live in ignorance – in all of its forms as they bleed into one another – that we are to enjoy the unalloyed fruits of knowledge. That is why dissent matters.

Dissent as a prophylaxis against ignorance

Dissent sits at the cross-roads (*krisis* Greek) of the manifold relations between knowledge and ignorance. (As Stijn De Cauwer observes, our notion of crisis descends etymologically from the *krisis*, a cross-roads requiring a judgement about which course to take: *crisis* is also connected to the practice of judgement (*krinein* Greek), which, e.g. a court has to decide on.) Knowledge is what ignorance seeks to deny by voluntary or involuntary means, or by acts or omission or commission. The practice of dissent helps to clarify the relations between knowledge/ignorance (De Cauwer 2018: 2). Dissent is the prophylaxis that helps us work out what is which. It also makes sense of the defence of the idea of politics as *agon/* conflict: we need in effect to enlarge the possibilities for permanent crisis in our political cultures.

The value of dissent: the liberal case

While it is true enough that the idea of freedom of speech is a pre-eminent political value in liberal-democratic polities, it is also where the fault lines in real liberal-democratic polities become all too apparent. As earlier chapters have argued when put to the test, delusions (and occasionally real concerns) about 'security' and the need to preserve 'order', consistently trump freedom of speech and the expression of dissent. So it can only ever be an ironical exercise to show how liberalism which has been shown wanting in so many ways both intellectually and as a political practice nonetheless still provides one of the best cases for dissent as a valuable, because disagreeable, activity.

John Stuart Mill offers a striking defence of freedom of thought, speech and action, a freedom he argues should be constrained only by his 'harm principle'. The rhetorical force of Mill's argument favouring freedom is exemplified in his claim that:

> If all mankind minus one were of one opinion, and only one person were of the contrary opinion, mankind would be no more justified in silencing that one person than he, if he had the power, would be justified in silencing mankind.
>
> (Mill 1998: 16)

As for the harm principle, it seems elegant and simple. In limiting freedom, the state ought to do so only to prevent harm to others: as Mill put it, 'the only purpose for which power can be rightfully exercised over any member of a civilized community, against his will, is to prevent harm to others' (Mill 1998: 9). Needless to say philosophers and commentators have made a meal of this ever since. Perhaps most egregiously, erstwhile liberals have changed the question Mill asked, i.e. 'why is dissenting speech valuable and why should it be freed from restriction' to loaded questions like 'How free should speech be?' and 'when is it justifiable to restrict it'? (Van Eekert 2017: 118). For that reason alone, it is useful to at least restate Mill's question and recall the answers he gave.

Mill's basic argument was that any liberal community should not merely tolerate, but embrace freedom of speech to promote critical even objectionable ideas and opinions *because it is good to do so*. In Mill's case, the good is the utilitarian good of promoting both individual and collective utility, i.e. well-being. For Mill as a utilitarian, truth is a necessary component of utility as evidenced by his suggestion that 'no belief which is contrary to truth can be really useful' (Mill 1998: 27). Perhaps a better way of putting this is to say that truth is a basic human good along with many others. This proposition is perhaps difficult for some post-modernists and/or those inclined to follow Foucault to swallow, given the tendency to treat truth as an effect of power. Stanley Fish, e.g. accepts that in most places in which we work, like corporations, government and non-government organizations, schools, shops or universities, we are governed by underlying rules and our thinking and speaking is supposed to fit in with these norms: '[r]egulation of free speech is a defining feature of everyday life' (Fish 1994: 129). Truth flies out one window as various kinds of ignorance rush in. Geert van Eekert (2017: 124) is right to insist that the value of truth is at the very centre of Mill's argument, something not always fully appreciated by his critics.

For those more interested in working out when and how to constrain the pursuit of truth, some have pointed to the difficulties with specifying what is to count as harm, or whether offensiveness is the clearer line which no-one should transgress (Feinberg 1984). Some have pointed to the problems like racially or homophobically motivated 'hate speech' (Fish 1994), or pornography that represents women in degrading and hurtful ways (MacKinnon 1987, 1995). Some like David van Mill (2017) start from a neo-Hobbesian position that we should not allow any relaxation of state interventions 'on speech or any other type of freedom, because once we do we are on the slippery slope to anarchy, the state of nature, and a life that Hobbes described in *Leviathan* as "solitary, poore, nasty, brutish, and short"' (Van Mill 2017: 3). Other more astute critics like Bernard Williams (1985) make the larger point that Mill's affiliation with utilitarianism as a system entails that apart from being internally inconsistent that like every attempt to develop a systematic, coherent principle for deciding how to live, Mill's utilitarianism is wrecked when encountering the rocks of messy and conflict-ridden reality.

While J.S. Mill made the political case that free speech is vital if the majority are not allowed to drown out the minority in any deliberative political process, he made a somewhat different case when he argued that free speech is epistemically valuable. As Ten Cate puts it, the 'central point of *On Liberty* is that tyrannical majorities must be prevented from silencing dissenting individuals'. This is because dissent promotes the good of truth.

Unlike later liberals, like Berlin and Rawls, Mill thinks the problem to start with is the problem of social conformity:

> … society can and does execute its own mandates: and if it issues wrong mandates instead of right, or any mandates at all in things with which it ought not to meddle, it practises a social tyranny more formidable than many kinds of political oppression, since, though not usually upheld by such extreme penalties, it leaves fewer means of escape, penetrating much more deeply into the details of life, and enslaving the soul itself. Protection, therefore, against the

tyranny of the magistrate is not enough: there needs protection also against the tyranny of the prevailing opinion and feeling; against the tendency of society to impose, by other means than civil penalties, its own ideas and practices as rules of conduct on those who dissent from them ....

(Mill 1998: 8–9)

In rejecting the idea that freedom of speech is intrinsically good, Mill argues that the freedom to dissent is vital for two related reasons. First, great minds flourish only in an atmosphere of freedom, making free speech particularly important in this respect. (Mill plainly could not envisage the capacity of tyrannical even totalitarian regimes to provoke the arts and literature of dissent). Second, freedom is needed in order 'to enable average human beings to attain the mental stature which they are capable of' (Mill 1998: 66–7). Indeed intellectual and social progress is achieved to a large extent as a result of the ability of 'calmer and disinterested bystander[s]' to consider and judge the value and merit of opposing opinions put forward by various minds as these opinions collide in a kind of intellectual free market. As Mill saw it:

... the peculiar evil of silencing the expression of an opinion is, that it is robbing the human race; posterity as well as the existing generation; those who dissent from the opinion, still more than those who hold it. If the opinion is right, they are deprived of the opportunity of exchanging error for truth: if wrong, they lose, what is almost as great a benefit, the clearer perception and livelier impression of truth, *produced by its collision with error*

(Mill 1998: 21)

On the question of how Mill thought about 'truth' and 'error', he seems to have believed in an invariant universal idea of truth linked to an Enlightenment faith in the capacity of positive science to reveal truth progressively:

As mankind improve, the number of doctrines which are no longer disputed or doubted will be constantly on the increase: and the well-being of mankind may almost be measured by the number and gravity of the truths which have reached the point of being uncontested

(Mill 1998: 49)

At the same time, Mill also thought that our decisions about how to live are not susceptible to being universally true. Here there is a kind of liberal preference for individual autonomy:

If a person possesses any tolerable amount of common sense and experience, his own mode of laying out his existence is the best, not because it is the best in itself, but because it is his own mode

(Mill 1998: 75)

Mill also seemed to make our fallibility a standing invitation to engage in endless exercises in Popperian-style refutation. As Mill put it, 'The beliefs which we have most warrant for, have no safeguard to rest on, but a standing invitation to the whole world to prove them unfounded' (Mill 1998: 26). This is because while he is committed to a project of liberal autonomy for the person he also wants to make the case that the ultimate justification for freedom of expression is found in the benefits a society gets collectively from exposure to dissent. This, as Geert van Eekert (2017) argues, looks a lot like Immanuel Kant's argument to the public use of reason.

For Kant, this begins with the exercise of our capacity for the use of reason glossed by Kant as the capacity to think for while claiming universal assent:

> Thinking for oneself means seeking the supreme touchstone of truth in one-self (i.e. in one's own reason); and the maxim of always thinking for oneself is enlightenment [...] To make use of one's own reason means no more than to ask oneself, whenever one is supposed to assume something, whether one could find it feasible to make the ground or the rule on which one assumes it into a universal principle for the use of reason
>
> (Kant 1786/1996: 146)

However, because even reason itself can fall into error or ignorance, reason itself needs critique.

All of Kant's major philosophical works testify to the importance of critique which I gloss as the identification of all the forms that ignorance can take. Kant insists that:

> Reason must subject itself to critique in all its undertakings, and cannot restrict the freedom of critique through any prohibition without damaging itself and drawing upon itself a disadvantageous suspicion. Now there is nothing so important be – cause of its utility, nothing so holy, that it may be exempted from this searching review and inspection, *which knows no respect for persons.*
>
> (Kant 1788/1998: 766–77)

The possibility of critique highlights the vital role played by a space of freedom which, in our time, Habermas (1989) has represented as the 'public sphere'. For Kant the possibility of truth achieved by reasoning and undergirded by critique needs freedom:

> The very existence of reason depends upon this freedom, which has no dicta-torial authority, but whose claim is never anything more than the agreement of free citizens, each of whom must be able to express his reservations, indeed even his veto, without holding back
>
> (Kant 1788/1998: 766–77)

The freedom to think and speak involves the courage to seek truth while freely choosing to submit one's opinions to the critical judgement of others. For Kant, this freedom to think freely is at odds with state regulation and social control:

> The freedom to think is opposed first of all to civil compulsion. Of course it is said that the freedom to speak or to write could be taken from us by a superior power, but the freedom to think cannot be. Yet how much and how correctly would we think if we did not think as it were in community with others to whom we communicate our thoughts, and who communicate theirs with us! Thus, one can very well say that this external power which wrenches away people's freedom publicly to communicate their thoughts also takes from them the freedom to think – that single gem remaining in us in the midst of all burdens of civil life, through which alone we can devise means of overcoming all the evils of our condition
>
> (Kant 1786/1996: 144)

This as Kant says in his 'puzzling' treatment of the difference between 'public' and 'private' requires nothing but freedom:

> … indeed the least harmful of anything that could even be called freedom: namely, freedom to make public use of one's reason in all matters. [...] The public use of one's reason must always be free, and it alone can bring about enlightenment among human beings…
>
> (Kant 1784/1996: 36–7)

This Kantian argument looks a lot like Mill's market-place of ideas argument. Mill says, e.g. that if a censored opinion is true, then censorship or suppression of dissent prevents the emergence of the truth. The more interesting aspect of this argument is his relational claim that it is the collision of knowledge and error (i.e. ignorance) that is really vital and valuable. As he put it:

> However unwillingly a person who has a strong opinion may admit the possibility that his opinion may be false, he ought to be moved by the consideration that however true it may be, if it is not fully, frequently, and fearlessly discussed, it will be held as a dead dogma, not a living truth
>
> (Mill 1998: 40)

In effect, whether suppressed opinions are true, partly true or false, all opinions are useful for reminding us of the basis of our knowledge, such that our opinions do not become dead dogma.

Mill clearly has, in mind, a lively space of discussion, refutation and dissent. Absent confrontation with error or falsehood, truths are likely to be held as mere opinions without supporting reasons. Presumably widespread errors or ignorance will also benefit from their collision with truth. Presumably, Mill believes that true beliefs atrophy into mere 'prejudice', and 'are apt to give way before the slight-est semblance of an argument' (Mill 1998: 41). While Mill allows that 'truths' could be taught, without allowing for the expression of dissenting falsehoods, this approach is not sufficient, especially 'when we turn... to morals, religion, politics, social relations, and the business of life'. Here 'three-fourths of the arguments for every disputed opinion consist in dispelling the appearances which favour some opinion different from it'. As Mill put his point pithily, 'He who knows only his own side of the case knows little of it' (Mill 1998: 42). This also presupposes a willingness to rigorous independent and critical thought:

> No one can be a great thinker who does not recognize, that as a thinker it is his first duty to follow his intellect to whatever conclusions it may lead. Truth gains more even by the errors of one who, with due study and preparation, thinks for himself, than by the true opinions of those who only hold them because they do not suffer themselves to think.
>
> (Mill 1998: 39)

Presumably, this entails a virtue like courage. Discussing the prohibition of her-esy, Mill asks, e.g.:

> Who can compute what the world loses in the multitude of promising intel-lects combined with timid characters, who dare not follow out any bold, vig-orous, independent train of thought, lest it should land them in something which would admit of being considered irreligious or immoral?
>
> (Mill 1998: 39)

In summary, Robert Solum (2000: 878) draws the right conclusion:

> Why should we value dissent that turns out to be erroneous? Because only in the day-to-day confrontation with error does truth become a living convic-tion with a firm grip on belief and a capacity to motivate action. Mill's two arguments form a complete case for the protection of dissent. When dissent is true or partially true, its suppression prevents the emergence of the truth. When dissent is false, even completely false, its suppression clouds the mean-ing of the truth and drains truth of its force. In either case, we have good reason to value dissent.

Conclusion

In any modern community characterized by what Isaiah Berlin and John Rawls called the 'fact of pluralism', we need to acknowledge that there is a non-remediable 'plurality of conflicting, and indeed incommensurable, conceptions of the mean-ing, value and purpose of human life' (Rawls 1984: 4). This pluralism should be celebrated not covered up by delusions about a single moral or epistemic order, just as the idea of truth is not trashed by treating truth as an effect of power. Against the many mealy mouthed liberals who start by giving up on truth and then start looking for ways to justify limiting dissent – and enchaining truth, we need to make deliberative dissent our default position.[7]

Dissent is valuable epistemically because it involves addressing some of the forms that ignorance takes whether this be as lies, deception, error, denial or presumed knowledge

Notes

1 In 2008, shortly after the world economy collapsed, Queen Elizabeth II asked what has become known as the 'Queen's question': 'Why did no one see it coming?' asked Queen Elizabeth II. Robert Skidelsky (2016:23) answers that the failure to see the abundant evidence of trouble looming before the 2008 Great Recession was a result of 'tightly held economic ideas, models and policies. The policy models used pre-2008 were wrong or seriously flawed'.

2 To be clear, I do not share the religious grounds on which Finnis chooses to stand. As Finnis (2012:31) himself notes '…practical reason's first principles can be understood and acknowledged, and their normative implications extensively unfolded into rich, substantive moral, political and legal theory without relying upon, presupposing or even adverting, to the existence of God or providential order'.

3 It is not limited, e.g. when it is accepted that not all kinds of knowledge are equally valuable, or that not all kinds of knowledge are equally valuable for each person. Equally, it is not the only good worth pursuing nor is it to be understood simply as a moral good.

4 It matters that we understand 'knowledge' as knowing, i.e. as an activity like enquiry. Too often we imagine that knowledge is simply reading or memorizing what is already known and can be 'found' in a book or report. While this shortcut is useful, this is also a sure route to the kind of ignorance called 'presumed knowledge'. Genuine enquiry is a praxis because what we may discover is highly likely at the start of our enquiry to be unknown.

5 Finnis distinguishes between different types of self-refuting (or 'self-negating') propositions, including logical self-refutation ('There is no such thing as truth') and operational self-refutation (e.g. saying 'I am not opening this door' even as I do so).

6 What is presented here is a substantially amended account first reprised in Watts (2016).

7 Robert Solum (2000: 879) notes that Rawls accepts that hat disagreement about the nature of the good or ultimate value is reasonable given the difficulties of arriving at a consensus about these questions. These difficulties include complex and conflicting evidence, disagreement about what is relevant and about how to weigh relevant considerations, the under-determinacy introduced by hard cases and the fact that different kinds of normative arguments may exist on both sides of a moral question.

Conclusion

Ours is a time marked by multiple signs of disruption and disaster from global warming, mounting inequality, all kinds of civil violence and war in too many places, to fundamental socio-technological transformation changing the very conditions and ways we have talked about human being. Liberal-democracies are not immune to these afflictions. The election of Donald Trump as America's forty-fifth President, the almighty mess that the Brexit campaign has unleashed in Britain, the mobilization of anti-immigrant sentiment by neo-Nazi and alt-right groups, the recrudescence of anti-science prejudice when people think about global warming are all best treated as symptoms of deep social, moral, economic, political and intellectual malaise in the great liberal-democratic heartlands.

In such a time, we need to recall the central argument made by John Maynard Keynes, one of the greatest liberals of the first half of the twentieth century. Writing in the 1930s, a decade full of omens of looming disaster including mass unemployment, poverty, war and the rise of ultra-nationalist, authoritarian states propelled by racist xenophobi, Keynes wrote, 'Civilization is a thin and precarious crust erected by the personality and will of a very few, and only maintained by rules and conventions skillfully put across, and guilefully preserved' (Keynes 1971–89 X: 446–7). Geoff Mann makes the perspicacious observation that, in this insight, we see the 'dialectic of hope and fear at the heart of Keynesianism' (Mann 2017: 14). Keynes understood all too well the tragic dimension of liberal capitalism 'an order fated to cultivate and celebrate the very freedoms' that 'inevitably and endogenously produce scarcity and poverty... capitalist modernity's internal dynamics erode the very fabric upon which it relies' (Mann 2017: 11).

There is nothing in Keynes' observation about the strengths of democracy, the wisdom of the people or popular sovereignty. What we have is Keynes reflecting on the kind of role played by small numbers of people just like him in preserving civilization. This role saw him mostly working to disagree with the dominant and all too complacent forms of ignorance then operating as received wisdom in economics and public policymaking. Keynes was one of the greatest dissenters, a role he played both skilfully and guilefully.

If nothing else, in our own season of discontent we will need more, not less, dissent of that kind.

I say this mindful of the fugitive existence this kind of dissent leads in too many modern academic disciplines and universities. In its own small way, this book has made the case for by-passing the ways so much conventional social science addresses politics, dissent and its criminalization.

The book has stressed that dissent encompasses a far more diverse range of activities than protest or social movements. Dissent is as various as all the possible ways people have of making sense of their world. Indeed, it is the recognition that we live in a world of difference that sparked this enquiry.

The essential problem which I have addressed is how to make sense of a situation which we find in any modern society namely an irreducible plurality of ideas and beliefs and values. In that sense, the persistence of disagreement or dissent is and ought to be utterly unsurprising. Equally what ought to be truly surprising and provoking of much more comment are the persistent attempts by liberal-democratic states to criminalize and suppress dissent. We should certainly not be taken in by claims made on behalf of liberal democracy that 'it' values dissent. Modern liberal-democratic societies don't.

I was also not interested in generating 'empirical' explanatory or predictive accounts of dissent or its suppression. I don't think that treating people and what we do as if we are billiard balls being ricocheted around a green baize table is all that illuminating. Drawing on the rich resources offered by Hannah Arendt and Pierre Bourdieu, I have offered a relational account of dissent and its criminalization.

The diversity or pluralism that Isaiah Berlin celebrated as do agonist theorists of the political like Chantal Mouffe albeit in difference ought to be something we all enjoy and add to. Yet somehow many people and institutions with resources to protect and the power to do so promote various imaginaries about the value of symbolic orders that deliver social and political order. The effect is to dissipate pluralism and to rely on several kinds of ignorance to promote fear and a preoccupation with security seem to impel many of the exercises that states engage in when they set out to suppress dissent in all of its many forms.

That said, suppressing and criminalizing dissent points to fundamental problems that cut into the heart of liberal democracy's claim to legitimacy. On the other hand, there is an irremediable contradiction between the sovereignty (or power) of the liberal-democratic state and its claim to legitimacy. The legal traditions of liberalism ground this claim in the idea of the rule of law though there is plenty of contestation between the legal positivists and those claiming some kind of ethical grounding. The claims for the political legitimacy of democracy are grounded in ideas of 'popular sovereignty' and some model of 'parliamentary' majoritarianism, which quickly rub up against the liberal insistence on the rule of law.

In either case, the essential bother is that modern liberal-democratic states excessively privilege order and security while criminalizing the vital practice of dissent.

This needs to be understood relationally. The one political theorist who has caught the essential relation, a relation of contradiction at work here, is Carl Schmitt. Schmitt understood better than anyone else the contradictions that have never gone away as various societies struggled historically and contingently to bring into being what we today call a modern nation-state. Carlo Galli (2015) reads Schmitt as tracing out through much of the twentieth century 'an originary crisis or better still an originary contradiction... the exhibition of two sides, two extremes' (Cited in Sitze 2015: xxiii). As Schmitt's work especially his *Political Theology* and the *Concept of the Political* suggests, the political is a kind of 'free floating energy' that simultaneously seeks to constitute order while undermining that order. This is the same ongoing tension that both Arendt (1958) and Ricoeur (1956) saw as the 'paradox of politics', namely the tension between 'novelty' and 'order' that was at work in the original Greek conception of *arche*.

As Adam Sitze puts it:

> Schmitt realised that modern political thought (and consequently too the liberal democratic institutions and practices whose modes of self-justifications it grounds and sustains) is divided against itself in a non-dialectical manner. Yet at the same time that it emerges from and even implicitly feeds on a crisis it is incapable of resolving, modern political though also accounts for this incapacity by suppressing the symptoms of this crisis.
>
> (Sitze 2015: xxiii)

One of the forms this suppression takes is the criminalization of dissent. This is one of the ways the resources of legitimation supplied in narratives of security and order can be put to work. It doesn't matter that these narratives of order and security are frequently delusional, incoherent and self-negating. For rather than acknowledge this, as Sitze notes, the liberal-democratic state will simply resort to more 'moralistic reaffirmations of the unquestionable necessity of its own explicit goals' (Sitze 2015: xxiii).

This explains something of the appeal Schmitt has had for agonistic theorists of democracy like Chantal Mouffe (2000, 2005) eager to reinvigorate democratic politics. Disagreement is central to the agonistic vocabulary because it exemplifies the *agon* or contest necessary to 'undo' the given and the hegemonic. On another level, it is exemplary because it attests to the pluralism constitutive of democratic life. Neither dispensable then, nor a problem to be solved, disagreement is constitutive of the political. Framed by pluralist interpretations of a democratic socio-political imaginary, disagreement challenges hegemonic ways of being and, according to agonistic theorists, ensures that democratic politics remains dynamic and perpetually alert. It points to the idea that a vibrant democracy might want to cultivate a permanent acceptance of contestation.

I have argued that dissent when it is pursuing truth is a valuable prophylaxis against many kinds of ignorance. However, this needs to be understood carefully. If the appeal to order is illusory, so too and no less is the idea of a polity forever bogged down in disagreement equally a fantasy. It might be enough simply to learn again to value disagreement and understand better the enormous value it has in dispelling ignorance.

Dissent is in effect the expression of the normal plurality of possibilities and evaluative frameworks in any political community and it ought to be especially valued in any liberal democracy.

References

Abbott, A., 1988, 'Transcending General Linear Reality'. *Sociological Theory*, 6: 169–186.

Abbott, A., 1995, 'Sequence Analysis: New Methods for Old Ideas'. *Annual Review of Sociology*, 21: 93–113.

ABS, 2015, *Prisoners in Australia, 2015*, ABS Cat No. 4517.0. Canberra: ABS.

ABS, 2016, *Corrective Services, Australia, March Quarter 2016*, ABS Cat No. 4512.0. Canberra: ABS.

ABS, 2018, *Prisoners in Australia, 2015*, ABS Cat No. 4517.0. Canberra: ABS.

Adbusters, 2011, 'Occupy Wall Street', 13 July, www.webcitation.org/63DZ1nIDl

Adell, R., 2011, 'La movilización de los indignados del 15-M. Aportaciones desde la sociología de la protesta'. *Sociedad y Utopía*, 38: 125–140.

Agamben, G., 1998, *Homo Sacer: Sovereign Power and Bare Life* (trans. Heller-Roazen, D.), Stanford, CA: Stanford University Press.

Agamben, G., 2005, *State of Exception* (trans. Attell, K.), Chicago and London: University of Chicago Press.

Aggarwal, B., 2012, 'The Bolt Case: Silencing Speech or Promoting Tolerance?', in Sykes, H., (ed.), *More or Less: Democracy and New Media*, Albert Park: Future Leaders.

Ake, C., 1969, 'Political Obligation and Political Dissent'. *Canadian Journal of Political Science*, 2 (2): 245–255.

Alexander, J. 1994, *Fin de Siècle Social Theory*, London: Verso.

Alexander, L., 2005, *Is there a Right to Freedom of Expression?* New York: Cambridge University Press.

Alexander, L., 2017, 'Sydney Squatters Turn a Hoarded House Into a Home', *ABC News*, 17 July, www.abc.net.au/news/2017-07-25/sydney-squatters-turn-a-hoarded-house-into-a-home/8728892

Alexander, M., 2010, *The New Jim Crow: Mass Incarceration in the Age of Colorblindness*, New York: The New Press.

Alford, F., 2001, *Whistleblowers: Broken Lives and Organizational Power*, Ithaca, NY: Cornell University Press.

Allan, G., and Dempsey, N., 2016, *Prison Population Statistics Briefing Paper*, House of Commons Library. Number SN/SG/04334, 4 July, www.parliament.uk/commons-library|intranet.parliament.uk/commons-library|papers@parliament.uk|

Amnesty International, 1992, *South Africa: State of Fear. Security Force Complicity in Torture and Political Killings, 1991–1992*, London: Amnesty International.

Amnesty International, 2003, December 11, *United Kingdom: Justice Perverted under the Anti-terrorism, Crime and Security Act 2001*, Electronic version http://web.amnesty.org/library/Index/ENGEUR450292003

Amster, R., 2006, 'Perspectives on Ecoterrorism: Catalysts, Conflations, and Casualties'. *Contemporary Justice Review*, 9 (3): 287–301.

Anastasakis, O., 2009, 'The New Politics of the New Century', in Economides, S., and Monastiriotis, V., (eds.), *The Return of Street Politics? Essays on the December Riots in Greece*, London: The Hellenic Observatory/LSE: 5.

Andersen, N., 2003, *Discursive Analytical Strategies: Understanding Foucault, Koselleck, Laclau, Luhmann*. Bristol: Policy Press.

Anderson, P., 2006, *The Origins of Postmodernity*, London: Verso.

Andrew, C., 2010, *The Defence of the Realm: The Authorized History of MI5*, New York: Vintage.

Annian-Welsh, R., and Williams, G., 2014, 'The New Terrorists: The Normalisation and Spread of Anti-Terror Laws in Australia'. *Melbourne University Law Review*, 38: 362–408.

Aoude, I., 2002, 'Arab Americans and the Criminalization of Dissent'. *Social Analysis: The International Journal of Social and Cultural Practice*, 46 (1): 125–128.

Appiah, K., 2018, *The Lies that Bind: Rethinking Identity*, New York: Profile Books.

Arendt, H., 1951, *The Origins of Totalitarianism*, New York: Schocken.

Arendt, H., 1958, *The Human Condition*, Chicago: University of Chicago Press.

Arendt, H., 1965, *On Revolution*, London: Penguin.

Arendt, H., 1968, 'What Is Freedom?' in her *Between Past and Future*, New York: Viking Press.

Arendt, H., 1971, 'Thinking and Moral Considerations'. *Social Research*, 38 (3): 428–445.

Arendt, H., 1972a, 'Civil Disobedience' in her *Crises of the Republic*, New York: Harcourt, Brace and Jovanovich.

Arendt, H., 1972b, *Crises of the Republic*, New York: Harcourt, Brace and Jovanovich.

Arendt, H., 1978, *The Life of the Mind*, New York: HBJ.

Arendt, H., 2003, 'Some Questions of Moral Philosophy', in Kohn, J., (ed.) *Responsibility and Judgment*, New York: Schocken Books.

Aristotle, 2017, *Politics: A New Translation* (trans. Reeve, D.), Indianapolis: Hackett.

Arnhart, L., 2013, 'George Anastaplo 1925–2014'. *Claremont Review*, www.claremont.org/crb/article/george-anastaplo-19252014/

Asch, S., 2004, *Relational Ontology: An Exploration through the Work of M. Foucault*, Unpublished M. Arts Thesis, Vancouver: University of Victoria.

Ashton, N., 2008, *King Hussein of Jordan: A Political Life*, New Haven, CT: Yale University Press.

Ashworth, A., 2009, *Principles of Criminal Law*, Oxford: Oxford University Press.

Ashworth, A., and Zedner L., 2008, 'Defending the Criminal Law: Reflections on the Changing Character of Crime, Procedure and Sanctions'. *Criminal Law and Philosophy*, 2: 21–51.

Ashworth, A., and Zedner, L., 2014, *Preventive Justice*, Oxford: Oxford University Press.

Ashworth, A., Zedner, L., and Tomlin, P., 2013, (eds.), *Prevention and the Limits of the Criminal Law*, Oxford: Oxford University Press.

Atkinson, A., 1987, 'On the Measurement of Poverty'. *Econometrica*, 55: 749–764.

Atkinson, A., 2015, *Inequality: What Can Be Done?* Cambridge: Harvard University Press.

Austin, J., 1995, *The Province of Jurisprudence Determined* (ed. Trumble, W.,), Cambridge: Cambridge University Press.

Austin, J. L., 1959, *How to Do Things with Words*, Cambridge, MA: Harvard University Press.

Bachelard, G., 1984, *The New Scientific Spirit*, Boston, MA: Beacon Press.

Bachelard, M., 2017, 'Free Speech the Loser in Australia's Defamation Bonanza', *Sydney Morning Herald*, 11 May, www.smh.com.au/national/free-speech-the-loser-in-australias-defamation-bonanza-20170511-gw2cnc.html

Bagguley, P., and Mann, K., 1992, 'Idle Thieving Bastards? Scholarly Representations of the "Underclass"'. *Work Employment and Society*, 6 (1): 113–126.

Bailey, R., 1973, *The Squatters*, London: Penguin.

Baines, P., and Rogers, P., 2007, *Edmund Curll: Bookseller*, Oxford: Oxford University Press.

Baker, J., 2008, 'Revisiting the Explosive Growth of Federal Crimes'. *Heritage Foundation*, https://www.heritage.org/report/revisiting-the-explosive-growth-federal-crimes

Bakhtin, M., 1993, *Toward a Philosophy of the Act* (trans. Liapunov, V. and Holquist, M.) Austin: University of Texas Press.

Banks, R., 2004, 'Racial Profiling and Antiterrorism Efforts'. *Cornell Law Review*, 89: 1201, http://scholarship.law.cornell.edu/clr/vol89/iss5/3

Banks, R., and Rudovsky, D., 2011, 'Racial Profiling and the War on Terror', *Penumbra, University of Pennsylvania Law Review*, 155: 173.

Barber, B., 1984, *Strong Democracy: Participatory Politics for a New Age*, Berkeley: University of California Press.

Barger, R., 2000, 'A Summary of Lawrence Kohlberg's Stages of Moral Development', University of Notre Dame, Notre Dame, www5.csudh.edu/dearhabermas/kohlberg01bk.htm

Bar-Joseph, U., 1995a, 'Israel's Intelligence Failure of 1973: New Evidence, New Interpretation and Theoretical Implications'. *Security Studies*, 4 (3): 584–609.

Bar-Joseph, U., 1995b, *Intelligence Intervention in the Politics of Democratic States: The United States, Israel, and Britain*, University Park: Pennsylvania State University Press: 9–35.

Bar-Joseph, U., 2005, *The Watchman Fell Asleep: The Surprise of Yom Kippur and its Sources*, Albany: State University of New York Press.

Barkan, S., 1984, 'Legal Control of the Southern Civil Rights Movement'. *American Sociological Review*, 49 (4): 552–565.

Barradori, G., 2004, *Philosophy in a Time of Terror: Dialogues with Jurgen Habermas and Jacques Derrida*, Chicago: Chicago University Press.

Bartee, W., and Bartee, A., 1992, *Litigating Morality: American Legal Thought and its English Roots*. New York: Praeger.

Bartelson, J., 1993, *A Genealogy of Sovereignty*, Cambridge: Cambridge University Press.

Bartelson, J., 2001, *Critique of the State*, Cambridge: Cambridge University Press.

Bartelson, J., 2014, *Sovereignty as Symbolic Form*, Abingdon: Routledge.

Bassiouni, M., 1971, *The Law of Dissent and Riots*, Springfield, IL: Charles C. Thomas.

Bedau, H., 1961, 'On Civil Disobedience'. *Journal of Philosophy*, 58: 653–665.

Begin, M., 1977, *The Revolt: The Story of the Irgun* (rev ed.), Tel Aviv: Steimatsky Agency.

Beiner, R., 1997, *Philosophy in a Time of Lost Spirit*, Toronto: University of Toronto.

Beiner, R., 1998, 'Forward', in Dyzenhaus, D., (ed.), *Law as Politics: Carl Schmitt's critique of liberalism*, Durham, NC: Duke University Press: vii–ix.

Beiner, R., 2014, *Political Philosophy: What it is and Why it Matters*, Cambridge: Cambridge University Press.

Benhabib, S., 1988, 'Judgment and the Moral Foundations of Politics in Arendt's Thought'. *Political Theory*, 16: 29–51.

Benhabib, S., 1996, *Democracy and Difference*, Princeton, NJ: Princeton University Press.

Benjamin, A., 2015, *Towards a Relational Ontology: Philosophy's Other Possibility* (SUNY series in Contemporary Continental Philosophy), Albany: State University of New York Press.

Benjamin, W., 1978, 'Critique of Violence', in *Reflections* (trans. Jephcott, E.), New York: Schocken Books.

Bentham, J., 1843, 'Principles of the Civil Code', in *The Works of Jeremy Bentham* (Vol I) (ed., Bowring, J.,), Edinburgh: William Tait.

Bentham, J., 1931, *Theory of Legislation*, New York: Harcourt and Brace.

Bentham, J., 1948, *A Fragment on Government with an Introduction to Morals and Legislation*, Oxford: Blackwell.

Bentham, J., 1954, *Economic Writings of Bentham* (ed. Stark, W.,) (3 Vols), London: Allen & Unwin.

Bentham, J., 1970, *Of Laws in General* (ed. Hart, H.,), London: The Athlone Press.

Berger, J., 1972, *Ways of Seeing*, London: Penguin.

Berlin, I., 1954, *Historical Inevitability*, Oxford: Oxford University Press.

Berlin, I., 1969, 'Two Concepts of Liberty', in his *Four Essays on Liberty*, Oxford: Oxford University Press: 118–172.

Berlin I., 1978, *Concepts and Categories: Philosophical Essays* (ed. Hardy, H.,), London: Hogarth Press.

Berlin, I., 1991, *The Crooked Timber of Humanity: Chapters in the History of Ideas* (ed. Hardy, H.,), New York: Knopf.

Berlin, I., 2002, *Liberty* (ed. Hardy, H.,), Oxford: Oxford University Press.

Bernstein, D., 2012, 'How FBI Monitored Occupy Movement', *Consortium News*, 31 December, https://consortiumnews.com/2012/12/31/how-fbi-monitored-occupy-movement/?print=print

Bertram, C., 2004, *Rousseau and the Social Contract*, London: Routledge.

Best, W., 1940, *Der Deutsche Polizei*, Darmstadt: L.C. Wittich Verlag.

Betts, R., 1982, *Surprise Attack: Lessons for Defense Planning*, Washington, DC: Brookings Institution.

Biggs, M., 2015, 'Size Matters: The Problems with Counting Protest Events', *Sociology Working Papers Paper Number 2015-05*, Oxford: Department of Sociology University of Oxford, doi:10.1.1.702.3860&rep=rep1&type=pdf

Bisley, N., 2018, 'Australia's Rules-Based International Order', *Australian Outlook*, July, Australian Institute for International Affairs. www.internationalaffairs.org.au/australianoutlook/australias-rules-based-international-order/

Bix, B., 2004, 'Legal Positivism', in Golding, M., and Edmundson, W., (eds.), *The Blackwell Guide to the Philosophy of Law and Legal Theory*, Oxford: Blackwell: 29–49.

Black, H., 1961, '366 US 82 In Re George Anastaplo', *Open Jurist*, https://openjurist.org/366/us/82/in-re-george-anastaplo

Bleiker, R., 2000, *Popular Dissent, Human Agency and Global Politics*, Cambridge: Cambridge University Press.

Bleiker, R. 2005, 'Seattle and the Struggle for a Global Democratic Ethos', in Eschle, C., and Maiguashca, B., (eds.), *Critical Theories, International Relations, and 'The Anti-Globalisation Movement': The Politics of Global Resistance*, London: Routledge: 195–211.

Bleiker, R., 2012, *Aesthetics and World Politics*, London: Palgrave-Macmillan.

Bleiker, R., 2013, 'The Visual Dehumanization of Refugees', (with D. Campbell, E. Hutchison and X. Nicholson), *Australian Journal of Political Science*, 48 (3): 398–416.

Blom-Cooper, L., 1997, *The Birmingham Six and Other Cases*, London: Duckworth.

Blum, L., 1980, *Friendship, Altruism and Morality*, London: Routledge and Kegan Paul.

Boehmer, E., 2005, 'Postcolonial Terrorist the Example of Nelson Mandela'. *Parallax*, 11 (4): 46–55.

Bohmann, J., 1996, *Public Deliberation: Pluralism, Complexity and Democracy*, Cambridge, MA: MIT Press.

Bolton, R., 2005, 'Habermas's Theory of Communicative Action and the Theory of Social Capital'. Association of American Geographers, Denver, Colorado, April, https://pdfs. semanticscholar.org/4d37/90471aaf0ea2280aa701651ec97ba920934d.pdf

Bonnefon, P., 1898, *Montaigne et ses Amis*, Paris: Armand Colin et Cie, (I): 103–224.

Botha, C., 2001, *Heidegger: Technology, Truth and Language*, Unpublished MA Dissertation, Pretoria: University of Pretoria, https://repository.up.ac.za/bitstream/handle/2263/30416/02

Bourdieu, P., 1977, *Outline of a Theory of Practice*, Cambridge: Cambridge University Press

Bourdieu, P., 1986, 'The Forms of Capital', in Richardson, J., (ed.), *Handbook of Theory and Research for the Sociology of Education*, New York: Greenwood: 241–258.

Bourdieu, P., 1990, *The Logic of Practice*, Stanford, CA: Stanford University Press.

Bourdieu, P., 1991, *The Political Ontology of Martin Heidegger* (trans. Collier, P.), Stanford, CA: Stanford University Press.

Bourdieu, P., 1993, *The Field of Cultural Production: Essays on Art and Literature*, Cambridge: Polity Press.

Bourdieu, P., 1994, In Conversation with T. Eagleton, 'Doxa and the Common Life: An Interview', in Žižek, S., (ed.), *Mapping Ideology*, London and New York: Verso: 265–277, 269.

Bourdieu, P., 1996, *The Rules of Art: Genesis and Structure of the Literary Field* (trans. Emmanuel, S.), Stanford, CA: Stanford University Press.

Bourdieu, P., 2000, *Pascalian Meditations*, Stanford, CA: Stanford University Press.

Bourdieu, P., (with Swain, H.,) 2000b, 'Move Over, Shrinks', *Times Higher Educational Supplement*, 14 April: 19.

Bourdieu, P., 2014, *On the State: Lectures at the College de France, 1989–1992* (Champagne, P., Lenoir, R., Franck Poupeau, F., and Riviere, M-C., trans. Fernbach, D.), Cambridge: Polity.

Bourdieu, P., 2017, *Manet: A Symbolic Revolution: Lectures at the Collège de France, 1999–2000* (trans. Collier, P., and Rigaud-Drayton, M.), Cambridge: Polity.

Bourdieu, P., and Wacquant, L., 1992, *An Invitation to Reflexive Sociology*, Cambridge: Polity Press.

Boyer, C., 2014, *Examining the Extent and Impact of Surveillance on Animal Rights Activists*, Unpublished M. Arts Thesis, Las Vegas: University of Nevada.

Boykoff, J., 2007, *Beyond Bullets: The Suppression of Dissent in the United States*, Oakland, CA: AK Press.

Brabazon, H. 2006, *Protecting Whose Security? Anti-Terrorism Legislation and the Criminalization of Dissent*, YCIS Working Paper 43, Toronto: York University.

Breen, K., 2016, 'Agonism, Antagonism and the Necessity of Care', in Schaap, A., (ed.), *Law and Agonistic Politics*, Abingdon: Routledge.

Brennan, J., 2016, 'When May We Kill Government Agents? In Defense of Moral Parity'. *Social Philosophy and Policy*, 32 (2): 40–61.

Brennan, J., 2019, *When All Else Fails: The Ethics of Resistance to State Injustice*, Princeton, NJ: Princeton University Press.

Bridgeman, P., 1927, *The Logic of Modern Physics*, New York: Macmillan.

Bromberg, Y., and Chevraud E., 2017, 'Anti-Trump Protesters Risk 60 Years in Jail. Is Dissent a Crime?', *The Guardian*, 17 November, www.theguardian.com/commentisfree/2017/nov/22/donald-trump-administration-punishing-dissent-protesters

Brown, D., 2013, 'Criminalisation and Normative Theory'. *Current Issues in Criminal Justice*, 25 (2): 605–625.

Brown, D., 2014, 'Criminal Law Reform and the Persistence of Strict Liability'. *Duke Law Journal*, 62: 285–339, http://scholarship.law.duke.edu/cgi/viewcontent.cgi?article=3358&context=dlj

Brown, D. M., 2013, 'Young People, Anti-Social Behaviour and Public Space: The Role of Community Wardens in Policing the 'ASBO Generation'. *Urban Studies*, 50 (3): 538–555.

Brown, E., 2011, *Criminal Justice and Neo Liberalism*, London: Palgrave Macmillan.

Brown, S., 1998, *Understanding Youth and Crime*, Buckingham: Open University Press.

Brown, W., 1995, *States of Injury: Power and Freedom in Late Modernity*, Princeton, NJ: Princeton University Press.

Brown, W., 2010, *Walled States, Waning Sovereignty*, Cambridge, MA: Zone Books.

Brown, W., 2017, 'Neoliberalism's Frankenstein: Authoritarian Freedom in Twenty-First Century "Democracies"'. *Critical Times*, 1 (1): 60–79.

Brown, B., and Jolivette, G., 2005, *Three Strikes: The Impact after More Than Decade*, Sacramento: California Legislative Analysts Office. https://lao.ca.gov/2005/3_strikes/3_strikes_102005.htm

Brown, A., Lewis, D., Moberly, R., and Vandekerckhove, W., (eds.), 2014, *International Handbook of Whistleblowing Research*, Cheltenham: Edward Elgar Publishing.

Brown, D., Farrier, D, Egger, S, McNamara, L., Steel, A. Grewcock, M., and Spears, D., 2011, *Criminal Laws: Materials and Commentary on Criminal Law*, Sydney: Federation Press.

Brownlee, K., 2007/2013, 'Civil Disobedience', in Zalta, E., (ed.), *The Stanford Encyclopedia of Philosophy*, https://plato.stanford.edu/archives/fall2017/entries/civil-disobedience

Brownlee, K., 2012, *Conscience and Conviction: The Case for Civil Disobedience*, Oxford: Oxford University Press.

Bruegel, S. von, 2014, *A Grammar of Atong*, Leiden: Brill, http://booksandjournals.brillonline.com/content/books/b9789004258938_009

Buchanan, J., 2003, *Public Choice: The Origins and Development of a Research Program*, Center for Study of Public Choice, Fairfax: George Mason University.

Buckle, S., 2013, 'The Blind Spot in Feminist Political Theory'. *Quadrant*, 57 (6): 68–71.

Buckler, K., 2008, 'The Quantitative/Qualitative Divide Revisited: A Study of Published Research, Doctoral Program Curricula and Journal Editor Perceptions'. *Journal of Criminal Justice Education*, 19: 383–403.

Bull, P., and Wells, P., 2012, 'Adversarial Discourse in Prime Minister's Questions'. *Journal of Language and Social Psychology*, 31 (1): 30–48.

Bureau of Prisons, 2018, 'Annual Determination of Average Cost of Incarceration', Federal Register, 83, 30 April, www.govinfo.gov/content/pkg/FR-2018-04-30/pdf/2018-09062.pdf

Burek, P., 2004, 'Adoption of the Classical Theory of Definition to Ontology Modeling', in Bussler, C., and Fensel, D., (eds.), *Artificial Intelligence: Methodology, Systems, and Applications*, AIMSA Lecture Notes in Computer Science, 3192, Berlin: Springer.

Burkhalter, S., Gersil, J., and Kelshaw, T., 2002, 'A Conceptual Definition and Theoretical Model of Public Deliberation in Small Face-to-Face Groups'. *Communication Theory*, 12 (4): 398–422.

Burnet, D., 2017, 'Why Religious Belief isn't a Delusion – in psychological Terms, at Least', *The Guardian*, 21 September. www.theguardian.com/science/brain-flapping/2017/sep/21/why-religious-belief-isnt-a-delusion-in-psychological-terms-at-least

Burrawoy, M., 2012, *Marxism Meets Bourdieu* in *Conversations with Bourdieu: The Johannesburg Moment*, Johannesburg: University of Witwatersrand Press.

Burrawoy, M., 2017, 'On Desmond: The Limits of Spontaneous Sociology'. *Theory and Society*, 46 (4): 261–284.

Burton J., 1984, *National Times*, 28 Sept – 4 October: 11.

Butler, J., 2004, *Precarious Life: The Powers of Mourning and Violence*. London: Verso.

Cain, F., 2004, 'Australian Intelligence Organisations and the Law: A Brief History'. *University of New South Wales Law Journal*, 2327 (2): 296.

Cameron, B., 2017, 'Antifa: Left-Wing Militants on the Rise', *BBC News*, 14 August, www.bbc.com/news/world-us-canada-40930831

Campbell, D., 1998, 'Why Fight: Humanitarianism, Principles and Post-Structuralism'. *Millennium*, 27 (3): 497–521.

Cane, L., 2015, 'Hannah Arendt on the Principles of Political Action'. *European Journal of Political Theory*, 14 (1): 55–75.

Carle, G., 2011, *The Interrogator: An Education*, New York: Nation Books.

Carlen, P., 1992, 'Crime, Feminism, Realism'. *Social Justice*, 7 (4): 106–123.

Carlen, P., 2008, 'Imaginary Penalities and Risk-Crazed Governance', in Carlen, P., (ed.), *Imagined Penalities*, Cullompton: Willan: 1–25.

Carlen, P., 2010, *Criminological Imagination*. Farnham: Ashgate.

Carley, M., 1997, 'Defining Forms of Successful State Repression: A Case Study of Cointelpro and the American Indian Movement'. *Research in Social Movements, Conflict, and Change*, 20: 151–176.

Carmi, G., 2008, 'Dignity Versus Liberty: The Two Western Cultures of Free Speech'. *Boston University International Law Journal*, 26: 277–371.

Carrington, D., 2018, 'Our Leaders Are Like Children, School Strike Founder Tells Climate Summit', *The Guardian*, 4 December, www.theguardian.com/environment/2018/dec/04/leaders-like-children-school-strike-founder-greta-thunberg-tells-un-climate-summit

Carson, J. V., LaFree, G., and Dugan, L., 2012, 'Terrorist and Non-Terrorist Criminal Attacks by Radical Environmental and Animal Rights Groups in the United States, 1970–2007'. *Terrorism and Political Violence*, 24 (2): 295–319.

Carvalho, H., 2017, *The Preventive Turn in Criminal Law*, Oxford: Oxford University Press.

Carvalho, H., and Norrie, A., 2017, '"In this Interregnum": Dialectical Themes in the Critique of Criminal Justice'. *Social & Legal Studies*, 26 (6): 716–734.

Castells, M., 2012, *Networks of Outrage and Hope: Social Movements in the Internet Age*, Malden, MA: Polity Press.

Castoriadis, C., 1993, *Philosophy, Politics, Autonomy: Essays in Political Philosophy* (trans. Ames, D.), Oxford: Oxford University Press.

Castoriadis, C., 1997, *World in Fragments: Writings on Politics, Society, Psychoanalysis, and the Imagination* (ed./trans. Curtis, D.), Stanford, CA: Stanford University Press.

Cavadino, M., and Dignan J., 2006, 'Penal Policy and Political Economy'. *Criminology & Criminal Justice*, 6 (4): 435–456.

Cavadino, M., and Dignan, J., 2007, *The Penal System: A Comparative Approach*, (4th ed.), London: Sage.

Cerny, P., 2010, *Rethinking World Politics: A Theory of Transnational Neopluralism*, Oxford: Oxford University Press.

Cesare, di D., 2018, *Heidegger and the Jews: The Black Notebooks*, (trans. Baca, M.,), Cambridge: Polity.

Chamayou, G., 2015, *A Theory of the Drone* (trans. Lloyd, J.), New York: The New Press.

Chambers, S., and Costain, A., (eds.), 2000, *Deliberation, Democracy and the Media*, Lanham, MD: Rowman & Littlefield.

Chambliss, W., 1964, 'A Sociological Analysis of the Law of Vagrancy'. *Social Problems*, 12: 67–77.

Chang, R., 2015, 'Value Pluralism', in Wright, J., (ed.), International Encyclopedia of the Social and Behavioral Sciences (Vol. 25), (2nd ed.), Amsterdam: Elsevier: 21–26.

Channing, I., 2015, *The Police and the Expansion of Public Order law 1829–2014*, Abingdon: Routledge.

Charters, D., 1989, *The British Army and Jewish Insurgency in Palestine, 1945–47*, London: Palgrave Macmillan.

Chenoweth, E., and Pressman, J., 2018, 'One Year after the Women's March on Washington, People Are Still Protesting En Masse. A Lot. We've Counted', *Washington Post*, 21 January, www.washingtonpost.com/news/monkey-cage/wp/2018/01/21/one-year-after-the-womens-march-on-washington-people-are-still-protesting-en-masse-a-lot-weve-counted/?noredirect=on&utm_term=.57c001de8be6

Chernilo, D., 2013, *The Natural Law Foundations of Modern Social Theory: A Quest for Universalism*, Cambridge: Cambridge University Press.

Cherniss, J., and Hardy, H., 2017, 'Isaiah Berlin', in Zalta, Edward N., (ed.), *The Stanford Encyclopedia of Philosophy*, https://plato.stanford.edu/archives/win2017/entries/berlin/

Chilcot, J., 2016, *The Iraq Inquiry*, (12 Vols.), London: HMG, https://webarchive.national archives.gov.uk/20171123123237/http://www.iraqinquiry.org.uk/

Church, A., 1956, *Introduction to Mathematical Logic*, Princeton: Princeton University Press: 3–9.

Coady, C. A., 1985, 'The Morality of Terrorism'. *Philosophy*, 60: 47–69.

Coady, C. A., 2008, *Morality and Political Violence*, Cambridge: Cambridge University Press.

Coady, C. A., and O'Keefe, M., (eds.), 2002, *Terrorism and Justice: Moral Argument in a Threatened World*, Melbourne: Melbourne University Press.

Coates, A., 1997, *The Ethics of War*, Manchester: Manchester University Press.

Cobain, I., 2018, 'UK's MI5 in Court for Covert Policy Allowing Agents to Commit Serious Crimes', *Middle East Eye*, 4 October, www.middleeasteye.net/news/uk-mi5-counter-terrorism-criminality-1551742704

Cobbett, W., and Cohen, R., 1988, *Popular Struggles in South Africa*, London: Zed Books.

Cocking, C., 2013, 'Crowd Flight in Response to Police Dispersal Techniques: A Momentary Lapse of Reason?' *Journal of Investigative Psychology and Offender Profiling*, 10 (2): 219–236.

Cohen, J., 1996, 'Deliberation and Democratic Legitimacy', in Hamlin, A., and Pettit, P., (eds.), *The Good Polity: Normative Analysis of the State*, Oxford: Blackwell: 17–34.

Cohen, M., 2009, 'Substances' in Anagnostopoulos, G., (ed.), *A Companion to Aristotle*. Oxford: Blackwell: 197–212.

Cohen, S., 1972, *Folk Devils and Moral Panics*, London: MacGibbon and Kee.

Cohen, S., 1992, *Against Criminology*, London: Transaction.

Cohen, S., 2001, *States of Denial: Knowing About Atrocities and the Suffering of Others*, Malden: Blackwell.

Cohen, J., and Arato, A., 1992, *Civil Society and Political Theory*, Cambridge: MIT Press.

Colander, D., Follmer, H., Haas, A., Goldberg, M., Juselius, K., Kirman, A., Lux, T., and Sloth, B., 2009, 'The Financial Crisis and the Systemic Failure of Academic Economics', University of Copenhagen, Dept. of Economics Discussion Paper No. 09-03.

Cole, D., 2003, 'Their Liberties, Our Security: Democracy and Double Standards', Washington University of Georgetown, https://scholarship.law.georgetown.edu/facpub/924/

Cole, D., and Dempsey, C., 2006, *Terrorism and the Constitution: Sacrificing Civil Liberties in the Name of National Security*. New York, London: The New Press.

Coleman, G., 2011, 'The Ethics of Digital Direct Action Denial-of-Service Attacks and Similar Tactics Are Becoming More Widely Used as Protest Tools', Aljazeera, www.aljazeera.com/indepth/opinion/2011/08/20118308455825769.html

Coleman, G., 2014, *Hacker, Hoaxer, Whistleblower, Spy: The Many Faces of Anonymous*, London: Verso.

Coleman, P., 2000, *Obscenity, Blasphemy and Sedition: The Rise and Fall of Literary Censorship in Australia*, Sydney: Duffy and Snellgrove.

College of Policing, 2013, *Guidance on the Amendments to Sections 5(1) and 6(4) of the Public Order Act 1986*, http://library.college.police.uk/docs/APPREF/Guidance-amendment-public-order-2013.pdf.

Collins, R., and Chaltain, S., 2011, *We Must Not Be Afraid to Be Free: Stories of Free Expression in America*, New York: Oxford University Press.

Connolly, W., 1995, *Ethos of Pluralization*, Minnesota: University of Minnesota.

Connolly, W., 2004, 'The Complexity of Sovereignty', in *Sovereign Lives: Power in Global Politics*, New York: Routledge.

Connover, M., Ferrar, E., Menczer, F., and Flammini, E., 2013, 'The Digital Evolution of Occupy Wall Street'. *PLOS One*, 8 (1): e64679. doi:10.1371/journal.pone.0064679

Constantin, I., 2012, 'Philosophy of Substance: A Historical Perspective'. *Linguistic and Philosophical Investigations*, 11: 135–140.

Constitution Society, 2017, *Sedition Act of 1798: An Act in Addition to the Act Intituled, An Act for the Punishment of Certain Crimes Against the United States*, www.constitution.org/rf/sedition_1798.htm

Cook, F., 1962, 'How they Shortchanged an American'. *Saga: The Magazine for Men*, 23 (6): 18–25, https://anastaplo.files.wordpress.com/2014/04/cook-how-they-shortchanged-an-american-george-anastaplo-saga-the-magazine-for-men-mar-1962-copy1.pdf

Cooper, C., Hamilton, R., Mashabela, H., Mackay, S., Sidiropoulos, E., Gordon-Brown, C., Murphy, S., and Markham, C., 1993, *Race Relations Survey, 1992/93*, Johannesburg: South African Institute of Race Relations.

Cooper, R., and Ellem, B., 2013, 'The State against Unions: Australia's Neo-liberalism, 1996–2007', in Gall, G., and Dundon, T., (eds.), *Global Anti-Unionism: Nature, Dynamics, Trajectories and Outcome*, Basingstoke: Palgrave Macmillan: 163–183.

Corr, A., 1999, *No Trespassing: Squatting, Rent Strikes and Land Struggles Worldwide*, Cambridge: South End Press

Cranston, M., 1967, 'Liberalism', in Edwards, P., (ed.), *The Encyclopedia of Philosophy*, New York: Macmillan and the Free Press: 458–461.

Crawford, C., 2009, 'Civil Liberties, Bjelke-Petersen and a Bill of Rights for Queensland: Lessons for Queensland'. *Bond Law Review*, 21 (2): 1–15, https://epublications.bond.edu.au/cgi/viewcontent.cgi?article=1357&context=blr

Creech, B., 2014, 'Digital Representation and Occupy Wall Street's Challenge to Political Subjectivity'. *Convergence: The International Journal of Research into New Media Technologies*, 20 (4): 461–477.

Crifasi, C., Pollack, K., and Webster, D., 2015, 'Effects of State Level Policy Changes on Homicide and Nonfatal Shootings of Law Enforcement Officers'. *Injury Prevention: Journal of the International Society for Child and Adolescent Injury Prevention*, 22 (4): 274–278.

Critchley, S., 2011, *Faith for the Faithless*, London: Verso.

Croft, W., and Cruse, D., 2004, *Cognitive Linguistics*, Cambridge: Cambridge University Press.

Crofts, T., and Loughnan, A., 2015, *Criminalisation and Criminal Responsibility in Australia*. Melbourne: Oxford University Press.

Crozier, M., Huntington, S., and Watanuki, J., 1975, *The Crisis of Democracy. Report on the Governability of Democracies to the Trilateral Commission*, New York: New York University Press.

Cuffaro, M., 2011, 'On Thomas Hobbes's Fallible Natural Law Theory'. *History of Philosophy Quarterly*, 28 (2): 175–190.

Cuozzo, Steve, 2011 'Mike Is Blowing It', *New York Post*, 11 November, http://nypost.com/2011/11/11/mike-is-blowing-it.

Dadusc, D., 2017, 'The Micropolitics of Criminalisation: Power, Resistance and the Amsterdam Squatting Movement', Unpublished Ph. D Thesis, Canterbury: University of Kent.

Dafnos, T., 2014, 'Social Movements and Critical Resistance: policing Colonial Capitalist Order', in Brock, D., Glasbeek, A., and Murdocca, C., (eds.), *Criminalisation, Representation Regulation: Thinking Differently about Crime*, Toronto: University of Toronto: 385–418.

Dahlberg, L., 2000, 'The Habermasian Public Sphere: A Specification of the Idealised Conditions of Democratic Communication'. *Studies in Social and Political Thought*, www.sussex.ac.uk/cspt/documents/10-1a.pdf

Dardot, P., and Laval, C., 2014, *The New Way of the World: On Neoliberal Society* (trans. Elliot, G.), London: Verso.

Davenport, C., 2000, 'Introduction', in Davenport, C., (ed.), *Paths to State Repression*, Lanham, MD: Rowman and Littlefield: 1–24.

Davenport, C., 2007a, 'State Repression and Political Order'. *Annual Review of Political Science*, 10: 1–23.

Davenport, C., 2007b, *State Repression and the Domestic Democratic Peace*, New York: Cambridge University Press.

Davidow, R., and O'Boyle, M., 1977, 'Obscenity Laws in England and the United States: A Comparative Analysis'. *Nebraskan Law Review*, 56 (2): 249–288, https://digitalcommons.unl.edu/nlr/vol56/iss2/3

Davis, B., and Dossetor, K., 2010, *(Mis)Perceptions of Crime in Australia*. Trends & Issues in Crime and Criminal Justice No. 396, Canberra: Australian Institute of Criminology. https://aic.gov.au/publications/tandi/tandi396

De Cauwer, S., 2018, (ed.) *Critical Theory at a Crossroads*, New York: Columbia University Press.

Deery, P., 2007, 'A Double Agent Down Under: Australian Security and the Infiltration of the Left'. *Intelligence and National Security*, 22 (3): 346–366.

de Jongh, N., 2000, *Politics, Prudery and Perversions: The Censoring of the English Stage, 1901–1968*, London: Methuen.

Della Porta, D., 1995, *Political Violence and the State*, New York Cambridge University Press

Della Porta, D., 2009, (ed.), *Democracy in Social Movements*, Houndsmill: Palgrave.

Della Porta, D., 2013, *Can Democracy Be Saved? Participation, Deliberation and Social Movements*, New York: Wiley.

Della Porta, D., 2015, *Social Movements in Times of Austerity*, Cambridge: Polity Press.

Della Porta, D., (ed.), 2017, *Global Diffusion of Protest: Riding the Protest Wave in the Neoliberal Crisis*, Amsterdam: Amsterdam University Press.

Della Porta, D., and Daniani, M., 2006, *Social Movements: An Introduction*, Oxford: Blackwells.

Della Porta, D., and Mattoni, A., 2014, *Spreading Protest: Social Movements in Times of Crisis*, Colchester: ECPR Press.

Della Porta, D., and Rucht, D., 1995, 'Left-Libertarian Movements in Context: A Comparison of Italy and West Germany, 1965–1990', in Jenkins, C. J., and Klandermans, B., (eds.), *The Politics of Social Protest. Comparative Perspectives on States and Social Movements*, London: UCL Press.

Della Porta, D., Peterson, A., and Reiter, H., (eds.), 2006, *The Policing of Transnational Protest*, Aldershot: Ashgate.

DeLuca, K., Lawson, S., and Sun, Y., 2012, 'Occupy Wall Street on the Public Screens of Social Media: The Many Framings of the Birth of a Protest Movement'. *Communication, Culture, and Critique*, 5 (4): 483–509.

Dépelteau, F., (ed.), 2018, *The Palgrave Handbook of Relational Sociology*, London: Palgrave-Macmillan.

Dépelteau, F., and Powell, C., (eds.), 2013, *Conceptualizing Relational Sociology: Ontological and Theoretical Issues*, New York: Palgrave Macmillan.

der Derian, J., 1998, 'Review: The Scriptures of Security': Reviewed Works: *Security Metaphors: Cold War Discourse from Containment to Common House* by Paul A. Chilton; *Imperial Encounters: The Politics of Representation in North-South Relations* by Roxanne Lynn Doty'. *Mershon International Studies Review*, 42 (1): 117–122.

Deranty, J-P., and Renault, E., 2016, 'Democratic Agon: Striving for Distinction or Struggle against Domination and Injustice?', in Schaap, A., (ed.), *Law and Agonistic Politics*, Abingdon: Routledge: 43–56.

Derman, J., 2012, *Max Weber in Politics and Social Thought: From Charisma to Canonization*, Cambridge: Cambridge University Press.

Derrida, J., 1992, 'Force of Law: The Mystical Foundations of Authority', in Cornell, D., Rosenfeld, M., and Carlson, D., (eds.), *Deconstruction and the Possibility of Justice*, New York: Routledge: 3–67.

Desmond, M., 2014, 'Relational Ethnography'. *Theory and Society*, 43: 547–579.

Dewey, J., and Bentley, A., 1949, *Knowing and the Known*, Boston: Beacon Press.

DiChristina, B., 1997, 'The Quantitative Emphasis in Criminal Justice Education'. *Journal of Criminal Justice Education*, 8 (2): 134–151.

Dikötter, F., 2010, *Mao's Great Famine: The History of China's Most Devastating Catastrophe, 1958–62*, London: Bloomsbury.

Donald, M., 1991, *Origins of the Modern Mind: Three Stages in the Evolution of Culture and Cognition*, Cambridge: Harvard University Press.

Donald, M., 2001, *A Mind So Rare: The Evolution of Human Consciousness*, New York: W.W. Norton.

Donati, P., 2010, 'Birth and Development of the Relational Theory of Society: A Journey Looking for a Deep 'Relational' Sociology'. www.relationalstudies.net/uploads/2/3/1/5/2315313/donati_birth_and_development_of_the_relational_theory_of_society.pdf

Donati, P., 2011, *Relational Sociology: A New Paradigm for the Social Sciences*, London: Routledge.

Donati, P., 2018, 'An Original Relational Sociology Grounded in Critical Realism', in Depelteau, F., (ed.), *The Palgrave Handbook of Relational Sociology*, London: Palgrave-Macmillan: 431–456.

Donati, P., and Archer, M., 2015, *The Relational Subject*, Cambridge: Cambridge University Press.

Dryzek, J., 2000, *Deliberative Democracy and Beyond: Liberals, Critics, Contestations*, Oxford: Oxford University Press.

Dryzek, J., 2010, *Foundations and Frontiers of Deliberative Governance*, New York: Oxford University Press.

Dryzek, J., Honig, B., and Phillips, A., 2011, 'Overview of Political Theory', in Goodin, R., (ed.), *The Oxford Handbook of Political Science*, www.oxfordhandbooks.com/view/10.1093/oxfordhb/9780199604456.001.0001/oxfordhb-9780199604456-e-002?print=pdf

Dubet, F., 1994, 'The System, the Actor, and the Social Subject'. *Thesis Eleven*, 38 (1): 16–35.

Duff, A., (ed.), 1998, *Philosophy and the Criminal Law*, Oxford: Oxford University Press.

Duff, A., 2005, 'Theorizing Criminal Law: A 25th Anniversary Essay'. *Oxford Journal of Legal Studies*, 25 (3): 353.

Duff, A., 2012, 'Towards a Modest Legal Moralism'. *Criminal Law and Philosophy Minnesota Legal Studies Research Paper* No. 12–28, 8, http://papers.ssrn.com/sol3/papers.cfm?abstract_id=2103317

Duff, K., 2016, Review of L. Finlayson, 2015, 'The Political Is Political: Conformity and the Illusion of Dissent in Contemporary Political Philosophy'. *Contemporary Political Theory*, 15, 50–53. London: Rowman & Littlefield International.

Duff, R., 2007, *Answering for Crime*. Oxford: Oxford University Press.

Duff, R., and Green S., (eds.), 2011, *Philosophical Foundations of Criminal Law*, Oxford: Oxford University Press.

Duff, R., Farmer, L., Marshall, S., Renzo, M., and Tadros, V., (eds.), 2010, *The Boundaries of the Criminal Law*, Oxford: Oxford University Press.

Duff, R., Farmer, L., Marshall, S., Renzo, M., and Tadros, V., (eds.), 2011, *The Structures of the Criminal Law*, Oxford: Oxford University Press.

Duff, R., Farmer, L., Marshall, S., Renzo, M., and Tadros, V., (eds.), 2013, *The Constitution of Criminal Law*, Oxford: Oxford University Press.

Duff, R., Farmer, L., Marshall, S., Renzo, M., and Tadros, V., (eds.), 2014, *Criminalization: The Political Morality of the Criminal Law*, Oxford: Oxford University Press.

Dumenil, G., and Levy, D., 2013, *The Crisis of Neo Liberalism*, Cambridge: Harvard University Press.

du Toit, A., and Manganyi, C., 1990, 'The Time of the Comrades: Reflections on Political Commitment and Professional Discourse in a Context of Political Violence', in Manganyi, C., and du Toit, A., (eds.), *Political Violence and the Struggle in South Africa*, London: Palgrave Macmillan.

Dworkin, R., 1978, *Taking Rights Seriously*, Cambridge: Harvard University Press.

Dyzenhaus, D., 1997, *Legality and Legitimacy: Carl Schmitt, Hans Kelsen and Hermann Heller in Weimar*, Oxford: Oxford University Press.

Dyzenhaus, D., 2001, 'The Permanence of the Temporary: Can Emergency Powers be Normalized?', in Daniels, R. J., Macklem, P., and Roach, K., (eds.), *The Security of Freedom: Essays on Canada's Anti-Terrorism Bill*, Toronto: University of Toronto Press.

Dyzenhaus, D., 2005, 'The Dilemma of Legality and the Moral Limits of Law', in Sarat, A., Douglas, L., and Umphrey, M., (eds.), *The Limits of Law*, Stanford: Stanford University Press.

Dyzenhaus, D., 2006, *The Constitution of Law: Legality in a Time of Emergency*, Cambridge: Cambridge University Press.

Dyzenhaus, D., 2016, 'Dworkin and Unjust Law', in Waluchow, W., and Sciaraffa, S., (eds.), *The Legacy of Ronald Dworkin*, New York: Oxford University Press: 131–164.

Dyzenhaus, D., and Poole, T., (eds.), 2015, *Law, Liberty and the State: Oakeshott, Hayek and Schmitt on the Rule of Law*, Cambridge: Cambridge University Press.

Earl, J., 2006, 'Introduction: Repression and the Social Control of Protest'. *Mobilization: An International Quarterly*, 11 (2): 129–143.

Earl, J., 2011, 'Political Repression: Iron Fists, Velvet Gloves, and Diffuse Control'. *Annual Review of Sociology*, 37: 161–184.

Earl, J., and Soule, S., 2006, 'Seeing Blue: A Police-Centered Explanation of Protest Policing'. *Mobilization: An International Quarterly*, 11 (2): 145–164.

Earl, J., Soule, S., and McCarthy, J., 2003, 'Protest under Fire? Explaining the Policing of Protest'. *American Sociological Review*, 68 (4): 581–606.

Economides, S., and Monastiriotis, V., (eds.), 2009, *The Return of Street Politics? Essays on the December Riots in Greece*, London: The Hellenic Observatory/LSE.

Eddy, E., 2005, 'Privatizing the Patriot Act: The Criminalization of Environmental and Animal Protectionists as Terrorists'. *Pace Environmental Law Review*, 22, 261–327.

Edwards, P., 2018, 'Counter-Terrorism and Counter-Law: An Archetypal Critique'. *Legal Studies*, 38 (2): 279–297.

Eekert, G., van, 2017, 'Freedom of Speech, Freedom of Self-Expression and Kant's Public Use of Reason'. *Diametros*, 54: 118–137.

El-Anany, N., 2014, 'Innocence Charged with Guilt: The Criminalization of Protest from Peterloo to Millbank', in Pritchard, D., (ed.), *Riot, Unrest and Protest on the Global Stage*, London: Palgrave-Macmillan: 72–97.

Elias, N., 1978, *What Is Sociology?* London: Hutcheson.

Elshtain, J., 2008, *Sovereignty: God, State and the Self*, New York: Basic Books.

Elster, J., 1989, *Nuts and Bolts for the Social Sciences*, Cambridge: Cambridge University Press.

Emirbayer, M., 1997, 'Manifesto for a Relational Sociology'. *American Journal of Sociology*, 103 (2): 281–317.

Emler, N., 1983, 'Morality and Politics; The Ideological Dimension', in Weinreich-Haste, W., and Locke, D., (eds.), *Morality in the Making: Thoughts Action and Context*, Chichester: Wile.

En.squat, 2018, https://en.squat.net/tag/melbourne/

Engelmann, D., 1993, *The Right to Dissent: Hannah Arendt's Defense of Civil Disobedience*, Unpublished Ph.D. Thesis, Marquette University.

Ercan, S., and Gagnon J-P., 2014, 'The Crisis of Democracy: Which Crisis? Which Democracy?' *Democratic Theory*, 1 (2): 1–10.

Espeland, W., 1997, 'Authority by the Numbers: Porter on Quantification, Discretion and Legitimation of Expertise'. *Journal of Criminal Justice*, 29: 389–405.

European Court of Human Rights, 1976, Case of Handyside v. the United Kingdom (Application no.5493/72) Judgment Strasbourg, 7 December, http://hudoc.echr.coe.int/eng?i=001-57499

Farron, T., 2017, 'Liberalism has eaten itself – it isn't very liberal any more', *The Guardian*, 17 November, www.theguardian.com/commentisfree/2017/nov/28/liberalism-eaten-itself-british-religious-liberty-christianity-tim-farron.

Fattah, E., 1997, *Criminology: Past, Present, and Future: A Critical Overview*, New York: St Martin's Press.

Featherstone, D., 2013, *Solidarity: Hidden Histories and Geographies of Internationalism*, London: Zed Books.

Feinberg, J., 1984, *Harm to Others: The Moral Limits of the Criminal Law*, Oxford: Oxford University Press.

Fernandez, L., 2008, *Policing Dissent: Social Control and the Anti-Globalization Movement*, Piscataway: Rutgers University Press.

Ferrier, M., 2017, 'Hat's That: Did the Queen's Headgear Allude to Brexit?' *The Guardian*, 21 June, www.theguardian.com/fashion/2017/jun/21/queens-hat-alludes-to-brexit

Festinger, L., 1957, *A Theory of Cognitive Dissonance*, Stanford: Stanford University Press.

Fidler, D., (ed.), 2015, *The Snowden Reader*, Bloomington: Indiana University Press.

Finnis, J., 1980, *Natural Rights and Natural Law*, Oxford: Oxford University Press.

Finnis, J., 1999/2000, 'On the Incoherence of Legal Positivism (1999–2000)'. *Notre Dame Law Review*, 75: 1597.

Finnis, J., 2012, 'Natural Law Theory: Its Past and Its Present', *Scholarly Works*. Paper 1085, http://scholarship.law.nd.edu/law faculty_scholarship/108

Fish, S., 1994, *There's No Such Thing as Free Speech...and It's a Good Thing Too*, New York: Oxford University Press.

Fish, S., 1999, *The Trouble with Principle*, Cambridge: Harvard University Press.

Fishkin, J., Keniston, K., and MacKinnon, C., 1973, 'Moral Reasoning and Political Ideology'. *Journal of Personality and Social Psychology*, 27: 109–119.

Flatau, P., Tyson, K., Callis, Z., Seivwright, A., Box, E., Rouhani, L., Lester, N., Firth, D., and Sze-Wan Ng, S-W., 2018, *The State of Homelessness in Australia's Cities*, Perth: Centre for Social Impact at the University of Western Australia.

Flew, T., 2009, 'The Citizen's Voice: Albert Hirschman's Exit, Voice and Loyalty and Its Contribution to Media Citizenship Debates'. *Media, Culture and Society*, 31 (6): 977–994.

Foucault, M., 1983, 'Afterword: The Subject and Power', in Dreyfus, H., (ed.), *Michel Foucault: Beyond Structuralism and Hermeneutics*, Chicago: University of Chicago Press.

Foucault, M., 2010, *The Government of Self and Others: Lectures at the Collège de France, 1982–1983*, New York: Picador/Palgrave Macmillan.

Foucault, M., 2011, *The Courage of Truth: The Government of Self and Other.* New York: Palgrave Macmillan.

Frankel, P., Pines, N., and Swilling, M., 1988, (eds.), *State, Resistance and Change in South Africa*, Johannesburg: Southern.

Frankfurt, H., 2005, *On Bullshit*, Princeton: Princeton University Press.

Fraser, N., 1990, Rethinking the Public Sphere: A Contribution to the Critique of Actually Existing Democracy'. *Social Text*, 25/26: 56–80.

Freeden, M., 2013, *The Political Theory of Political Thinking: The Anatomy of a Practice.* Oxford: Oxford University Press.

Frege, G., 1952, 'On Sense and Reference', in Geach, P., and Black, M., (eds.), *Translations from the Philosophical Writings of Gottlob Frege*, Oxford: Basil Blackwell: 56–78.

Friedman, M., 2002, *Capitalism and Freedom* (with Friedman, D.), Chicago: University of Chicago Press.

Fromm, E., 1941, *Fear of Freedom*, London: Routledge and Kegan Paul.

Fromm, E., 1981, *On Disobedience and Other Essays*, New York: Harper and Row.

Fuchs, C., 2003, 'Some Implications of Pierre Bourdieu's Works for a Theory of Social Self-Organization'. *European Journal of Social Theory*, 6 (4): 387–408.

Fuchs, E. 2013, "Time Warner Cable Site Defaced with Gorilla Over Its New Anti-Piracy Policy," *Business Insider*, www.businessinsider.com.au/time-warner-hacked-by-nullcrew-2013-3

Fukuyama, F., 1989, 'The End of History?' *The National Interest*, 16: 3–16.

Fukuyama, F., 1992, *The End of History and the Last Man*, New York: Free Press.

Fuller, L., 1958, 'Positivism and Fidelity to Law – A Reply to Professor Hart'. *Harvard Law Review*, 71 (4): 630.

Fuller, L., 1964, *The Morality of Law*, Yale: Yale University Press.

Fuller, S., 2004, *Kuhn vs Popper: The Struggle for the Soul of Science*, New York: Columbia University Press.

Fultner, B., 2003, 'Translators Introduction', in Habermas, J., *Truth and Justification* (ed. and trans. Fultner, B.), Cambridge: MIT Press: vii–xxii.

Furedi, F., 1997, *Culture of Fear: Risk Taking and the Morality of Low Expectation*, London: Continuum.

Furedi, F., 2005, *The Politics of Fear. Beyond Left and Right*, London: Continuum.

Galli, P., 2015, *Janus's Gaze: Essays on Carl Schmitt*, Duke University Press.

Galston, W., 2005, *The Practice of Liberal Pluralism*, Cambridge: Cambridge University Press.

García-Albacete, 2014, *Young People's Political Participation in Western Europe: Continuity or Generational Change?*, London: Palgrave-Macmillan.

Gardner, J., 2001, 'Legal Positivism: 5-1/2 Myths'. *American Journal of Jurisprudence*, 46: 199–227.

Garkawe, S., 2003, 'The South African Truth and Reconciliation Commission: A Suitable Model to Enhance the Role and Rights of the Victims of Gross Violations of Human Rights.' *Melbourne University Law Review*, 27, www.mulr.com.au/issues/27_2/27_2_3.pdf

Garland, D., 1990, *Punishment and Modern Society: A Study in Social Theory*. Oxford: Clarendon Press.

Garland, D., 1996, 'The Limits of the Sovereign State'. *The British Journal of Criminology*, 36, (4): 445–471.

Garland, D., 2001, *The Culture of Control: Crime and Social Order*, Oxford: Oxford University Press.

Garland, D., 2009, 'Disciplining Criminology'. *Sistema Penal & Violencia*, 1 (1): 114–125.

Gaydosh, B., 2017, *Bernhard Lichtenberg: Roman Catholic Priest and Martyr of the Nazi Regime*, Lanham: Lexington Books.

Gelber, K., 2002, *Speaking Back: The Free Speech Versus Hate Speech Debate*, Amsterdam: John Benjamins.

Genova, C., 2018, 'Youth Activism in Political Squats between Centri Sociali and Case Occupate'. *Societies* 8 (77): 1–25. doi:10.3390/soc8030077

Gerbaudo, P., 2016, 'The Indignant Citizen: Anti-Austerity Movements in Southern Europe and the Anti-Oligarchic Reclaiming of Citizenship'. *Social Movement Studies*, 16, 36–50.

Gerbaudo, P., 2017, *The Mask and the Flag: Populism, Citizenism, and Global Protest*, Oxford: Oxford University Press.

Gessen, M., 2018, 'The Fifteen-Year-Old Climate Activist Who Is Demanding a New Kind of Politics', *The New Yorker*, 2 October, www.newyorker.com/news/our-columnists/the-fifteen-year-old-climate-activist-who-is-demanding-a-new-kind-of-politics

Gillard, M., and Flynn, L., 2012, *Untouchables: Dirty cops, bent justice and racism in Scotland Yard*, London: Bloomsbury.

Gilleman, L., 2014, *John Osborne: Vituperative Artist*, London: Routledge.

Gillers, S., 2007, 'A Tendency to Deprave and Corrupt: The Transformation of American Obscenity Law from Hicklin to Ulysses II'. *Washington University Law Review*, 85: 215, http://openscholarship.wustl.edu/law_lawreview/vol85/iss2/1

Gilham, P., Edwards, B., and Noakes, J., 2011, 'Strategic Incapacitation and the Policing of Occupy Wall Street Protests in New York City, 2011'. *Policing and Society*, 23 (1): 81–102.

Gimmler, A., 2001, 'Deliberative Democracy, the Public Sphere and the Internet', *Philosophy and Social Criticism*, 27 (4): 21–39.

Glass, A., 2013, 'Occupy Wall Street Began', *Politico*, 17 September, www.politico.com/story/2013/09/this-day-in-politics-096859

Glasser, C., 2011, *Moderates and Radicals under Repression: The US Animal Rights Movement, 1990–2010*, Irvine: University of California Press.

Global Freedom of Expression, 2016, *The Case of Satirist Jan Böhmermann*, New York: Columbia University, https://globalfreedomofexpression.columbia.edu/cases/the-case-of-satirist-jan-bohmermann/

Golder, B., and Williams, G., 2004, 'What Is Terrorism – Problems of Legal Definition'. *University of New South Wales Law Journal*, 27 (2): 270–295.

Goodin, R., 2006, *What's Wrong with Terrorism?* Oxford: Polity Press.

Goodman, J., 2007, 'Shielding Corporate Interests from Public Dissent: An Examination of the Undesirability and Unconstitutionality of Eco-Terrorism Legislation'. *Journal of Law and Policy*, 16, 823.

Gordon, J., 2010, 'A Developing Human Rights Culture in the UK? Case Studies of Policing'. *European Human Rights Law Review*, 6: 609–620.

Grace, J., 2018, 'A Balance of Rights and Protections in Public Order Policing: A Case Study on Rotherham'. *European Journal of Current Legal Issues*, 24 (1).

Graeber, D., 2013, *The Democracy Project: A History, a Crisis, a Movement*, New York: Spiegel & Grau.

Graham, D., 2015, 'Heraclitus'. *Stanford Encyclopedia of Philosophy*, https://plato.stanford.edu/entries/heraclitus/#Flu

Gray, J., 1983, *Mill on Liberty: A Defence*. London: Routledge and Kegan Paul.

Grayling, A., 2006, *Among the Dead Cities: Was the Allied Bombing of Civilians in WWII a Necessity or a Crime?* London: Bloomsbury.

Green, P., and Ward, R., 2004, *State Crime: Governments, Violence and Corruption*, London: Pluto Press.

Green, T. H., 1907, *Lectures on the Principles of Political Obligation*, London: Longmans.

Greenberg, I., 2011, 'The FBI and the Making of the Terrorist Threat'. *Radical History Review*, 111: 35–50.

Greenberg, I., 2012, *Surveillance in America: Critical Analysis of the FBI, 1920 to the Present*, Lanham: Lexington Books.

Greenwald, G., 2014, *No Place to Hide: Edward Snowden, the NSAA and the US Surveillance State*, London: Hamish Hamilton.

Greenwalt, K., 1989, *Speech, Crime and the Uses of Language*, Oxford: Oxford University Press.

Gross, M., and McGoey, L., (eds.), 2015, *Routledge International Handbook of Ignorance Studies*, Abingdon: Routledge.

Grotius, H., 1960, *[De Indis] De jure Praedae Commentarius. Commentary on the Law of Prize and Booty* (trans. Williams G., and Zeydel, W.), London: Wildy & Sons.

Gulli, B., 2009, 'The Sovereign Exception: Notes on Schmitt's Word that Sovereign Is He Who Decides on the Exception'. *Glossator*, 1 (1): 23–29.

Gusfield, J., 1963, *Symbolic Crusade: Status Politics and the American Temperance Movement*. Urbana: University of Illinois Press.

Gutmann, A., and Thompson, D., 2002, *Why Deliberative Democracy?* Princeton: Princeton University Press.

Guthrie, C., and Quinlan, M., 2007, *Just War: The Just War Tradition: Ethics in Modern Warfare*, London: Bloomsbury.

Haan, N. 1972, 'Activism as Moral Protest: Moral Judgments of Hypothetical Moral Dilemmas and an Actual Situation of Civil Disobedience', in Kohlberg, L., and Turiel, E., (eds.), *The Development of Moral Judgment and Action*, New York: Holt, Rinehart & Winston.

Haas, J., and Vogt, K., 2015, 'Ignorance and Investigation', in Gross, M., and McGoey, L., (eds.), *Routledge International Handbook of Ignorance Studies*, Abingdon: Routledge: 17–32.

Habermas, J., 1971, 'The Classical Doctrine of Politics in Relation to Social Philosophy', in *Theory and Practice*, Boston: Beacon Press: 41–81.

Habermas, J., 1977, 'Hannah Arendt's Communications Concept of Power'. *Social Research*, 44: 3–24.

Habermas, J., 1989, *Structural Transformation of the Public Sphere: An Inquiry into a Category of Bourgeois, Society* (trans. Burger, T., and Lawrence, F.), Cambridge: MIT Press.

Habermas, J., 1991, 'The Public Sphere', in Muckerji, C., & Schudson, M., (eds.), *Rethinking Popular Culture: Contemporary Perspectives in Cultural Studies*, Berkeley: UCP.

Habermas, J., 1992, 'Concluding Remarks', in Calhoun, C., (ed.), *Habermas and the Public Sphere*, Cambridge: MIT Press: 462–479.

Habermas, J., 1996, *Between Facts and Norms: Contributions to a Discourse Theory of Law and Democracy* (trans. Rehg, W.), Cambridge: MIT Press.

Habermas, J., 2003, *Truth and Justification* (trans., Fultner, B.), Cambridge: MIT Press

Hacking, I., 1998, *Mad Travellers: Reflections on the Reality of Transient Mental Illness*, Richmond: University of Virginia Press.

Hacking, I., 2001, *Historical Ontology*, Cambridge: Harvard University Press.

Hall, S., Critcher, C., Jefferson, T., Clarke, J., and Roberts, B., 1977, *Policing the Crisis*, London: Macmillan.

Hamilton, C., 2016, *What Do We Want: The Story of Protest in Australia*, Canberra: The National Library of Australia.

Hampton, J., 1986, *Hobbes and the Social Contract Tradition*, Cambridge: Cambridge University Press.

Hancock, R., 1975, 'Kant and Civil Disobedience'. *Idealistic Studies*, 5: 164–176.

Handel, M., 1977, 'The Yom Kippur War and the Inevitability of Surprise'. *International Studies Quarterly*, 21: 461–501.

Handel, M., 1984, 'Intelligence and the Problem of Strategic Surprise'. *Journal of Strategic Studies*, 7 (3): 229–281.

Handel, M., 1987, 'The Politics of Intelligence'. *Intelligence and National Security*, 2 (4): 5–46.

Handley, M., Shellard, D., and Nicholson, S., 2004, *The Lord Chamberlain Regrets...: A History of British Theatre Censorship*, London: British Museum.

Hansen, M., 1993, 'Foreword' to O. Negt, O., and Kluge, A., *Public Sphere and Experience: Toward an Analysis of the Bourgeois and Proletarian Public Sphere* (trans. Labinyi, P., Daniel, J., and Oksiloff, A.), Minneapolis: University of Minnesota Press.

Hansen, S., and Jensen, J., 1971, *The Little Red School Book*, New York: Pocket Books.

Harcourt, B., 2012, 'Punitive Preventive Justice: A Critique', *Public Law and Legal Theory Working Paper no. 386*, Chicago: Law School University of Chicago.

Harman, C., 2008, 'Theorising Neoliberalism'. *International Socialist*, 117 (Winter), www.marxists.org/archive/harman/2008/xx/neolib.htm#n82

Hart, H., 1958, 'Positivism and the Separation of Law and Morals'. *Harvard Law Review*, 71 (4): 593–629.

Hart, H., 1961, *The Concept of Law*, Oxford: The Clarendon Press.

Hart, H., 1983, 'Positivism and the Separation of Law and Morals', in Hart, *Essays in Jurisprudence and Philosophy*, Oxford: Clarendon Press.

Harvey, D., 2005, *A Short History of Neoliberalism*, Oxford: Oxford University Press.

Hauhart, R., 2012, 'Toward a Sociology of Criminological Theory'. *The American Sociologist*, 43 (2): 153–171.

Hayek, F., 1982, *Law, Legislation and Liberty: A New Statement of the Liberal Principles of Justice and Political Economy*, (Vol. II), London: Routledge and Kegan Paul.

Hayhurst, R., 2014, 'Arrests and Charges under Section 5 of the Public Order Act', *What Do They Know?* www.whatdotheyknow.com/request/arrests_and_charges_under_sectio_2

Hayner, P., 2010, *Unspeakable Truths: Transitional Justice and the Challenge of Truth Commissions*, Abingdon: Routledge.

Heffernan, M., 2011, *Wilful Blindness: Why We Ignore the Obvious at Our Peril*, New York: Walker & Co.

Heidegger, M., 1971. 'The Thinker as Poet', in *Poetry, Language, Thought* (trans. Hofstadter, A.,), New York: Harper & Row.

Heidegger, M., 1977. 'Letter on humanism', in Heidegger, M., Krell, D., (ed.), *Basic Writings*. New York: Harper & Row.

Heidegger, M., 1978, 'The Essence of Truth', in Heidegger, M., (ed.), *Basic Writings* (ed. Krell, D.), London: Routledge: 111–138.

Heidegger, M., 1996, *Being and Time: A Translation of Sein und Zeit*, Albany: State University of New York Press.

Heidegger, M., 2015, *The History of Beyng* (W. McNeill and J. Powell) Bloomington: Indiana University Press.

Heilpern, J., 2007, *John Osborne a Patriot for Me*, New York: Vintage.

Held, V., 2008, *How Terrorism Is Wrong: Morality and Political Violence*, Oxford: Oxford University Press.

Hempel, C., 1942, 'The Function of General Laws in History'. *Journal of Philosophy*, 39 (2): 35–48.

Henriques, D., 2012, *The Wizard of Lies*, New York Henry Holt and Winston.

Herald, Sun, 2018, 'Planned Student Strike for Climate Change Prompts PM's Call for 'More Learning, Less Activism' in Schools', *Herald Sun*, 27 November, www.heraldsun.com.au/news/national/planned-student-strike-for-climate-change-prompts-pms-call-for-more-learning-less-activism-in-schools/video/5c7889bd952da601ae8dad2f645c062b

Hill, M., 2010, 'United States v. Fullmer and the Animal Enterprise Terrorism Act: True Threats to Advocacy'. *Case Western Reserve Law Review*, 61 (3): 981–1048.

Hirschman, A. 1970, *Exit, Voice and Loyalty: Responses to Decline in Firms, Organizations, and States*. Cambridge: Harvard University Press.

Hirst, P., 1988, 'Carl Schmitt — Decisionism and Politics'. *Economy and Society*, 17 (2): 72–82.

Hislop, I., 2011, 'Statement of Ian Hislop', *The Levenson Inquiry*, https://webarchive.nationalarchives.gov.uk/20140122165058/http://www.levesoninquiry.org.uk/wp-content/uploads/2012/01/Witness-Statement-of-Ian-Hislop.pdf

Hislop, I., and Hockenhull, T., 2018, *I Object: Ian Hislop's Search for Dissent*, London: British Museum.

Hobbes, T., 1971/1681, *A Dialogue between a Philosopher & a Student of the Common Laws of England*, Chicago: The University of Chicago.

Hobbes, T., 1985, *Leviathan*, London: Penguin.

Hobbes, T., 1998, *On the Citizen [De Cive]* (Ed. Tuck, R., and Silverthorne, M.,) Cambridge: Cambridge University Press.

Hochschild, A., 2016, *Strangers in their Own Land: Anger and Mourning on the American Right*, New York: The New Press.

Hocking, J., 1993, *Beyond Terrorism: The Development of the Australian Security State*, Sydney: Allen and Unwin.

Hocking, J., 2003, 'Counter-Terrorism and the Criminalisation of Politics: Australia's New Security Powers of Detention, Proscription and Control'. *Australian Journal of Politics and History*, 49: 355–371.

Hoernlé, R., 1945, 'A Theory of Liberty', in his *Race and Reason; Being Mainly a Selection of Contributions to the Race Problem in South Africa*, (ed., MacCrone, I. D.). Johannesburg: Witwatersrand University Press.

Hoffman, J., and Rosenkrantz, G., 1997, *Substance: Its Nature and Existence*, London: Routledge.

Hogg, R., 1983, 'Perspectives on the Criminal Justice System', in Findlay, M., Egger, S., and Sutton, J., (eds.), *Issues in Criminal Justice Administration*, Sydney: Allen and Unwin.

Holmes, M., and Taggart, W., 1990, 'A Comparative Analysis of Research Methods in Criminology and Criminal Justice Journals'. *Justice Quarterly*, 7 (2): 421–437.

Honderich, T., 2003, *After the Terror*, Edinburgh: Edinburgh University Press.

Honderich, T., 2006, *Humanity, Terrorism, Terrorist War*, London and New York: Continuum.

Honig, B., 1993, *Political Theory and the Displacement of Politics*, Ithaca, NY: Cornell University Press.

Honig, B., 2008, 'Between Decision and Deliberation: Political Paradox in Democratic Theory'. *Netherlands Journal of Legal Philosophy*, 2: 115–136.

Horner, D. 2014, *The Spy Catchers: The Official History of ASIO 1949–1963*, Canberra: AWM.

House of Commons Home Affairs Committee, 2009, *Policing of the G20 Protests: Eighth Report of Session 2008–09*, Report, London: House of Commons.

Huddleston, R., and Pullum, G., 2006, *A Student's Introduction to English Grammar*. Cambridge: Cambridge University Press.

Hughes, T., 1976, *The Fate of Facts in the World of Men: Foreign Policy and Intelligence Making*, New York: Foreign Policy Association.

Hulnick, A., 1991, 'Controlling Intelligence Estimates', in Hastedt, G., (ed.), *Controlling Intelligence*, London: Frank Cass: 81–96.

Husak, D., 2008, *Over Criminalization: The Limits of the Criminal Law*, Oxford: Oxford University Press.

Ioannidis, J., 2005, August, 'Why Most Published Research Findings Are False'. *PLoS Medicine*, 2 (8): e124.

Ignatieff, M., 1997, *Warrior's Honour: Ethnic War and the Modern Conscience*, New York: Henry Holt.

International Network of Civil Liberties Organizations, 2013, October, *Take Back the Streets: Repression and Criminalization of Protest Around the World*. New York: International Network of Civil Liberties Organizations.

InterOccupy.Net, 2012, 'FBI Documents Reveal It Monitored Occupy as a Criminal and Terrorist Threat', http://interoccupy.net/blog/fbi-documents-reveal-it-monitored-occupy-as-a-criminal-and-terrorist-threat/

Isin, E., 2002, *Being Political: Genealogies of Citizenship*. Minneapolis: University of Minnesota Press.

Isin, E., 2005, 'Engaging, Being, Political'. *Political Geography*, 24: 373–387.

Isin, E., 2008, 'Theorizing Acts of Citizenship', in Isin, E., and Nielsen, G., (eds.), *Acts of Citizenship*, London: Palgrave Macmillan: 15–43.

Isin, E., 2018, 'Acts', Engin Isin, http://enginfisin.net/acts.html

Jackson, W., 2011, 'Liberal Intellectuals and the Politics of Insecurity', in Neocleous, M., and Rigakos, G., (eds.), *Anti-Security*, Ottawa: Red Quill.

Janis, I., 1972, *Victims of Groupthink*, Boston: Houghton Mifflin.

Janis, I., 1982, *Groupthink: Psychological Studies of Policy Decisions and Fiascos*. Boston: Houghton Mifflin.

Jansson, K., 2007, *British Crime Survey – Measuring Crime for 25 Years*, London: BCS, nationalarchives.gov.uk/20110218135832/rds.homeoffice.gov.uk/rds/pdfs07/bcs25.pdf

Jenness, V., 2004, 'Explaining Criminalization: From Demography and Status Politics to Globalization and Modernization'. *American Review of Sociology*, 30: 147–171.

Joas, H., and Knobl, W., 2009, *Social Theory: Twenty Introductory Lectures*, Cambridge: Cambridge University Press.

Johnson, C., 2016, 'Christian Brother 'gyrated' Against Me: Catholic Sexual Abuse Victim', *The Age*, 22 February, www.theage.com.au/victoria/christian-brother-gyrated-against-me-catholic-sexual-abuse-victim-20160222-gn09q7.html

Johnson, P., 1991, *Darwin on Trial*, Washington, DC: Regnery Gateway.

Johnson, P., 1995, *Reason in the Balance: The Case against Naturalism in Science, Law and Education*, Downers Grove: InterVarsity Press.

Johnstone, L., 2018, 'Apartheid As Seen By the Boers: The Population History of South Africa', *The Occidental Observer*, 1 March, www.theoccidentalobserver.net/2018/03/01/white-refugees-from-third-world-barbarism-the-case-of-south-africa-part-2/

Jones, J., 2018, '"Joyless in the Extreme" – I Object: Ian Hislop's Search for Dissent Review', *The Guardian*, 4 September. www.theguardian.com/artanddesign/2018/sep/04/i-object-ian-hislop-search-for-dissent-review-british-museum

Kahn, R., 2009, 'Operation Get Fired: A Chronicle of the Academic Repression of Radical Environmentalist and Animal Rights Advocate-Scholars'. *Academic Repression: Reflections from the Academic Industrial Complex*: 200–215.

Kahneman, D., and Tversky, A., 1972, Subjective Probability: A Judgment of Representativeness, *Cognitive Psychology*, 3 (2): 430–451.

Kahneman, D., and Tversky, A., 1979, 'Prospect Theory: An Analysis of Decision under Risk'. *Econometrica*, 47 (2): 263–291.

Kam, E., 1988, *Surprise Attack: The Victim's Perspective*, Cambridge: Harvard University Press.

Kalyvas, A., 2016, 'The Democratic Narcissist: The Agonism of the Ancients Compared to that of the (post)Moderns', in Schaap, A., (ed.), *Law and Agonistic Politics*, Abingdon: Routledge: 15–42.

Kant, I., 1781–87/1998, *Critique of Pure Reason*, trans. Wood, A., and Guyer, P., Cambridge: Cambridge University Press.

Kant, I., 1784, 'What is Enlightenment?' (trans. Smith, M.), New York: Columbia University. www.columbia.edu/acis/ets/CCREAD/etscc/kant.html

Kant, I., 1784/1996, 'An Answer to the Question: What Is Enlightenment?' (trans. Gregor, M.,), in Kant, I., (ed.), *Practical Philosophy*, Cambridge: Cambridge University Press: 11–22.

Kant, I., 1786/1996, 'What Does It Mean to Orient Oneself in Thinking?' (trans. Wood, A.), in Kant, I., (ed.), *Religion and Rational Theology*, Cambridge: Cambridge University Press: 7–20.

Kaplan, W., 2017, Why Dissent Matters: Because Some People See Things the Rest of Us Miss. Montreal: McGill-Queens University Press.

Katz, J., 1977, 'A Proper Theory of Names'. *Philosophical Studies: An International Journal for Philosophy in the Analytic Tradition*, 31 (1): 1–80.

Katz, J., 1988, *Seductions of Crime*, New York: Basic Books.

Kauzlarich, D., and Kramer, R., 1998, *Crimes of the American Nuclear State: At Home and Abroad*, Boston: North Eastern University Press.

Keen, S., 2015, *Developing an Economics for the Post-Crisis world*. London: College Publications.

Kelsen, H., 1945, *General Theory of Law and State* (trans. Wedberg, A.), New York: Russell and Russell.

Ketchen, J., 1999, 'Legality and Legitimacy in the Hart-Fuller Debate', Unpublished Ph.D., London: University of Western Ontario.

Keynes, J., 1971–1989, *Collected Writings (Essays in Biography)* (Vol. X), Cambridge: Cambridge University Press.

King, M., and Waddington, D., 2004, 'Coping with Disorder? The Changing Relationship between Policer Public Order Strategy and Practice: A Critical Analysis of the Burnley Riot'. *Policing and Society*, 14 (2): 118–137.

Kinsey, A., Pomeroy, W., and Martin, C., 1948, *Sexual Behavior in the Human Male*, Boston: Saunders.

Kirkby, R., 2014, 'Men against Power: Antistatism, Grassroots Organizing, and the Vietnam Veterans Against the War, Unpublished Ph.D. Thesis, Waterloo: University of Waterloo.

Kleck, G., Tark, J., and Bellows, J., 2006, 'What Methods Are Most Frequently used in Research in Criminology and Criminal Justice?' *Journal of Criminal Justice*, 34 (2): 147–152.

Klugg, F., Starmer, K., and Weir, S., 2003, *The Three Pillars of Liberty: Political Rights and Freedoms in the United Kingdom*, London: Routledge.

Knauer, J., 1980, 'Motive and Goal in Hannah Arendt's Concept of Political Action'. *The American Political Science Review*, 74: 721–733.

Knuckey, S., Glenn, K., and MacLean, E., 2016, *Suppressing Protest, Human Rights Violations in the US Response to Occupy Wall Street*, New York: New York University School of Law and Fordham Law School.

Kohlberg, L., 1973, 'The Claim to Moral Adequacy of a Highest Stage of Moral Judgment'. *Journal of Philosophy*, 70 (18): 630–646.

Kohlberg, L., 1981, *Essays on Moral Development, Vol. I: The Philosophy of Moral Development*, San Francisco: Harper & Row.

Kolnai, A., 2004, 'What Is Politics About?' in Balázs, Z., and Dunlop, F., (eds.), *Exploring the World of Human Practice. Readings In and About the Philosophy of Aurel Kolnai*, New York: Central European University Press: 17–44.

Körösényi, A., 2005, 'Politics of Friendship versus Politics of Enmity'. *ECPR Workshop on 'The Politics of Friendship'*, Granada, April, https://ecpr.eu/Filestore/PaperProposal/126e3742-7d60-4761-9441-6b3040300d8d.pdf

Koskenniemi, M., 2006, 'By Their Acts You Shall Know Them… (And Not by Their Legal Theories)'. *German Law Journal*, 7: 155.

Kosselleck, R., 2002, *The Practice of Conceptual History: Timing History, Spacing Concepts*. Series: Cultural Memory in the Present (trans. Samuel, T.), Stanford: Stanford University Press.

Krasner, S., 1999, *Sovereignty: Organized Hypocrisy*, Princeton: Princeton University Press.

Krastev, I., 2014, *Democracy Disrupted: The Politics of Global Protest*, Philadelphia: University of Pennsylvania.

Kronman, A., 1975, 'Hart, Austin, and the Concept of a Legal System: The Primacy of Sanctions'. *Yale Law Journal*, 84 (3): 584–607.

Kuhn, T., 1970, *The Structure of Scientific Revolutions* (2nd ed.), Chicago: University of Chicago Press.

Kunstler, S., 2012, 'The Right to Occupy—Occupy Wall Street and the First Amendment'. *Fordham Urbana: Law Journal*, 39: 989.

Kupperwasser, Y., 2007, *Lesson's From Israel's Intelligence Reforms*, Washington: Brookings Institute.

La Boétie, E., 1975, *The Politics of Obedience: The Discourse of Voluntary Servitude* (Intro. Rothbard, M.; trans. Kurz, H.), Auburn: Mises Institute.

Lacey, N., 2004, 'Criminalisation as Regulation: The Role of Criminal Law', in Parker, C., et al. (eds.), *Regulating Law*, Oxford: Oxford University Press: 144–167.

Lacey, N., 2008, 'Philosophy, Political Morality, and History: Explaining the Enduring Resonance of the Hart-Fuller Debate'. *New York University Law Review*, 83 (4): 1059.

Lacey, N., 2009, 'Historicising Criminalization: Conceptual and Empirical Issues'. *Modern Law Review*, 72: 936.

Lacey, N., 2010, 'Out of the 'Witches' Cauldron?: Reinterpreting the Context and Reassessing the Significance of the Hart-Fuller Debate', in Cane, P., (ed.), *The Hart-Fuller Debate in the Twenty-First Century*, Oxford: Hart Publishing: 1–42.

Lacey, N., 2012a, 'Principles, Policies, and Politics of Criminal Law', in Zedner, L. and Roberts, J., (eds.), *Principles and Values in Criminal Law and Criminal Justice*, Oxford: Oxford University Press.

Lacey, N., 2012b, 'What Constitutes Criminal Law', in Duff, R., Farmer L., Marshall S., Renzo, M., and Tadros, V., (eds.), *The Constitution of Criminal Law*, Oxford: Oxford University Press.

Lacey, N., 2013, 'The Rule of Law and the Political Economy of Criminalization: An Agenda for Research'. *Punishment & Society*, 15 (4): 349–366.

Lacey, N., 2016, *In Search of Criminal Responsibility: Ideas Interest Institutions*, Oxford: Oxford University Press

Laclau, E., and Mouffe, C., 1985, *Hegemony and Socialist Strategy*, London: Verso.

Lakoff, G., 1972, 'Hedges: A Study in Meaning Criteria and the Logic of Fuzzy Concepts'. *The 8th Regional Meeting of the Chicago Linguistic Society*: 183–228.

Lakoff, G., 1987, *Women, Fire, and Dangerous Things: What Categories Reveal About the Mind*, University of Chicago Press.

Lakoff, G., 1993, 'The Contemporary Theory of Metaphor', in Ortony, A., (ed.), *Metaphor and Thought* (2nd ed.), Cambridge: Cambridge University Press: 20–51.

Lakoff, G., 2006, 'Conceptual Metaphor', in Geeraerts, D., (ed.), *Cognitive Linguistics: Basic Readings*, Berlin/New York: Mouton de Gruyter Geeraerts: 185–238.

Landau, P., 2012, 'The ANC, MK, and 'The Turn to Violence' 1960–1962'. *South African Historical Journal*, 64 (3): 538–563.

Lapham, L., 2004, *Gag Rule: On the Suppression of Dissent and the Stifling of Democracy*, New York: Penguin.

Larsen, O., 2009, *The Right to Dissent: The Critical Principle in Ethics and Deliberative Democracy*, Copenhagen: University of Copenhagen/Museum Tusculanum Press.

Lau, F., 2016, 'The Treatment of High Value Detainees under the United States' Extraordinary Rendition Program: A Case of Crimes against Humanity for the International Criminal Court'. *UNSW Law Journal*, 39 (3): 1261.

Lavis, S., 2015, 'The Conundrum of Nazi Law: An Historiographical Challenge to the Anglo-American Jurisprudential Representation of the Nazi Past', Unpublished PhD thesis, Nottingham: University of Nottingham.

Law Council of Australia, 2017, 'Anti-Terror Laws', www.lawcouncil.asn.au/policy-agenda/criminal-law-and-national-security/anti-terror-laws

Leadbetter, C., 1999, *Living on Thin Air: The New Economy*, London: Penguin Viking.

Leary, C., 2014, *Occupy Wall Street's Challenge to an American Public Transcript*, Unpublished Ph.D. thesis, New York: City University of New York, https://academicworks. cuny.edu/cgi/viewcontent.cgi?referer=https://www.google.com/&httpsredir=1&article= 1323&context=gc_etds

Leary, C., 2015, 'Erasing the Material Base of Occupy Wall Street: When Soft Means Fail'. *KOME – An International Journal of Pure Communication Inquiry*, 3 (2): 44–63.

Lee, R., (ed.), 2010a, *Questioning Nineteenth-Century Assumptions about Knowledge, Determinism*, New York: SUNY Press.

Lee, R., (ed.), 2010b, *Questioning Nineteenth-Century Assumptions about Knowledge, Reductionism*, New York: SUNY Press.

Lee, R., (ed.), 2010c, *Questioning Nineteenth-Century Assumptions about Knowledge, Dualism*, New York, SUNY Press.

Leeuwen, A., Klandermans, B., and Stekelenburg, J., 2015, 'A Study of Perceived Protest Atmospheres: How Demonstrators Evaluate Police- Demonstrator Interactions and Why'. *Mobilization: An International Quarterly*, 20 (1): 81–100.

Leming, J., 1974, 'Moral Reasoning, Sense of Control and Social Political Activism Among Adolescents'. *Adolescence*, 9, 507–528.

Leppänen, J., 2016, *A Political Theory of Dissent: Dissent at the Core of Radical Democracy*. PhD. Dissertation, Helsinki: University of Helsinki.

Levite, A., 1987, *Intelligence and Strategic Surprises*, New York: Columbia University Press.

Levitov, A., 2016, 'Normative Legitimacy and the State'. *Oxford Handbook OnLine*, doi:10.1093/oxfordhb/9780199935307.001.0001/oxfordhb-9780199935307-e-131

Lewis, T., 1989, 'On Using the Concept of Hypothetical Consent'. *Canadian Journal of Political Science*, 22: 793–807.

Limond, D., 2012, 'The UK Edition of *The Little Red Schoolbook*: A Paper Tiger Reflects'. *Sex Education*, 12 (5): 523–534.

Linn, R., 1989, *Not Shooting and Not Crying: Psychological Inquiry into Moral Disobedience*, Westport: Greenwood Press.

Linn, R., 1996, *Conscience at War: The Israeli Soldier as a Moral Critic*, Albany: State University of New York Press.

Lloyd, S., 2001, 'Hobbes's Self-Effacing Natural Law Theory'. *Pacific Philosophical Quarterly*, 82: 285–308.

Locke, J., 2002 [1689], *Two Treatises of Government* (ed., Laslett, P.,) Cambridge: Cambridge University Press.

Lockley, A., and Ismail, I., 2016, *Policing Protests in Rotherham; Towards a New Approach*, www.southyorkshire-pcc.gov.uk/Document-Library/Publications/Review-of-Police-Community-Relations.pdf

Lopez, M., 2018, 'The Politics of Squatting, Time Frames and Social-Spatial Contexts', in Lopez, M., (ed.), *The Urban Politics of Squatters Movements*, London: Palgrave Macmillan: 1–22.

Lopez, M., and Bernardos, A., 2015, 'The Occupation of Squares and the Squatting of Buildings: Lessons From the Convergence of Two Social Movements'. *ACME: An International E-Journal for Critical Geographies*, 14 (1): 157–184.

Loughlin, M., 2015, 'Nomos', in Dyzenhaus, D., and Poole, T., (eds.) *Law Liberty and the State: Oakeshott, Hayek and Schmitt on the Rule of Law*. Cambridge: Cambridge University Press: 65–95.

Luban, D., 1999, 'Contrived Ignorance'. *Georgetown Law Journal*, 87: 957.

Lyddon, D., 2018, 'Why Trade Union Legislation and the Labour Party Are Not Responsible for the Decline in Strike Activity'. *International Socialism*, http://isj.org.uk/why-trade-union-legislation-and-the-labour-party-are-not-responsible-for-the-decline-in-strike-activity/

Lynch, S., 2002, 'Aristotle and Derrida on Friendship'. *Contretemps*, 3: 98–108.

Lyon, D., 1994, *The Electronic Eye: The Rise of Surveillance Society*, Minneapolis: University of Minnesota Press.

Lyon, D., 2007, *Surveillance Studies: An Overview*, Cambridge: Polity Press.

Lyon, D., 2015, *Surveillance After Snowden*, Cambridge: Polity Press.

Lyons, D., 1972, 'Logic and Coercion in Bentham's Theory of Law'. *Cornell Law Review*, 57: 335–362. https://scholarship.law.cornell.edu/cgi/viewcontent.cgi?article=3985&context=clr

MacBride, S., Falk, R., Asmal, K., Bercusson, B., de Pradelle, 1983, *Israel in Lebanon: Report of the International Commission to Enquire into Reported Violations of International Law by Israel During its Invasion of the Lebanon*, London: Ithaca Press.

MacIntyre, A., 1981, *After Virtue*, Notre Dame: University of Notre Dame Press.

MacIntyre, A., 1984, *After Virtue* (2nd ed.), Notre Dame: University of Notre Dame Press.

MacKinnon, C., 1987, *Feminism Unmodified*, Cambridge: Harvard University Press.

MacKinnon, C., 1995, *Only Words*, London: Harper Collins.

MacKinnon, D., 2014, 'The Criminalization of Political Dissent: A Critical Discourse Analysis of Occupy Vancouver and C-90', Unpublished M. Arts Thesis, Vancouver: Simon Fraser University.

Macpherson, C., 1962, *The Political Theory of Possessive Individualism: Hobbes and Locke*, Oxford: The Clarendon Press.

Mair, P., & van Biezen, I., 2001, 'Party Membership in Twenty European Democracies'. *Party Politics*, 7 (1): 5–21.

Mandela, N., 1962, *Address by Nelson Mandela on Behalf of the ANC Delegation to the Conference of the Pan-African Freedom Movement of East and Central Africa*, Nelson Mandela Foundation, http://db.nelsonmandela.org/speeches/pub_view.asp?pg=item&ItemID=NMS004&txtstr=1962

Mandela, N., 1964, 'I Am Prepared to Die'. *Nelson Mandela Archives*, http://db.nelsonmandela.org/speeches/pub_view.asp?pg=item&ItemID=NMS010

Mann, G., 2017, *In the Long Run We Are All Dead: Keynesiansim, Political Economy and Revolution*, London: Verso.

Manning, R., 1980, 'The Origins of the Doctrine of Sedition'. *Albion: A Quarterly Journal Concerned with British Studies*, 12 (2): 99–121.

Margolits, E., and Lawrence, S., 1999, (eds.), *Concepts: Core Readings*, Cambridge: MIT Press.

Marshall, J., 1994, *John Locke, Resistance, Religion and Responsibility*, Cambridge: Cambridge University Press.

Martin, L., 1997, 'Jeremy Bentham: Utilitarianism, Public Policy and the Administrative State'. *Journal of Management History*, 3 (3): 272–282.

Martin, R., 2013, *Government by Dissent: Protest Resistance and Radical Democratic Thought* New York: New York University Press.

Martínez, M., 2007, 'The Squatters' Movement: Urban Counterculture and Alter-Globalisation Dynamics'. *South European Society and Politics*, 12 (3), 379–398.

Martínez, M., 2013, 'The Squatters' Movement in Europe: A Durable Struggle for Social Autonomy in Urban Politics'. *Antipode*, 45 (4): 866–887.

Martínez, M., 2014, 'How Do Squatters Deal with the State? Legalization and Anomalous Institutionalization in Madrid'. *International Journal of Urban and Regional Research*, 38 (2): 616–674.

Martínez, M., 2016, Squatters and Migrants in Madrid: Interactions, Contexts and Cycles. *Urban Studies*, 54, 24–72.

Mason, E., 2018, 'Value Pluralism', in Zalta, E., (ed.), *The Stanford Encyclopedia of Philosophy* (Spring 2018, ed.), forthcoming, https://plato.stanford.edu/archives/spr2018/entries/value-pluralism/

Matthews, R., 2005, 'The Myth of Punitiveness'. *Theoretical Criminology*, 9 (2): 175–201.

Mayer, J., 2008, *The Dark Side: The Inside Story on How the War on Terror Turned into a War on American Ideals*, New York: Doubleday.

McAlpine, K., and Roberts, S., 2017, 'The Future of Trade Unions in Australia', www.aierights.com.au/wp-content/uploads/2017/02/Future-of-unions.pdf

McKay, G., 1998, 'D-i-Y Culture: Notes Towards an Intro', in G. McKay (ed.), *DiY Culture. Party & Protest in Nineties Britain*, London: Verso: 1–53.

McMahan, J., 2009, *Killing in War*, New York: Oxford University Press.

McNamara, L., 2015, 'Criminalization Research in Australia: Building a Foundation for Normative Theorizing and Principled Law Reform', in Crofts, T., and Loughnan, A., (eds.), *Criminalization and Criminal Responsibility in Australia*, Melbourne: Oxford University Press: 33–51.

McNamara, L., Quilter, J., Hogg, R., Douglas, H., Loughnan, A., and Brown, D., 2018, 'Theorising Criminalisation: The Value of a Modalities Approach'. *International Journal for Crime, Justice and Social Democracy*, 7 (3): 91–121.

Mead, D., 2010, *The New Law of Peaceful Protest: Rights and Regulation in the Human Rights Act Era*, London: Bloomsbury Publishing.

Mead, G., 2017, 'Forms of Knowledge and the Love of Necessity in Bourdieu's Clinical Sociology'. *The Sociological Review*, doi:10.1177/0038026116674883

Mertens, T., 2002, 'Radbruch and Hart on the Grudge Informer: A Reconsideration'. *Ratio Juris*, 15: 186.

Mertens, T., 2007, Review Essay – Continuity or Discontinuity of Law? – David Fraser's Law after Auschwitz: Towards a Jurisprudence of the Holocaust, *German Law Journal*, 8: 533.

Merton, R., 1938, 'Social Structure and Anomie'. *American Sociological Review*, 3 (5): 672–682.

Michaelson, C., 2006, 'Balancing Civil Liberties against National Security? A Critique of Counterterrorism Rhetoric'. *University of New South Wales Law Journal*, 29 (2): 13.

Michalowski, R., 1985, *Order, Law and Crime: An Introduction to Criminology*, New York: Random House.

Michelman, F., 1997, 'Must Constitutional Democracy Be Responsive?' *Ethics*, 107 (4): 706–723.

Midgley, M., 2001, *Wickedness*, London: Routledge.

Milgram, S., 1974, *Obedience to Authority; An Experimental View*, New York: Harper & Row.

Miles, B., 2010, *London Calling: A Countercultural History of London since 1945*, London: Atlantic Books.

Mill, J. S., 1859/1998, *On Liberty*, in *On Liberty and Other Essays* (ed. and Intro., Gray, J.,), Oxford: Oxford University Press.

Miller, H., 2011, 'Rep. Peter King Calls Occupy Wall Street Protesters "Ragtag Mob," "Anarchists"', *Huffington Post*, 7 October, www.huffingtonpost.com/2011/10/07/peter-king-occupy-wall- street_n_1000318.html.

Miller, W., 2006, *Eye for an Eye*, New York: Cambridge University Press.

Milligan, T., 2016, *The Next Democracy? The Possibility of Popular Control*, New York: Rowman and Littlefield.

Milne, A., 1983, *The Right To Dissent*, Cambridge: Cambridge University Press.

Mirowski, P., 1989, *More Heat than Light: Economics as Social Physics, Physics as Nature's Economics*, Cambridge: Cambridge University Press.

Modrak, D., 2002, *Aristotle's Theory of Language and Meaning*, Cambridge: Cambridge University Press.

Mommsen, W., 1989, *The Political and Social Theory of Max Weber*, Oxford: Blackwell.

Moore, N., 2005, 'Secrets of the Censors: Obscenity in the Archives'. Paper given at the National Archives of Australia in Canberra on 2 May, www.naa.gov.au/about-us/grants/margaret-george/moore-paper.aspx

Moore, T., 2010, 'The Paradox of the Political: Carl Schmitt's Autonomous Account of Politics'. *The European Legacy*, 15 (6): 721–734.

Morris, B., and Black, I., 1991, *Israel's Secret Wars: A History of Israel's Intelligence Services*, New York: Grove Press.

Morris, N., 2006, 'Blair's 'Frenzied Law Making': A New Offence for Every Day Spent in Office'. *The Independent*, 16 August, www.independent.co.uk/news/uk/politics/blairs-frenzied-law-making-a-new-offence-for-every-day-spent-in-office-412072.html

Mortensen, C., 2007, 'Zeno's Paradoxes', in Close, E., Tsianikas, M., and Couvalis, G., (eds.), *Greek Research in Australia: Proceedings of the Sixth Biennial International Conference of Greek Studies*, Adelaide: Flinders University: 11–18.

Moss, S., 2018, 'Ian Hislop in Dissent: It's Cathartic to Say 'This is rubbish'', *The Guardian*, 28 August, https://pdfs.semanticscholar.org/1c40/4f4b615d4df7d2eff8854d2deee5351d08d5.pdf

Mouffe, C., 2000, *The Democratic Paradox*, London: Verso.

Mouffe, C., 2005, *On the Political*, London: Routledge.

Moulin-Doos, C., 2015, *Civic Disobedience: Taking Politics Seriously, a Democratic Theory of Political Disobedience*, London: Bloomsbury.

Mudu, P., 2013, 'Resisting and Challenging Neoliberalism: The Development of Italian Social Centers', in Squatting Europe Kollective (eds.), *Squatting in Europe, Radical Spaces, Urban Struggles*, Wivenhoe: Minor Compositions: 61–88.

Muller, J., 2016, *What Is Populism?* London: Penguin.

Mueller, J., and Stewart, M., 2012, September 11, 'The Terrorism Delusion: America's Overwrought Response'. *International Security*, 37 (1): 81–110.

Mueller, J., and Stewart, M., 2016a, *Chasing Ghosts: The Policing of Terrorism*, New York: Oxford University Press.

Mueller, J., and Stewart, M., 2016b, 'Misoverestimating ISIS Comparisons with Al-Qaeda'. *Perspectives on Terrorism*, 10 (4): 30–39.

Mullins, P., 2018, *Tiberius with a Telephone: The Life and Stories of William McMahon*, Melbourne: Scribe.

Mulvaney, B., 2012, 'Red Teams: Strengthening Through Challenge'. www.hqmc.marines.mil/Portals/138/Docs/PL/PLU/Mulvaney.pdf

Mumford, M., Schanzenbach, D., and Nunn, R., 2014, *The Economics of Private Prisons*, The Hamilton Project, www.hamiltonproject.org/papers/the_economics_of_private_prisons

Muncie, J., 2000, 'Decriminalising Criminology, Proceedings. Volume 3. Papers from the British Criminology Conference: Selected Proceedings. Volume 3. Papers from the British Society of Criminology Conference', Liverpool, July 1999, http://britsoccrim.org/new/volume3/010.pdf

Muncie, J., 2006, 'The 'Punitive Turn' in Juvenile Justice: Cultures of Control and Rights Compliance in Western Europe and the USA'. *Youth Justice*, 8 (2): 107–121.

Muniz-Fraticelli, V., 2014, *The Structure of Pluralism: On the Authority of Associations*, Oxford: Oxford University Press.

Murphy, C., 2010, *A Moral Theory of Political Reconciliation*, New York: Cambridge University Press.

Murphy, M., 1995, 'Was Hobbes a Legal Positivist?' *Ethics*, 105: 846–873.

Nardin, T., 2008, 'Theorising the International Rule of Law'. *Review of International Studies*, 34: 385–401.

Nathanson, S., 2010, *Terrorism and the Ethics of War*, Cambridge: Cambridge University Press.

Nederman, C., and Laursen, J., (eds.) (1990), *Difference and Dissent: Theories of Tolerance in Medieval and Early Modern Europe*, New York: Rowman & Litlefield.

Nelson, R., 2001, *Economics as Religion: From Samuelson to Chicago and Beyond*, University Park: Penn State University Press.

Neocleous, M., 2000, 'Against Security'. *Radical Philosophy*, 100: 7–15.

Neocleous, M., 2008, *Critique of Security*. Edinburgh: Edinburgh University Press.

Neocleous, M., 2011, 'Security as Pacification', in Neocleous M., and Rigakos, G., (eds.). *Anti-Security*, Ottawa: Red Quill.

Neuwirth, R., 2005, *Shadow Cities: A Billion Squatters, a New Urban World*, Abingdon: Routledge.

Neuwirth, R., 2007, 'Squatters and the Cities of Tomorrow'. *City*, 11 (1): 71–80.

New York General Assembly, 2011, Declaration of the Occupation of New York City.

New York Times, 1970, 'A Mock Trial Here On 'Housing Crimes' Censures Lindsay', *NYT*, 7 December, www.theguardian.com/books/2017/mar/16/the-autonomous-city-by-alexander-vasudevan-review-squatting

Nielsen, K., 1981, 'Violence and Terrorism: Its Uses and Abuses', in Leiser, Burton M., (ed.), *Values in Conflict*, New York: Macmillan, 435–449.

Niewert, D., 2017, *Alt America: The Rise of the Radical Right in the Age of Trump*, London: Bloomsbury.

Nock, G., 1995, 'On the Dissent Theory of Political Obligation'. *Polity*, 28 (2): 141–157.

Nolasco, C., Vaughan, M., and del Carmen, R., 2010, 'Toward a New Methodology for Legal Research in Criminal Justice'. *Journal of Criminal Justice Education*, 21 (1): 1–23.

Norrie, A., 1993, *Crime Reason and History*, London: Butterworths.

Norrie, A., 2009, 'Citizenship, Authoritarianism and the Changing Shape of the Criminal Law', in Norrie, A., Bronitt, S., and McSherry, B., (eds.), *Regulating Deviance: The Redirection of Criminalisation and the Futures of Criminal Law*, Oxford: Hart: 213–234.

Norrie, A., 2014, *Crime, Reason and History: A Critical Introduction to Criminal Law*, Cambridge: Cambridge University Press.

Northcott, C., 2007, 'The Role, Organization, and Methods of MI5'. *International Journal of Intelligence and Counter Intelligence*, 20 (3): 453–479.

Nowotny, S., 2003, *The Condition of Becoming Public* (trans. Derieg, A.), http://eipcp.net/transversal/1203/nowotny/en

NullCrew. 2013, @NullCrew_FTS twitter, https://twitter.com/NullCrew_FTS/status/309172610204315648

Numbers, R., 2006, *The Creationists: From Scientific Creationism to Intelligent Design*, Cambridge: Harvard University Press.

Oakley, J., 1994, *Morality and the Emotions*, Abingdon: Routledge.

Oakley, J., and Cocking, D., 2002, *Virtue Ethics and Professional Roles*, Cambridge: Cambridge University Press.

OECD, 2012, *How's Life in Australia?* Paris: OECD, www.oecd.org/general/Better-life-index-2014-country-reports.pdf

Office of the Director of National Intelligence, 2018, *Statistical Transparency Regarding Use of National Security Authorisation*. Calendar year 2017, www.dni.gov/files/documents/icotr/2018-ASTR----CY2017----FINAL-for-Release-5.4.18.pdf

Ogden, C., 1959, *Bentham's Theory of Fictions*, Paterson: Littlefield Adams & Co.

O'Keefe, M., and Schumaker, P., 1983, 'Protest Effectiveness in South East Asia'. *American Behavioural Scientist*, 26 (3): 375–394.

Oliver, E., and Woods, T., 2014, 'Conspiracy Theories and the Paranoid Style(s) of Mass Opinion'. *American Journal of Political Science*, 58 (4): 952–966.

Ollman, B., 1971, *Alienation: Marx's Conception of Man in Capitalist Society*, Cambridge: Cambridge University Press.

Olney, C., 2016, 'Justice and Legitimacy: Rawls, Schmitt and the Normativity of Law'. *Law, Culture and the Humanities*, 12 (1): 49–69.

Olson, K., 2007, 'Paradoxes of Constitutional Democracy'. *American Journal of Political Science*, 51 (2): 330–343.

Owen, J., 2005, 'The Tolerant Leviathan: Hobbes and the Paradox of Liberalism'. *Polity*, 37 (1): 130–148.

Owen, S., 2017, 'Monitoring Social Media and Protest Movements: Ensuring Political Order through Surveillance and Surveillance Discourse'. *Social Identities*, 23 (6): 688–700.

Palmer, R., 1959/1963, *The Age of the Democratic Revolution: A Political History of Europe and America, 1760–1800* (2 vols), Princeton: Princeton University.

Parekh, B., 1981, *Hannah Arendt and the Search for a New Political Philosophy*, London: Palgrave-Macmillan.

Parker, R., 2001, *The October War: A Retrospective*, Fort Lauderdale: University of Florida.

Parks, D., and Daniel, M., 2010, 'Political Protest, Mass Arrests and Mass Detention'. *Journal of Prisoners on Prisons*, 20 (2): 155–170.

Pascal, B., 1670/1995, *Pensees* (trans. Krailsheimer, T.), London: Penguin.

Penney, J., and Dadas, P., 2014, '(Re)Tweeting in the Service of Protest: Digital Composition and Circulation in the Occupy Wall Street'. *New Media & Society*, 16 (1): 74–90.

Perraudin, F., 2016, 'Far-Right Protests Draining Police Resources, Figures Reveal', *The Guardian*, 26 December. www.theguardian.com/uk-news/2016/dec/25/far-right-protests-draining-police-resources-figures-reveal

Peterson, A., and Wahlstrom, M., 2015, 'Repression: the Governance of Domestic Dissent', in della Porta, D., and Diani, M., (eds.), *The Oxford Handbook of Social Movements*, Oxford: Oxford University Press.

Picketty, T., 2014, *Capital in the Twenty-First Century*, Cambridge: Harvard University Press.

Pickrell, J., and Kinsky, J., 2012, 'Why Does Occupy Matter?' *Social Movement Studies: Journal of Social, Cultural, and Political Protest*, 11 (3–4): 279–287.

Pigou, P., 2001, 'The Apartheid State and Violence: What has the Truth and Reconciliation Commission Found?' *Politikon: South African Journal of Political Studies*, 28 (2): 207–233.

Piotrowski, G., 2014, 'Squatting in the East: The Rozbrat Squat in Poland, 1994–2012', in Steen, B., Katzeff, A., and Hoogenhuijze, L., (eds.), *The City Is Ours: Squatting and Autonomous Movements in Europe from the 1970s to the Present*, Oakland: PM: 233–254.

Pocock, J., 1992, 'The Concept of a Language and the *Metier d'historien*: Some Considerations on Practice', in Fildeler, P., and Mayer, T., (eds.), *Political Thought and the Tudor Commonwealth: Deep Structure, Discourses and Disguise*, London: Routledge: 19–38.

Popper, K., 1963, *Conjectures and Refutations: The Growth of Scientific Knowledge*, London: Routledge.

Porpora, D., 2018, 'Critical Realism as Relational Sociology', in Depelteau, F., (ed.), *The Palgrave Handbook of Relational Sociology*, London: Palgrave Macmillan.

Potter, W., 2008, 'The Green Scare'. *Vermont Law Review*, 33: 671.

Potter, W., 2011, *Green Is the New Red: An Insider's Account of a Social Movement under Siege*, San Francisco: City Lights Publishers.

Postema, G., 1982, 'Coordination and Convention at the Foundations of Law'. *Journal of Legal Studies*, 11: 165–203.

Powell, C., and Dépelteau, F., 2013, *Conceptualizing Relational Sociology: Ontological and Theoretical Issues*, New York: Palgrave Macmillan.

Prandini, R., 2015, 'Relational Sociology: A Well-Defined Sociological Paradigm or a Challenging 'Relational Turn' in Sociology?' *International Review of Sociology: Revue Internationale de Sociologie*, 25 (1): 1–14.

Prison Reform Trust, 2015, *Race*, www.prisonreformtrust.org.uk/ProjectsResearch/Race

Proctor, R., and Schiebinger, L., 2008, *Agnotology: The Making and Unmaking of Ignorance*, Stanford: Stanford University Press.

Pruijt, H., 2012, 'The Logic of Urban Squatting'. *International Journal of Urban and Regional Research*, doi:10.1111/j.1468-2427.2012.01116.x

Pruijt, H., 2013, 'Culture Wars, Revanchism, Moral Panics and the Creative City. A Reconstruction of a Decline of Tolerant Policy: The Case of Dutch Anti-Squatting Legislation'. *Urban Studies*, 50 (6): 1114–1129.

Pruijt, H., 2014, 'The Power of the Magic Key: The Scalability of Squatting in the Netherlands and the United States', in Cattaneo, C., and Martinez, M., (eds.), *The Squatters' Movement in Europe. Commons and Autonomy as Alternatives to Capitalism*, London: Pluto: 110–135.

Public Policy Polls, 2013, 'Democrats and Republicans Differ on Conspiracy Theory Beliefs', *Public Policy Polling*, 2 April, www.publicpolicypolling.com/polls/democrats-and-republicans-differ-on-conspiracy-theory-beliefs/

Radbruch, G., 2006, 'Statutory Lawlessness and Supra-Statutory Law (1946)' (trans. Litschewski, P., and Bonnie, Paulson, S.) *Oxford Journal of Legal Studies*, 26: 1–11.

Ranciere, J. 2010, *Dissensus: On Politics and Aesthetics*, London: Continuum.

Ranciere, J., 2003, September 16–17, 'The Thinking of Dissensus: Politics and Aesthetics', Paper presented at Fidelity to the Disagreement: Jacques Ranciere and the Political. Goldsmiths College, London: Political Studies Association of the UK.

Rawls, J., 1971, *A Theory of Justice*, Cambridge: Belknap Press of Harvard University Press.

Rawls, J., 1993, *Political Liberalism*, New York: Columbia University Press.

Rawls, J., 1984, 'Legal Obligation and the Duty of Fair Play', in White, Joe P., (ed.), *Assent/Dissent*, Dubuque: Kendallmunt: 45–56.

Rawls, J., 1999, *A Theory of Justice* (Rev. ed.), Cambridge: The Belknap Press of Harvard University.

Raz, J., 1979, *The Authority of Law: Essays on Law and Morality*, Oxford: Oxford University Press.

Raz, J., 1986, *The Morality of Freedom*, Oxford: Oxford University Press.

Raz, J., 2003, *The Practice of Value*, Oxford: Clarendon Press.

Raz, J., 2009, *The Authority of Law: Essays on Law and Morality*, New York: Oxford University Press.

Reeve, K., 2005, 'Squatting since 1945: The Enduring Relevance of Material Needs', in Somerville, P., and Sprigings, N., (eds.), *Housing and Social Policy*, London: Routledge: 197–216.

Reeve, K., 2011, *Squatting: A Homelessness Issue: An Evidence Review*, Centre for Regional Economic and Social Research, Sheffield: Sheffield Hallam University.

Reidel, B., 2017, 'Enigma: The Anatomy of Israel's Intelligence Failure Almost 45 Years Ago', *Brookings Report*, 25 September, Washington: Brookings Institution, www.brookings.edu/research/enigma-the-anatomy-of-israels-intelligence-failure-almost-45-years-ago/

Reinach, A., 1913/1983, 'The a Priori Foundations of Civil Law' (trans. Crosby, J.) *Aletheia*, 3: 1–142.

Reiner, R., 2007, *Law and Order: An Honest Citizen's Guide to Crime and Control*, Cambridge: Polity.

Richards, A., 2014, 'Conceptualizing Terrorism'. *Studies in Conflict & Terrorism*, 37 (3): 213–234.

Richards, R., 2010, *The Species Problem: A Philosophical Analysis*, Cambridge: Cambridge University Press.

Richardson, J., 2015, 'Alex Jones: Father Knows Best, Updated for the Apocalypse', *Esquire*, 5 December, www.esquire.com/news-politics/news/a24349/alex-jones-interview/

Ricketts, A., 2017, Anti-Protest Laws: Lock Up Your Nannas'. *Alternative Law Journal*, 42 (2): 107–111.

Ricoeur, P., 1965, 'The Political Paradox', in his *History and Truth*, Evanston: North-Western University Press: 247–270.

Ricoeur, P., 2003, *The Rule of Metaphor, the Creation of Meaning in Language*, London: Routledge.

Ricoeur, P., 2004, *Memory, History, Forgetting* (trans. Blamey, K., and Pellauer, D.), Chicago: University of Chicago Press.

Riley, D., 2008, *Engineering and Social Justice*, San-Rafael, CA: Queens University/Morgan & Claypool

Riley, P., 2009, 'The Legal Philosophy of Thomas Hobbes', in Pattaro, E., Canale, D., Grossi, P., Hofmann, H., and Riley, P., (eds.), *A Treatise of Legal Philosophy and General Jurisprudence. Vol. 9: A History of the Philosophy of Law in the Civil Law World, 1600–1900*, London: Springer: 379–401.

Risen, J., 2006, *State of War: The Secret History of the CIA and the Bush Administration*, New York: Free Press.

Roche, S., 2007, 'Criminal Justice Policy in France: Illusions of Severity'. *Crime and Justice*, 36 (1): 471–550.

Rokoff, J., 2018, 'Hail to the Chief', Review of Paul, J., *Without Precedent: John Marshall and His Times*, New York: Riverhead, *New York Review of Books*, LXV (18): 40–43.

Rorty, R., 1989, *Contingency Irony and Solidarity*, Cambridge: Cambridge University Press.

Rosch, E., 1975, 'Cognitive Representation of Semantic Categories'. *Journal of Experimental Psychology*, 104 (3): 192–233.

Rose, J., 1996, *States of Fantasy*, Oxford: Oxford University Press.

Rosenblatt, H., 2018, *The Lost History of Liberalism: From Ancient Rome to the Twenty-First Century*, Princeton: Princeton University Press.

Ross, J., 2012, *An Introduction to Political Crime*, Bristol: Policy Press.

Rothbard, M., 1975, 'Introduction', in La Boetie, E., (ed.), *The Politics of Obedience: The Discourse of Voluntary Servitude* (intro. Rothbard, M.; trans. Kurz, H.), Auburn: Mises Institute.

Rousseau, J., 1997, *Social Contract and Other Political Writings* (Gourevitch, Victor, ed.), Cambridge: Cambridge University Press.

Royal Commission into Institutional Responses to Child Sexual Abuse, 2012–17, *Report of Case Study No. 28: Catholic Church Authorities in Ballarat*. www.childabuseroyalcommission.

gov.au/sites/default/files/case_study_28_-_findings_report_-_catholic_church_authorities_in_ballarat_catholic_church_authorities_in_ballarat2.pdf

Royal Commission into the Intelligence Services, 1977, *Report*, Canberra: AGPS: (Vol. 4), 116–125.

Rubino, K., 2017, 'Ruth Bader Ginsburg Claps Back at Neil Gorsuch', *Above the Law*, 4 October, https://abovethelaw.com/2017/10/ruth-bader-ginsburg-claps-back-at-neil-gorsuch/

Ruggie, J., 1993, 'Territoriality and Beyond: Problematizing Modernity in International Relations'. *International Organization*, 47 (1): 139–174.

Ruggiero, V., 2000, 'New Social Movements and the "Centri Sociali" in Milan'. *Sociological Review*, 48 (2): 167–185.

Rumsfeld, D., 2002, 'DoD News Briefing – Secretary Rumsfeld and Gen. Myers', US Department of Defence, http://archive.defense.gov/Transcripts/Transcript.aspx?TranscriptID=2636

Rundle, K., 2012, 'Law and Daily Life – Questions for Legal Philosophy from November 1938'. *Jurisprudence*, 3 (2): 429.

Ruse, M., 2018, 'Creationism', in Zalta, Edward N., (ed.), *The Stanford Encyclopedia of Philosophy* (Winter 2018 ed.), https://plato.stanford.edu/archives/win2018/entries/creationism/.

Ryle, G., 1949, *The Concept of Mind*, London: Hutchinson University Library.

Salem, A., 2013, 'Action and Communication in Niklas Luhmann's Social Theory'. *Sociologija Mintis ir veiksmas*, 2 (33): 70–89.

Salter, C., 2011, 'Activism as Terrorism: The Green Scare, Radical Environmentalism and Governmentality'. *Anarchist Developments in Cultural Studies, Ten Years After 9/11: An Anarchist Evaluation*, 1: 211–238.

Sandel, A., 2014, *The Place of Prejudice: A Case for Reasoning within the World*, Cambridge, MA: Harvard University Press.

Sanson, M., Anthony, T., and Worswick, D., 2009, *Connecting with Law*, Oxford: Oxford University Press: 148–149.

Sarkar, A., 2018, 'What Therese May said in South Africa is an Insult to Everyone Who Protested Apartheid', *The Independent*, 18 August, www.independent.co.uk/voices/theresa-may-apartheid-south-africa-comments-conservatives-thatcher-robben-island-a8513186.html

Sassen, S., 2006, *Territory, Authority, Rights: From Medieval to Global Assemblages*, Princeton: Princeton University Press.

Sassen, S., 2016, *Expulsions: Brutality and Complexity in the Global Economy*, Cambridge: Harvard University Press.

Sauerbray, A., 2016, 'Erdogan and Merkel's Comic Comeuppance', *New York Times*, 16 April www.nytimes.com/2016/04/16/opinion/erdogan-and-merkels-comic-comeuppance.html

Saussure, F., 1977, *Course in General Linguistics*, (trans. Baskin, W.,), Glasgow: Fontana/Collins.

Savage, S., 1990, 'A War on Crime?', in Savage, S., and Robins, L., (eds.), *Public Policy Under Thatcher*, London: Macmillan.

Schaap, A., 2016, (ed.), *Law and Agonistic Politics*, Abingdon: Routledge.

Schatzki, T., 2001, 'Introduction: Practice Theory', in Schatzki, T. R., Knorr-Cetina, K., and Savigny, E., (eds.), *The Practice Turn in Contemporary Theory*, London: Routledge: 1–23.

Schauer, F., 1982, *Free Speech: A Philosophical Enquiry*, Cambridge: Cambridge University Press.

Scheuerman, W., 2006, 'Emergency Powers and the Rule of Law after 9/11'. *Journal of Political Philosophy*, 14: 61–84.

Schiffrin, S., 1999, *Dissent, Injustice and the Meaning of America*, Princeton, NJ: Princeton University Press.

Schmitt, C., 1932/2007, *The Concept of the Political* (trans. Schwab, G.), Chicago: University of Chicago Press.

Schmitt, C., 1976, *The Concept of the Political*, New Brunswick, NJ: Rutgers University Press.

Schmitt, C., 1985, *Political Theology: Four Chapters in the Concept of Sovereignty* (trans. Schwab, G.), Chicago: University of Chicago Press.

Schmitt, C. 1988, *The Crisis of Parliamentary Democracy* (trans. Kennedy, E.), Cambridge, MA: MIT Press.

Schmitt, C., 2003, *The Nomos of the Earth in the International Law of the Jus Publicum* (trans. Ulmen, G.), New York: Telos.

Schumpeter, J., 1951, *Ten Great Economists: From Marx to Keynes*. New York/Oxford: Oxford University Press.

Schwartz, B., 1950, 'Imperative Theory of the State'. *Notre Dame Law Review*, 25: 438.

Search Amelia, 2010, 'Land of 40,627 Laws and Regulations More'. *Search Amelia*. www.searchamelia.com/land-of-40627-laws-and-regulations-more

Searle, J., 1958, 'Proper Names'. *Mind*, LXVII (266): 166–173.

Shaff, C., 2014, 'Is the Court allergic to *Katz*? Problems Posed by New Methods of Electronic Surveillance to the 'Reasonable-Expectation-of-Privacy' Test'. *Southern California Interdisciplinary Law Journal*, 23: 409, 410.

Shaikh, A., 2003, 'Who Pays for the 'Welfare' in the Welfare State?' *Social Research*, 70 (2), http://homepage.newschool.edu/~AShaikh/welfare_state.pdf

Shantz, J., 2010, *Racial Profiling and Borders: International, Interdisciplinary Perspectives*, Lake Mary: Vandeplas.

Shantz, J., (ed.), 2011, *Law Against Liberty: The Criminalization of Dissent*, Lake Mary: Vandeplas Publishing.

Shapiro, I., 2016, *Politics against Domination*, Cambridge, MA: Belknap Press of Harvard University Press.

Shapiro, S., 2001, 'On Hart's Way Out', in Coleman, J., (ed.), *Harts' Postscript*, Oxford: Oxford University Press: 149–192.

Shapiro, S., 2011, *Legality*, Cambridge, MA: Harvard University Press.

Sharp, G., 1973, *The Politics of Nonviolent Action* (3 vols.), Boston, MA: Porter Sargent.

Sharp, G., 1979, 'Types of Principled Nonviolence', in *Gandhi as a Political Strategist, with Essays on Ethics and Politics*, Boston: Porter Sargent Publishers: 201–234.

Sharp, G., 1990, 'The Role of Power in Nonviolent Struggle', in Crow, R. Grant, P., and Ibrahim, S., (eds.), *Arab Nonviolent Political Struggle in the Middle East*, Boulder, CO: Lynne Rienner Publishers.

Sharp, G., 2005, *Waging Nonviolent Struggle: 20th Century Practice and 21st Century Potential*, New York: Extending Horizons Books.

Shelton, D., 1999, 'The Promise of Regional Human Rights Systems', in Weston, B., and Marks, P., (eds.), *The Future of International Human Rights*, Ardsley: Transnational: 351–398.

Sicker, M., 1978, 'Jeremy Bentham on Law and Jurisprudence'. *Modern Age*, Summer: 277–284.

Siggelakis, S., 1992, 'Advocacy on Trial'. *American Journal of Legal History*, 36 (4): 499–516.

Simmons, A., 2001, *Justification and Legitimacy: Essays on Rights and Obligations*, Cambridge: Cambridge University Press.

Simpson, G., 2004, *Great Powers and Outlaw States: Unequal Sovereigns in the International Legal Order*, Cambridge University Press.

Singer, P., 1973, *Democracy and Disobedience*, Oxford: Oxford University Press.

Sitze, A., 2015, 'Introduction', in Galli, P., (ed.), *Janus's Gaze: Essays on Carl Schmitt*, Durham, NC: Duke University Press: xi–xiii.

Sitze, A., 2018, 'The Opposite of Apartheid: Further Notes on Mandela and the Law'. *Discourse* 40 (2): 143–164.

Skidelsky, R., 2016, 'Answering the Queen's Question: New Approaches to Economic Challenges', in OECD (ed.), *Debate the Issues: New Approaches to Economic Challenges*, Paris: OECD Insights.

Skinner, Q., 1978, *The Foundations of Modern Political Thought: The Age of Reformation* (Vol. II), Cambridge: Cambridge University Press.

Skinner, Q., 1988, 'Meaning and Understanding in the History of Ideas', in Tully, J., (ed.), *Meaning and Context: Quentin Skinner and His Critics*, Princeton: Princeton University Press: 29–67.

Skinner, Q., 2002, *Visions of Politics: (Vol I) Regarding Method*, Cambridge: Cambridge University Press.

Slee, J., 1990, 'Sydney as World Libel Capital'. *Press Council of Australia Newsletter*, 2 (1): 1.

Slomp, G., 2003, 'Carl Schmitt and Thomas Hobbes on Violence and Identity'. Paper presented at the 53rd annual conference of the Political Studies Association, 'Democracy and Diversity', University of Leicester, 15–17 April.

Smith, A. 1979, *Inquiry into the Nature and Causes of the Wealth of Nations* (1776) (ed. Campbell, R. H., Skinner, A. S., and Todd, W. B.), Indianapolis: Liberty Fund.

Smith, A., 1982, *Lectures on Jurisprudence* (1762–1764) (ed. Meek, R. L., Raphael, D. D., and Stein, P. G.), Indianapolis: Liberty Fund, 405, 412, 540, 722–723, 944.

Smith, R., 2008, 'Ecoterrorism: A Critical Analysis of the Vilification of Radical Environmental Activists as Terrorists'. *Environmental Law*, 38, 537–576.

Sober, E., 1980, 'Evolution, Population Thinking and Essentialism'. *Philosophy of Science*, 47: 250–283.

Solnit, D., and Solnit, R., 2008, *The Battle of the Story of the Battle of Seattle*, Edinburgh: AK Press.

Solum, R., 2000, 'The Value of Dissent' (reviewing Steven Shiffrin, H., 1999). *Dissent, Injustice, and the Meanings of America. Cornell Law Review*, 85: 859–881.

Sommerlad, J., 2018, 'Alex Jones: Who is the Ranting Alt-Right Radio Host and What Are His Craziest Conspiracy Theories?' *The Independent*, 9 August, www.independent. co.uk/news/world/americas/us-politics/alex-jones-radio-show-us-alt-right-conspiracy-theories-youtube-infowars-illuminati-frogs-a8483986.html

Sonderegger, R., 2012, 'Negative versus Affirmative Critique: On Pierre Bourdieu and Jacques Rancière', in de Boer, K., and Sonderegger, R., (eds.), *Conceptions of Critique in Modern and Contemporary Philosophy*, London: Palgrave Macmillan: 248–270.

Sorkin, A., 2012, 'Occupy Wall Street: A Frenzy That Fizzled', *New York Times*, 17 September, https://dealbook.nytimes.com/2012/09/17/occupy-wall-street-a-frenzy-that-fizzled/

Sorenson, J., 2009, 'Constructing Terrorists: Propaganda about Animal Rights'. *Critical Studies on Terrorism*, 2 (2): 237–256.

Soreen, P., 2016, 'The 'Schoolkids' Oz, Soho, and the Downfall of the 'Dirty Squad'', *Flashbak*, 9 March, https://flashbak.com/the-schoolkids-oz-dirty-books-and-the-downfall-of-the-dirty-squad-56477/

Soule, S., and Davenport, C., 2009, 'Velvet Glove, Iron Fist, or Even Hand? Protest Policing in the United States, 1960–1990'. *Mobilization: An International Quarterly*, 14 (1): 1–22.

South African Institute of Race Relations, 1986, *Survey of Race Relations*, Johannesburg: The Institute.

Southern Poverty Law Centre, 2018, 'About Alex Jones', Southern Poverty Law Centre, Mongomery, www.splcenter.org/fighting-hate/extremist-files/individual/alex-jones

Sreedhar, S., 2010, *Hobbes on Resistance: Defying the Leviathan*. Cambridge: Cambridge University Press.

Starr, A., Fernandez, L., Amster, R., Wood, L., and Caro, M., 2008, 'The Impacts of State Surveillance on Political Assembly and Association: A Socio-Legal Analysis'. *Criminology and Criminal Justice*, 31 (1): 251–270.

Steen, B., Katzeff, A., and von Hoogenhuij, L., 2014, The City is Ours: Squatting and Autonomous Movements in Europe from the 1970s to the Present, Amsterdam: PM Press.

Steinhoff, U., 2007, *On the Ethics of War and Terrorism*, Oxford: Oxford University Press.

Steinmetz, G., 2005, *The Politics of Method in the Human Sciences: Positivism and Its Epistemological Others (Politics, History and Culture)*, Durham: Duke University Press.

Stolzenberg, L., and D'Alessio, S., 1997, 'Three Strikes and You're Out: The Impact of California's New Mandatory Sentencing Law on Serious Crime Rates'. *Crime and Delinquency*, 43 (4): 457–469. doi:10.1177/0011128797043004004

Strauss, L., 1936, *The Political Philosophy of Hobbes: Its Basis and Its Genesis* (trans. Sinclair, Elsa M.), Oxford: The Clarendon Press.

Strauss, L., 1959, *What Is Political Philosophy? and Other Studies*, Glencoe: The Free Press.

Strauss, L., 1996 [1932], 'Notes on Carl Schmitt "The Concept of the Political"', in Schmitt, C., (ed.), *The Concept of the Political*, Chicago: University of Chicago Press: 81–107.

Strayer, J., 1970, *On the medieval origins of the modern State*, Princeton: Princeton University.

Streeck, W., 2013, *The Politics of Public Debt Neoliberalism, Capitalist Development, and the Restructuring of the State*, MPIfG Discussion Paper 13/7, Cologne: Max Planck Institute, www.mpi-fg-koeln.mpg.de/pu/mpifg_dp/dp13-7.pdf

Streeck, W., 2016: *How Will Capitalism End?* London: Verso.

Sussman, N., 2013, 'Can Just War Theory Delegitimate Terrorism?' *European Journal of Political Theory*, 12 (4): 425–446.

Sutherland, J., 1983, *Offensive Literature: Censorship in Britain, 1960–1982*, Boston: Rowman & Littlefield.

Swartz, N. 1997, *Definitions, Dictionaries and Meaning*, www.sfu.ca/philosophy/swartz/definitions.htm#part2.1 (1997)

Sweet, W., 2013, 'R.F.A. Hoernlé and Idealist Liberalism in South Africa'. *South African Journal of Philosophy*, 29 (2): 178–194.

Swift, A., 2017, 'In U.S., Belief in Creationist View of Humans at New Low'. *Gallup*, 22 May. https://news.gallup.com/poll/210956/belief-creationist-view-humans-new-low.aspx

Swilling, M., and Phillips, M., 1988, *The Politics of State Power in the 1980s*, Johannesburg: Centre for Policy Studies.

Sylvestre, M., 2014, 'Crime and Social Classes: Regulating and Representing Public Disorder', in Brock, D., Glasbeek, A., and Murdocca, C., (eds.), *Criminalisation, Representation Regulation: Thinking Differently about Crime*, Toronto: University of Toronto: 217–246.

Szabo, M., 2006, 'Politics Versus the Political: Interpreting 'Das Politische' in Carl Schmitt'. *Distinktion: Journal of Social Theory*, 7 (1): 27–42.

Tarrow, S., 2011, *Power in Movement: Social Movements, Collective Action, and Politics* (3rd ed.), New York: Cambridge University Press.

Tashima, W., 2008, 'The War of Terror and the Rule of Law'. *Asian American Law Journal*, 15: 245.

Taylor, C., 1992, *The Ethics of Authenticity*, Cambridge: Harvard University Press.

Tchir, T., 2017, *Hannah Arendt's Theory of Political Action: Daimonic Disclosure of the 'Who'*, London: Palgrave Macmillan.

Ten Cate, I., 2010, 'Speech, Truth, and Freedom: An Examination of John Stuart Mill's and Justice Oliver Wendell Holmes's Free Speech Defenses'. *Yale Journal of Law & the Humanities*, 22 (1), Article 2: 35–47.

Terreblanche, S., 2002, *A History of Inequality in South Africa, 1652–2002*, Pietermaritzburg: University of Natal Press.

Terrill, R., 1989, 'Margaret Thatcher's Law and Order Agenda'. *American Journal of Comparative Law*, 37 (3): 429–456.

Teschke, B., 2003, *The Myth of 1648: Class, Geopolitics and the Making of Modern International Relations*, London: Verso.

The Economist Intelligence Unit, 2013, 'Rebels Without a Cause: What the Upsurge in Protest Movements Means for Global Politics'. A report from The Economist Intelligence Unit.

The Real News, 2018, 'The Kochs and ALEC Behind Criminalization of Dissent Bills in Five States', *The Real News*, 18 March, https://therealnews.com/stories/kochs-and-alec-behind-criminalization-of-dissent-bills-in-five-states

Thomassen, S., 2018, 'History of the Christiania Area', www.bygst.dk/english/knowledge/christiania/history-of-the-christiania-area/?AspxAutoDetectCookieSupport=1

Thompson, J., 2004, 'Terrorism, Morality and right Authority in Textor, M., Kemmerling, A., and Meggle, G., (eds.), *Ethics of Terrorism & Counter-Terrorism*. Amsterdam: De Gruyter: 151–160.

Thoreau, H., 1991, 'Civil Disobedience', in Bedau, H., (ed.), *Civil Disobedience in Focus*, London: Routledge.

Tilly, C., 1995a, 'To Explain Political Processes'. *American Journal of Sociology*, 101: 1594–1610.

Tilly, C. 1995b, *Popular Contention in Great Britain, 1758–1834*, Cambridge: Harvard University Press.

Tilly, C., 2003, *The Politics of Collective Violence*, Cambridge: Cambridge University Press.

Todorov, T., 1980, *The Conquest of America*, Houston: University of Texas.

Toit, du A., 1993, 'Understanding South African Political Violence: *A New Problematic?*', UNRISD Discussion Paper 43, The United Nations Research Institute for Social Development, http://unrisd.org/80256B3C005BCCF9/(httpAuxPages)/6FC92D92DCDF-2CE680256B67005B64B7/$file/dp43.pdf

Tonry, M., 2011, *Punishing Race: A Continuing American Dilemma*, Oxford: Oxford University Press.

Topper, K., 2011, 'Arendt and Bourdieu between Word and Deed'. *Political Theory*, 39 (3): 353–377.

Tooze, A., 2018, *Crashed: How a Decade of Financial Crises Changed the World*, London: Random House.

Trotsky, L., 1929, *The Defence of Terrorism: A Reply to Karl Kautsky*, London: George Allen and Unwin.

Truth and Reconciliation Commission, 1998, *Report*, (Vol. 5), Testimony of Craig Williamson, Armed Forces Hearings, Day 3: 'South African Police', 9 October 1997.

Tsekeris, C., 2008, 'The Public Sphere in the Context of Media Freedom and Regulation'. *Humanity and social Sciences Journal*, 3 (1): 12–17.

Tuck, R., 1978, *Natural Rights Theories: Their Origin and Development*, Cambridge: Cambridge University Press.

Tuck, R., 1993, *Philosophy and Government 1572–1651*, Cambridge: Cambridge University Press.

Tuck, R., 1999, *The Rights of War and Peace: Political Thought and International Order from Grotius to Kant*, Oxford: Oxford University Press.

Tuck, R., 2016, *The Sleeping Sovereign: The Invention of Modern Democracy*, Cambridge: Cambridge University Press.

Tucker, M., 2016, 'Two Kinds of Value Pluralism'. *Utilitas*, 28 (3): 333–346.

Turner, B., 2010, 'John Stuart Mill and the Antagonistic Foundation of Liberal Politics'. *The Review of Politics*, 72: 25–53.

Undercover Policing Inquiry, 2018a, *The Inquiry into Undercover Policing Strategic Review*, May 2018, www.ucpi.org.uk/wp-content/uploads/2018/06/20180510-strategic_review.pdf

Undercover Policing Inquiry, 2018b, 'Cover Names', www.ucpi.org.uk/cover-names/

Unicorn Riot, 2018, 'DC Police Face Class Action Lawsuit Over Trump Inauguration Mass Arrest', *Its Going Down*, 18 January, https://itsgoingdown.org/dc-police-face-class-action-lawsuit-trump-inauguration-mass-arrest/

United States Supreme Court, 1925, 268 U.S. 652, Gitlow v. People of the State of New York. https://openjurist.org/268/us/652

United States Supreme Court, 1942, Chaplinsky v. New Hampshire, 315 U.S. 568 https://supreme.justia.com/cases/federal/us/315/568/

United States Supreme Court, 1962, United States Supreme Court 366 US 82 in re Anastaplo, No. 58. Argued: December 14, 1960. Decided: April 24, 1961, https://openjurist.org/366/us/82

Vaihinger, H., 1935, *The Philosophy of 'As If': A System of the Theoretical, Practical and Religious Fictions of Mankind* (trans. Ogden, C. K., 2nd ed.), London: Routledge & Kegan Paul.

Vallet, E., 2014, *Borders, Fences and Walls. State of Insecurity?* London: Ashgate.

Valls, A., 2000, 'Can Terrorism Be Justified?', in Valls, A., (ed.), *Ethics in International Affairs: Theories and Cases*, Lanham, MD: Rowman and Littlefield: 65–80.

Van der Walt, A., 2009, *Property in the Margins*, Portland: Hart.

Vandenberghe, F., 1999, 'The Real is Relational': An Epistemological Analysis of Pierre Bourdieu's Generative Structuralism'. *Sociological Theory*, 17 (1): 32–67.

Vandenberghe, F., 2018, 'The Relation as Magical operator: Overcoming the Divide between Relational and Processual Sociology', in Depelteau, F., (ed.), *The Palgrave Handbook of Relational Sociology*, London: Palgrave Macmillan: 35–58.

Varoufakis, Y., 2005, 'A Most Peculiar Failure: On the Dynamic Mechanism by which the Inescapable Theoretical Failures of Neoclassical Economics Reinforce Its Dominance', www.sfecon.com/2_Theory/23_Stability/233_Equilibrium/A&V.pdf

Vasudevan, A., 2017, *The Autonomous City: A History of Urban Squatting*, London: Verso.

Vine, I., 1983, 'The Nature of Moral Commitments', in Weinreich-Haste, W., and Locke, D., (eds.), *Morality in the Making: Thoughts Action and Context*, Chichester: Wiley.

Visser, M., 2008, *The Gift of Thanks: The Roots and Rituals of Gratitude*, New York: Harper Collins.

Vlastos, G., 1983, 'The Socratic Elenchus'. *Oxford Studies in Ancient Philosophy*, 1: 27–58.

Vlastos, G., 1991, *Socrates, Ironist and Moral Philosopher*, Ithaca, NY: Cornell University Press.

Voice, P., 2013, 'Consuming the World: Hannah Arendt on Politics and the Environment'. *Journal of International Political Theory*, 9 (2): 178–193.

Vollrath, E., 1995, 'Hannah Arendt: A German – American Jewess Views the United States and Looks Back to Germany', in Kielmanslegg, P., Mewes, H., and Glaser-Schmidt, E., (eds.), *Hannah Arendt and Leo Strauss: German Emigres and American Political Thought after World War II*, Cambridge: Cambridge University Press: 45–60.

Wacquant, L., 2009, *Punishing the Poor: The Neoliberal Government of Insecurity*, Durham, NC: Duke University Press.

Wagner, P., and Rabuy, B., 2016, 'Mass Incarceration: The Whole Pie 2016', *Prison Policy Initiative*, www.prisonpolicy.org/reports/pie2016.html?gclid=CKC565LQ7c0CFc1uGwodZWYLHg

Wagner, P., and Sawyer, W., 2018, 'Mass Incarceration: The Whole Pie 2018', *The Prison Initiative*, www.prisonpolicy.org/reports/pie2018.html

Walby, K., and Monaghan, J., 2011, 'Private Eyes and Public Order: Policing and Surveillance in the Suppression of Animal Rights Activists in Canada'. *Social Movement Studies*, 10 (01): 21–37.

Waldron, J., 2008, 'The Concept and the Rule of Law'. *Georgia Law Review*, 1: 43.

Waldron, J., 2010, 'Legal Pluralism and the Contrast Between Hart's Jurisprudence and Fuller's', in Cane, P., (ed.), *The Hart-Fuller Debate*, Oxford: Hart Publishing.

Walker, A., Kershaw, C., and Nicholas, 2006, *Crime in England and Wales 2005/06*, www.homeoffice.gov.uk/rds/index.htm

Walker, C., 2002, *The Anti-Terror Legislation*, Oxford: Oxford University Press.

Walzer, M., 1970, *Obligations: Essays on Disobedience, War and Citizenship*, Cambridge, MA: Harvard University Press.

Walzer, M., 1977, *Just and Unjust Wars: A Moral Argument with Historical Illustrations*, 4th ed., New York: Basic Books.

Walzer, M., 1988, *The Company of Critics*, New York: Basic Books.

Walzer M., 1991, 'Constitutional Rights and the Shape of Civil Society', in Calvert, R., (ed.), *The Constitution of the People: Reflections on Citizens and Civil Society*, Lawrence: University Press of Kansas.

Walzer, M., 2006, 'Terrorism and Just War'. *Philosophia*, 34: 3–12.

Wates, N., and Wolmar, C., (eds.), 1980, *Squatting: The Real Story*, London: Bay Leaf.

Watts, R., Bessant, J., and Hil, R., 2008, *International Criminology: A Critical Introduction*, London: Routledge.

Watts, R., 2014, 'Truth and Politics: Thinking About Evidence-Based Policy in the Age of Spin'. *Australian Journal of Public Administration*, 73 (1): 34–46.

Watts, R., 2016, *States of Violence and the Civilizing Process: On Criminology and State Crime*, London: Palgrave-Macmillan.

Watts, R., Bessant, J., and Hil, R., 2008, *International Criminology: A Critical Introduction*, Thousand Oaks: Sage.

Weber, M., 1978, *Politik als Beruf*, Berlin: Universal Bibliotheck: 1–47.

Weber, M., 1904/1949, 'Objectivity in Social Science and Social Policy', in Shils, E., and Finch, H., (eds. and trans.), *The Methodology of the Social Sciences*, New York: Free Press.

Weber, M., 1964, *The Theory of Social and Economic Organization* (ed., Parsons, T.,), New York: Free Press.

Weber, M., 2011, 'Politics as a Vocation', http://anthropos-lab.net/wp/wp-content/uploads/2011/12/Weber-Politics-as-a-Vocation.pdf

Weiner, T., 2007, *Legacy of Ashes: The History of the CIA*, New York: Doubleday.

Weiskopf, R., and Tobias-Mersch, Y., 2016, 'Whistleblowing, Parrhesia and the Contestation of Truth in the Workplace'. *Organisation Studies*, 37 (11): 1621–1640.

Whitebrook, P., 2015, *John Osborne: Anger is Not About...*, London: Oberon Books.

Whiteley, P., 2009, 'Where Have All the Party Members Gone? The Dynamics of Party Membership in Britain'. *Parliamentary Affairs*, 62 (2): 242–257.

Widick, R., 2003, 'Flesh and the Free Market: (On taking Bourdieu to the Options Exchange)'. *Theory and Society*, 32 (5–6): 679–723.

Wildeman, C., 2009, 'Parental Imprisonment, the Prison Boom, and the Concentration of Childhood Disadvantage'. *Demography*, 46 (2): 265–280.

Wilkins, L., 1965, *Social Deviance*, London: Tavistock.

Wilkinson, M., 2018, *Authoritarian Liberalism: The Conjuncture Behind the Crisis*. LSE Law, Society and Economy Working Papers 5/2018, London: London School of Economics and Political Science Law Department, http://eprints.lse.ac.uk/87542/1/Wilkinson_Authoritarian%20Liberalism_Author.pdf

Williams, B., 1985, *Ethics and the Limits of Philosophy*, Cambridge: Harvard University Press.

Williams, B., and Smart, J., 1973, *Utilitarianism: For and Against*, Cambridge: Cambridge University Press.

Williams, G., and Golder, B., 2004, 'What is "Terrorism"? Problems of Legal Definition'. *University of New South Wales Law Journal*, 27: 270–295.

Williams, G., and Lynch, A., 2006, *What Price Security? Taking Stock of Australia's Anti-Terror Laws*, Kensington: UNSW Press.

Williams, G., 2011, 'A Decade of Anti-Terror Laws'. *Melbourne University Law Review*, 35 (3): 1136–1176.

Williams, G., Lynch, A., and McGarrity, N., 2015, *Inside Australia's Anti-Terrorism Laws and Trials*, Kensington: NewSouth.

Wilson, E., 2008, *Savage Republic: De Indis of Hugo Grotius, Republicanism, and Dutch hegemony within the Early modern World System (c. 1600–1619)*, Leiden: Martinus Nijhof.

Wilson, J., and Herrnstein, R., 1985, *Crime and Human Nature*, New York: Basic Books.

Wittgenstein, L., 1958, *Philosophical Investigations* (trans. Anscombe, G. E.), Oxford: Blackwell.

Wolin, S., 1990, 'Hobbes and the Culture of Despotism', in Dietz, M., (ed.), *Thomas Hobbes and Political Theory*, Lawrence: University Press of Kansas: 9–36.

Woolf, R., Moore, B., and Marcuse, H., 1968, *A Critique of Pure Tolerance*, Boston, MA: Beacon.

Workers Solidarity Movement, 2018, 'Thoughts on Squatting & Social Centers', www.wsm.ie/c/thoughts-dublin-squatting-social-centers

Worrall, J., 2000, 'In Defence of the Quantoids: More on the Reasons for the Quantitative Emphasis in Criminal Justice Education and Research'. *Journal of Criminal Justice Education*, 11: 353–361.

Wright, C., 2013, *The Forgotten Rebels of Eureka*, Melbourne: Text Publishing.

Wroe, M., 1995, 'Martin Wroe Talks to Ian Hislop', *Third Way*, March https://books.google.com.au/books?id=Cg5gAS_YdyEC&pg=PA12&redir_esc=y#v=onepage&q&f=false

Yang, Y., 2014, 'Bourdieu, Practice and Change: Beyond the Criticism of Determinism'. *Educational Philosophy and Theory*, 46: 1522–1540.

Youth Justice Board, 2016, *Youth Justice Statistics 2014/15: England and Wales*, London: Ministry of Justice, www.gov.uk/government/uploads/system/uploads/attachment_data/file/495708/youth-justice-statistics-2014-to-2015.pdf

Zaitchik, A., 2011, 'Meet Alex Jones', *Rolling Stone*, 2 March, www.rollingstone.com/culture/culture-news/meet-alex-jones-175845/

Zedner, L., 2007, 'Pre-Crime and Post-Criminology'. *Theoretical Criminology*, 11 (2): 261.

Zedner, L., 2009, 'Fixing the Future? The Pre-Emptive Turn in Criminal Justice', in McSherry B, Norrie, A., and Bronnit, S., (eds.), *Regulating Deviance: The Redirection of Criminalisation and the Futures of Criminal Law*, Oxford: Hart Publishing.

Zerilli, L., 2012, 'Truth and Politics', in Elkins, J., and Norris, A., (eds.), *Truth and Democracy*, Philadelphia: University of Pennsylvania Press: 54–75.

Zizek, S., 1994, (ed.), *Mapping Ideology*, London: Verso.

Zizek, S., 2012, 'Occupy Wall Street: What is to be Done Next?', *The Guardian*, 24 April, www.theguardian.com/commentisfree/cifamerica/2012/apr/24/occupy-wall-street-what-is-to-be-done-next

Index